THE CAMBRIDGE CULTURAL HISTORY

VOLUME 2   MEDIEVAL BRITAIN

The Cambridge Cultural History

The Cambridge Cultural History of Britain

edited by
BORIS FORD

VOLUME 2

MEDIEVAL BRITAIN

CAMBRIDGE
UNIVERSITY PRESS

Published by the Press Syndicate of the University of Cambridge
The Pitt Building, Trumpington Street, Cambridge CB2 1RP
40 West 20th Street, New York, NY 10011–4211, USA
10 Stamford Road, Oakleigh, Victoria 3166, Australia

First published 1988 as *The Cambridge Guide to the Arts in Britain: The Middle Ages*
First paperback edition 1992

Printed and bound in Great Britain by
BPCC Hazells Ltd
Member of BPCC Ltd

British Library cataloguing in publication data
A catalogue record for this book is available from the British Library.

Library of Congress cataloguing in publication data

Cambridge guide to the arts in Britain.
The Cambridge cultural history/edited by Boris Ford.
   p. cm.
Previously published as: The Cambridge guide to the arts in Britain. 1988–1991.
Includes bibliographical references and indexes.
Contents: v.1. Early Britain – v.2. Medieval Britain – v.3. Sixteenth-century
Britain – v.4. Seventeenth-century Britain – v.5. Eighteenth-century Britain –
v. 6. The Romantic Age in Britain – v. 7. Victorian Britain – v.8. Early
twentieth-century Britain – v.9. Modern Britain.
ISBN 0-521-42881-5 (pbk.: v.1). – ISBN 0-521-42882-3 (pbk.: v.2). – ISBN
0-521-42883-1 (pbk.: v.3). – ISBN 0-521-42884-X (pbk.: v.4). – ISBN 0-521-42885-8
(pbk.: v.5). – ISBN 0-521-42886-6 (pbk.: v.6). – ISBN 0-521-42887-4 (pbk.: v.7). –
ISBN 0-521-42888-2 (pbk.: v.8). – ISBN 0-521-42889-0 (pbk.: v.9)
1. Arts, British.   I. Ford, Boris.   II. Title.
[NX543.C36   1992]
700'.941–dc20   91–43024
                                                       CIP

ISBN 0 521 30975 1 hardback
ISBN 0 521 42882 3 paperback

Contents

Notes on Contributors

Richard Axton is a Fellow of Christ's College and Lecturer in English at Cambridge University. He is General Editor of 'Tudor Interludes' and author of *European Drama of the Early Middle Ages*. He was a founding director of Medieval Players Ltd.

Nicola Coldstream is a Deputy Editor of the *Macmillan Dictionary of Art* and her publications include *Masons and Sculptors*, in the *Medieval Craftsmen* series.

Barrie Dobson is Professor of Medieval History at the University of Cambridge. His publications include *Politics, Patronage and the Church in Fifteenth-Century England*, (ed.), *The Peasants' Revolt of 1381*, *Durham Priory, 1400–1450*, and *The Jews of Medieval York and the Massacre of March 1190*.

T.A. Heslop is a Lecturer in the History of Art at the University of East Anglia, specialising in the art of Venice and the Middle Ages. He contributed to C. Norton and D. Park, eds., *Cistercian Art and Architecture in the British Isles*, and to the *Burlington Magazine* and *Art History*.

Carol Meale is a Lecturer in Medieval England at the University of Bristol. Her publications include studies of Malory and medieval patronage, and she is co-editor of and contributor to *Romance in Medieval England*, and is editor of and contributor to *Women and Literature in Britain, 1150–1500*.

Stephen Medcalf is Reader in English in the School of European Studies at the University of Sussex. He edited *The Later Middle Ages* and *Joseph Glanvill's 'The Vanity of Dogmatizing'*. He wrote *William Golding*, and is now writing a study of T.S. Eliot, *An Anatomy of Consciousness*.

Nigel Nicolson, a former Member of Parliament who lives at Sissinghurst Castle, Kent, is a publisher and the author of *Great Houses of Britain*, *Portrait of a Marriage*, and *Mary Curzon*. He edited the letters of Virginia Woolf in six volumes.

Christopher Page is Senior Research Fellow in Music at Sidney Sussex College, Cambridge. He directs the ensemble 'Gothic Voices', making recordings and giving concerts in Britain and abroad. He is the author of *Voices and Instruments of the Middle Ages*.

Derek Pearsall, formerly Professor of English and Co-Director of the Centre of Medieval Studies at the University of York, is now Professor of English at Harvard University. His books include *Old English and Middle English Poetry* and *The Canterbury Tales*.

Nick Sandon is Professor of Music at University College Cork. He has published widely on Medieval and Renaissance music and has created numerous reconstructions of liturgical ceremonies for live performance, broadcast and recording.

Tom Williamson is a Lecturer in Landscape History and Material Culture at the Centre of East Anglia Studies at the University of East Anglia. He is the co-author, with Liz Bellamy, of *Ley Lines in Question* and *Property and Landscape*.

General Introduction

BORIS FORD

If all people seem to agree that English literature is pre-eminent in the world, the same would not often be claimed for Britain's arts as a whole. And yet, viewed historically, Britain's achievements in the visual and decorative arts and in architecture and music, as well as in drama and literature, must be the equal, as a whole, of any other country.

The Cambridge Cultural History of Britain is not devoted, volume by volume, to the separate arts, but to all the arts in each successive age. It can then be seen how often they reinforce each other, treating similar themes and speaking in a similar tone of voice. Also it is striking how one age may find its richest cultural expression in music or drama, and the next in architecture or the applied arts; while in a later age there may be an almost total dearth of important composers compared with a proliferation of major novelists. Or an age may provide scope for a great range of anonymous craftsmen and women.

The nine volumes of this *Cambridge Cultural History* have been planned to reveal these changes, and to help readers find their bearings in relation to the arts and culture of an age: identifying major landmarks and lines of strength, analysing changes of taste and fashion and critical assumptions. And these are related to the demands of patrons and the tastes of the public.

These volumes are addressed to readers of all kinds: to general readers as well as to specialists. However, since virtually every reader is bound to be a non-specialist in relation to some of the arts under discussion, the chapters do not presuppose specialist knowledge.

This volume on the medieval arts in Britain is not altogether typical of the series as a whole. In the first place it covers a great span of 400 years, or as long as from Chaucer till the present day, and so records great developments and changes of style in all the arts. Then a great deal of medieval art – of popular non-notated music, for instance, or wall paintings, or the bright colours in which much architecture and many sculptures were painted – has not survived. As a result, much of our information about these arts is based on contemporary descriptions rather than on the evidence of our own eyes and ears.

Finally, a great deal of medieval art was created by anonymous artist-craftsmen and women, whose creative role and status was unlike that of the individual virtuoso artists of later ages. Only a few great artists are known to us by name, like the poets Chaucer and Langland, the composers Dunstable and Powell, and the master-builder, Henry Yevele. It is our fortune that so many masterpieces of medieval art have survived, like *Sir Gawain and the Green Knight* and the *Opus Anglicanum* embroideries and a mass of carols. Above all, the cathedrals, whoever built them and filled them with music and carvings and paintings, are among the greatest creations in the history of British and European art.

This volume, with a considerably more detailed bibliography, was originally published in a hardcover edition as *The Middle Ages*, under the series title *The Cambridge Guide to the Arts in Britain*.

Part I
The Cultural and Social Setting

Decorated initial page from the Grey Fitspayne Book of Hours *(c.1300)*

The Cultural and Social Setting

DEREK PEARSALL

Introduction

A cultural history of Britain in the Middle Ages uses the records of the past in order to build up a picture of the artistic life of the community. It works with a variety of material, from magnificent buildings that everyone is familiar with to tiny scraps of evidence unearthed by painstaking research, and the facility it principally exercises is that of the historical imagination. To recognise how things were different, how even the things that remain apparently the same were differently responded to and understood, is a vital part in this activity of the historical imagination, and one useful way of beginning this process of making things familiar – whilst reminding oneself constantly that they are unfamiliar – is to ask what form the present project for a 'Cultural History of Britain' would have taken in the medieval period. The answer, of course, is that it would have taken no form at all, would have had no possible existence, since the terms of reference we are using are, naturally enough, modern ones.

There was, for instance, no such thing as 'Britain', certainly no political unit which can be thought of as operating in any coherent or integrated way in the arts. (It may be that this is still, to some extent, true.) What we shall find ourselves mostly talking about and thinking about, and from time to time bashfully denying the fact, is England, and principally those parts of England of which most is known and of which most has been written – the South East, East Anglia and the Midlands. Wales was annexed to the English crown when Edward I defeated Llywelyn ap Gruffydd in 1282, but remained in most ways a cultural enclave within the larger unit, retaining its own language and literature despite the attempt at plantation, and prone to break out in revolt when the opportunity offered. Wales has more in common, culturally, with Brittany and Ireland than with England. Scotland, by contrast, is two nations: a Gaelic-speaking one, of which we are accustomed to hear next to nothing; and the English-speaking lowlands and southern border country, which were originally part of Anglian Northumbria and only joined Scotland (as Lothian) in 1018. The reign of David (1124–53) confirmed Scotland's role as essentially a tributary of the Anglo-Norman kingdom, a role it continued to fill, in relation to England, throughout the Middle Ages, whether or not in postures of aggressive defiance. Its literature and art are intimately bound up with those of England; the best poems are either inspired by English models or else by the historical struggle against English suzerainty; the 'old alliance' with France is a political convenience.

As to England itself, it begins the period as part of an Anglo-Norman kingdom and, though it is never a cultural dependency, it remains in the shadow of France throughout the Middle Ages. Normandy, and, after the loss of Normandy in 1204, France and Burgundy, are the main channels through which England, a comparative backwater, absorbs the influences of Continental literary forms, decorative and architectural styles, intellectual and spiritual innovation. It is true that there was at times a specifically English response to these influences through which they were transformed and through which, on occasion – in architecture, in sculpture, in manuscript illumination, eventually in literature and music – the models were transcended. But nevertheless it is impossible to separate England, in any significant way, from the Continent.

The 'arts' must be similarly thought of as a subject of study brought into existence by modern ideas of what is appropriate to the activity of study and by the accidents of survival. A good book has been written, by R.M. Wilson, about the 'lost literature' of medieval England; it is not in all ways a better book than those that have been written about what survives, but it indicates something of the haphazard and fragmentary nature of the latter, at least up to the end of the fourteenth century. The paintings and manuscripts and sculptured objects that survive are likewise a mere fraction, and inevitably not a representative one, of what existed. The buildings are perhaps the most enduring monument of the age, since even the ones that fell down tended to get rebuilt, but they appear to us in a guise quite different from their original appearance in the Middle Ages, with elaborate and colourful schemes of internal wall-decoration reduced to muted stone greys and white washes, and the profusion of gilded, painted and enamelled images remembered only in empty niches. What remains is of an unmedieval austerity; and likewise ornaments, objets d'art, alabaster figurines and ivory panels, which once had a living context in houses, palaces and churches, are now unnaturally sealed in the antiseptic hush of museums and galleries.

This is no mere accident of survival, of course, but rather a form of historical appropriation. In fact it could be said that there are no 'accidents' of survival, and the biggest non-accident of all is the almost complete removal from our purview of the expressive forms, the games and ceremonies, of popular and social life. Of popular song and dance and secular dramatic entertainment we know virtually nothing, except what is presented in the distorting mirror of preachers' execrations (like Robert Mannyng's famous account, in his penitential treatise *Handlyng Synne*, c.1303, of the churchyard dancers of Colbek who found themselves dancing willy-nilly into hell) or what in other ways is strained to a didactic purpose (like the versions of folk and mumming plays embedded in the doctrinal structure of the fifteenth-century mystery cycles as examples of coarse or depraved behaviour). What survives of popular culture is inevitably denatured in the written record, over which the educated classes, namely the clergy, have a near-monopoly until near the very end of the Middle Ages.

From another point of view, too, the picture we have of 'the arts' in the Middle Ages is a narrow and perhaps a complacent one, skilfully adjusted to reflect post-Renaissance ideas of the 'fine arts' as a subject of connoisseurship. To a member of the upper classes in the Middle Ages, it may well have seemed that the romance, the love-song, the beautiful objet d'art, were not objects of appreciation in themselves but accessories in that ceremonialisation of social life which made social life itself a form of art. The tournament, the hunt, the feast, the 'art' of love, the 'art' of war, are far more important to medieval sensibility and to our understanding of it than the permanent yet paradoxically ephemeral tokens that survive. Even the work of literature itself, the romance that survives in its written text, whole and complete, is but an index to the total experience of listening, participating, discussing, of which it was part.

Happily, it is possible to read a musical score and, without ever having heard a performance, to reconstruct something of what that performance might be; and so it is with the records, objects and monuments that survive from the Middle Ages. They can mean something if the life that they contributed to can in some way be relived in the imagination. The following pages will attempt to provide some materials for that understanding. It will not be a systematic 'history', since chronology is a straitjacket one would wish to wear as loosely as possible: rather a series of important sources of stimulus and momentum in the arts will be explored, inevitably with some overlap and some arbitrary categorisation.

Royal and aristocratic patronage

One important part of the history of the cultural and social setting of the arts in Britain in the Middle Ages is the history of the interests and tastes of the ruling classes, especially as those interests and tastes were embodied in or fashioned by the monarch. In an age when a large proportion of the disposable wealth of the country was in the hands of these classes – though this was progressively less true by the fifteenth century – it is inevitable that they will have considerable influence on the volume and nature of artistic production, especially in those arts that involve the use of costly materials. There are reasons for believing that this influence was particularly strong in Britain. One reason is the exceptional degree of centralisation of government achieved by the Anglo-Norman kings and maintained to a greater or lesser extent by their successors. The conquest and subjugation of the country by William I (reigned 1066–87), the plantation of a new Anglo-Norman aristocracy, numbering no more than 5,000 persons, bound to the person of the king by the system of holding land in exchange for military service, the virtual elimination of the provinces as potential alternative centres of culture (with some exceptions, as we shall see), established this dominance, and it was consolidated by Henry I (1100–35) and Henry II (1154–89), partly by military means, but more importantly by the introduction of a governmental administration and a system of law which again centred in the person of the king. France, Germany, Spain, Italy were by contrast federalised and fissiparous.

Another reason for the relatively greater importance of royal and aristocratic patronage in Britain might be the 'colonial' nature of its economy in the twelfth and thirteenth centuries, which meant that there were no real urban rivals to the pre-eminence of the metropolis, which is where the court soon became established, albeit at Westminster rather than London. The principal, almost the sole English export was wool, though hides also became important, and the principal import was manufactured cloth; the trade was run by foreign merchants, with better know-how and capitalisation than the natives; the finance was largely provided by foreign bankers; industry was primitive compared with Flanders and Tuscany. Such were not the conditions for the development of powerful towns which might act as competing artistic centres, and the largest towns of the early medieval period, such as York, Lincoln and Norwich, though they were much more than oversized market towns, had only a limited role as independent urban centres. Even the spate of church-building that followed the Conquest can be seen in a way as an aspect of royal policy. William 'Normanised' the church by converting the bishoprics and larger abbacies into feudal baronies, and filling them with his appointees. Their building projects were the indirect product of his patronage. So, later, Ranulph Flambard, having acted as Henry I's trusted adviser in his war against his brother Robert, returned to be Bishop of Durham after the battle of Tinchebrai in 1106, and set to the building of the great nave on a scale to match the new choir and transepts.

There was no systematic attempt to stamp out Anglo-Saxon culture by the Anglo-Norman kings, though it may have seemed like it to some monastic observers. Certainly the monks of Glastonbury did not take kindly to the introduction of a new kind of chant by their newly-appointed Norman abbot. But the pre-Conquest art of manuscript illumination continued at Winchester and Canterbury, perhaps because much of its had already been absorbed by the Norman monks before they came to England, and in other arts, such as metalwork, the Anglo-Saxons civilised their conquerors. The Bayeux tapestry, though it was made for a Norman patron, was done to a Canterbury design, using English embroidery techniques. Of the great building schemes of the Normans, even, it could be said that they were as much the product of the determination and the ability to raise the necessary money as of any attempt at cultural imperialism. But the Norman Conquest did act decisively to turn England for ever away from Scandinavia and towards France: Anglo-Saxon England had its contacts with the Continent, but England was now part of the Continent, and no very important part.

Above all, the Norman Conquest, in planting a new aristocracy, supplanted the old language of literary culture. English continued to be spoken by the great majority of people in the country, but the language of the ruling classes was now Norman-French or, as it was called in its later developed form, Anglo-Norman, whilst the territories of learning, historical writing, science and law, which had been, quite exceptionally, taken over by the vernacular during the Anglo-Saxon period, were re-annexed to Latin. English was relegated, and played a subordinate role for the next three centuries. It remained, of course, the dominant spoken language, perhaps in all but the most exalted circles, and everyone who had contact with those who spoke only English would have needed some fluency. Many would have been bilingual, if not possessing equal fluency in both the vernaculars. Even in an aristocratic household there would have been situations – with the servants, with the children, in bed – when English might come more promptly to the tongue. The situation was complex, and cannot be described simply as a war for supremacy.

Nor is it helpful to take the written record as evidence of what was spoken: records of law-cases and parliamentary proceedings were nearly always kept in Latin or French throughout the period, but it is obvious that English would often have been spoken on such occasions. Even in the literary status of the two languages, as written vernaculars, there are some ambiguities. They seemed to have co-existed at times, in certain clerical circles for example, on a more or less equal basis, and a poem like *The Owl and the Nightingale* (c.1200) concedes nothing in wit and sophistication to contemporary Anglo-Norman poetry, while *The Proverbs of Alfred*, the *Bestiary*, and Layamon's *Brut* have the closest relationships with their Anglo-Norman sources and analogues. There does seem to be a new stridency in the late thirteenth century and onwards in the comments of certain popular romance and homiletic writers about the privileged status of French, and Ranulph Higden's remarks about the unnatural practice of teaching children in a language other than their mother-tongue are famous (as are John Trevisa's assurances in 1387, sixty years later, that all is now put right). There is ebb and flow in the relations of the two languages, and perhaps Anglo-Norman reached its high point in the reign of Henry III (1216–72).

However, with all these complexities and ambiguities, one thing seems to be clear: there was no English court between Harold Godwinson (1066) and Richard II (1377–99) at which English would have been the language of formal spoken discourse or of polite literature. English was thus excluded from the activity of that royal and aristocratic patronage of literature which would be usually thought of as the most important social determinant of literary production. English poetry and prose were being written, but it tended to be provincial or clerical work, or both, and the courtly romance, which was the principal secular entertainment of upper-class households, whether recited, read aloud or read privately, was represented in English in generally simpler and cruder forms, suited to what a popular audience might perceive of the manners of their social superiors. Even well into the fourteenth century, all of the books of romance owned, or recorded as having been owned, by the aristocracy were French versions of stories such as those of Lancelot and Tristan, and it was not until the latter part of the century that sophisticated courtly romances got to be written in English. By this time, ironically, the genre was almost exhausted.

But, though English did not prosper, literature and the arts received much from the stimulus of court and aristocratic patronage during these early medieval centuries, especially during the reigns of Henry II (1154–89) and

Henry III. In the twelfth century the very nature of the Angevin kingdom, as well as its crusading activities, promoted a wealth of Continental contacts, and scholars, poets and artists, as well as lords and warriors, moved freely between England, France, Spain and Italy. Adelard of Bath, who dedicated a treatise on falconry to Henry II, had studied at the cathedral schools of Tours and Laon, travelled extensively in Greece and Italy, especially Sicily, and knew both Greek and Arabic; John of Salisbury, the principal English scholar of his day (d.1180), studied at Paris and Chartres, was in the household of Archbishop Theobald of Canterbury during the years 1147–61, and made many journeys to the papal court, crossing the Alps (and taking no pleasure whatsoever in the experience) ten times.

Contacts with the Norman kingdom of Sicily were particularly important, since they provided the channel through which a fresh and strong Byzantine influence could be communicated to English artists. The Albani Psalter, done at St Albans 1119–46, is a witness to the stimulus of these contacts, as are the Bury Bible, done at Bury St Edmunds 1121–48, and other manuscripts done at Canterbury and Hereford, as well as the famous wall-paintings in the former. The Sicilian connection inspired also the aristocratic Anglo-Norman romance of *Ipomedon*, set in southern Italy, and written by Hue de Rotelande about 1185.

The monarchs were themselves mostly busy about other matters. It was not to Henry I, called Beauclerc because he could almost sign his name, but to his queen, Maud, that the poet-bishops, Marbod of Rennes and Hildebert of Lavardin, dedicated their Latin eulogies, and it was his sister, Adela of Blois, who maintained the more sumptuous and cultivated court. She passed on her taste for artistic patronage to her son, Henry of Blois, who was Bishop of Winchester during Stephen's troubled reign, and an excellent representative of the essentially aristocratic interests of a great churchman of the time. He managed, despite many distractions, to build palaces, indulge his taste for imported menageries, transport to England a whole shipload of artefacts collected among the ruins of Rome, and commission the Winchester Psalter, made in 1150–60. He may also have had something to do with the making of the great Winchester Bible in 1160–70, the giant of twelfth-century English Romanesque manuscripts, a book which Henry II himself coveted.

Amongst the opposition party, there was patronage of a more traditional kind in the encouragement that Robert of Gloucester, supporter of the rival claim to the English throne of the Empress Matilda, gave to the Anglo-Latin historians William of Malmesbury and Geoffrey of Monmouth. Later in the century, Richard I (1189–99) kept court mostly in France, at Poitiers and Argentan, sponsored poets like Bertrand de Born, even composed a *sirventes* (a Provençal lyric poem) or two himself; John (1199–1216) to had his French protégés, and Gerald of Wales dedicated his *Conquest of Wales* too him.

But it is Henry II and his queen, Eleanor of Aquitaine, who provide the most significant evidence of the cultural influence of the court. Eleanor kept her connections with south France, and with poets like Bernart de Ventadour, and perhaps brought to England something of the spirit and habit of such literary patronage. The *Roman de Brut* of the Jerseyman Wace, a version in French octosyllabics of Geoffrey of Monmouth's *Historia Regum*

Britanniae, was written for Henry II, and maybe Eleanor too, about 1155, and his *Roman de Rou*, a glorification of Henry's Norman ancestors, was commissioned in 1166. He received a canonry at Bayeux for his efforts. An Anglo-Norman verse chronicle of the king's Scottish wars was written for Henry II by Jordan Fantosme in 1175. Two of the most prolific writers of the day, Gerald of Wales and Peter of Blois, were royal chaplains, appointments that must be seen as a form of patronage, and there are works dedicated to Henry and Eleanor – less perhaps as the product of patronage than in the hope of favours to come – by writers as diverse as Adelard of Bath, Aelred of Rievaulx, Henry of Huntingdon, Joseph of Exeter, and Walter Map. Even if we thought that Henry was most solidly satisfied with the dedication of two works that in a way celebrated his own political achievement, Ranulph Glanville's treatise on the laws of England and the *Dialogus Scaccarii*, or *Dialogue on the Exchequer* (a monument to the newly established civil service, also attributed to Glanville), the stimulus and rewards that he and Eleanor proffered are undeniable. The Anglo-Norman poet Thomas may have written his noble romance of *Tristan* for Eleanor, and Marie de France too has a connection with Henry, dedicating to him her *Lais* (she is also perhaps his half-sister).

The spread of Arthurian romance itself, if we can trace its origins to the Angevin kingdom (and perhaps particularly to those Welsh interpreters or 'latimers' whose business it was to transmit the legends of their own people in the current lingua franca), may have had much to do with the marriage of Henry's and Eleanor's daughters, Eleanor, Matilda and Joanna, to, respectively, Alfonso VIII of Castile, Henry Duke of Saxony, and William II of Sicily.

Patrons, of course, expect some return on their (usually inconsiderable) investment, and it is not impossible that we should see some sort of cultural propaganda at work in royal sponsorship of literary works. It is difficult to see how Geoffrey's *Historia*, glorifying the Celtic British at the expense of the Anglo-Saxons, could have given particular satisfaction to the new Norman overlords, but the encouragement offered in England to Arthurian romance, as distinct from the baronial opposition of great magnates celebrated in French *chansons de geste* such as *Ogier le Danois* and *Girard de Vienne*, and distinct too from the particular kind of Arthurian romance favoured in France (where Arthur fades to a *roi faineant*), does suggest an interest in promoting a glorified image of centralised monarchy.

There are other ways, too, in which the dominant literary form of romance can be seen in relation to dominant social and political interests. The 'ancestral' romance, in which a very respectable set of adventures is invented to grace the imaginary forebears of a family, was one of the principal types of literary work commissioned by the newly established Anglo-Norman nobility in the thirteenth century. Likewise, the popularity of the 'exile-and-return' motif, in which the hero is dispossessed and returns to claim his inheritance by force, and of other types of story in which a younger and disadvantaged son wins through to fame and fortune, does suggest some attempt at an imaginative resolution of certain tensions present in a hierarchical society based on primogeniture. Maybe it was not so much a fantasy either:

tournaments flourished in the twelfth and thirteenth centuries, despite papal prohibitions, and a young landless knight could make a fortune in prizes and ransoms, as did William Marshall, Earl of Pembroke, in the late twelfth century. These tournaments were great social occasions, lasting several days, with much pageantry and feasting as well as fighting, and they came to be called, in allusion to Arthurian romance, 'Round Tables'. Such was the tournament held by Roger Mortimer at Kenilworth in 1279. Literature embodies, but is also embodied in, the life of its aristocratic sponsors.

The reign of Henry III has already been alluded to. Though castigated by historians for his lack of interest in constitutional monarchy, Henry is without much doubt the greatest royal patron of the arts in medieval England (though he would no doubt appear less great if his work had not been faithfully sustained and completed by his son), and it was he who established the expectation that the royal court should be the natural centre of cultural life and the fount of artistic patronage. It was not, in Henry's case, literature that was his chief interest as a patron, though he extended his usual generosity to Henry of Avranches, a kind of itinerant professional Euro-laureate who wrote eulogies for a pope, two emperors, three kings, six archbishops and a dozen or so assorted bishops. He had clearly mastered the art of winning patrons, and he wrote for Henry lives of St George and St Edward (the latter possibly the Anglo-Norman *Estorie de Seint Aedward le Rei* of 1245) for which he received the handsome stipend of 20*s.* a month in 1243–4. From 1255 he received 3*d.* a day as *magister Henricus versificator*, which, with the regular grant of wine, suggests that he had become almost a court official. There are twenty-three records of grants to him between 1243 and 1260.

Such royal favour must inevitably have provoked envy, and Michael of Cornwall was prompted to a long diatribe against the supercilious and cosmopolitan Master Henry, representing himself as the proud provincial taking up arms against a court of Frenchified sycophants. There is a reminder here of the opposition, trumped up or not, that Henry III aroused through the favour he showed to southern French poets at court, many of them brought there by his queen, Eleanor of Provence.

Henry III's patronage of the arts can be seen in two phases. In the early part of his reign he was the benefactor whose generosity assisted the projects of others with money, materials, and other kinds of support: during the period up to 1240 he gave aid for construction purposes to 350 institutions, and a further 170 received precious gold or silver utensils and vestments. After 1240 nearly all his energies and wealth were devoted to Westminster Abbey, to the purchase of every kind of ceremonial or decorative object, to the ennoblement of the shrine of Edward the Confessor, and to the enlargement of the building. Henry's piety and devotion to his chosen saint are unquestioned, as are his extravagance and love of beauty, but emulation too played a part. It was France, as always, that pricked English royal ambition most sharply. The reception of the relic of the Holy Blood in 1247 and its presentation to Westminster Abbey seems a direct imitation of the enshrinement of the Crown of Thorns by Louis IX in the Sainte Chapelle in Paris in 1239. Henry's meeting with Louis in 1254 influenced him

profoundly. To all these spurrings to endeavour, the rebuilding of
Westminster Abbey, mostly 1245–69, at his direct personal instigation, was
Henry's answer. It was a revolution: a great monument of religious art
constructed under the auspices of a secular connoisseur.

No expense was spared. Purbeck marble was shipped from the new quarries
in Dorset for columns and effigies, and at one time in 1253 Henry had forty-
nine marblers and fifteen polishers at work in London. A new 'court school'
emerged, attracting the best craftsmen from all over the country. To Edward
of Westminster, his artistic administrator, Henry sent a constant stream of
requests and instructions for building, carving, jewelwork, and he diverted
money for the task from wardships and special taxation of the Jews. During
the 1240s and 1250s quite a large part of the national revenue was going into
this national monument.

General and particular circumstances conspired to assist Henry's
enterprise. The country was wealthier than it had ever been, and was going
through a period of general economic expansion that was to allow the
population to expand to over three million by 1300 (as against one-and-a-half
million in 1100), only to end abruptly in the disastrous harvests and cruel
winters of 1317–19. English manufactured cloth and also grain were now
beginning to be exported, and imports of furs, wine and spices were
increasing. Mining as well as the textile industries was expanding, and
increasing trade encouraged the growth of ports like Bristol, Lynn, Hull and
Newcastle. Henry may also be said to have been specially fortunate in some
of the people he had working for him, as administrators, suppliers and
producers. Edward of Westminster, in particular, was the kind of king's clerk
who could faithfully convert Henry's wishes into reality, taking charge often
of a whole commission, and working out the details himself. At another level
there was the London draper, Adam de Basing, who between 1238 and 1260
received over £2,500 in payment for cloths and vestments, and Mabel of St
Edmunds, an embroiderer of rare skill, who was treated with characteristic
generosity by Henry. The records give some reality to this uniquely
integrated and consistent act of royal patronage, and it is well that they do,
for much has been lost, including even parts of the building itself, such as the
front of the north transept, heavy with statuary ('time-eaten sculpture', we
are told in 1723, now justly pared away by 'the ingenious Mr Dickinson').

Prosperity bred a general confidence as the thirteenth century advanced,
and images of aristocratic life and heraldic splendour began to burgeon in
wall-paintings in palaces, on tiles from the Chertsey Abbey workshops, on
bosses and spandrels (the spaces between the shoulders of adjacent arches). It
is a time of lavish decoration, exemplified in the richly illuminated
manuscripts, deriving from London and East Anglian workshops, that now
began to be commissioned by members of the nobility and even the local
gentry (witness, somewhat later, the Luttrell Psalter, c.1340) as well as by
religious houses, and exemplified too in the 'Eleanor crosses' erected by
Edward I (1272–1307) to mark the stages of his dead queen's journey from
Lincolnshire to Westminster in 1290. Commonly said to mark the beginnings
of the 'Decorated' style, these crosses, with their elaborately functionless
ogival (or onion-shaped) arches, and decorative crocketings and finials, were

perhaps inspired by the similar series of crosses made for St Louis twenty years before, while the life-sized effigies of Eleanor and his father that Edward I had commissioned for Westminster Abbey (1291–3) imitate a series of sixteen that Louis did of his ancestors (1263–4) and proclaim the prestige of the monarchy in the same way. The tomb of Edmund Crouchback (d.1296) at Westminster is one of the most notable: elaborate as it is, it was designed to look even more extravagant, when the crestings and pinnacles were gilt and the canopy inlaid with stained glass set upon tinfoil.

Edward was less fortunate than his father in some respects: he ran out of court masons and sculptors for the crosses, since they were being done in such a hurry, and some of them had to be done by sub-contractors. He showed more interest in literature than Henry, though, especially Arthurian literature: he had a volume of French romance with him when he went on crusade just before his accession, and held an elaborate Round Table in 1284 to celebrate his conquest of Wales; a French Arthurian romance of *Escanor* (1277–82) was dedicated to his queen, Eleanor of Castile.

Edward's contribution to the completion of his father's schemes at Westminster was very important, and should not be underestimated, but his most enduring legacy, and the one area of royal patronage – or at least expenditure – where he vied with his father, is the series of royal castles in North Wales. Eight of these were built between 1277 and 1301, costing over £60,000. With their curtain walls with flanking half-round towers, great double-towered gateways and turreted tops, they are most people's idea of what a 'castle' should be. They bring to an end the development of the military fortress, and Caernarfon (begun 1283), which was designed to be also a future royal residence, has been called 'aesthetically perhaps the most satisfying secular building of its size which the Middle Ages have left to us' (this may be less of a recommendation than it seems).

Another aspect of royal patronage can be seen in the feast organised by Edward I to celebrate the knighting of his son in 1306. An unusual surviving record lists ninety-two minstrels who were present at the feast, including nineteen trumpeters, six taborers, twenty-six harpers, and twenty-two string-players. These minstrels were not permanently resident at court, but might stay in service for long spells when they were called. Trumpeters went around with the king to enhance his dignity, 'cornours' (horn-players) blew the night-watches, announced meals, and warned of departure or fire, taborers and fifers served as a dance-band, and the stringmen played like a café orchestra at mealtimes, or in private rooms, or if the king were ill or recovering after blood-letting. Minstrels were especially important at great feasts, where they organised shows and spectacles. Some of them went on campaign too, composing victory songs when appropriate.

Such a record alerts us to the important part played by music in the aristocratic household – and reminds us too of the equally important part it played in the life of those classes of society whose music-making leaves less of an imprint on the documents. One should add, too, that music could function not only for secular entertainment and religious devotion, but also for what might loosely be called 'political' purposes. The musical compositions performed at ceremonial and state occasions could have an important

propaganda purpose in asserting the stability of the regime, while by contrast
– but still 'political' – versions of the divine office would be composed to
celebrate the 'martyrdom' of figures such as Simon de Montfort (d.1265) and
Thomas of Lancaster (d.1319).

At the same time, however, that one asserts the importance of music at this
period, one must also recognise that England remained rather insular in
terms of musical development. Henry III had been quite prominent as a
patron of music, but during the latter part of the thirteenth century and the
first half of the fourteenth there was little contact with music in France, or
evidence of the influence of the extraordinary developments in the polyphonic
elaboration of the motet that were taking place there. It was perhaps the
establishment of choirs at the new royal chapels, such as that of St Stephen's,
Westminster, by Edward III in 1348, that, as one factor at least, eventually
led to the resurgence of English music under the early Lancastrian kings.

The son so promisingly launched at the feast of 1306 did not turn out too
well, and it was left to Edward III (1327–77) to resume the role of royal
patron and provider. This he did in a very positive manner, giving his
support to (though not actually paying for) the rebuilding of the choir at
Gloucester cathedral, where the body of his murdered father was buried,
with the result that the new 'Perpendicular' style of architecture,
characterised by flat rectilinear blind panelling and window tracery,
developed by masons of the court school in their continuing work at
Westminster (particularly St Stephen's Chapel, completed at vast royal
expense in 1348, and painted 1352–61, so as to be 'one universal blaze of
splendour and magnificence'), was extended for the first time to the provinces.
Edward, though, was generally more interested in pageantry, ostentation and
comfort than piety: 'Round Tables' proliferated in his day, the most notable
being that at Windsor in 1358, where two captive kings, David Bruce of
Scotland and John of France, were put on display. Heraldic trappings of
feast and tournament grew richer, and coats of arms and badges appeared
everywhere – on plate, brooches, hangings and beds. Costume became more
extravagant, with much purfiling (or decorative edging), particoloured
striping, slitting and dagging of sleeves, and plate-armour reached its greatest
magnificence, exemplified in the funeral achievements of the Black Prince
(d.1376) at Canterbury.

Above all, Edward introduced a building programme for the royal palaces
the organisation of which rivalled that of his great-grandfather. He had an
energetic administrator in William of Wykeham (who exercised his own
personal patronage in the building of Winchester and New Colleges) as Clerk
of the King's Works, and by the end of his reign there are established posts
for King's Mason and King's Carpenter, and also established royal painters.
Windsor was transformed from a castle into a palace (1350–77), with
refurbishing of the royal lodgings on the most sumptuous scale. A chronicle
says:

Almost all the masons and carpenters throughout the whole of England were brought
to that building, so that hardly anyone could have any good mason or carpenter,
except in secret, on account of the king's prohibition.

At Eltham, Edward III built a new range of royal lodgings (1350–9). He made improvements at King's Langley (1359–77), including the installation of a quite large and elaborate bath-house with hot running water. He built virtually a new palace at Sheen (1358–70), with much glass and elaborate decoration in the new chambers. Leeds and Rotherhithe were other royal castles where the residential quarters were upgraded, and a completely new royal castle, all trace of which has now disappeared, was built at Queenborough, on the Isle of Sheppey.

Richard II (1377–99) continued this work, though it is difficult to credit him with the same boldness as a royal patron as his grandfather, Edward III. He had some fancy additions made at Sheen, which was his favourite residence and the one he caused to be demolished in 1395 after the death of Queen Anne. At Eltham he added (1384–8) a new bath-house, a painted chamber, a dancing chamber, a spicery, and a saucery. Much of the time he was working with an already existing organisational machinery which more or less ran itself. However, the king's influence is never less than very significant, as is illustrated by the manner in which funds for building works, which were cut off while Richard was more or less in the hands of his opponents in 1388–9, were renewed when he resumed power. In 1393 he began rebuilding the Great Hall of Westminster, employing the old King's mason, Henry Yevele, as his chief architect, and Hugh Herland as the carpenter for the great hammer-beam roof. It is Richard II's most magnificent legacy, and was completed more or less in time for his deposition there in 1399.

For the rest, Richard's tastes ran to more personal kinds of ostentation, such as may have prompted the commissioning of the Wilton Diptych, and the colossally expensive gilded bronze effigies of himself and his queen in Westminster Abbey, and to lavish expenditure on objets d'art and clothes. He probably spent more money than any other king, but much of it was spent, in an attempt to keep up with France, on the import of foreign-made goods: the decline of *Opus Anglicanum*, the traditional English embroidery, can probably be traced to the taste for imported clothes, while the deterioration in the quality of English illuminated manuscripts (the ones that Richard II commissioned, such as the *Liber Regalis*, a memento of his coronation, do not even represent the best that was available) may similarly owe something to the preferment of the French style. Though Richard can be credited with creating an atmosphere of luxury and refinement, and encouraging his own kinds of extravagance in a few others (John of Gaunt's rebuilding of Kenilworth Castle as a lavishly appointed residential palace would be an example), he did nothing to establish a machinery for the distribution of royal patronage, as did Henry III and Edward III.

Something similar would have to be said about his role in the great flowering of poetry in his reign. Chaucer (d.1400) was a member of his court, certainly, and received royal patronage in the form of employment, annuities and grants. But the jobs were not sinecures, and there is no sign anywhere in Chaucer's poetry, nor in the manuscripts that survive, of such characteristic tributes and recognitions as are usually thought to be the proper return for patronage. *The Legend of Good Women* is playfully submitted to Queen Anne, and *The Book of the Duchess* must surely have been done under Gaunt's auspices, but there is no mention anywhere in Chaucer's poetry of Richard. On the contrary, the circle of readers that Chaucer acknowledges is that of men much like himself in status – civil servants, diplomats, country gentlemen, lawyers – and not that of the royal and aristocratic entourage.

The traditional role of the 'court-poet' was to be a member of the household, rewarded in the same way as other servants for his services – such was Froissart at the court of Edward III's queen, Philippa of Hainault, as late as 1369, and such will be Lydgate, with some differences, in the next century. But though the importance of this role and this relationship must be acknowledged, it does not seem to be an appropriate account of Chaucer. Chaucer himself, of course, pretends to the incompetence of a professional entertainer, toying with the image of himself as a poor hack, but more properly what he gives evidence of is the emergence of the 'man of letters' – educated, independent and bound to no service. Gower (d.1408) is not dissimilar: he seems to choose his patrons, rather than they him, and he discards Richard, one feels, not because Richard failed to reward him but because he did not come up to John Gower's expectations.

The age of Chaucer and Gower was the era in which English poetry emerged to take over the commanding heights of the cultural economy, after having been long condemned to play second or third fiddle to Anglo-Norman and French, and to be preoccupied mostly with the entertainment and edification of non-aristocratic audiences. But the influence of royal and aristocratic patrons seems to have played little part in this take-over. Humphrey de Bohun, Earl of Hereford, gave his permission for the English romance of *William of Palerne* to be made for him in the 1350s (and commissioned the only series of illuminated MSS that can be compared in quality with those produced earlier in the century), and there may be other aristocratic patrons in the west. But the crucial changes seem to be taking place without the active connivance of the traditional patrons of literature – perhaps a sign that their traditional role has been eroded. By a historical coincidence, English floods back into the areas of literary activity evacuated by Anglo-Norman at just the point when the aristocratic household culture that sustained that activity is in decline.

The splendours of Richard's patronage, hollow as they may seem in some respects, nevertheless look like splendours from the perspective of his Lancastrian successors in the fifteenth century. A lavish feast could always be put on for the right occasion, as for the coronation of Henry VI in 1429 –

Here follows the second course: Meat blanched, barred with gold. Jelly divided by the writing and musical notation, Te Deum Laudamus. Pig gilded. Crane. Bittern. Rabbits; chickens gilded. Partridge. Peacock adorned. Great bream. White leach, with an antelope of red carved therein, a crown about his neck with a chain of gold. Flampayne powdered with leopards and fleurs de lis of gold. Fritters, a leopard's head, with two ostrich feathers . . .

but the Lancastrian kings seem generally to have been short of money. Others may have profited from the wars with France, like Sir John Fastolf, building Caister Castle and purchasing a good library on the proceeds, but not the Henries. Henry V (1413–22) seems to have been conscious of the need to promote English, and he encouraged Lydgate in a new elaborate style in liturgical writing as well as acting as his patron for the *Troy Book*, but he was too preoccupied with the French war, and reigned too briefly, to take it far. Henry VI's (1422–61) own patronage took a sober form, being chiefly remembered in the foundation of Eton and King's College, and perhaps it was his taste as much as his straitened circumstances that led him to declare of his two foundations, in 1448:

I wol that the edification of my same College proceed in large form clear and substantial, setting apart superfluity of too great curious works of entaille and busy moulding.

In all this, an exception has to be made for music, which during the era of the Lancastrian kings was one of England's principal glories. There may be incidental reasons for this – the elaborate polyphonic styles may have been encouraged, as an assertion of orthodoxy, by the opposition of the Lollards to all forms of musical display and ornamentation, and certainly the increasing number of chantries, dedicated to the singing of masses, must have had an influence – but royal patronage played a very significant part. The establishment of the choir at St Stephen's Chapel, Westminster, by Edward I in 1348 has already been mentioned, but it was Henry IV and his sons who were famous for their love of music. Henry V seems to have taken a special interest in the new forms of elaborated liturgical style, in both words and music, and may have worked with Edmund Lacy, Dean of the Royal Chapel at Windsor (1414–17), later Bishop of Exeter (1420), to encourage John Lydgate to compose appropriate words to new musical settings to be sung in the Royal Chapel; the Old Hall MS, the major surviving manuscript of English music of the Middle Ages, was probably made for or in the household of his next oldest brother, Thomas, Duke of Clarence (1338–1421). Clarence's own chapel was where Lionel Power (d.1445), perhaps a figure as important in his way as a musical composer as John Dunstable (c.1390–1453?), spent his formative years, while Dunstable himself was in the employ of Henry V's next oldest brother, John, Duke of Bedford (1389–1435), principally in France. For all of these politically shrewd Lancastrian kings and dukes, music was not only a form of devotion and a source of pleasure, but also well recognised for the part it could play in enhancing the prestige of the regime through ceremonial.

Humphrey of Gloucester, Henry V's younger brother, and one of the most important figures in the country's affairs from his brother's death until his own in 1447, had the family interest in music, but in other respects he is clearly in a class of his own. He has the reputation of being the greatest patron of letters of the English Middle Ages, and he certainly had dealings with many of the writers of his day, including Lydgate, Hoccleve, Capgrave and the anonymous translator of Palladius *De Re Rustica* (a Roman treatise on horticulture). This last gives evidence of Humphrey's keen interest in his work, and of his habit of stopping by to give advice on metre, while Lydgate tells us how Humphrey asked for moralising envoys to be added to the stories of the *Fall of Princes* (as if Lydgate needed asking) and at one point brought in a copy of a recent work by the Italian humanist Coluccio Salutati to provide some stimulus for the ageing poet. With all this, Humphrey seems to have been reluctant to give Lydgate the financial rewards he expected: one of Lydgate's best poems is the comical begging epistle he addresses to Humphrey as he moves into Book II of the *Fall*, but it had little effect, and Lydgate finished the poem in 1436 more or less gloomily acknowledging that nothing much would be forthcoming.

Humphrey was an avid collector of books, and had his agents on the Continent buying and commissioning books for him, a large number of which he eventually bequeathed to the University of Oxford. He seems, however, to have done remarkably little to encourage book production at home, and this criticism might be levelled against aristocratic patronage generally in the fifteenth century. Though this was an age when manuscripts of the English poems of Gower, Chaucer, Lydgate, Hoccleve and others were beginning to be produced in some quantity, and with some degree of opulence, it was only comparatively rarely that aristocratic patrons were involved. The baton seems to have passed to the classes of new readers among the urban burgesses and the country gentry, and it is notable that Caxton too, when he began printing at Westminster in 1476, though he paid fulsome tribute to the encouragement he had received from royalty and members of the nobility, and invented occasions for such tribute when they were otherwise lacking, addressed himself principally to the tastes of this larger and more amorphous audience.

The aristocracy, of course, were not inactive in literary patronage, even if they spent some significant part of the century squabbling over the division of their increasingly precarious revenues. The Lord Berkeley gave important encouragement to John Trevisa in his work of translating the Latin encyclopaedias of Higden (the *Polychronicon*) and Bartholomaeus Anglicus (*De Proprietatibus Rerum*) in the latter part of the fourteenth century, and his daughter Elizabeth commissioned the verse translation of Boethius by John Walton, canon of Oseney, in 1410, and probably also his prose translation of Vegetius *De Re Militari*. It was a daughter, too, Elizabeth, daughter of the Earl of Warwick, for whom Lydgate wrote his *Guy of Warwick* in celebration of the family's putative ancestor. This was one of a number of commissions that Lydgate received from aristocratic ladies, for lives of favourite saints, expositions of the liturgy, and properly serious meditations on the mutability of things. In fact, Lydgate seems to have absorbed most of the aristocratic patronage that was on offer in the first half of the fifteenth century. In addition to the works already mentioned, he wrote Mummings for court and other entertainments, much of the official verse for the festivities surrounding Henry VI's coronation, a versified *Title and Pedigree of Henry VI*, at the instigation of the Earl of Warwick, and a translation of Deguileville's *Pilgrimage of the Life of Man* for the Earl of Salisbury. He wrote, let it be said, for every other class of society as well, and the aristocracy can claim no special credit nor accept any special responsibility for him.

Lydgate wrote some poetry that might conceivably be associated with the 'game of love' as played at the court – that social, cultural and erotic 'game' of which the surviving written poetry, such as Chaucer's Prologue to the *Legend of Good Women*, may give us such a pale reflection – including *The*

Complaint of the Black Knight. His literary factotum, John Shirley, has the plausible opinion that one of his love-ballades was made at the instance of 'a squire that served at Love's court'. But there is little to attach these poems to, and indeed some mystery surrounds the court-poetry of the fifteenth century generally. A fair quantity of it is written, including allegorical love-visions of the traditional type and upgraded courtly romances employing the new Chaucerian style, and some of it can be associated with particular kinds of aristocratic environment, like the translation of Alain Chartier's *La Belle Dame sans merci* by Sir Richard Ros, whose career as a soldier, diplomat and courtier conforms to a classic pattern. But there is not much that can be located and given a provenance in this way, and it is one of the ironies of the fifteenth century that the most sophisticated court poetry of the day in English is written by foreigners who happen to find themselves in English prisons – Charles of Orleans and King James I of Scotland.

It seems on the face of it likely that the households of Humphrey of Gloucester, or of Margaret of Anjou after she became Henry VI's queen in 1446, would have done something to stimulate the production of poetry, if only the verse of the 'game of love'. But nothing very much can be produced in evidence, apart from the poems in Bodleian Library MS Fairfax 16 attributed to the Duke of Suffolk, and a good deal of the poetry has the faded 'literary' air of writing being done not in a living social environment but in imitation of what that environment might be thought to be like. The real influences on artistic production, in literature, architecture, sculpture and manuscript painting, are now, it seems, being exerted elsewhere, outside the households of king and aristocracy.

There are exceptions, of course. The Lancastrian kings and dukes did much to encourage music, and it was in the household of John, Duke of Bedford, that the greatest composer of the English Middle Ages, John Dunstable, flourished, though this may be as much because Bedford spent his best years in France (most of Dunstable's music survives in Continental manuscripts) as anything. The Warwick chapel erected in memory of Richard Beauchamp (d.1439) is a splendid piece of traditional aristocratic patronage of the arts, with a magnificent copper effigy of the Earl.

For a time, too, Edward IV (1461–83) seems to have asserted something of the traditional royal authority. He put the royal finances on a sounder footing, partly by raising money for fighting wars in France and never fighting any, partly by improving the administration of the royal estates, and he took great pains to elevate the status of the king and appear magnificent: a German visitor in 1465 is properly impressed. The tournament between Lord Scales and the Bastard of Burgundy in 1467 is one of the grand ceremonial occasions of the fifteenth century, with the minutest attention to every detail of accoutrement and procedure. Edward also, taking as his model the practice of his Burgundian hosts observed during his exile in 1470–1, bought some expensive books and established the first real royal library. But there was little consistency to his activity as a patron and, apart from the library, little long-term consequence.

The Church

The influence of the Church on artistic production is pervasive and ubiquitous, the more so in the surviving record; there are 100 surviving medieval churches for every medieval house, 1,000 or more manuscripts containing religious writing for every scrap of secular song or verse. It is not so much a matter of 'cultural and social setting' as of the motive, inspiration and sole subject-matter of art and literature. Most of what has been spoken of in relation to royal and aristocratic patronage is connected with the Church, and nearly all that has to be said of commercial and provincial production will be too.

The Church in the Middle Ages was a vast multinational corporate institution, employing an army of clerics (perhaps 60,000 in England), including nearly all those with any pretension to education, administering estates covering, in England, about a third of all the cultivated land in the country, exercising a dominance both physical, through the sheer scale of its buildings in relation to what lay about them, whether the parish church in the village or the cathedral in the town, and also mental, through the universal acceptance of its doctrines and codes. In such circumstances it is not possible to do more than sketch in a broad role for the Church in influencing literary, musical and artistic production, to draw attention to some important changes in that role, and perhaps to hint at some matters of more particular interest.

Pious devotion, a more elaborately developed processional liturgy, and superior building techniques provided the motive, the need and the practical means for the erection of the great Norman cathedrals (Durham, Winchester and Norwich, for instance), which at their smallest were about twice the size of the largest Anglo-Saxon cathedral (at North Eltham), but it was money and organisation that made it possible. The professionalisation of the clergy under archbishop Lanfranc, appointed by William I in 1070, and the conversion of the bishoprics and larger abbeys into feudal baronies, concentrated power in a more effectively disposable manner, while the presence of a small number of rich Norman overlords instead of a large number of Anglo-Saxon thanes made endowment also more effective.

The great growth of monastic houses in the twelfth century (between 1066 and 1154 the number of houses rose from 48 to about 300, and the number of monks from 850 to 5,000) depended upon similar factors. The Cistercians received a very large share of the endowments, and they got it because they were well organised to demonstrate they could put it to good use, as well as because they were evidently very pious: the austerity and lack of decoration of early Cistercian architecture may have helped to fortify this impression. A good deal of wealth changed hands during the strife of Stephen's reign without too much nice observance of propriety, and one would expect that the new possessors, without being conscience-stricken, would be concerned that their endowments should go to institutions whose piety would guarantee a good investment.

It was the possession of endowments such as this, and the ability of monastic and secular chapters to attract more gifts of the same kind, that made possible the erection of the great cathedrals such as those at Canterbury, Ely, Gloucester, Lincoln and York over the next 200 years, and especially during the century from 1250 to 1350. In most cases, building and rebuilding went on for centuries, as money became available, and Exeter and Salisbury are exceptional in being built in a single burst of a few decades.

Shrines and the cult of relics were very important: at Canterbury, between 1198 and 1213, offerings to the shrine of St Thomas brought in twenty-five per cent of the cathedrals whole revenue, and, though most of this had of course to be spent on the shrine, some could be diverted to the fabric of the building. In 1224, at the end of a successful advertising campaign for St Wulfstan, the bishop and chapter at Worcester set in hand the eastern extension of their cathedral. Lincoln was glad to have St Hugh, York St William, and Westminster, as we have seen, St Edward. When the body of Edward II was accepted for burial by the Abbot of Gloucester in 1327, his was an act of considerable courage, but it was one for which he was amply rewarded. Edward III fostered the cult of his father, less out of filial piety than out of a desire to emulate the cult of St Louis, so effectively exploited by the French kings, and more and more pilgrims made their way to the shrine to make offering. The choir was rebuilt to house the shrine more suitably and the monastery history comments that 'it was the common opinion that if all the offerings thus made had been spent on the church, it could have been rebuilt easily from the foundations'.

The presence of such shrines added impetus to the desire of the wealthy to have tombs in the near vicinity, another source of income for the church. The shrines have all gone, the tombs remain, contributing to the impression the modern observer might have that a church is a kind of funeral parlour, and equally to the impression he has in Catholic countries that the churches are full of bric-a-brac. So they were in the English Middle Ages, stuffed with crucifixes, cult images, statues, which, being made mostly of wood, have not survived. As for the tombs, from being the prerogative of royalty (the oldest that survives is that of King John in Worcester, 1225, the most famous those of Henry III and Queen Eleanor, 1291–3, and Edmund Crouchback, 1296, in Westminster Abbey), they became more and more the common property of knights and gentry.

One of the sore complaints against the friars made by the monastic orders and secular clergy was that they had usurped this right of burial and the endowments that went with it. The friars, in fact, had succeeded to the reputation that the Cistercians had had in the twelfth century: the friars represented themselves as, and seemed to be, more authentic witnesses to the pure apostolic faith, and a better investment against the perils of the future than the luxury-loving monks and indolent parish priests. The Franciscan church described in the late fourteenth century anti-mendicant poem, *Pierce the Ploughman's Crede*, is profuse with funerary ornament. Another late fourteenth-century poem, *Piers Plowman*, has a graphic passage describing a friar selling confession in exchange for endowments, and promising to have the name of the donor inscribed in the window that he has paid for. Langland, the author of the poem, clearly regards this as a corrupt practice, though it becomes common enough.

What we do not get any mention of, and certainly no longer see, since the mendicant churches have virtually all disappeared, is the light and air and unity of space of the hall-churches built for the friars to preach in, such as the vast London church of the Franciscans in Newgate begun in 1306. This church may have played an important part in the development of Perpendicular architecture.

Such trends as these are general, and in danger of becoming abstractions. It may be worth stressing the importance of individual bishops and other churchmen in providing the initiative, the drive or the money for particular programmes of church-building. After the Lincoln fire of 1141, for instance, it was Bishop Alexander of Blois (d.1148) who set himself the task of repairing the damage and adorning the west front of the cathedral with the statuary that still, happily, survives. He showed what a wealthy and determined prelate could do. The similarly magnificent west front at Wells was likewise set in hand by the individual initiative of Bishop Joscelin and carried out by his energetic building administrator, Elias of Dereham. John Grandisson, Bishop of Exeter 1327–69, was a typically wealthy ecclesiastical patron of the arts, and he pushed ahead vigorously with the reconstruction of the nave. He did not always, unfortunately, manage to get very good sculptors.

The history of York Minster is instructive in illustrating some of the human factors, as well as economic realities, that lie behind a long programme of church building. The enlargement of the church began with the building of the new south and north transepts during the archepiscopate of Walter Gray (1215–45), who was both generous and energetic and also enormously wealthy, and had the added advantage of being in office for a long time and therefore able to recover from the colossal expenses of going to Rome for his pallium. Work on the chapter-house and nave progressed during the later part of the century, receiving unexpected support from the contributions of those passing through York on their way to and from the Scottish wars (the shrine of St John of Beverley profited in the same way, his banner having been found particularly effective in battle). The west window was paid for by Archbishop William de Melton (1317–40), who otherwise spent most of his money endowing his brother's family; and, though we should not underestimate the part played by the residentiary canons in prompting and encouraging, it was left again to the individual initiative of another Archbishop, John Thoresby (1352–73), to push ahead with the now sorely needed new choir. He put this in hand at a chapter session in 1361, paid £2,600 toward it himself, and even got the chapter clergy to accept a levy on their earnings to help pay for it.

Archbishop Scrope (1398–1405) contributed in an unusual way, for the offerings at his shrine, after he had been summarily executed as a rebel by Henry IV's forces, were diplomatically diverted to the fabric fund and the less contentious St William by the cathedral clergy. Archbishop Henry Bowet (1407–23) managed to get local aristocrats and ecclesiastics to contribute to the completion of the great east window. Not much came from the burghers of York, though this may have been as much because they were excluded as because they were reluctant to contribute: this had a spectacular effect on the York parish churches.

It may be that social and economic factors of this kind are what we are likely to hear about from the extant records, and that larger trends are still more important. General prosperity, as in the late thirteenth century, must have played a very significant part, and one would assume that the Black Death must have had at least some temporary effect on programmes of church-building, though there is little evidence that it did (at Beverley it does seem to have coincided with the end of a style, presumably because of the death of the craftsmen who were working then). Generalisation is easy and usually dangerous (witness the many uses to which the Black Death has been put in 'explaining' the development of Gothic art), especially when the evidence that survives is of a multitude of personal and practical decisions and activities. The flourishing of highly naturalistic foliage carving in the late thirteenth and early fourteenth century, at Lincoln, Exeter, York and Southwell, has often been acclaimed as a revolution in the perception of the natural world and fitted into histories of art that go in for such revolutions of perception. But it was a fashion of very brief duration and the whole style of carving at Exeter, for instance, changed with the arrival of new craftsmen in 1308.

One might think of more homely and practical reasons at work: the tastes of individual craftsmen and the spread of a fashion within what must have been a close-knit craft community; the influence of pattern books; the enjoyment of the opportunities given for precision and deep undercutting by a new supply of stone-cutting drills. Likewise, the unusually fine and elaborate carving in some twelfth-century Herefordshire churches, notably Shobdon and Kilpeck, is evidence of the availability of contacts with Southern France; but more specifically it is evidence of the travels of one talented craftsman and his ability to absorb what he had seen and to communicate it both in his own carving and in the example he gave to others. Even a powerful and ambitious patron might depend for success upon the availability of the right craftsmen: Henry III was fortunate as well as energetic.

Churches of course were more than stocks and stones and they contributed something more to the strengthening of faith than the witness they gave of the amount of money and energy some were prepared to spend on it. They were in a very real sense the books of the laity, who would see around them in church, whilst their attention remained undistracted by services in Latin they could barely understand, the complete programme of Christian history. In the west window, or on the west wall, or over the chancel arch, would be the representation of Doomsday; above the altar the Crucifixion, the events leading up to which would be commemorated in painting or statuary of the stations of the Cross; along the walls of the nave would be ranged sequences of pictures in which Old Testament scenes on one side would be set in correspondence to their typological New Testament fulfilment on the other. Some churches would have still more specific kinds of moralistic instruction or exhortation set forth in wall-painting or glass: the church at Hoxne in Suffolk is one of the few surviving representatives of many that must have had similar cycles illustrating the seven deadly sins, the seven works of mercy, the seven ages of man, the seven sacraments, as well as Judgement

The Crucifixion of Christ, from the Evesham Psalter (c.1250).

and Crucifixion. A great cathedral could be a complete education in the Christian faith, a series of lessons to be read, in bench-ends, roof-bosses, carvings on capitals, tympana (the spaces between the top of doors and the arch), even exterior gargoyles, as well as wall-paintings, glass and statuary.

In some cases, it is true, the lesson could not be read, only apprehended to be present. High in the transepts and angel choir of Norwich Cathedral, and seen only by cleaners and repairers before modern days of binoculars and floodlighting, are roof-bosses carved with infinite delicacy, lines and dots, for instance, representing the writing in books held in the hands of figures, and the hawthorn berries precisely carved down to their black tips. Roof-bosses, it should be noted, are a disproportionately important source of knowledge about medieval carving, surviving in unusual quantity because they were generally out of reach of depredators at the time of the Reformation and Commonwealth. Their remoteness may also have encouraged a certain element of fantasy and irrelevance on the part of the carvers, though generally speaking they are no more fanciful than carved objects much nearer at hand, such as misericords, which seem generally to have been handed over to secular subjects. Sometimes we may be dealing with natural ebullience on the part of the craftsman, sometimes, particularly in the case of roof-bosses and misericords, with the constraints placed upon the craftsman by the medium and the near-impossibility of doing anything that does not look, as a whole, fantastic. It is possible that some cocking of snooks at authority was involved too, especially if we recall that these craftsmen are laymen.

This effect is more pronounced in illuminated manuscripts: previously copied and decorated more or less exclusively in monasteries, with all the severe constraints on the illustrative programme that this implies, manuscripts are by the late thirteenth century illuminated more and more by lay artists, whether working as itinerants in monastic scriptoria, or in their own ateliers. They give some scope to invention in their elaboration of marginal grotesques, some of which may but not all of which can be associated with the iconography of text or main picture, and they provided what was no doubt a very acceptable form of diversion and distraction to the cultivated owners of such manuscripts.

Again, it would not do to generalise this as a trend or to forget the role that continues to be played by monastic ateliers in the production of illuminated manuscripts. The most important manuscript produced in England in the late fourteenth century, the Carmelite Missal, was done at the London Whitefriars, and a named painter like John Siferwas, who did the Sherborne Missal and also the Gospel Lectionary for Salisbury Cathedral commissioned as a gift by Lord Lovell (d.1408), was most probably a monk at Sherborne itself. A Carthusian manuscript of the same period (British Library MS Add. 37049) provides a reminder of the strictest kind of monastic control over production: a collection of devotional and penitential texts, it is illustrated by precise, aesthetically unpleasing pictures that function in the most practical manner as mnemonic diagrams of such points of doctrine as the significance of the Crucifixion, the function of the sacraments and the nature of the seven deadly sins. The tradition if not the excessively austere manner of such a manuscript can be traced back to the

The Crucifixion of Christ, from the Sherborne Missal (c.1405).

manuscripts of works such as the *Hortus Deliciarum* and the *Somme le Roi*, which attempt to illustrate in memorably graphic form such allegorical concepts as the ladder of virtue and the tree of vices and virtues.

Something that can be the subject of more confident generalisation is the change in the social and cultural circumstances of English literary production in the fourteenth century. Up till about 1350, nearly all writers were clerics and the matter of nearly all their writing is religion. The popular romances constitute the sole substantial exception to this generalisation and even there it would appear that many of the authors, as of romances like *Havelok*, must be clerics, and it has been commonly observed that the English romances as a whole have a strongly pious and didactic cast as distinct from their French and, to a lesser extent, Anglo-Norman originals and analogues.

Be that as it may, it is clear that in the twelfth and thirteenth centuries the Church, and particularly the monasteries, dominate all aspects of English writing. Nearly everything that survives from the twelfth century – the continuation of the Anglo-Saxon Chronicle, the collections of sermons, the debate of the Body and Soul that forms one of the Worcester fragments – is known to come from monasteries, and works like *The Proverbs of Alfred* and the *Bestiary* can best be associated with small religious houses. Orm, Lincolnshire author of English verse-translations of the gospels (c.1200) was an Augustinian canon. Layamon was a parish priest, and the author of the *Owl and the Nightingale* was certainly a cleric of some kind.

The decrees of the 4th Lateran Council of 1216, imposing penance and confession as a requirement upon all Christians, triggered a spate of manuals of penitential instruction, homiletic writings, legendaries of saints and biblical paraphrases, treatises on the seven deadly sins, some in prose, most in verse, which all together constitute the great bulk of English writing before Chaucer. Examples are the vast *South English Legendary* (c.1280, but constantly added to); the *Cursor Mundi* (c.1300), a verse paraphrase of biblical history; the penitential treatise, *Handlyng Synne*, begun 1303 by Robert Mannyng, Gilbertine canon of Sempringham; the *Northern Homily Cycle* (c.1360, but again constantly added to); and, perhaps the most notable of all, *The Prick of Conscience*, an 8,000-line poem of remorseless doctrinal instruction which survives in more manuscripts (124) than any other English poem of the Middle Ages. One of the manuscripts in which it appears, the Vernon MS (Oxford, Bodleian Library, MS eng.poet.a.1), written down probably at Bordesley Abbey in Worcestershire about 1380, can be taken as summing up this phase in the history of English poetry. Weighing nearly half a hundredweight, its contents almost entirely English verse, the Vernon MS contains everything that anyone could possibly want for 'sowle hele' ('soul's health'), and more.

Meanwhile, though, the tradition of clerical instruction that it represents, which had dominated English poetry since the Conquest, was showing signs of fragmentation. Chaucer was the poet who set the models for the fifteenth century, even for monks like Lydgate, and he was not a cleric, nor was all of his writing concerned with penitential instruction, however much his modern exegetes may strive to make it seem so.

There are other strands in the network of clercial dominance that need drawing out before brief mention is made of the role of the Church in the fifteenth century. The friars, from the time of their arrival in England in the 1220s, exerted a considerable influence, particularly on the development of short devotional religious poems and songs in the vernacular. There are a number of manuscript miscellanies attributed to them in which are gathered together songs and lyrics in praise of the Virgin or celebrating the Passion, stories and treatises to read aloud, verse-sermons, exempla and proverbs to incorporate in sermons, as well as odd copies of things not at all edifying that the friars found interesting for their own sake. The tone is generally less heavy than in monastic and related compilations.

Nevertheless, manuscripts such as these testify to the overwhelmingly clerical cast of English culture during the period – and this is as true of music as of literature. These manuscripts contain some of the few examples of notated non-liturgical music that survive from the fourteenth and fifteenth centuries, and demonstrate how resistant, generally, England was to the new developments in secular music that were taking place in France. The secular polyphony of the motet, which was a dominant form in France during these centuries, was virtually unknown in England until about 1400, and secular polyphonic song did not become established – as far as can be determined from surviving records (music manuscripts suffered exceptionally severe depredations at the time of the Reformation) – until half a century later.

The friars were also chiefly responsible for popularising in literary form the kind of affective devotion that took its beginnings from St Anselm and St Bernard in the twelfth century but which the Franciscans especially had made their special cult in the thirteenth. The Virgin is represented as a loving mother, singing lullabies to her infant son, or pleading with him at the foot of the Cross, while Christ is represented in his suffering humanity, scourged and bleeding, beseeching man for his love. These are the themes of medieval English devotional lyrics, as inspired particularly by the friars, and they are developed even more fully in the fourteenth century, as the enormously influential *Meditations on the Life of Christ*, written in Latin by an Italian Franciscan in the late thirteenth century, begins to be more widely known. The *Meditations* are an emotionally highly charged narrative of Christ's life, appealing directly to the reader to visualise and share in Christ's suffering, and to respond with an almost human love.

Many narratives of the Passion drew inspiration from this account, as did the Mystery plays in the fifteenth century, and developments in religious art are clearly related. A nativity of the thirteenth century shows the child displayed on a kind of altar, separated from the Virgin, who gazes intently before her, regardless of her son, meditating on the mystery of which she is part and the prophecy which has come to pass. In the fourteenth century she becomes more human, radiant with maternal pride, entwining eyes with her son and sometimes visited by even more touching displays of feeling. Likewise, earlier representations of the crucified Christ show him standing firm with open eyes and lifted head, while the fourteenth century characteristically emphasises the suffering, the closed eyes, the drooping form. The earlier artist thought less of stirring emotions than of recalling the dogma of the Redemption: the one creates monuments that witness to a spiritual truth, the other seeks, often restlessly and with a tendency to sentimentality, for an emotionally affective visual language.

It would not be implausible to associate these developments with a growth in the sense of the importance of the individual in the fourteenth century, and to recognise the profound disturbance that such a sense might make within the established institution of the Church. A demand for a more intense kind of personal devotion, a closer imitation of Christ, a return to a life of apostolic purity, had been recurrent in the Middle Ages as a symptom of newly aroused religious fervour. So it had been with the Cistercian revival in the twelfth century and with the Franciscan movement in the thirteenth century and the Church had always had the flexibility to absorb these waves of fervour into its structures and institutionalise them.

Now, however, in the fourteenth century, the Church no longer seemed able to do this, whether because it had grown too wealthy or too corrupt or too rigid in its long-established procedures, and the effect was to cast out as heretical and to marginalise what formerly would have been welcomed as a source of renewal. In its most acceptable form, the fervour can be seen in the growth of mysticism in the fourteenth century, in Richard Rolle, Walter Hilton, Julian of Norwich and the author of *The Cloud of Unknowing* and related treatises. Mystical writing in its most authentic form has little to do with the institutionalised Church and the prerogatives of its priesthood, and these writers tend to step very carefully when they allude to such matters as the authority of the Church, Julian especially. The emergence of the woman–mystic, in Julian, should be noted: it is not a new phenomenon from a European point of view, but it seems new in England since such women had traditionally been excluded from the kind of education that would enable them to write in the appropriate language, Latin, and had generally expected to be written for and down to in English, as by the author of the *Ancrene Wisse* and by Rolle, rather than to write themselves.

Langland's *Piers Plowman* is expressive of a similar kind of religious fervour, but one that finds much greater difficulty in accepting the Church as it is. Langland's protest against the fossilisation of the Church in its institutionalised practices, the greed and venality of its officers, is vehement, and it is interesting that the friars bear the brunt of it. It was because the friars were felt to have betrayed the cause – of poverty, purity of life, care for the oppressed – for which they were believed specially to stand that they came in for such fierce condemnation. Langland's attack is mild compared with that of Wycliffe, who showed the way to those who wished to make a break with the established Church and deny its authority. Understandably, this was the form of protest that the Church found least acceptable, and Wycliffe's followers, the Lollards, were condemned as heretics and destroyed by persecution, or at least driven underground.

The exhaustion of these waves of fervour, the rigidity of the Church, and the rigour of its suppression of heresy, made the fifteenth century, though not for these reasons alone, a generally unpromising one for religious art. The Church retained, of course, much of its traditional role in literary production. The most prolific author of English religious lyrics in the Middle Ages was a Franciscan friar, James Ryman, and the most prolific English author of all time was a Benedictine monk, John Lydgate. Osbern Bokenham, author of an extensive series of *Legends of Holy Women*, John Audelay, Benedict Burgh, Henry Bradshaw, were all members of religious houses, though it must be admitted that they were beginning to be outnumbered by authors of secular origin. The occasions for writing were still often religious – a commission for a saint's legend such as Lydgate received from St Albans, or Bokenham from a large part of Suffolk society, a request for a devout meditation on the Crucifixion or for some exposition of doctrine. There is, however, much less writing of doctrinal instruction than there had been: perhaps the increase in copying made what had already been written more generally available so that the need was satisfied in that way.

An important change in the fifteenth century was the 'rhetoricisation' of religious writing, as in the variations wrought by Lydgate on the stylistic models for Marian eulogy and saint's legend provided by Chaucer. Lydgate's *Life of Our Lady* is perhaps the high point of the fifteenth-century 'flamboyant' style: such an association of religious subject-matter with self-conscious stylistic display would have been unthinkable in England in previous centuries. Equally characteristic of the century are poems like *The Court of Sapience* and *The Assembly of Gods*: the subject-matter is essentially religious still but it is presented in a learned and literary and allusive manner, suggesting that the reader is expected to enjoy the rhetorical display as well as welcome the instruction.

In general, the Church was becoming less central to the concerns of the state, and there were no major figures with an influence comparable with that of earlier churchmen. It is not possible to imagine Archbishops of Canterbury like Henry Chichele (1414–43) or Thomas Bourgchier (1454–86) standing up to the king of the day or doing much to rock the boat in which the Church so comfortably slept. Great prelates, like William of Wykeham or Cardinal Beaufort, tended to be more conformist, more involved in day-to-day politics, not disturbed by untoward piety. Notable abbots tended to be good managers, as had been increasingly true in the fourteenth century, and the kind of building they went in for was splendid residential quarters for themselves, as at Thornton Abbey in Lincolnshire (after 1382), or spectacular follies like the tower at Fountains Abbey, completed just before the dissolution. There was little outside endowment of new monastic building, and what little there was generally went to the new order of Carthusians.

People preferred to spend their money on more personal kinds of investment. Elaborate tombs became more popular and brasses commonplace, whilst the growth of the practice of founding chantry chapels, where a priest could be paid to say masses in perpetuity for the soul of the benefactor, showed the benefit to the Church of the doctrine of purgatory. The Warwick Chapel (1453) is the finest example, while at Westminster the court sculptors were engaged throughout the 1430s and 1440s on the stonework for Henry V's chantry. It was with such appurtenances that the churches grow increasingly filled in the fifteenth century. Major cathedral building had still been going on in the late fourteenth century – at Winchester, Canterbury, York – but there was little in the fifteenth century, apart from the towers at Canterbury and Gloucester and the east end at York.

Like Henry VI, some patrons turned to educational foundations: Archbishop Chichele founded All Souls' College in 1438, and Bishop Wayneflete of Winchester founded Magdalen College (Oxford) in 1448. The Church indeed no longer had a monopoly on education: a Sevenoaks grocer left money in 1432 for the endowment of a school and to provide as teacher 'a Bachelor of Arts but by no means in holy orders to teach and instruct all boys whatsoever coming there for learning'. The Inns of Court in London, by contrast with Oxford and Cambridge, provided now an essentially lay education, and more and more court officials, following the example of Chaucer, who may himself have received his education at the Inns of Court, were laymen.

In terms of church building, finally, it was the development of parish churches, depending more on the common wealth of the parish community, less on individual ecclesiastical or aristocratic endowments, that is most notable in the fifteenth century, especially in those areas, such as Gloucestershire and Suffolk, that had profited most from economic change.

Commercial developments

Court and Church between them monopolised the arts in the twelfth and thirteenth centuries, and continued to be dominant in the fourteenth and fifteenth, but from about the end of the thirteenth century other influences began to be exerted. It was partly a matter of the growth of commercialised production techniques and of export–import trade in 'works of art'; but it was essentially a matter of the growth of a class, whether of urban burgesses or country gentry, wealthy enough to begin to have a say in production and style. Hints and suggestions are all that are to be found in the fourteenth century, but 'bourgeoisification' (or 'gentrification') was a dominant theme that had to be developed for the fifteenth century.

The evidence of change can perhaps first be detected in the practice of manuscript illumination, a highly-skilled craft in which monks could not be guaranteed to excel. Of the two thirteenth-century illuminators whose names we know, one, Matthew Paris, was a monk of St Alban's, the other, more or less contemporary, William de Brailes, was a clerk who worked freelance in Oxford c.1220–40. William may even have run a workshop, in which miniatures were painted on separate vellum pages and then pasted on to the text pages of manuscripts copied elsewhere. The next stage was the employment of itinerant groups of secular artists, such as those who did the Peterborough Psalter about 1300 for a monastic patron; the next the setting up of secular, professional, urban workshops, which must have happened first in London, though the first evidence comes from Norwich; and the last stage was the commissioning of manuscripts from these workshops by secular patrons, as in the case of the Luttrell Psalter (c.1340). The pattern of production and the nature of the commission are surely reflected in the increasing secularisation of decorative marginal motifs in such a manuscript, where grotesque zoomorphic forms, allusions to fabliau and bestiary motifs, courtly and hunting scenes, find themselves in bizarre conjunction.

By the 1330s, then, there were non-monastic scribes and illuminators working professionally to execute commissions for secular, non-aristocratic patrons. The Auchinleck MS provides further evidence of the same kind: it may not have been produced in a single workshop (that is, all the operations in making it performed on the same premises), but it was coherently planned, professionally executed by a number of scribes, and adequately illustrated with simple miniatures. It was designed, one must presume, for a purchaser who belonged to the class of the aspirant London bourgeoisie, literate enough to have a taste for versions of fashionable romance, not sophisticated enough to desire to have them in French. There is virtually no French in the manuscript, which is very unusual for any kind of miscellany of the period. The book gives evidence of the kind of book production in which the bourgeoisie might have been involved: it also indicates the kind of tastes they had, especially in romance, and provides some sort of explanation of the vogue of the English popular romances. It would not do to generalise too much about the audience of these romances – after all, Chaucer read them, and there are some which might have passed muster in a noble household – but the absence of extended analysis of love-sentiment, the fairly peremptory way with niceties of chivalric conduct and court life, the prevailing tone of piety, might suggest a generally 'middle-class' audience of London merchants and country gentlemen and their households.

Tomb-sculpture and memorial brasses were other areas where non-aristocratic patronage began to be of importance from about the 1350s on, that is, from the time the Northamptonshire quarries started to turn out quantities of alabaster, and from the time that latten sheets for brasses began to be imported from the metal factories of the Rhineland and Flanders. It was aristocratic patrons who set the fashion and the middle classes who adopted it when a degree of mass-production and economical marketing brought it within their means. The first important use of alabaster, a material so much easier to carve than stone or Purbeck marble, is for the effigy of Edward II at Gloucester, while the finest brass of the first half of the fourteenth century is that at Elsing in Norfolk (1347–8) of Sir Hugh Hastings, an important military leader in the French wars, with strong court connections. Soon, though, brasses were being produced in quantity (they were popular too with church officials, because, being set in the floor, they took up less room) to standardised patterns, at various prices, often in advance of orders. Over a thousand survive. Most are monotonously repetitive, and some of the finest brasses are of foreign workmanship, especially those imported from North Germany through Hanseatic merchants; but there are fine English ones too, such as those made for Eleanor Bohun, widow of the Duke of Gloucester (d.1399) or for Thomas Beauchamp, Earl of Warwick (d.1401). The fashion declined after the mid-fifteenth century, though there is a fine custom-made brass for John Portey (d.1458), one of the Cotswold woolmen, in Northleach, Gloucestershire, showing him with his feet resting on a sheep and a wool-sack, and his merchant's mark, with which he distinguished his sacks, in a medallion on either side of him.

Alabaster figures for tombs were likewise produced in quantity for a broad range of patrons, and there was no attempt at portraiture unless special arrangements and payment were made. One can understand how aristocratic patrons, anxious to preserve class distinction, would be impelled to go abroad to find something different: how the effigy of Richard Beauchamp in the Warwick chapel, for instance, is clad in the latest type of imported Milanese armour instead of the usual standardised armour. Over 350 tomb alabasters survive, as well as many of those alabaster figurines and carved panels and retables (altar-pieces) in which there was a brisk export trade.

There were other kinds of 'mass-production' too, through which the tastes of a larger and less discriminating purchasing group could be supplied. Painted wooden panels such as are found in East Anglian churches, done to standardised patterns with traditional scenes of the Annunciation and Crucifixion, were done by travelling journeymen for local ecclesiastics, or for ambitious gentry or burgesses who wished to make their mark with a gift to the local church.

Manuscript production itself could never be said to have got to the stage of commercial mass-production, but it certainly became more commercialised in the fifteenth century, with some practice of distribution of portions of an exemplar to different scribes for more rapid copying, or of making up a volume to the tastes of a customer from already copied fascicules or 'booklets'. Buying new books, though, remained a pretty expensive business, and it remained so during Caxton's time and indeed until Wynkyn de Worde at the end of the century saw the means to appeal to a much wider audience by cutting costs and printing more cheaply. One reason for the comparatively slow development of manuscript book production in England was the import trade from Flanders in Latin books for which there was a regular demand, such as school books and Books of Hours. In Flanders, such books were produced on a genuinely commercial basis, 'on spec', for sale in bulk.

These developments generally began in the fourteenth century and became widespread in the fifteenth century when the economic factors that contributed to the rise of the 'middle' classes (if in such a term we can include the country gentry as well as the urban burgesses), and made them more of a force in the determination of artistic production and style, were more fully in operation. One of these factors was the continuing growth of the cloth industry and of commerce, which made merchants wealthier and land less important as a source of wealth. In 1523, Thomas Spring the clothier, of Lavenham, was reckoned the wealthiest man in Suffolk after the Duke of Norfolk. Another factor was the decline in demesne cultivation by lords, and the putting out of more and more land to rent, which made for an increasingly prosperous group of free tenants, such as franklins, who broadened the base of the class of country gentry. The latter class plays a very significant part in the shifting pattern of cultural patronage, and we happen to know something of their activities, in the letters and other documents that survive from families such as the Pastons, the Celys and the Plumptons.

Economic change thus tends to erode the old sources of patronage – courts, noble households, monasteries, cathedrals – and to give strength to a broader group rather than to create the equivalent of the Italian and Flemish ducal and merchant patrons. The effect is not always one of mediocrity, as the great parish churches of Suffolk such as Long Melford and Lavenham, essentially the product of this new kind of patronage, would testify. In Coventry, where commerce developed spectacularly in the fifteenth century (Margaret of Anjou was given oranges when she visited there), two local merchants, in the late fourteenth century, are said to have paid £100 a year for twenty-one years to build the tower of St Michael's. William Camynges, a Bristol merchant, rebuilt the church of St Mary Redcliffe after the spire fell down in 1446. In York, and above all in London, which expanded rapidly in the fifteenth century, the city burgesses were much involved in the building and beautifying of the parish churches, while the guilds built splendid meeting-halls, which in London vied with the town houses of the nobility, and also acted as patrons for the production of a whole range of objects such as plate, illuminated charters, civic regalia, tapestries and hangings. In York and Coventry and other cities, the guilds also put on the cycles of Mystery plays.

In domestic building, too, it was the new classes that made the running, and there was some ostentatious building by men who would have been thought in previous centuries to be of very moderate status. William Grevel's house in Chipping Campden, and Icomb Place in Gloucestershire, are Cotswold examples, the latter built with fine indefensible gatehouse and oriel windows. Sir John Fastolf made himself rich in the French wars and built Caister Castle in Norfolk (1432): he would certainly have been considered nouveau riche, as would Ralph Cromwell, treasurer to Henry VI, who built at Tattershall (1434) the most magnificent of all fifteenth-century pseudo-castles, with a great keep-like tower full of windows, arcades leading to fine rooms with elaborate fireplaces, and a household of one hundred. The decline of chivalry, lament for which becomes something of a theme of the fifteenth century, could be very comfortably contemplated in such quarters. Later in the century, Oxburgh Hall, Norfolk, built in the 1480s, kept up this tradition of the fortified mansion, or castle de luxe. (See Chapter 2.)

The great expansion of literary activity, of composing, compiling and copying, in the fifteenth century cannot be attributed entirely, nor even principally, to the expansion of the middle class, but it plays an important and well-documented part. Poets were often both non-clerical and non-aristocratic, and among those who followed in Chaucer's footsteps are Thomas Hoccleve, George Ashby, Peter Idley and Stephen Hawes, all civil servants in one capacity or another. Henry Lovelich, a London merchant, wrote two very long Arthurian verse romances (c.1425). Lydgate, in the midst of all his aristocratic commissions, also did verses to accompany painted cloth hangings in a citizen's house (*Bycorne and Chychevache*) and in the hall of a craft-guild (*The Legend of St George*), and a *Mumming at Bishopswood* for a civic picnic.

The copying of miscellanies and anthologies containing romances, religious verse, instructional pieces, medical recipes and other oddments can be well understood to cater for the needs and tastes of households where books were not to be had in large numbers, while the large amount of translation into English of standard encyclopaedic and informational works in Latin and

French is presumably to do with the same more broadly based reading public. Workaday copies of Chaucer are not uncommon, and even some of the more handsome copies of Chaucer, Gower and Lydgate are known to have been made for provincial gentry of moderate status. No attempt should be made to minimise the traditional sources of aristocratic and ecclesiastical influence on literary production and dissemination, but clearly the commercialisation of book production was well advanced even before the invention of printing introduced the technology of commercial mass-production.

The provinces

The purpose in this final section is to draw particular attention to some regional variations in the patterns of artistic activity, and to suggest some tentative explanation for them. Britain did not seem such a small country in the Middle Ages as it does now, and it is as important to be aware of *where* as it is to be of *when*. (There will be some reference back to what has been spoken of already, and some overlap, but this is necessary for the purposes of giving the different perspective.)

King William's policy after the Conquest was to eliminate any active opposition – the harrying of the north after a rebellion there in 1070 left it waste for decades – but not to interfere gratuitously with what did not incommode him. He seems to have got on well with Bishop Wulfstan of Worcester, and Worcester remained, therefore, during St Wulfstan's episcopacy (1062–95), which spanned and long survived the Conquest, a most important centre for the preservation of Old English learning. Wulfstan's life was written in the vernacular by his secretary Coleman (no text survives), and the scriptorium at Worcester continued to turn out copies of liturgical and homiletic texts in Old English well into the twelfth century. The evidence of contemporary glosses (in the 'tremulous hand' of the Worcester glossator) suggests an attempt by a scholar or teacher to make the texts intelligible, through Latin glosses, to his colleagues or students.

It is tempting to see a link between these authentic surviving traditions and the flourishing of writing in English in the west in the early thirteenth century, at a time when Anglo-Norman was dominant in the rest of the country, and a further link with the reflourishing of alliterative verse in the west in the fourteenth century. The early thirteenth century saw the production of a series of learned and sophisticated religious treatises (*Sawles Warde, Hali Meidenhad*) and saints' legends (*St Juliana, St Margaret, St Katherine*), known as the 'Katherine group', along with a number of elaborate prose and verse effusions on the love of Christ and the Virgin (*The Wooing of Our Lord* group), and a treatise for the instruction of anchoresses, the *Ancrene Wisse*, one of the finest pieces of prose in the English language. The last-named is known to have been written for a group of noble ladies who went into seclusion in Herefordshire in the early 1200s, and the other works may all be associated with composition for (less likely, by) women recluses and nuns. Composition for women helps to explain the use of the vernacular, though Anglo-Norman would be expected for ladies of high birth.

Remoteness from the metropolitan centres of Anglo-Norman and French is evidently a further factor in the survival of these English traditions. But something must be due to continuities in which Worcester may have played a part: the connection of the Katherine group with Old English rhythmical homiletic prose is one such continuity, and another is the distinctly developed literary character of the language used, suggesting a tradition of composition going back directly to West Mercian originals.

What follows from this is very important: the continuity of a predominantly regional tradition of English writing and the ability of alliterative forms of prose and verse to manifest themselves vigorously in a variety of metamorphoses. It is, we may presume, no accident that a translation of Wace's *Roman de Brut* into English alliterative verse in the first half of the thirteenth century should have been made by Layamon, parish priest of Arley Kings, a few miles up the Severn from Worcester; nor that some of the later developments in alliterative writing in rhyme and elaborate stanzaic form are most fully and sometimes uniquely represented in a manuscript of the early fourteenth century (British Library MS Harley 2253) known to have been written by a Shropshire scribe and associated closely as to its contents with the south-west Midlands and the Welsh marches. The poems of Harley 2253 are confident, sophisticated and stylistically highly wrought: the existence of such a compilation contemporary with a London manuscript of such a completely different character as the Auchinleck MS suggests that English had a traditionally higher prestige in the West than important, socially and artistically, than in the rest of the country.

Whether this will do to 'explain' the revival of alliterative poetry in the unrhymed long line in the fourteenth century (the first poems begin to appear in the 1350s) is unsure. Certainly, this writing, particularly in poems of such sophisticated quality and high literary sensitivity as *Sir Gawain and the Green Knight* and *Pearl*, implies an audience of considerable cultivation, and suggests that English had a traditionally higher prestige in the West then elsewhere. Particular influences may have been important, and the markedly serious, learned and historical cast of much of the writing of the revival (*The Destruction of Troy, The Parliament of the Three Ages, Patience, Cleanness*) might suggest a connection with monastic traditions. One should not forget how important monasteries were as places of hospitality; how commonly it was the practice for royalty and nobility, on their way to the Welsh wars, or holding parliament in the provinces, to be entertained at a large monastery, with provision of suitable entertainment (in alliterative verse?); how the Abbot of Worcester complained in 1350 at the expenses the abbey was being put to in providing such hospitality, Worcester having the only bridge over the Severn between Gloucester and Bridgnorth.

It would not be historically accurate to represent the alliterative revival as an isolated phenomenon restricted to the west: the *Morte Arthure* was written in Lincolnshire, and of course Langland carries his own kind of alliterative verse to London and makes it popular throughout the country. But something definitely western and non-metropolitan there is about the main body of alliterative verse of the revival, not so much in its themes as in its language, which would have been in certain cases almost unintelligible to a Southerner, and in its forms.

The West Midlands are perhaps the strongest evidence of a regional development in literary culture, and it is perhaps in literary culture that such developments are most likely to take place, since the influences of architecture, sculpture and painting are so much more readily transmitted. Nevertheless, the burst of production of illuminated psalters in East Anglia in the last years of the thirteenth century and the first half of the fourteenth remains a striking phenomenon. It is difficult to know why they stand out so sharply, even given the usual accidents of survival. Some are for monastic patrons, some for members of the East Anglian gentry, like the Luttrell Psalter, and the St Omer Psalter, done for the St Omer family of Mulbarton in Norfolk; though copied by monastic scribes, they seem to have been illustrated by groups of travelling artists, one group, the 'Fenland' group (the Ramsey, Gough and Barlow Psalters and the Crowland Apocalypse), by a secular, professional, urban workshop, perhaps in Norwich.

But these were the conditions that presumably pertained in London, and it is hard to know why they should give rise to a particularly characteristic group of manuscripts in East Anglia. It may be that London was at this time preoccupied with the new influences coming in from France, where Psalters were already superseded by Books of Hours, and that the East Anglian Psalters are in some way archaic and for that reason provincial; it may be that centres like Norwich and Peterborough exerted a particularly strong regional influence; it may be that more needs to be known of the provenance of individual manuscripts.

It is tempting to look for something similarly regional in literary production. East Anglia, at least the more remote parts of it in Norfolk and Suffolk, was sufficiently distinct as a region, and certainly Londoners were very conscious of 'Norfolkisms' in the speech of immigrants from that area, as both Chaucer and Langland attest. A vigorous attempt has been made to associate with East Anglia the writing of romance in a particular kind of tail-rhyme stanza, and to suggest the existence of a distinctive East Anglian culture based in Norwich, but it does not work too well. Quite simply, not enough is known about the provenance of individual romances to make such a theory any more than an intriguing speculation.

Lincolnshire is another region that might have been expected to show signs of a regional literary culture: it was one of the richest farming areas in the country and had one of the densest populations, and yet was sufficiently remote from metropolitan influences. There are some suggestions of such a kind: *Havelok* is a very assertively Lincolnshire poem, offering a romantic explanation of the origin of the name Grimsby amongst other things, and there are links with Robert Mannyng of Brunne (Bourne in South Lincolnshire), canon of Sempringham priory (also in Lincolnshire), who included on his own initiative an account of the Havelok story in his translation (1338) of the Anglo-Norman chronicle of Peter of Langtoft. There are, much later in the mid-fifteenth century, possible stylistic echoes of the romance of *Havelok* in the poetry of John Capgrave, Augustinian prior of Lynn, just across the fens from Lincolnshire in West Norfolk.

It is always important to be on the alert for particular outbursts of regional artistic activity, for the influences of little schools of local craftsmen such as gave us the twelfth-century carvings at Shobdon and Kilpeck in Herefordshire, or the late thirteenth-century leaves at Southwell, or the East Anglian rood screens of the fifteenth century, coming in perhaps as a result of North German influence communicated through the thriving port at Lynn. The local response to court and metropolitan influences may itself produce something distinctive. The famous (and controversial) 'sword-drawing' knight effigy at Dorchester, in Oxfordshire, made in the Abingdon workshop, has been thought by some to show the influence of the late thirteenth-century court style, but transformed into something altogether more free and adventurous, less refined and decorous. There seems to have been at the same period a particularly 'Yorkshire' style of figure sculpture. Yet always the mobility of medieval masons, particularly in the employment of the king or of high ecclesiastics, should be remembered.

It is to literary culture that one is recurrently drawn in the attempt to elicit patterns of regionality. The north, laid waste by William in 1070, did not begin to make any mark until the late thirteenth century, when the enormous 'run-through' of world history, the *Cursor Mundi*, was composed in Durham or even further north, but the following centuries witnessed much activity. The writing of Richard Rolle in Latin prose and verse shows him to be a highly educated European scholar, but his most characteristic work in the vernacular, much of it for devout women recluses, is in a very strongly marked northern dialect. With some later writing, such as the *Northern Passion*, the *Northern Homily Cycle*, and the translation of the pseudo-Bonaventuran *Meditationes Vitae Christi* by Nicholas Love, prior of Mount Grace in North Yorkshire, it suggests the existence of a powerful regionally defined spiritual vernacular, maybe even that the northern dialect spoke of devotion in some specially authentic way (Rolle's continuing influence, well into the fifteenth century, would be important here).

The cycles of mystery plays that survive from York and Wakefield draw heavily on such sources as the *Northern Passion*. These plays, with other cycles or parts of cycles that survive from Chester, Coventry, Newcastle, Beverley and other towns, testify also, perhaps, to another kind of specifically regional religious culture, and may also be considered to be important evidences of regional culture in another way. It is characteristic of the Corpus Christi cycles of York and Wakefield, as of other towns from which cycles or parts of cycles survive, that they were put on by the craft and trade guilds of the city. Each guild would be allocated its own play or 'pageant', and on the appointed day the pageant-waggons would follow each other through the streets and the whole cycle of biblical history be enacted.

It is not difficult to recognise this as a major civic cultural and religious activity and to see in it some attempt to express, on the part of these important and growing, predominantly northern towns (a line drawn from the Severn estuary to the Wash would include to the north-west nearly all the places that have or had cycles), a nascent sense of civic pride and prestige. For a guild to have a play was a sign that it had 'arrived'; for a town to have a cycle was a sign that it too had arrived.

There is the further possibility that the importance attached to the plays by the municipal authorities, as evidenced by the surviving records, was partly because they provided a means of articulating the control of the merchant oligarchy over the smaller and more volatile trade and craft guilds. The municipal authority would not always have been popular (witness the outbreaks against the richer merchants of York and Beverley at the time of the Peasants' Revolt in 1381), but it would have been evident to all that some authority had to be responsible for organising the plays.

Further north, in Scotland, or at least in that part of Scotland that figures in this history, there was little, or at least little that survives, that was distinctively Scottish. A tradition of anti-English historical writing in verse is evidenced in Barbour's *Bruce* (1375) and Blind Hary's *Wallace* (c.1478), but the forms of romance and allegorical writing that survive, for instance, the *Kingis Quair*, the *Buik of Alexander*, *Lancelot of the Laik*, seem only accidentally to be in the Scottish dialect. Towards the end of the fifteenth century, though, in the work of Robert Henryson and William Dunbar, and later in Gavin Douglas, Sir David Lindsay and others, there appeared a kind of Scots verse for which no real English parallel can be found and which indeed is superior to anything produced in England throughout the period from Chaucer's death to 1550.

It is not altogether easy to explain this late and powerful expression of Scottish cultural life and artistic independence. Something must be attributed to the influence of the court of James IV of Scotland (1488–1513), whose wilful and glamorous character and ravenous appetites and interests certainly stimulated Dunbar; something might have been due to one of those happy conjunctions when the language of everyday speech and the language of literary discourse for a moment coincide, where in England, by contrast, an exactly contemporary poet like Hawes could find no meeting ground between tawdry aureation and coarse colloquialism. Whatever the reason, Scotland had for fifty years the literary advantage of England.

Part II
Studies in the Individual Arts

Durham Cathedral, the nave (1128–33).

1 Architecture

NICOLA COLDSTREAM

Introduction

'He had the work preached through many episcopal dioceses, and relics carried around, . . . and he collected quite a lot of money.' In the later years of the twentieth century we are well used to restoration appeals on behalf of our great medieval churches, and, save for the reference to relics, this quotation could come from the report of just such an appeal. It is in fact from a contemporary account of the efforts made by a thirteenth-century abbot of St Albans to raise money to finish building his abbey church, a church which dominates to this day the city over which it presides. Even in this era of tower-blocks, many of our towns lie in the shadow of a medieval castle or cathedral whose bulk and eminence still dictate the character of the community.

These huge stone buildings are scarcely typical even of the period in which they were built, when ordinary people lived in dwellings made of wood and plaster, at the most one or two storeys high. Enormous resources of men and materials were required to build them, but they governed people's lives in more than an economic sense: they symbolised the power of the great feudal landholders to whom nearly everyone was bound, however remotely, and of the Church, responsible for the salvation of people's souls in the life to come. Thus, although the buildings we will look at in this chapter may seem to be highly specialised, they represent aspects of life which touched those people whose physical surroundings no longer survive, and whom we can no longer approach so closely. Stretching over a span of nearly 400 years, they reflect great changes in attitudes to life. This Introduction describes the stylistic development of architecture in general over the whole period, so that the buildings discussed in more detail in later parts of the chapter may be fitted into a context; but there we shall be able to explore more fully some of the ideas only touched on here.

Church architecture forms the theme of the Introduction for two reasons. The first is simply a matter of survivals: most medieval architecture in Britain is ecclesiastical, cathedrals, parish churches and monasteries.

Monasteries, like most of the castles, survive only as ruins. At the Reformation their sites were plundered for building stone, often for houses which rose on the monastic foundations, as at Netley (Hampshire). Some monastic churches were adapted for parish worship: at Binham (Norfolk), where only the nave was used, the choir fell into decay, but Selby (Yorkshire) survives intact as the parish church, and St Albans Abbey is now a cathedral.

Castles exist in reasonable numbers, some dismantled, some incorporated into later buildings, others ruined. Several, including the Welsh castles discussed at the end of this chapter, continued in use until after the Civil War in the seventeenth century; but they were already decaying by the end of the Middle Ages, and they have been saved only by extensive restoration.

The greatest loss is houses, and with them traces of the domestic life of all but the wealthiest classes. Wood and plaster are less durable materials than the ashlar (or squared) masonry used for castles and churches; and even the few stone houses tended to vanish, for they were the victims of change in the style and standard of living, and were often rebuilt; modern research does, however, suggest that medieval timber halls are the concealed basis of many houses that were previously supposed to date from the sixteenth or seventeenth century.

The second reason that church architecture will be particularly emphasised is that, although castle design required the highly specialised skills of engineer-architects trained in warfare, it is in churches that we find the work of the skilled workers in the fine arts, foliage and figure carving, delicate mouldings, patterned window tracery and vaults. Ideas about the appropriate appearance of a building were most fully expressed in churches, because of strongly held beliefs about what a church should look like, and new stylistic ideas were usually explored there first.

Over the four centuries covered by this book, the liturgical life of the Church was much elaborated, and this is also reflected in the architecture. Each type of church had a particular function, expressed in its layout and degree of decoration. The cathedral, centre of the diocese and dominant in the religious life of the lay people, was a great church on a large scale, as imposing within as without. Its internal arrangements carefully defined those parts of the church, the choir and beyond it the presbytery with the high altar, which were the domain of the clergy; the nave was set aside for the laity and for processions on Sundays and feast days, and the procession paths and chapels round the transepts and choir were open to the laity on certain occasions. The monastic church varied in size according to the community: some, such as Rievaulx (see p. 73), were enormous, others much smaller. A monastic church, too, placed great emphasis on the choir in which the monks passed so much time. The monastery was a closed community, and the laity were forbidden to go beyond the great screen in the nave, above which hung the Rood (the crucified Christ with SS Mary and John). If there was a great shrine behind the high altar, as at Durham or St Albans (see p. 54), the reliquary containing the holy bones was carried in procession on the saint's feast day; but as the centuries went by more provision was made for pilgrims to go into the eastern parts of the church and approach the shrine. In most churches the altar is at the east end, and in this chapter it will be assumed to be at the east, even where (as at Rievaulx) the church is not sited on an east–west axis.

Parish churches took many forms, but their divisions, although simpler, were as clear. The larger parish churches of the late Middle Ages were either collegiate churches built by a particular family and served by a college of priests, or they were the large urban parish churches which, in new towns such as Hull or Winchelsea, were built in preference to the conglomeration of small parishes and their churches in old-established towns such as Norwich or York.

Most medieval churches have been much altered since they were first built. Parts have been replaced or extended, especially the eastern arm with the presbytery and choir, which had to accommodate changes in liturgical practice, such as increased processions, the growing cult of the Virgin and the need for more chantry altars for masses for the souls of the dead. Repairs were often necessary: in the nave of Gloucester Cathedral a fourteenth-century vault sits above an Anglo-Norman elevation. Larger windows were often cut through old walls. Extra aisles were added to parish churches generations after the churches were first built. But if there were additions, much has been swept away. Chapels, especially Lady chapels, were vulnerable at the Reformation and later puritanical moments in our history. Restorers such as Wyatt at Salisbury could be ruthless in their prunings and tidyings of chapels and tombs. Owing to iconoclasm and the passage of time we have lost what was most important in the life of the medieval Church, the shrines and reliquaries, the stained glass and sculpture, and, above all, the colour. While surviving dark marbles can give us some idea of the medieval love of colour and texture, they cannot recreate the medieval church interior, with its whitewashed walls in sombre darkness, the rich glint of gilded statues, reliquaries and panel paintings, and the glowing, jewel-like stained glass.

Only monastic orders such as the Cistercians would, in the early days, not have had these rich interiors, although by the end of the Middle Ages even they had succumbed. The Cistercians and orders like them believed that ornament was a distraction from contemplation, and they forbad all sculpture and most paint. Their stained glass was an opaque grey, with geometric figures designed to guide the monks through their spiritual exercises and contemplation.

The architectural setting is, however, left to us. English medieval architecture was intensely insular, but its insularity was fed by a series of stylistic influences from the Continent, which were absorbed and redeployed in a characteristically English way. Over the period as a whole the strongest influence came from France, where the Gothic style was invented; but England's cultural affiliations were very wide, and in the early days France was by no means pre-eminent, and even Norman influence was diluted. Many post-Conquest churchmen came from the Low Countries and Rhineland; there were constant journeys to Rome; and the Cluniac and Cistercian orders of monks were based on Burgundy. Even while political links with Normandy were still close, details of Anglo-Norman architecture such as the cushion capital or the cylindrical pier were associated with these areas rather than Normandy; and the forms of early Gothic came, not through Normandy, but through north-east France. Sometimes English masons were in such close touch with architectural developments abroad that they copied quite intricate details when they returned; but they confined themselves to details applied to a traditional structural framework.

English buildings tended to be long and low, ignoring the possibilities of height expressed in French Gothic architecture. The squat profile was usually balanced by towers: the great lantern towers built by the Normans, together with the twin-towered façades such as Southwell (Nottinghamshire) and Canterbury, were developed by later generations, which sometimes added stone spires as at Salisbury in the fourteenth century. The preferred plan for the choir was rectangular, either with a flat, cliff-like east wall, or with a single-storey extension built out a few bays beyond it. From the late twelfth century these box-like choirs replaced the Anglo-Norman choirs ending either in three semi-circular apses (of which good traces remain at Peterborough) or an apse with an ambulatory and chapels radiating from it, surviving in the crypt at Gloucester. The former proved too inconvenient for circulation, and the latter was overcome by the taste, already evident in Anglo-Saxon times, for square-ended churches. By the late twelfth century the ambulatory and chapels were expressed on the floor by screens rather than in the architecture itself. Westminster is a rare example of a genuine French ambulatory plan.

Until the end of the thirteenth century, church interiors were dictated by the use of a traditional wall structure and an elevation design which was not well adapted to the demands of French Gothic. The Anglo-Norman elevation lived on as the ghostly basis of many a later remodelling. Many post-Conquest great churches, such as Winchester and St Albans, were based on William the Conqueror's abbey at Caen: the arcade and deep, vaulted gallery above it were of almost equal height, with a row of squat clerestory windows at the top. The elevation was built as a thick-wall structure, a technique introduced under Norman influence, in which the wall is composed of two skins of ashlar masonry with a rubble filling. A passage is cut through the thickness of the wall at clerestory level. This type of wall is very stable; with some extra buttressing it can easily support a stone vault. In modified form this structure lived on in English architecture until the fourteenth century, partly because the pattern of rebuilding forced alterations and replacements to conform to the proportions and structure of earlier buildings. At Ely (Cambridgeshire) the thirteenth-century choir extension continues the lines of the Anglo-Norman bays to which it was attached; the fourteenth-century replacement of the early work perpetuates the Anglo-Norman proportions and wall-passage.

If we are seeking a continuous theme to tie the Anglo-Norman world to that of the early Tudors, the love of surface decoration provides one. The English response to architectural developments abroad was primarily decorative, explored across surfaces, through foliage and figure sculpture, through arch mouldings, vault patterns and window tracery. Structure and decoration were already closely linked in the Anglo-Norman period. Although the figure sculpture is not up to Continental standard, the decoration of arches and

Peterborough Cathedral, the nave (c.1150).

vault mouldings with zigzag chevrons, lozenges and beakheads was much
more inventive. While these were being developed in the first half of the
twelfth century the canon of proportion described above was being varied
too: at Gloucester tall cylindrical piers pushed the two upper storeys right up
under the roof; in East Anglia the logical Norman relation of pier to arch
moulding was abandoned in favour of oval and octagonal piers, pier shafts
which led to no corresponding arch mouldings, and arch mouldings
unsupported by shafts. Bay divisions were emphasised by a half-column on
each pier rising uninterrupted to the ceiling.

Lincoln Cathedral, St Hugh's Choir (1190s).

The English response to French Gothic began decoratively and largely remained so. By the late twelfth century churches such as Notre Dame, Paris or Chartres Cathedral were very high, with thin walls, large windows and stone vaults largely kept in place by arched flying buttresses. Inside, the flat elevation was composed of pointed arches with a reduced middle storey, separated by narrow shafts rising to the cross-ribbed vault, which linked the two sides into an integrated composition. Accustomed as they were to Anglo-Norman arched elevations, English masons had been attracted to the grouped arches from the start, but they applied them to their own thick walls, which, if the windows were small and the height not excessive, could easily support stone vaults. At Byland (Yorkshire) the Cistercians, who helped to bring Gothic forms to the north, decorated areas of flat wall with arches and detached shafts, and by c.1180 a three-storey elevation with pointed arches and rib vaults was under way at Canterbury and Wells, both showing strong French influence in detail and in some of their proportions.

As the thirteenth century moved on, the English form of early Gothic known as Early English became established: the clerestory remained short and the gallery storey correspondingly high and deep, and the depth of the wall was emphasised with complex pier and arch mouldings, which articulated the sharply pointed arches. Dark 'marbles' were used for piers, detached shafts, capitals and bases. Capitals were now either plainly moulded or carved with the beautiful stiff-leaf foliage, where a bunch of stylised leaves curls over flat stalks. The visual relation of pier and vault, upon which the appearance of French Gothic depends, was broken by terminating the vault shaft at the level of the gallery. Some buildings, such as Wells and Salisbury, positively exploited a layered, horizontal effect; others, such as Whitby and Rievaulx, explored the effects of deeply moulded arches and shafts. A simultaneous shift towards paler and greyer colours in stained glass allowed more light in to play on the mouldings.

Salisbury and the choir of Rievaulx were not built until well into the thirteenth century, but the seeds of the future had already been sown in a building of the 1190s, St Hugh's choir at Lincoln Cathedral. Here the conventional three-storey structure with a wall passage is heavily decorated in marble and foliage. The aisle wall is lined by a blind arcade in two layers, the second row of arches arranged in counterpoint. The whimsicality of the decoration is emphasised by the vault, which has a longitudinal ridge rib, to which the cross ribs are attached at intervals. In each bay one of the ribs is split like a hairpin, casting all symmetry aside and abandoning any idea that the vault is a series of cross-arches which tie the building together: any such notion is here denied.

At Lincoln, then, the urge to decorate extended even to the vault. The nave vault, designed in the 1220s, has several ribs springing from each pier, which gives a more regular appearance; this design appears in several great churches built over the next hundred years, for example at Ely, Old St Paul's (London) and at Exeter. There is evidence that at Lincoln in the 1230s they were experimenting with a simple form of window tracery, in which the lancet is divided with a Y shape. When, therefore, French patterns of window tracery were introduced at Westminster in the 1240s, English masons were ready for them.

Westminster reflects the desire of Henry III and Edward I to use art and architecture for personal display, in emulation of their French royal cousins. Apart from the use of window tracery, it affected English architecture in another way, by heightening the inward concentration of the building. It did this through applied interior decoration: rosette diaper in relief all over the wall surface, foliage sculpture, and large figure sculptures. As a highly decorated shrine church it was a direct imitator of the Sainte-Chapelle in Paris, and its 'illuminated' interior was a pointer to the future.

The Angel choir of Lincoln responded immediately to Westminster, with an interior richly ornamented with foliage and figure sculpture, and decorated wall surfaces, but with a wholly traditional wall structure. Until the end of the thirteenth century ornamental detail and window tracery held all the masons' interest: the flat end walls were opened up as huge windows filled with trefoil and quatrefoil patterns, even a rose window at St Paul's. Tintern Abbey (Monmouth), rebuilt c.1290, has the latest patterns of tracery in its east and west windows, and at Southwell the beautiful naturalistic foliage sculpture in the chapter house shows the masons' sympathy with a style of carving found all over Europe. Structurally, however, we are still in a world of thick walls, deep galleries and short (although wider) windows. Even St Paul's, which used the very latest Parisian tracery designs, had a traditional wall structure, and a vault pattern two generations old.

The turning point, when English architecture finally shed its Anglo-Norman past and entered its late medieval phase, came in the years around 1300, from which there emerged new ideas about proportion and wall

Lincoln Cathedral, the Angel Choir (1256–80)

structure. Indeed, the Anglo-Norman proportions of the nave at Winchester were so subtly altered by their late fourteenth-century recasing that the existence of the earlier work was forgotten for centuries. Several developments seem to have contributed to the change. New churches were smaller than before, partly because all the cathedrals had now been built, and few large monasteries were being founded; and partly owing to the advent of the friars, and to a taste for small, personal family churches which went with the shift towards a more personal religion. The highly decorated chapel, emulated on so large a scale in Westminster Abbey, was manifest in a normal size in St Stephen's Chapel in the Palace of Westminster (refounded 1292, destroyed 1834), and in St Etheldreda's, chapel of the bishops of Ely in Holborn, London (which still exists); to be followed a generation later in the Lady chapel at Ely. These reflect Edward I's taste for miniaturist, encrusted architecture, a style closely related to tomb and reliquary sculpture. It was rapidly adopted, as is evident at Ely, by the bishops and other members of the royal household, spreading on shrines and tombs as well as on buildings. The two-storeyed, thin-walled friars' churches, with their slender piers and large windows, set a fashion for parish church architecture which persisted until the end of the period: it influenced the style of the new town parish churches such as Hull and Winchelsea, the former having an early version of a quatrefoil-shaped pier, universal in later parish churches, which we now know to have been introduced by the friars.

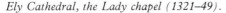

Ely Cathedral, the Lady chapel (1321–49).

The so-called Decorated style, which shared motifs with tombs, reliquaries and screens, was scarcely at all concerned with architectural structure as such: it formed the ornamental background to the countless sculptured and painted representatives of the Kingdom of Heaven which once filled niches and stood on pedestals. Their architectural setting is all we have left of a style in which the human and angelic figures were once paramount. This setting is formed of curvilinear tracery based on the ogee, or reversed, curve; the three-dimensional 'nodding' ogee over tabernacles and niches; the seaweed-like foliage which creeps and curls over roof bosses, capitals, woodwork and tombs. Vault ribs are now arranged in net patterns over shallow surfaces, and mouldings are carved with undulating lines as if from soap. When architects interested themselves in structural problems it was to build fantastic creations like the octagonal crossing at Ely with its great wooden lantern tower, the intricately planned east end of Wells or the openwork vaulting of Bristol Cathedral.

The Decorated style had taken French decorative ideas and recast them in its own way; and from one strand of it emerged the last phase of English medieval architecture, the Perpendicular. The taste for decorating all surfaces with tracery, glass or paint was common to all early fourteenth-century buildings, but in some it was expressed in a flatter, more rectilinear manner, perhaps directly related to French architecture, but, again, recasting it. It is known to have been pioneered at St Stephen's, Westminster, but it now survives in an early stage at Gloucester. The fence of thin, rectilinear tracery panels encasing the choir is not yet ready to support monumental architecture, but later in the century the choir of York and the nave of Canterbury were rebuilt with high, thin walls covered in blind panels of tracery.

In Perpendicular buildings windows are much bigger, the wall surfaces often panelled with tracery of the same pattern as that used in the windows; vaults were now designed with straighter, squarer patterns. Piers, capitals and bases were clearly defined and sharply faceted, moulded with dips and hollows. Arches gradually flattened into the familiar four-centred shape. These buildings of the late fourteenth and fifteenth centuries are rarely on a huge scale; they are thin, open, clear and light.

Perpendicular architecture went through its own short cycles of austerity and richness, with Henry VII's burial chapel at Westminster showing how luscious it could be. The aim was still to integrate all surfaces and forms of decoration, perhaps most excitingly achieved by the fan vault, with its panelled cones reaching across the ceiling. Used charmingly and on a relatively small scale in the cloister of Gloucester in the 1370s, the earliest certain appearance of fan vaults over a wide span is c.1425 at Sherborne Abbey. By the time the new eastern work at Peterborough and King's College Chapel, Cambridge, were built, the fans show all the serenity of masons confident in their art. Late Perpendicular, flat, thin and integrated, may look very different from the rotund massiveness of Durham; but the underlying decorative spirit is much the same.

Salvation and pilgrimage: shrine, tomb and chantry

To the clergy and monks the focal point of the church was likely to be the high altar, but to the laity, especially pilgrims, it was more likely to be the great shrine. Before turning to the architecture itself, therefore, we must look in more detail at the importance of shrines in medieval life and at the hopes of salvation which they brought with them.

In Protestant Britain it is not always easy to reconstruct the significance of shrines. The reliquaries themselves have vanished, taken apart at the Reformation for the value of their metal and jewels. The holy bones within were usually buried near the original place, but the stone bases upon which the reliquaries were kept were smashed to pieces. What we see today are the empty spaces where the shrines once stood, sometimes marked, as at Durham, by a modern inscribed slab set in the floor. We can, however, understand something from the few shrine bases which do survive.

By no means all churches had a major shrine (Wells, for instance, did not), and they tended to be in monasteries rather than secular cathedrals, for many of the saints had themselves been monks and missionaries, and their bodies were cared for in their own monasteries. All churches had a collection of lesser relics, and a typical pilgrimage would include visits to several places on the way to the great shrine. Pilgrimage was an essential part of medieval life. By journeying to the Holy Land or to places nearer home, to the holy places associated with Christ himself or to the shrines of saints who bore witness to the faith, pilgrims did penance for their sins, hoped to cure their bodily ills, and tried to ensure their salvation in the life to come. Late medieval descriptions of pilgrimages often give the impression of people on holiday, away from daily care. This sense of freedom can be read in *The Canterbury Tales*, and parts of *The Book of Margery Kempe* betray the cheerful, inquisitive tourist.

The Church had many reasons for promoting shrines, of which one was undoubtedly mercenary, for money could be made from a properly-managed cult. But too much should not be made of this aspect, as the popularity of many shrines was relatively shortlived, and the shrine of Becket at Canterbury was unusual in taking so much revenue for so long. The real reasons for encouraging the cult of the saints were two-fold: to create and maintain faith, and to ensure salvation. The cult of the saints can be traced back to the second century; the first saints, often martyrs, confirming the existence of Jesus and the continuity of Christian belief. Through the holiness of the saints, the faithful could approach the reality of Christ. After the conversion of the peoples of northern Europe, who were far removed in time and place from the events of the New Testament, relics of the apostles and martyrs were highly valued for their power to reinforce and maintain faith. Great efforts were made to acquire them, and thefts of relics are the subject of some of the most enjoyable medieval anecdotes, like the story told about the future saint Hugh of Lincoln, who is said actually to have bitten pieces off the arm of St Mary Magdalen at Fécamp in his eagerness to possess a relic of her.

The holy bones also offered a path to salvation, the saint acting as intercessor between Heaven and the earthbound sinner. The most powerful intercessor of all was held to be the Virgin Mary, universally venerated, especially from the twelfth century, and the patron saint of the entire Cistercian order. Owing to her bodily Assumption, the Virgin had left no bones, hence the appearance of such improbable relics as her robe or drops of her milk. Like the apostles and early martyrs such as Stephen, the Virgin was a universal saint, but there were many local saints, and in Britain nearly all the major shrines were of local saints.

St Albans Cathedral, base of the shrine of St Alban (1305–8)

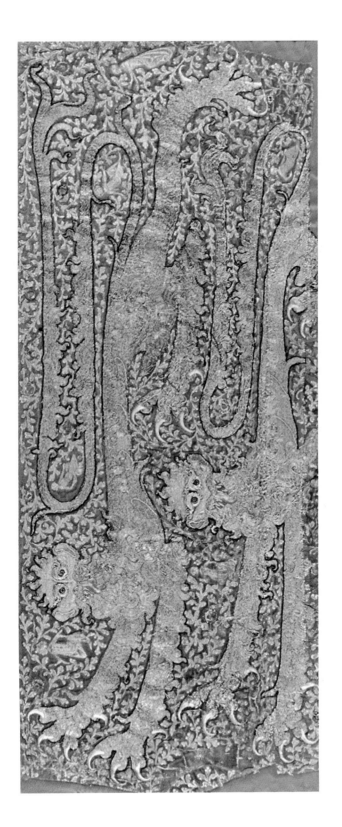

1. 'Leopards of England' embroidery (c.1350).

2. *Chaucer reading* Troilus and Criseyde *to the Court: Criseyde being handed over by the Trojans to the Greeks. From an early fifteenth-century edition of* Troilus and Criseyde.

anuuam mcam;
Gloua pam.
Dñs Galfridus louterell me fieri
fecit

3. *Knight on horseback, from the Luttrell Psalter (c.1340).*

quame a uoue a terre ueimir en oubler
a prist la sapience du mont a gquester
faire les agais ⁊ sa gent ozdener
gduire ses ofts ⁊ trelbien deuiser

4. *Performer in a beast skin, perhaps the* cervulus *of ancient Saturnalia, an ancestor of
the hobby horse.*

5. Moses expounding the Law, from the Bury Bible (c.1125–37).

6. *Combat boss, in the muniment room, Westminster Abbey (c.1260).*

Lot's flight from Sodom. Window, by the Methuselah Master, in Canterbury Cathedral (c.1178).

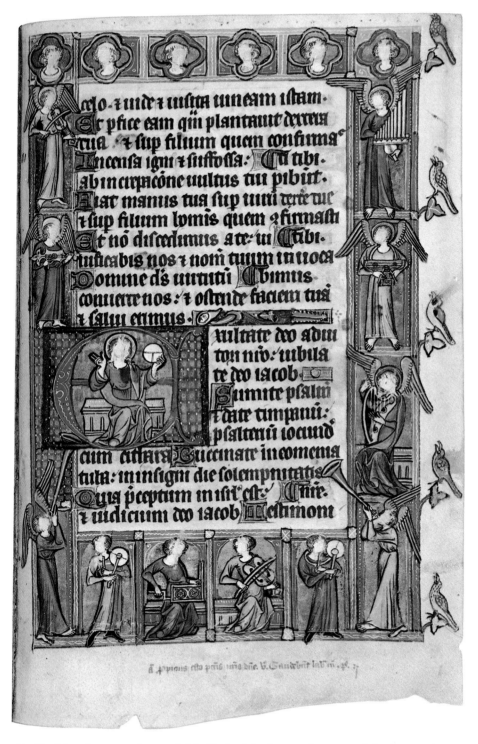

8. *Musicians from a psalter copied in England in the second quarter of the fourteenth century.*

9. *Oxburgh Hall from the north-west (late fifteenth century)*.

Most of the pre-Conquest saints whose cults survived to be enshrined in the Anglo-Norman great churches had borne witness to the faith through the holiness of their lives: such were St Cuthbert of Durham, St Etheldreda of Ely and St Swithun of Winchester. But Britain also had her martyrs, for example St Edmund at Bury, St Alban and St Thomas Becket. Becket, murdered in 1170, was the latest and most famous, but historically St Alban is more significant, as there is evidence that his cult was continuous from at least the fifth century, and as a witness to the early Church he is unrivalled in this country. From our point of view he is additionally significant, for the base of his shrine survives, restored to its medieval place, in St Albans Abbey; and there we can study the great shrine behind the high altar, and its relation to the other eastern altars.

The great shrine was the most important among the host of reliquaries which were kept about the church. Every altar had a relic, and some reliquaries were kept high up on special beams. At St Albans the nave piers have traces of the paintings marking the position of the nave altars, to which the lay people would have had daily access. The great shrine was, however, at the heart of the liturgical activity, especially after the new choir extension was built out beyond it in the thirteenth century, to accommodate four small altar spaces and the big eastern Lady chapel.

The main shrine was first associated with the high altar in late sixth-century Rome, but relics were then normally kept in a subterranean crypt, with the high altar directly above. In Anglo-Saxon England relics were often kept in the main body of the church, but it was not until after the Conquest that the great shrine was placed behind the high altar. St Cuthbert, who had lodged temporarily in the cloister at Durham, was translated to his new shrine in 1104. In Anglo-Saxon Winchester, St Swithun had been interred in a special western block attached to the cathedral, and part of his remains were kept in a reliquary in the church itself, probably on the high altar. In 1093 the saint (apparently reunited) was translated to his place behind the high altar of the Anglo-Norman cathedral, but the site of his tomb was preserved from the demolished Anglo-Saxon building, and a separate cult was maintained there until the Reformation.

A high shrine was in two parts: the reliquary, a wooden box covered in precious metals, enamels and jewels, stood on a specially built stone base, high enough for the reliquary to be seen over the top of the altar by the celebrating priest. The reliquary was covered by a cloth or canopy, removed only on feast days; at Durham the canopy was suspended from the roof, and as it was drawn up there sounded a peal of silver bells. The early shrine bases were slabs of stone supported on tall columns, often made of dark 'marble'; we know from the records that the first shrine bases of SS Cuthbert, Alban and Thomas Becket were like this. After the middle of the thirteenth century the design changed. A few of the later bases survive, and they fall into two types. The first, represented by the shrine of St Thomas Cantilupe at Hereford, is a solid block with an upper tier of open arcading. The second, still to be seen at Westminster and St Albans, is a tall block with niches in the sides into which the pilgrims could creep to come as close as possible to the holy bones which would give them relief from disease and

pain. This type of base became the most popular in the late Middle Ages.
Bases could be made of ordinary stone, but Edward the Confessor's shrine at
Westminster was decorated with geometric patterns of coloured marbles, and
the early fourteenth-century shrine of St Alban is made of Purbeck 'marble'
and still bears traces of gilding and paint. It was decorated with sculptured
figures showing the martyrdom of the saint, and its stylistic details show it to
be in the vanguard of contemporary fashion.

The setting of the high shrine at St Albans and Westminster is the late
medieval arrangement, for in the later fourteenth century it became
fashionable to block the view from the west by placing a tall screen between
the high altar and the shrine. These screens also survive at Winchester and
Durham. It is not entirely clear why this change was made, but evidence
from York suggests that the late medieval shrine of St William was heavily
screened on all sides. Fears about the security of the precious reliquary may
have contributed: the watching loft at St Albans suggests something of the
sort.

Burial near the high altar was believed to enhance the likelihood of
salvation in the hereafter. Many monasteries were founded for the burial of
the patron, a privilege extended to successive patrons as monasteries changed
hands; the series of tombs round the choir of Tewkesbury (Monmouthshire)
include those of the Despensers, who acquired the patronage of Tewkesbury
through marriage into the Clare family. But in a monastic cathedral with a
shrine (see Durham, p. 61) the bishops and priors reserved the best places
for themselves. At Canterbury, for instance, no lay person was admitted for
burial near the shrine of St Thomas until the interment of the Black Prince
in 1376.

Westminster still preserves a shrine base encircled by tombs. Henry III
had provided for his own burial in the tomb of Edward the Confessor, now
made empty by the translation of his relics to the shrine; but Edward I
converted the sanctuary and shrine chapel into a royal mausoleum, arranging
for the burials of his father, his brother, his first wife and himself. They were
to be joined by the remains of Edward III and his queen, Richard II and
Anne of Bohemia, and, finally, Henry V, whose sculptured chantry chapel
forms a bridge across the ambulatory.

The earliest surviving sculptured tombs are those of the highest nobility,
such as Gundrada, Countess of Warenne and founder of Lewes Priory,
bishops and abbots, with knights and ladies making their appearance in the
thirteenth century. The twelfth-century tombs are flat grave slabs, carved
with foliage and crosses; the series of bishops at Wells (see p. 66) are among
the earliest effigies, carved in shallow relief with stylised faces and draperies.
The deeper, more box-like tomb of Archbishop Hubert Walter at
Canterbury, c.1205, has details which closely resemble a contemporary metal
shrine, and with the development in the middle of the thirteenth century of
the great sculptured canopies which were placed over tomb boxes, the
tendency increased to equate the tombs of higher clergy with reliquaries.

In the tomb of Archbishop Walter de Grey at York a shallow niche was
created round the effigy, which lies stiffly, wearing a mitre and holding a
crozier, but given no individuality. Eight tall, slender columns support a

York Minster, tomb of Archbishop Walter de Grey (c.1255).

stone canopy decorated with gables, foliage, trefoil arches and foliate
pinnacles. The ensemble closely recalls an early shrine base with a reliquary
on top, and it is as if the dead archbishop were being prepared for future
canonisation. This was a common occurrence: the shrine of St Thomas
Cantilupe was made many years before he was finally canonised, and at
Wells, where there was a move to canonise the unpopular Bishop March
(d.1302), his elegantly carved wall-tomb in the south transept could have
acted as a shrine. The tomb of Edward II at Gloucester, an equally unlikely
candidate for canonisation, is the most shrine-like of them all, with a canopy
of delicate and slender pinnacles.

Under strong French influence, canopies were placed over the tombs of lay people from the late thirteenth century, now sharing and exchanging decorative motifs with church architecture as well as shrines. The reliquaries were decorated with spires and pinnacles, the churches covered in the miniaturist, jewel-like ornament of the Decorated style. Small weeper figures were placed along the sides of the tomb-box, and there was an effigy, now fully three-dimensional, of bronze, wood, stone or alabaster. The draperies, which had earlier been carved to take no account of the pose, now fell in folds natural to a recumbent figure. Knights took hold of their swords: the bomb-shattered group made of Purbeck stone in the Temple church in London are perhaps the earliest of the series of cross-legged knights who appear to be rising from the tomb.

In this context, the plain black sarcophagus of Edward I (d.1307) is a surprising contrast, but it hints at his own attitude to salvation and perhaps to a sense, which he inherited from his father, of identifying with a past figure. Henry III had wanted to acquire some of Edward the Confessor's holiness by being buried in his empty tomb, and Edward may have wanted something similar for himself. We know from a description that one other tomb exactly matched his: the tomb of Arthur, ordered for Glastonbury by Edward I and placed in the choir with some ceremony in 1278. Edward's interest in Arthur is well-attested, and he may have fashioned his own self-image in Arthur's reputation for chivalrous, Christian kingship. Like Henry III, Edward perhaps wanted to be buried in the shadow of his mentor, and because he could not be buried with Arthur, he ordered a duplicate tomb.

Oxford, interior of Divinity Schools (1340s; vault 1479).

Edward I's queen, Eleanor of Castile, had left her heart to be buried in the Dominican church in London, and there is no doubt that royalty led the tendency during the late Middle Ages for the wealthy city dwellers to entrust their bodies and souls either to the new urban parish churches or to the mendicant orders. They no longer wished to buy their way into monasteries. The building of the new town churches encouraged the endowment of chantries, either at altars in the building or in chapels built alongside.

Chantries have been mentioned before in these pages, and we shall see how the east end of Durham was transformed to provide nine altars for masses to be said for the souls of the dead. A private chantry would be endowed for a priest to serve it in perpetuity; a member of the gentry or a well-born priest, such as Richard de Potesgrave, royal chaplain and rector of Heckington (Lincolnshire), would rebuild the chancel of a church and install his tomb there. Failing that, an aisle would be added to an existing nave. In the later Middle Ages a noble family who earlier would have founded a monastery now built a church served by a college of secular priests, which acted both as the family burial church and as the parish church. Many of these collegiate churches survive, shorn of their college buildings, although Ewelme (Oxfordshire), founded in the 1430s by Alice de la Pole, Duchess of Suffolk, still has its almshouses and school building. The palace at Ewelme has disappeared, but at Tattershall (Lincolnshire) the castle and church built from the 1430s by Ralph Cromwell, Treasurer of England, survive as a group, evoking the care taken by one man to provide for himself while living, and in death. Tombs themselves now placed great emphasis on morbidity and decay, often having an open base containing a memento mori, a realistic carving of the future skeleton.

An alternative to a simple altar or to a collegiate church, which was adopted by a few great laymen and much favoured by bishops, was to build a freestanding chantry chapel either, as at Warwick, attached to the church, or actually inside it. Sometimes, as in the sumptuous chantry chapels of Bishops West and Alcock at Ely, an existing chapel would simply be redecorated. But a chantry chapel was often an entirely separate miniature building, and as the fashion for them coincided with the Perpendicular style, they exhibit the characteristics of that style at its delicate best. The chantry chapel of Bishop William of Wykeham (d.1404), who finished the nave of Winchester Cathedral, is placed between two of the nave piers and it reaches to the top of the arcade. It has three bays, the middle one slightly canted outwards; the solid lower part is trellised with Perpendicular panelling, and the interior is decorated with blind panels and a vault, with a pattern of short (lierne) ribs, the tomb and altar fitting snugly into the floor space. In the mid-fifteenth century two chantry chapels were built in the eastern extension of the cathedral, near the shrine of St Swithun. That of Cardinal Beaufort (d.1447) has little fan vaults and acutely angled mouldings that closely recall metalwork.

So we finish where we began, near the shrine. The Church comprised all its members, living or dead, and by the end of our period there was a sense of the presence of the whole community, enshrined in reliquaries or depicted in sculpture, glass and paint. Those holy ones who had gone before were invoked to help to ease the way through Purgatory to the eternal life. The heavenly kingdom was present on earth, recreated in the church building. In the next two sections we will look at three great church buildings, each with a different approach to God: a Benedictine monastery with a great shrine, a secular cathedral, and, as a contrast, the greatest Cistercian monastery in the north.

The Cathedrals of Durham and Wells

The sees of Durham and Wells both date back into Anglo-Saxon times, but there the resemblance ends. Durham was a monastic cathedral, an institution peculiar to England, in which the cathedral was attached to and served by monks. It possessed the shrine of St Cuthbert, greatest saint of the north, and although the monastery was refounded as part of the post-Conquest reform of the Church, the continuity of cult was not disturbed until the Reformation. Wells was a secular cathedral, served by priests, and it had no great shrine. Moreover, in the late eleventh century the see was moved to Bath, and Wells did not regain its cathedral status until c.1220. The cathedral bears interesting traces of this dispute, showing how our understanding of a building can be greatly enhanced by some knowledge of its history.

At both Durham and Wells the bishops were active promoters of the building programme, but considered as churches set in a landscape the two groups of buildings could hardly be more different. Durham is set on a high rock, a defensive site in a loop of the River Wear. The monastic buildings, presided over by the prior, lie to the south of the church, while the bishop's residence guarded the neck of the peninsula a few hundred metres to the north. The bishop had no powers within the monastery. His residence, a strongly fortified castle, emphasised the secular interests of a Norman bishop. Castle and cathedral are also sited close together at Rochester and Winchester, but Durham was different in that the bishop was lord of the county palatine, and his lands marched with the Scottish border, which it was his duty to defend. The castle at Norham (Northumberland), built in the later twelfth century by Bishop Hugh of Le Puiset, is another stark, solidly-built reminder of the secular side of the bishop's life.

Wells Cathedral stands in a spacious, low-lying green, near to the Roman springs and holy well beside which the earliest church was founded in Anglo-Saxon times. The clergy houses lie to one side and on the other is the cloister, with the bishop's palace divided from it by a moat. Here the bishop's palace is a tranquil house, whose original medieval parts are rambling, and unfortified until the 1340s.

The two cathedrals are interesting to study together, for their building phases are largely complementary, and between them they give an almost complete view of the architecture of our whole period. Durham is mainly Anglo-Norman, with some late twelfth-century work, and a major new building of the mid-thirteenth century. At Wells, as it happened, building took place when nothing was going on at Durham: begun in the late twelfth

century, its west front was built c.1220–40, and the great new Lady chapel
and retrochoir at the east end were put up in the fourteenth century, in the
Decorated style of which there is scarcely a trace at Durham. They both have
some late medieval work.

Durham Cathedral

Durham Cathedral is famous as the earliest surviving church to be vaulted
throughout in rib vaults, and it is a building about whose quality there has
never been any argument. The church was begun in 1093, the relics of St
Cuthbert were translated to his new shrine behind the high altar in 1104,
and the nave vault was finished by 1133. What makes Durham unusual
among English great churches is its apparent homogeneity, with the four
main arms of the building, choir, transepts and nave, still the original work.
Parts have been added, but none of the main elevations has been rebuilt in a
later style. As the visitor approaches from the north he first sees the great
bulk of the Anglo-Norman nave with its evenly spaced, round-headed
windows. As he enters by the north door, the Romanesque sanctuary knocker
(now a replica) in the form of a demonic head, reinforces the stylistic
impression, and the image is fixed for ever by the first view of the massive
nave piers. As is inevitable in so large and ancient a building the stone has
been worked over and renewed, but although the restorers, Wyatt and Scott,
are often vilified for the changes they made, especially to the liturgical
furnishings, they were simply following the fashion of their time; and their
efforts have preserved for us one of the most magnificent Romanesque
churches in Europe.

The building we have today has two additions, the western Galilee and the
eastern chapel of the Nine Altars, both of which reflect the later elaboration
of the liturgy and new cults and uses for altars. The building of 1093 had an
aisled choir of four bays, ending in three apses, transepts with eastern aisles,
and an aisled nave of eight bays with two western towers and a ceremonial
entrance between them. The monks' choir stalls were in the crossing, with
the presbytery and high altar in the eastern arm, and the shrine of St
Cuthbert in the central apse, raised on high as described above (pp. 55–6). As
in other Anglo-Norman churches of this type it was not long before space at
the east end became restricted.

In the 1170s Bishop Hugh of Le Puiset tried to extend the east end of the
church in some way, probably in an effort to provide greater access to the
relics and easier circulation; but the monks objected, blaming their wish not
to be disturbed on Cuthbert's recorded dislike of women, and Bishop Hugh
built a new chapel at the west end instead, incidentally blocking the
ceremonial entrance to the cathedral. The Galilee chapel had several
functions: a Galilee is the place where the clergy re-assembled before
entering the church after the Sunday procession, symbolising Christ's journey
from Galilee to Jerusalem, but the Durham Galilee was also the bishop's
ecclesiastical court, it had an altar to the Virgin, and the relics of the early
churchman Bede were moved there from their previous place beside the shrine

of St Cuthbert. The Galilee thus represents Bishop Hugh's efforts to establish his episcopal rights within the monastery, and reflects the growing interest during the twelfth century in the cult of the Virgin and the reorganisation of relics.

Emphasis on the relics is given as the reason why the chapel of the Nine Altars was built to replace the eastern apses in the 1240s: it was said to be intended as a grand new setting for the shrine of Cuthbert. The high vault of the choir was structurally unsound, procession paths non-existent, and the new bishop, Richard Poore, had come directly from planning the new cathedral at Salisbury, where liturgical reform had demanded ample space behind the high altar. Although the new work allowed freer circulation round the shrine and provided an adequate processional way, its main purpose was to give space to nine new chantry altars (see below, p. 65) to supply the increasing demand for soul masses from lay patrons. The chapel of the Nine Altars, a long hall lying north–south across the east end, is based on the only other one of its kind, at Fountains Abbey (Yorkshire). At Fountains it was so positioned for reasons of space, at Durham perhaps because they admired Fountains. The new chapel gave Durham all the space it needed, so that by the middle of the thirteenth century the building was substantially as we have it today. The central tower was rebuilt in the fifteenth century, and alterations were made to many of the windows, especially on the main facades, which were redesigned to suit later medieval taste.

Stylistically the main church, the Galilee and the chapel of the Nine Altars are quite distinct, although there were two building campaigns in the church itself. As often happened with a monastic church, once the monks' choir was completed building stopped for a while. The building began at the south transept (attached to the cloister and dormitory) followed by the choir and the north transept, which was half finished together with some bays of the nave when the relics were translated in 1104. It took another thirty years to complete the church. The main elevation, the types of piers and the presence of rib vaults are almost the same throughout the church, but the details of the two campaigns are quite different, merging only in the transept, which experienced both.

As originally designed, Durham was in some ways a conventional Anglo-Norman building in the mood of the second generation of post-Conquest churches. The choir plan was one of the two standard types, and the sequence of piers, alternating plain columns with cruciform compound piers, followed established practice. The alternating system, which had a long history, appeared in the Anglo-Norman world simultaneously at Jumièges (Normandy) and Westminster in the mid-eleventh century, and by 1100 it was being adapted for piers of many shapes in the great churches of East Anglia. Durham follows the earlier model in keeping the double bay form, where the bay divisions are marked out by vertical shafts on the compound piers only, so that each 'bay' of the elevation encompasses two arcade arches. The Durham elevation has the traditional three storeys, arcade, tribune gallery and clerestory windows, with a clerestory passage in the transepts and nave. Durham is a classic thick-wall building, each storey resting on and slightly set back from the one beneath, with the main wall over two metres thick.

In other ways, however, Durham breaks tradition. The three storeys are not treated after the manner of Caen and Canterbury, with arcade and gallery of roughly equal height, but adopt a pattern in which the arcade is much taller, pushing the gallery and clerestory up towards the roof and allowing the elevation to be dominated by the astonishing piers. With other English churches, Durham uses the cushion capital, derived from the Rhineland and almost unknown in Normandy itself. But Durham takes its connections with the Rhineland and Low Countries a good deal further: like the cushion capital, the concave arches which ornament the exterior are derived from the imperial church at Speyer, which was being vaulted in groin vaults at the same time as the first phase at Durham. The deeply incised patterns on the cylindrical piers of Durham are the earliest in Britain, their closest precedents being at Deventer and Utrecht in Holland, where they may have marked the site of a special altar or shrine.

The first phase of building markedly lacks other forms of surface decoration; there is some shafting, but also large expanses of plain wall. The vault of the north transept (and by inference that of the choir, now replaced) has a plain roll moulding, and it is the chevron decoration of the later south transept vault which prepares us for the burst of decoration in the nave. Here, in the main part of the later campaign, the piers are incised with lozenges and zigzags, an intersecting blind arcade lines the aisle walls, and there are deep chevrons on vault and arch mouldings. In the second bay an extra order was added to the gallery arches to emphasise the moulded surfaces. If the choir represents a phase in transition from the austere buildings of the immediate post-Conquest period, the nave leads the fashion for a new generation, with heavily ornamented surfaces. Many of the devices we see here passed into common use.

Not so the vaults. There is evidence that few Anglo-Norman buildings besides Durham had rib vaults, and Durham was the earliest, pre-dating the series of rib vaults built in Normandy itself after 1100. Anglo-Norman choirs could have barrel vaults, but the transepts and nave were invariably roofed in wood. Differences between the nave and choir at Durham suggest that here, too, only the choir was originally prepared for vaulting: there is no wall passage, the compound piers are massively broad, and the buttresses concealed under the gallery roof are full semi-circular arches, all of which contrasts with the nave where there is a wall passage, compound piers of a normal size and concealed buttresses of quadrant (i.e. half) arches. Although the argument is complicated by other details it does look as if the masons thought that the choir vault needed a lot of extra masonry to support it.

The presence of a rib vault does not make Durham a forerunner of the Gothic style. It is part of a flourishing tradition of rib-vaulted Romanesque churches, found in Italy as well, where the ribs were built to stiffen a groined cross vault. The Gothic system of ribbing is partly structural and partly visual, but in a Gothic building the structure is a balanced frame of thrust and counter-thrust. At Durham there is no such sophistication. The vaults sit on top of the wall, which is thick enough to absorb extra stresses, and the short vault shafts are unrelated to the main groups of shafting dividing the bays. In the nave the appearance of the vault was improved by the use of pointed transverse arches, which ensured that their keystones and those of the cross-ribs were all at the same level; and the pattern created by two sets of cross-ribs over each double bay is reinforced by the extra decoration of chevrons and cat masks.

The delicacy and thinness of the Galilee is the greatest contrast to the articulated monumentality of the nave. The Galilee is divided by thin walls into five aisles, with a wooden roof. The decoration is not confined to architectural moulding: there are traces of painted chevrons, as well as large human figures, showing how all types of decoration could be used, sometimes interchangeably, in a medieval building. The wide round arches have roll mouldings flanked by deep chevrons, and they are supported on clusters of slender colonnettes in opposing pairs of limestone and Purbeck 'marble', cut *en délit* (i.e. with vertical instead of horizontal grain). The huge exterior buttresses were added in the fifteenth century, and the gabled roof line was cut down, but the interior does seem to reflect the personal taste of Bishop Hugh, whose other buildings show the same mixture of delicate structure and florid ornament. The details are derived both from Cistercian buildings and from one of the most significant lost churches of the twelfth century, Archbishop Roger Pont L'Eveque's new choir of York Minster. The chevronned arches almost certainly come from York, which shared with Cistercian buildings of this time the shafts *en délit* and the broad, flat waterleaf capital.

Durham Cathedral, the Galilee (1170).

Durham Cathedral, the Chapel of Nine Altars (1240s).

The Galilee can be described as late Romanesque, but the chapel of the
Nine Altars is a classic representative of early Gothic architecture in the
north. The details of this large unaisled hall reflect the fashion of the time for
tall lancet windows with steeply pointed arches, bunched shafts in contrasting
stones, with stiff-leaf capitals, a blind arcade with trefoil arches and punched
quatrefoils above giving a jewel-like surface texture. Passages were cut
through the thick wall at two levels. The vault, now with the nervous, finely-
cut mouldings of the thirteenth century, is decorated with rosettes and
pyramidal dog-tooth ornament. Where the ribs cut into each other round the
great open keystones, little figures are carved into them, an example of
turning necessity to advantage, for the ground measurements of the chapel
(which for some reason are exactly the same as at Fountains) did not allow
for even-sized vault bays, and the vaults had to be adjusted to fit. The great

north window is not part of the original design: with its intersecting Y-tracery and foiled circles it is a fine example of late thirteenth-century window tracery, marking the introduction of window tracery to Durham.

The decorative and stylistic qualities of the three main parts of Durham Cathedral are easily distinguished. Major building operations were now over, and apart from the central tower the later additions were mostly windows and furnishings. Here the clergy moved with the times. In the late fourteenth century the shrine area was refurbished with a new base for the shrine, and a new altar screen reflecting the late medieval taste for concealing rather than revealing the shrine. The Neville screen, made in London and shipped to Durham, is in a miniaturist, fantastic style typical of London, with faceted niches and small metal figures which would have gleamed and sparkled in the candlelight; and this taste for the mildly fantastic is also seen in the intersecting vault of the monastery kitchen, which balances structural necessity equally with fantasy, a quality which we will see in the later work at Wells and perhaps not entirely alien to the cathedral of Durham.

Wells Cathedral

Wells is a more fundamentally English building than Durham, for in it we can see very clearly the absorption of foreign influences and their redeployment in an English idiom. The transepts and nave of the church begun c.1180 survive untouched by later remodelling; the choir, extended in the fourteenth century, was more radically altered than at Durham, but as the view of it is blocked from the west by the great scissor arches under the crossing, the visitor's overwhelming first impression is of a unified church.

The church was being built while Wells was fighting to regain its status as an episcopal see, a status finally won back by Bishop Jocelin (1206–42), who was responsible for part of the nave and for the west front. The conception of the building was deliberately grandiose, planned with a cloister and chapter house, neither necessary in a secular church, but present in all the great cathedrals. The set of eight effigies of Anglo-Saxon bishops, which were carved soon after 1200 and set up on the choir screen, was perhaps intended as a tangible reminder of the ancient traditions of the see.

The cathedral was built on a new site a few feet to the north of its Anglo-Saxon predecessor, and it could therefore be laid out without the restrictions imposed by earlier buildings; the plan shows none of the underlying inconsistencies and adaptations of Durham. It was spacious, with east and west aisles to the transept and a rectangular choir of three bays with a low eastern ambulatory. A chapel may have projected east from the ambulatory, but in any event the plan reflects the English twelfth-century development towards choirs with straight east ends, a plan also favoured by the Cistercians, to whose buildings Wells is related.

The apparent unity of the transepts and nave is deceptive; as at Durham there are signs of development within the design. The main elevation has all the superficial characteristics of a Gothic church, with three storeys, the middle one a series of shallow arches, a quadripartite rib vault, and all arches sharply pointed. The arch mouldings, set in multiple clusters, are sharp and

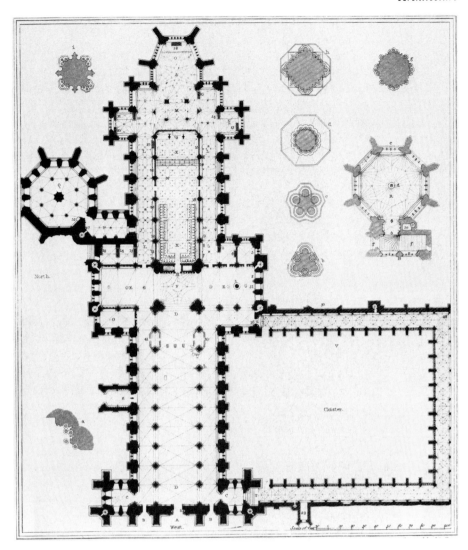

Ground plan of Wells Cathedral as it stands today.

thin. But while the massive roundness of Romanesque is absent, Gothic this building is not. It is low and squat, with consistent emphasis on bulk and depth. The main wall is more than a metre thick, deep enough for a wall passage. The depth of the cruciform piers is emphasised by the groups of triple shafts attached to the faces and corners. As far as possible the vertical line has been eradicated.

Wells is designed in horizontal layers. Although the rib vault implies the existence of the bay as a unit, the vaults are actually corbelled in at the clerestory, and everything below that denies the bay structure. There are no vertical bay divisions, and in the nave the middle storey is an uninterrupted sequence of tall, narrow arches which carry the eye forward rather than upward. This horizontality was a deliberate aim, for in the choir and

Wells Cathedral, the nave (c.1200).

transept, which were built before the nave, they kept some sense of the bay
structure by bringing the vault shafts down to the base of the gallery,
dividing the gallery arches into pairs and breaking the continuous line.

The absence of capitals and bases on the gallery arches and the applied
wall sculptures relate Wells to a group of churches scattered widely across the
south and west of England, built by a workshop which was primarily
interested in decoration. It is these details that connect the buildings, but in
most of them we find the same re-use of forms of incipient French Gothic in
an English recipe. At Wells the sculpture styles developed as the building
progressed westwards. In the late twelfth-century west bays of the choir the

foliage capitals are based on the acanthus leaf, under identifiably French influence; but in the nave the leaves are blown out into the stiff-leaf form made famous by these examples at Wells. The small figures of men and animals lurking among the foliage are not purposeless; for example, the man removing a thorn from his foot is a symbolic reference to sin.

The north porch, which was the public entrance, was probably decorated by a different sculptor, but its rectangular plan, wall arcading and figured capitals are very much to English taste. Although the break in the building associated with the Interdict of 1208, when the Pope banned all administration of the Sacraments in Britain, occurs just west of the north porch, there was no change of style until the builders reached the west front, now the main, once the ceremonial, entrance. Façades wider than the body of the church were favoured in England from the immediate post-Conquest period, in the western transepts of East Anglia and the great fortified structure at Lincoln. Lincoln and one or two other English churches had shown interest in the sort of figured decoration currently being developed in France, but Wells was the first to adopt on any scale the idea of a facade decorated by a programme of symbolic images. Much of the great image screen here shares both the style and the iconographic content of its French contemporaries, but at Wells the designer almost reversed the main ideals of French design: here, instead of three dominant sculptured doorways related to two western towers, we see tower bases set outside the line of the building, three tiny doors like mouseholes, and the figure sculpture spread all over the façade. The same idea was pursued later at Salisbury, but only at Wells does the original sculpture survive, albeit depleted and eroded. The purpose of the sculpture is the same wherever it is positioned. It is to represent, to teach and to warn. Saints, priests, kings, angels and biblical scenes, set in niches and roundels, lead the eye to the central figure of Christ in Majesty (a modern replacement) high in the gable. They represent a symbolic interpretation of Christ in his Church, a reminder of the life to come and of the church building as the embodiment of the kingdom of Heaven.

For want of definite evidence it is normally said that the iconographic programme of the west front was devised by Bishop Jocelin and the design made by Adam Locke, master mason of Wells until 1229. Unlike Durham, the master masons of Wells are reasonably well documented; we know the names of several, and the later masters, Thomas of Witney, William Joy and William Wynford, are recorded at other surviving buildings. In theory we should be able to recreate their careers as architects in the same way as we do for later figures such as Wren and Hawksmoor; so adaptable was the medieval mason, however, that so far it has been difficult to trace consistent internal development in the work of these men, but for those who dislike the anonymity of much medieval building, the documentation of these masters is reward enough.

Although a start was made on the chapter house before 1250, the great staircase from the north choir aisle and the chapter room itself were built only from the late thirteenth century, and they form a suitable prelude to the rebuilding campaign at the east end. By the 1290s the buildings of London were acting as a powerful stimulus to regional imagination, and the Wells

Wells Cathedral, the chapter house (c.1300).

The retrochoir and Lady chapel (c.1320).

chapter house combines London details with a west-country taste, seen also at Exeter, for copious bulky decoration. They loved the moulded work of vaults and tracery. Here the huge central column has sixteen marble shafts from which thirty-two ribs spring to meet their counterparts from the walls. Linked by a ridge rib, all intersections are masked by heavy foliate keystones. The window embrasures are thick with the studded ornament known as ball-flower, complex tracery patterns fill the windows, which once contained stained glass. All secondary shafting is in contrasting marble. Following the fashion set by Westminster and London, the intensity of the interior decoration is much heightened, and here some of the details such as tracery patterns are of London origin.

The heightened interior concentration of the chapter house prepares us for the choir and eastward extension. As at Durham, the reason for the rebuilding was liturgical. In the late thirteenth century Wells adopted a liturgy based on the new one at Salisbury, which required elaborate processional and altar space which the old choir and ambulatory were unable to provide. The resulting fusion of the client's requirement with the architect's inspiration is one of the glories of English medieval architecture.

The ambulatory was removed and the high choir extended to six bays, beyond which spread a low, single-storey eastern transept, processional way (the rectrochoir) and Lady chapel, glimpsed through the choir arches as a forest of slender piers set against gigantic traceried windows. Where the late twelfth-century design was simple, with neat right angles and no ambiguities, the new work substituted polygons for rectangles and abandoned clarity and precision in favour of ambiguity and concealment. The chapels in the eastern transept and at the end of the aisles lead in echelon to the Lady chapel, which is an irregular octagon set into the retrochoir like an egg into a cup: five sides project clear, but the other three push into the retrochoir space, even displacing the piers. At ground level the complete absence of solid walls allows people to move freely between the chapels and the retrochoir.

This love of polygonal plans and ambiguous spaces is characteristic of the Decorated style of which Wells is an outstanding example. It is equally characterised in the big windows with their fishscale tracery, the delicately moulded piers with seaweed-like foliage capitals, and in the vaulting. At Wells the long tiercerons and short liernes which make up the secondary ribs are used in the Lady chapel to make a star pattern which beautifully solves the problem posed by the irregular sides; their patterns and clusters do the same in the confused spaces of the retrochoir; in the aisles they make clear, cruciform patterns, while in the choir the smooth barrel-like surface is intersected with regular diagonal ribs interrupted by a series of lozenge shapes.

The design of the Lady chapel has been attributed on stylistic comparisons to Thomas of Witney, also master at Exeter, but the choir itself is the work of William Joy. After the ingenuity of the surrounding spaces it might seem paradoxical to call the rectangular, boxy choir the climax of the design, but in their terms it was. This is the liturgical focus of the building, and surrounding the enlarged space, with the altar moved to the new east wall, the windows and niches were filled with figures of saints, patriarchs, bishops and donors, all witnesses to the rite, glowing with colour and gilding. In the vault, the window embrasures and the niches so cleverly used to mask the join of the new choir bays to the old, consistent decoration has been used over all surfaces. So consistent is it that the window tracery is beginning to resemble the panel-like niche shapes on the walls, and the east window in particular seems to anticipate the slightly later work at Gloucester. Here again, coloured marble, stained glass, decorated vaulting and painted surfaces act together to draw in the spectator, but in the generation since the building of the chapter house the mouldings are further refined, with many facets to reflect gold and candlelight.

In the choir, which was finished c.1340, William Joy was clearly responding to the move towards the rectilinear which had been emphasised at St Stephen's, Westminster, and would be reaffirmed at Gloucester. But the huge scissor arches which he afterwards inserted between the tower piers, whose ogival shape and ogival mouldings are in a purely Decorated idiom, warn us that we should not distinguish too sharply between what we see as two styles at this time; the masons themselves moved happily between one and the other and as yet saw no great stylistic revolution. The arches were designed to prevent the collapse of the central tower, an aim they fulfil admirably, for although they look entirely frivolous they are in fact engineered with great precision, ideally designed to counteract and absorb the pressure exerted by the piers.

In a sense these arches are the climax of the building work at Wells; the last big undertaking, the facade towers, are dull by comparison. William Wynford designed the south-west tower c.1390, and its northern twin was added about forty years later. Dull though the south tower is, it is both

Wells Cathedral, the choir (1330s).

discreet and harmonious. It is famous for its influence on many fifteenth-century parish church towers in Somerset, and its understated design perhaps shows that Wynford had a somewhat unmedieval sense that the new towers should not dominate the masterpiece of which they are the crown, the sculptured hymn to the glory of God which is harbinger to the building within.

Rievaulx: a Cistercian monastery

'Strong and weak alike [shall] find in Rievaulx a haven of peace, a spacious and calm home.' Thus Ailred, Abbot of Rievaulx Abbey, the earliest Cistercian foundation in Yorkshire and the mother house of the Cistercians in Scotland. Rievaulx, our third building, is a complete contrast to the glories of secular Wells and Benedictine Durham. It was founded in 1132 directly from Clairvaux in Burgundy, home of Bernard, whose dominant personality was to mould the Cistercian movement into one of the formative influences on twelfth-century life and spirituality.

Unlike other monastic orders, the Cistercians were closely governed from their original centre, and from the annual General Chapter, which every abbot was supposed to attend, came a series of statutes giving rules for the conduct of Cistercian life. Some of them concern architecture, many concern liturgical objects and furnishings; and while the influence of the former has been somewhat exaggerated, in the early days the latter had a strong effect. In their life and surroundings the Cistercians cut out all unnecessary distractions: they used a reduced, simplified liturgy, there was no form of sculptured decoration, no paint beyond whitewash, and when stained glass became widespread in the thirteenth century the Cistercians allowed in their windows only geometric patterns in monochrome grisaille which could act as an aid to contemplation and prayer.

Rievaulx Abbey, North Yorkshire.

The founder of Rievaulx, Walter L'Espec, was one of the most powerful barons in the north, and the new foundation carried the blessing of the Archbishop of York, King Henry I and the Pope. For the rest of the century Rievaulx was the spiritual leader of the Cistercian movement in the north, and its grip on men's imagination was immediate and strong: within ten years there were 300 monks at Rievaulx itself, and eleven new foundations had been colonised from it. The first monastic buildings on the site were wooden, but the church itself, finished c.1145, was built of beautiful ashlar masonry, and sited on a terrace cut into the hill, itself a considerable feat of engineering.

The Rievaulx of today consists of the ruins of the first church and later additions, with the conventual buildings rebuilt in stone and modified several times. Insofar as it represents a period in the abbey's history it catches the moment of the Dissolution of the monasteries; after the Dissolution the Earl of Richmond acquired the site and removed much of the building stone for use elsewhere. The great beauty of the site evokes a powerful emotional response, but in the layers of ruins we can trace across the centuries the changes in Cistercian attitudes.

The architecture of Rievaulx repeats a pattern which has been observed in Cistercian buildings throughout Britain: at first there was a conscious desire for simplicity, which could produce a form of Romanesque so reduced as to seem archaic. This phase was followed by a move towards contemporary architectural values, still austere, but now in the main current of development. The first phase can be seen in the nave and lower levels of the transept, the second in the upper transept and the choir.

The style of the first phase, finished c.1145, is not only reduced and plain, but it is also closely related to Cistercian work on the Continent. The plan of the first church was cruciform, with a rectangular sanctuary, three rectangular chapels on each arm of the transept and an aisled nave of nine bays. As there was no central tower, there was no crossing, and the main arcade ran through to the sanctuary. The aisles were narrow in proportion to the central nave. Although the exterior is decorated with regularly spaced horizontal string courses and shallow buttresses, still visible on the transept walls, the inside walls of the nave are devoid of articulation. The piers are square, with the corners slightly chamfered, and the windows (visible in the transept) small, roundheaded and unmoulded. The main elevation had two storeys, with no passage in the thin wall, and a wooden roof. In the south aisle enough traces remain to show that the aisles were vaulted by barrel vaults set at right angles to the main vessel.

The absolute simplicity and the thin-walled two-storey structure at once set Rievaulx apart from its Anglo-Norman contemporaries: Durham was finished the year after Rievaulx was founded. But the plan of choir and transept, the transverse barrel vaults in the aisles and the small porch at the west end place Rievaulx in the so-called Bernardine group of churches, whose more mature form, barrel-vaulted throughout and with no clerestory, can be seen today at Fontenay in Burgundy. The wooden roof and clerestory of Rievaulx have been ascribed to English influence, but it shares these features with several early Bernardine churches on the Continent. It can plausibly be argued that in these early days churches affiliated to Clairvaux adopted a standard layout, and there is evidence that monks from the mother-houses went to supervise not only the spiritual welfare but also the building of the new daughter-houses. It is this evidence that the Cistercians' attempts at centralised control actually worked that makes them a remarkable phenomenon.

The immense length of the nave was needed to accommodate the lay brothers, men who had not taken full monastic vows, but who did much of the manual work needed to support a life of self-sufficiency. They lived in the west range of the cloister, and attended mass in their own choir, sited in the nave to the west of the choir monks' stalls, separated from them by the rood screen. The true laity were strongly discouraged from entering the church at all (there are few public entrances to a Cistercian church and none is welcoming). The Cistercians did not at this early date encourage pilgrims and therefore had no important shrines. In the thirteenth century this was to change, although at Rievaulx the main shrine, of William, their first abbot, was placed in the chapter house and was not for public view; but the relic list of Rievaulx compiled at the Dissolution records a substantial quantity of minor and improbable relics in the church itself. Nor did the Cistercians encourage lay burials, although by the early thirteenth century this, too, was to change. After 1200 the Cistercians were being drawn inexorably towards the general monastic world in which patrons required Cistercians as well as Benedictines to accept their bodies for burial and say masses for their souls. As at Durham, more monks were ordained priests, and more altars were needed.

Rievaulx was not the first Cistercian house to build an enormous choir, for Byland had led the way in the north in the 1170s, with Jervaulx and Fountains following in the years around 1200. Byland and Jervaulx were new church buildings, but the Fountains choir, like Rievaulx, replaced an earlier one. It is in all these buildings that we see the beginning of the shift in Cistercian architecture away from their own stylistic preoccupations and towards current local styles.

At this time the rectangular aisled choir was becoming the most popular English type, and Jervaulx (with Fountains in a modified form) helped to promote it in the north. The rectangular plan was chosen for Rievaulx c.1220, and the choir building itself is in every way a contrast to the nave. The transept was also substantially rebuilt above the ground floor, and now a proper crossing, supporting a low central tower, was introduced, again following a recognisable Cistercian trend. The new work has three storeys, and the choir was vaulted throughout in rib vaults (the absence of preparation for a vault in the upper levels of the transept shows that it had a wooden roof). The choir has an arcade, a big gallery with twin arches opening to the main vessel, and a clerestory with a passage in the thickness of the wall.

The piers are clustered, the form already introduced by the Cistercians and adopted all over the north; and the pointed arches are deeply and finely moulded. Mouldings of the same quality are used in the gallery, together with 'nailhead' studded ornament and ornamental detached shafts with flat, strip-like fillets on them. Little quatrefoil shapes are cut out in the spaces above the arches. Each bay of the clerestory has twin lancet windows, and the wide arch opening to the main vessel is flanked by narrow blind arches. The east wall has a set of six fine lancets in two groups of three. Five altars were set against the east wall, with the high altar two bays to the west, allowing for access to the eastern altars. At some time after this the monks' choir was moved, most unusually, to the east side of the crossing, leaving the nave clear.

This heavily moulded style places Rievaulx in the centre of architectural development in the north of England. Although there is scarcely any purely decorative sculpture, the choir has an intensely decorated feel to it, as if the older ideas of reduced simplicity had been abandoned. Compared to its closest parallels, the Abbeys of Hexham and Whitby and the transepts of York Minster, Rievaulx is more austere, but it is nevertheless a lovely example of early Gothic architecture in the north. The clerestory passage and the gallery opening to a lean-to roof over the aisle show the acceptance of much that had been rejected nearly a century before. Except for details such as the pairing of gallery openings, the transept design is closest to the choir of Whitby, and the choir elevation, modified for vaulting, is still a close cousin.

The conventual buildings were altered more often than the church, but in a more piecemeal fashion. During the twelfth century the wooden buildings round the cloister were replaced in stone, although the cloister walks were roofed in wood. Owing to the presence of the lay brothers in the west range, Cistercian refectories were sited at right angles to the south range, to leave room for the kitchens. The refectory of Rievaulx, built c.1200, opens straight off the cloister, but it has an undercroft to compensate for a sharp fall in the ground level; thus, as in other Cistercian abbeys, the refectory is an upper room, symbolising the room where the Last Supper took place. The walls are articulated by a blind arcade with detached shafts and a row of arches once screened the reading desk in the side wall. Well lit by tall lancet windows and regularly buttressed on the outside, the refectory in its restrained splendour is a prelude to the slightly later finery of the choir.

The Rievaulx chapter house, used for a daily reading from the Rule of St Benedict, was most unusual. Cistercian chapter houses are normally rectangular and vaulted in six or nine bays with three large openings to the east walk of the cloister. At Rievaulx the chapter house was an unvaulted square room with an apse, surrounded by an ambulatory and aisles leading from a vestibule. A chapter house was traditionally the burial place of the abbots; the shrine of the canonised first abbot of Rievaulx is a little gabled structure with a vaulted canopy in the west wall.

Changes to the buildings reflect the smaller number of monks in the late Middle Ages, and their weakened ideals of a truly communal life. The apse of the chapter house was walled off, and the Infirmary, for instance, was divided into cubicles and fireplaces were provided. This may also have been done in the destroyed dormitory on the upper floor of the east range. In the early sixteenth century the Infirmary was converted to the abbot's lodging, and a niche with a sculptured Annunciation group, a well-known symbol of humility, was put in above the door. It may seem ironical to have such a symbol on a new house for the abbot, but Rievaulx made these changes towards grandeur and privacy later than did many of her sister houses. By the Dissolution the monks may have been far from the founders of 400 years earlier in their aspirations as well as in time, but for many people in the twentieth century the atmosphere of Rievaulx remains redolent of her early ideals.

The art of the carpenter: Westminster Hall and Mildenhall Church

In the three great churches we have looked at, the art of the stone mason seemed to dominate, but in this period the carpenter was just as important a figure. Master carpenters reached the same high status at about the same time as stone masons, earning the same wages. The working life of a few individuals can be traced from the early fourteenth century, although an Irish carpenter of the thirteenth century is famous, chiefly from his criminal record. For houses timber framing was cheaper than stone, and more convenient, for a house built of timber and plaster could be dismantled and rebuilt somewhere else. This was the frequent fate of buildings such as royal hunting lodges, which would be in use for only short periods.

Woodwork and stonework were closely related. A church building is incomplete without its fittings of choir stalls, misericords, screens and pew ends, all of wood and surviving in considerable numbers even today. The stone building was structurally incomplete without its roof, and the weight of the massive wooden frame supporting the pitched roof above the vaults had to be calculated when stresses on the stonework were being considered. Carpenters and stone masons therefore worked closely together: for several years after William Hurley's timber lantern was built over the stone octagonal crossing of Ely Cathedral Hurley was paid an annual retainer, presumably to be at hand to advise over difficulties which might develop as the building settled. When the wooden throne for the Bishops of Exeter was made from 1313, the Master Thomas de Winton, who advised on the choice of timber, was almost certainly Thomas of Witney, whose stone building we have seen at Wells, and who was shortly to become master mason of Exeter Cathedral.

Carpenters and masons imitated each other's styles. The lantern at Ely rises from a cantilever arrangement whose underside, visible from below, is in the form of wooden vaults. There was a long tradition of wooden vaults, of which those in York Minster are famous, and the wooden vaults at Lichfield Cathedral pleased Henry III so much that he stipulated that the roof of his new chapel in Windsor Castle should be made in imitation of them. Meanwhile masons tried to reproduce in stone the decorative qualities of timberwork: the entrance to the vestibule of the chapter house at York has an arrangement in stone which markedly resembles part of a timber roof truss, and the openwork vaults in the south aisle of Bristol cathedral are supported on horizontal members in a manner compared by several scholars to carpentry. The late fifteenth-century Divinity Schools and cathedral ceiling at Oxford have pendant vaults, where a carved boss hangs from the centre of each cone of a fan vault (see p. 58). This is almost certainly derived from a form of timber roof, surviving at Eltham Palace and Hampton Court, with similar bosses hanging from the wooden beams.

The friars' churches and the parish churches which they inspired were light and thin-structured with wooden roofs. As the fourteenth century gave way to the fifteenth, the arches adopted the depressed, shallow, four-centred shape typical of the later Perpendicular style, and the same shape was used in the roof beams. By the late Middle Ages a church roof could be a work of art in its own right, but because carpentry was rooted in the strong domestic tradition of houses, halls and barns, many new techniques were first developed in secular buildings.

Timber-framed buildings, like stone ones, were built in bays, with the longitudinal framework which made up the side walls supported at intervals by cross-frames or trusses which ran across the building. Depending on the size of the building, timber frames could be constructed in different ways, but they were put together before they were raised into position. The method depended on the width of the building, for in practice a roof truss cannot span a width bigger than the normal length of timbers, but for a building which was not too wide the roof truss rested on the main posts of the exterior frame, leaving the interior of the building open and unimpeded by internal supports. An alternative to this method was cruck framing, in which the cross frames consisted of huge curved timbers which rose to meet at the crown of the roof, strengthened by tie beams.

When the building was too wide to support a roof truss on the outer walls it was aisled; the main frame supporting the roof became the internal arcade, with aisles attached on each side. Roof trusses can sit as happily on a stone wall or arcade as over a timber frame. The late twelfth-century hall at Oakham Castle (Rutland) is a stone building with a wooden roof and divided into aisles; it was in an effort to find ways of managing without the internal supports to achieve an open interior that the glory of late medieval timber roofing, the hammer-beam roof, was developed.

Westminster Hall

The great hall is the only part of the medieval Palace of Westminster to survive intact the fire of 1834, and although it has been much restored we can see the building essentially as it was modified in the reign of Richard II. The hall was originally built as an aisled hall with a wooden roof by William Rufus in the 1090s; from 1394 it was converted under the direction of the king's master mason, Henry Yevele, into a huge aisle-less space, with new windows and a heraldic cornice on the side walls. A more significant figure, however, was Hugh Herland, the king's master carpenter, for he it was who designed the enormous timber roof which floats above the floor, spanning nearly twenty metres with no central support.

In this roof the longitudinal timbers supporting the roof trusses, which would have run above the arcade piers, are now themselves supported by a different method: a short horizontal (hammer) beam, bedded into the top of the outside wall, projects inwards on a cantilever principle, braced and steadied by a series of curved timbers. From the end of the hammer beam rises the hammer post, a short post in the position of the old piers, which supports the roof truss. The entire roof system now rides well clear of the ground.

This ingenious solution did not originate at Westminster; a plain and crudely-worked hammer-beam roof probably dating from c.1325 survives in the Pilgrim's hall at Winchester, and in the 1380s John Holland, half-brother to Richard II, built a hammer-beam roof over his new hall at Dartington (Devon). But at Westminster the structural engineering is presented in fully decorated form, with moulded timbers, openwork tracery panels and, at the ends of the hammer beams, angels bearing shields of the king's arms.

Westminster Hall, interior (1390s).

Mildenhall Church

Late medieval parish churches were rarely vaulted in stone; the calm
simplicity of the Perpendicular parish church is usually complemented by a
timber roof, sometimes panelled and ceiled, often with some sort of timber
frame, and, especially in East Anglia, hammer-beam roofs adorned with
angels. Some, such as March (Cambridgeshire), have a double-hammer-beam
roof, with two sets of angels on the hammer beams and a third at the foot of
the wall posts.

The roof of the parish church at Mildenhall (Suffolk) cannot produce quite
such an array of angels, but it is a triumph of the carpenter's art, covered
with relief carvings and freestanding figures. The church building is of
different periods, the chancel built in the thirteenth century, the quatrefoiled
tracery of the east window just predating the spread of ogival (flowing)
tracery in the fourteenth. The nave, with its roof, was built by Sir Henry
Barton from 1420. Over the main vessel, horizontal tie beams supported by

Mildenhall Parish Church, Suffolk, single hammer-beam roof with carved angels (1420s).

curved arches alternate with hammer beams, from the underside of which have been carved out large figures of angels. This is unusual, as the angel was normally carved separately (at Westminster they cost fifteen shillings each), but here only the wings were carved from separate pieces of wood. The angels hold shields with symbols of the Passion, a contrast to the self-regarding decoration by Richard II at Westminster Hall. Smaller angels sit on the tie beams and the wall plates along the sides of the roof. Surviving traces of paint show that the roof was originally coloured and gilded.

The lean-to roofs of the aisles are supported at their outer edge by hammer beams, of which the group in the north aisle are particularly rich in ornament. At the foot of each wall post stands the figure of an apostle or saint protected by a flying angel above. The draperies, falling in abundant folds to the feet, are loose and graceful. The curved braces supporting the hammer beams are solid, carved in shallow relief by a different sculptor, with figures and scenes in the mixture typical of the period: Old and New Testament scenes such as Abraham with Isaac and the Baptism of Christ; demons playing the organ; heraldic emblems. Elsewhere in the roof there are similar scenes, including a reference to St Edmund, king and martyr, whose shrine at Bury was the source of some wealth to East Anglia. It is a truism that on misericords, pew ends and other purely decorative parts of the church the sculptors produced all sorts of fanciful designs, scenes of daily life, popular tales and legends. Today at Mildenhall the meaning of some of these scenes eludes us, but the great skill and importance of the medieval carpenter is plain to see.

The castle builders: Harlech and Caernarfon

A medieval castle was not strictly speaking a military fortress, but it was the fortified residence of a king or great lord, either lay, or, as we saw at Durham, ecclesiastical. It was the dwelling house and the seat of administration, and in the castles chosen to illustrate this chapter both military and non-military functions were clearly differentiated. These Welsh castles of Edward I are far removed in size and plan from the donjon of Norman times; they are one-period castles, representing late thirteenth-century thinking about castle design, with no substantial additions or alterations. Dover, for instance, or the Tower of London, were both adapted, the Norman donjon surrounded by later defensive walling systems.

Enough British castles survive, albeit ruined, for their development to be studied from the earliest motte-and-bailey castles built by the advancing Normans, where the donjon was raised upon a mound surrounded by a defensive ditch, to the more complex gatehouses and curtain walls of the later Middle Ages. Most castles should also be studied for their aesthetic character, for they were clearly designed to please the eye, with attention to tower plans (often polygonal) and elegant details. Castle builders were also church builders, and although the same degree of decoration was not appropriate to a castle, the same standard of building was applied.

Harlech and Caernarfon were largely built during the years of intense activity following the Welsh defeat of 1283, when Edward I finally conquered the intractable region of Snowdonia and brought it under control with his 'ring of castles'. Thousands of pounds (the equivalent of tens of millions today) were spent, and masons and labourers were impressed in astonishing numbers from all over the country. Collecting at Chester they were poured into north Wales to build Conwy, Harlech and Caernarfon. Rhuddlan and Flint had already been built after the Welsh campaign of the 1270s; Beaumaris was to follow the uprising of 1295. These buildings gave Edward I the chance to perfect the planning of various types of castle, based on wide experience from his extensive travels. Edward was the most widely travelled English king since Richard I: he visited the south of France, Italy, Sicily and the Holy Land, and, like Richard, he absorbed many of the latest ideas on defence.

Harlech is an isolated castle, Caernarfon has a walled town attached to it, and they have been chosen as classic examples of two distinct types of castle which were built extensively in the late thirteenth century. Isolated strongholds using much the same defensive devices as Harlech were being built, with Edward's permission and often with his help, by several great magnates of the realm; and in Gascony especially both Edward and his French opponents built fortified towns known as *bastides*, to which Caernarfon is related. Reflecting the personality of their patron, the Welsh castles do not innovate; rather, they consolidate existing forms into new patterns. The curtain wall with regularly spaced towers and the strong gatehouse had both been deployed before, and the principle of the concentric castle, in which two or more circles of defence repeat one another line for line, had been established in the Crusader kingdoms before the end of the twelfth century. Edward I and his architect combined these ideas in various ways to create castles of formidable strength and great beauty, both visible and abstract. While a castle often has to follow the configuration of the site, this is not always so; the groundplans of Rhuddlan, Harlech and Beaumaris, and the gatehouse of Denbigh, are in themselves geometric figures quite as beautiful as the buildings which rose upon them.

As we have seen at Wells, the collective methods of medieval building, the time taken and the sheer number of masons involved, make it rarely safe or wise to attribute a building to a single designer; but we do know that the man who controlled the building of these and most of Edward's other works in Wales was Master James of St George, a mason who worked for Edward's cousins the Counts of Savoy in the Alps near Turin. The castle of St Georges d'Esperanches, whence Master James took his name, has several details in common with the north Welsh castles. Master James appeared in the records of the king's works in 1278, and he died c.1309. His title was 'Master of the King's Works in Wales', and he almost certainly laid out the designs of all the Welsh castles. For several years he was based in Conwy, and in 1290 he became Constable of Harlech for three years, perhaps living in the gatehouse he himself designed.

Master James would have designed the layout of the plan and such details as mouldings, which were then carved and built by his assistants. It is impossible to apportion the exact roles of master and assistants, as the master was often absent, and an assistant could take the master's ideas elsewhere. The names of several prominent assistants are known, some from Savoy, and their presence may explain why some continental methods of construction were used, such as, for example, the inclined or spiral arrangement of scaffolding holes, clearly visible in the south towers of Harlech, when it was the English custom to place them horizontally. Master James' main English assistant was Walter of Hereford, who took over at Caernarfon in 1295; he also built several important churches patronised by royalty, including the Franciscan church in London. It was Walter who took the idea of polygonal towers, designed by Master James for Caernarfon, and used them at Denbigh.

These castles were still so effective even in the seventeenth century that Harlech was the last castle to fall in the Civil War and an order was given to dismantle Caernarfon at the Restoration in 1660. Harlech survived the attentions of the Cromwellians, and the order at Caernarfon was never carried out. Restored though they both are, they remain essentially buildings of their time.

Harlech Castle

Harlech Castle, standing on its rocky outcrop against the seashore, guardian of the coastal route to the Snowdon range which forms its background, has a remote past properly described in Welsh legend. It is doubtful whether any earlier buildings were on the site in May 1283, when Edward I's friend and associate, Sir Otto de Grandisson, advanced on it from Castell y Bere, and sealed the conquest of the southern approaches. The castle was built in two phases, but it was practically completed in seven building seasons, finished by 1290 when Master James of St George was appointed Constable.

Harlech is an example of the concentric plan made famous by Edward I and his architect, who, though they did not invent it, certainly perfected it. The plan has two defensive circuits: the main building, enclosing the inner ward, is not quite square, the east side being slightly longer than the west. There is a strong round tower at each corner with the main strength concentrated on the gatehouse in the middle of the east wall. The outer curtain encloses the inner structure almost line for line. Outworks protect the corner towers, the side entrance on the north wall is guarded by its own bastion, and the two towers of the gatehouse are reflected in the twin turrets of the protective barbican or outer fortification. On the north side the ground falls away sharply, and the sea lapped the west; on the south and east side was dug a deep defensive ditch, with a bridge across it to the barbican and gatehouse.

The empty appearance of the inner ward is deceptive, for built up against the walls were the great hall, chapel and kitchens, all now stripped to their foundations. They were probably built in the second building campaign, which also concentrated on adding to the height and thickness of walls already in place. On the south curtain, especially on a sunny afternoon, the masonry break masking the two phases shows clearly, running along the wall

Harlech Castle, gatehouse from the west (1283–90).

about 4.5m above ground level. Vertical breaks, showing where the wall was thickened, can easily be picked out in the windows of the west curtain.

At Harlech, however, attention should properly be focused on the gatehouse. It is a deep block, three storeys high, with extra floors in the towers. It consists of a rectangular rear section, with twin towers built out in front where it joins the curtain wall. The towers are rounded at their outer edges, but squared off at the entrance door to help form the passage which runs through at ground level. As so often in Master James's gatehouses, military and domestic requirements are most satisfactorily combined. The gatehouse is designed to keep people out, the passage fitted with three sets of doors and three portcullises, with arrow slits in the guard rooms through which soldiers could attack anyone who penetrated the first portcullis. The passage doors were controlled from the guardrooms, which themselves could be entered only from the inner end of the passage.

The symmetry of windows and stringcourses on the outer towers is some preparation for the great elegance of the non-military part of the gatehouse. The upper rooms were reached by staircases in the corner turrets of the main block, and by an outer stair which formed a sort of forebuilding at the back, giving added protection to the passage entrance. The two sets of rooms on the upper floors have fireplaces and privies, with a small chapel overlooking the barbican. These sets of rooms were presumably the apartments for the Constable and distinguished visitors.

The inner side of the gatehouse contrasts strongly with the menacing twin-towered outer side. Here, protected by the staircase turrets, are six enormous windows, once with shallow segmental arches and a simple pattern of window tracery. Horizontal moulded stringcourses ran round the turrets and across the facade at battlement level and beneath the windows. This side of the gatehouse looks what it is, a strengthened but gracious house of a nobleman. All Master James' gatehouses are as elegantly detailed as they are defensively strong, and at Beaumaris a few years later he was able to develop the Harlech design on a larger scale. The design reflects the reality of castle life: that every so often the full strength of the castle may be needed to withstand attack, but the gatehouse and curtain walls are designed for this. In the meantime the daily and administrative life of the castle can be peacefully conducted in civilised surroundings.

Access to the sea helped Harlech to survive the rebellion of 1295, and after that the outer defences were built to strengthen the sea gate. Harlech has fallen to siege and to cannonade, but Master James' gatehouse has withstood all assaults.

Caernarfon Castle

The Statute of Wales (1284) established Caernarfon as the seat of English government in north Wales, the centre of the administration of justice and the collection of taxes. The idea was to create a sphere of English influence in the Welsh heartland, and as also at Denbigh the fortified town was to be populated solely by English burgesses. At Conwy and Caernarfon the castle is set at one edge of the town but within and attached to the walls. This is a development of the earlier French type of *bastide* such as Aigues Mortes in Provence, which Edward I had visited, where the residential tower is set outside the main fortified square and is connected to it by a bridge. The round tower and rectangular enclosure of Flint Castle are clearly influenced by Aigues Mortes. Caernarfon Castle was meant from the beginning to house a governor (or Constable). It could be reached easily by sea, and there had already been a Norman castle on the site, taken over by the Welsh in 1115. But there may have been additional reasons for choosing it, for there are indications in Caernarfon's history and architecture that its symbolic function was to be as significant as its administrative role.

On the town walls, the towers are the round ones seen on every other Edwardian castle in Wales except Denbigh; but right from the start the series of linked towers and gatehouses which make up the castle itself were polygonal. Where the contemporary castle at Conwy was whitewashed, at Caernarfon the walls were banded with a reddish stone. The nearest parallel to the combined phenomenon of polygonal towers and striped walls is the Theodosian wall at Constantinople (Istanbul). Just after the castle was begun some bones were discovered which were alleged to be those of the father of Constantine. It has been suggested that Edward I deliberately exploited the association with the first Christian Emperor of Rome and the founder of Constantinople, the imperial connotations being further emphasised by the stone eagles placed on the battlements of the Eagle tower; that he deliberately chose Caernarfon as the birthplace in 1284 of the son whom in 1301 he created Prince of Wales. Now the eagles are more likely to be associated with the arms of a member of the Grandisson family, and there was no guarantee that the baby born in 1284 would not be a girl, or that the infant Prince would become Prince of Wales (his elder brother Alfonso was still alive at the time); but allowing for some scepticism, to present Caernarfon as a building of Christian and Imperial significance is typical of Edward I himself. A devout Christian, he habitually turned Christianity to his own advantage, and this treatment of Caernarfon fits well with his other acts of conquest, both symbolic and actual, towards the Welsh.

Caernarfon, like Harlech, was built in two main phases, only more drawn out, not being finished for half a century. The town walls and the south curtain of the castle were done first, forming a fortified ring; but the walls were penetrated and largely destroyed in the Welsh uprising of 1295 which also threatened Harlech. The immediate result of that episode, which the English won only with difficulty, was the building of Beaumaris Castle on the opposite bank of the Menai Strait, and the completion of the north curtain of Caernarfon Castle with mural towers and a strong gatehouse. Where the Beaumaris gatehouses are full of ingenious devices to trap the invader, the King's Gate at Caernarfon relies on strength: the plan, with two polygonal towers backed by square rooms, is not unlike Harlech, but the entrance passage has six portcullises, with murder holes in the vaults above, through which arrows and missiles could fall upon attackers. The arrow slits in the battlements overlooking the entrance each allowed two archers to fire through them at the same time, an arrangement invisible from outside. As at Harlech, the chapel was above the passage, and here two of the portcullises would, if ever raised, have come up into it. But for all its strength and military preparedness the gatehouse is designed with symmetry and balance, the beautifully moulded entrance arch an Imperial tribune like the great arch in Charlemagne's palace chapel at Aachen. The topmost windows have delicate tracery patterns, and in 1321 a statue of Edward of Caernarfon (now Edward II) was placed in a niche above the door.

Once through the gatehouse the visitor experiences the same change of mood as at Harlech. Inside, the castle is given over to comfortable living.

Caernarfon Castle, from the south-west (1280s).

The plan is a rough figure of eight, the narrow central part lying between the King's Gate and the Chamberlain Tower, which guarded the entrance to the lower ward and access to the Constable's rooms in the Eagle Tower. The upper ward bulges out to enclose the old Norman motte, against which the builders revetted the walls and towers. These towers are defended by battlements and wall walks, but in the thickness of the lower walls are passages lit by arrow slits, which allow circulation between the towers without having to go outside, a great blessing in rainy north Wales. The great hall between the Queen's Tower and the Chamberlain Tower has gone, but in the towers themselves are signs of provision for permanent and ceremonious residence. The towers have several storeys with strong basements and big central rooms; some have extra rooms and passages in the thickness of the walls, and they all have privies and fireplaces. Sir Otto de Grandisson crowned his career of conquest by becoming Justiciar of north Wales, based on Caernarfon, and his residence was commensurate with the dignity of his office.

Oxburgh Hall, the arched gateway within the courtyard (late fifteenth century).

2 Oxburgh Hall, Norfolk

NIGEL NICOLSON

Oxburgh Hall, seven miles south-west of Swaffham in Norfolk, was built in the 1480s by Edmund Bedingfeld as a castellated moated manor-house, and was given to the National Trust by Lady Bedingfeld who died in 1985 at the age of 101. Longevity was not a characteristic of the Bedingfelds, but it is of the house. Its continuous occupation by the same family for 500 years (they still live in part of it) is one reason for its survival. They cared for it, made it more comfortable internally, but only once, by pulling down the great hall in the eighteenth century, violated its integrity. When they replaced parts of the building or embellished it, they did so in a manner that is well adapted to its original character. It remains our loveliest evidence of how a castle was gradually transformed into a house, and of the waning influence of military and church architecture upon domestic building.

The view from the northern approach is the best. We confront the most magnificent feature of Oxburgh, the gatehouse. Twin octagonal turrets 80 feet high are attached each side of a central tower which contains two superimposed rooms marked by great windows. The intention was clearly dramatic. The tower proclaims the authority and audacity of its builder, but also his romanticism, his attachment to the past, for the skyline is serrated by battlements, the facade laced at intervals by firm Gothic loops, and the windows designed to suggest both welcome and defiance. The proportions, height and distancing of the turrets are the result of careful forethought, to create an impression of grandeur, permanence and sublimity. The traditional medieval entrance, squeezed narrowly between the cheeks of rotund towers, is replaced by a glorious achievement of architectural pageantry. The reverse side of the gatehouse, within the courtyard, is treated quite differently. The pair of turrets stop short of the parapet, and two watch-towers, corbelled outwards at the angles, carry the eye upwards.

On each side of the gatehouse extend lower two-storeyed wings, the windows patterned irregularly like stamps in an album, and centrally gabled, in a manner that is clearly more house than castle. This north front marries an ancient to a novel style, breaking with a tradition while paying tribute to it, and makes more habitable and hospitable a building which fifty years earlier would have been constructed in stone and designed mainly to resist attack. Oxburgh is a highly imaginative work of architecture in its balance of different shapes. It makes a deliberate attempt to please if not to charm, and possesses a composure, an Englishness, which castles subsequently acquired only by ruin and sentimental associations.

Its situation is an odd one. It lies only a few feet above sea-level at the very edge of fens that were not properly drained till the eighteenth century, but was linked by a low spur to a navigable tributary of the Ouse. While not a fortified harbour like Beaumaris in Anglesey, nor a coastal fort like Bodiam in Sussex, Oxburgh did form a bastion to mark and vaguely defend the line where the gently swaying heaths of Norfolk met the rivers and the swamps. No previous castle occupied the site, but there was a substantial mansion on the higher ground just east of the present village of Oxborough (Hall and village now spell the name differently), and this came to the Bedingfelds, a Suffolk family by marriage to the sister of the previous owner, Sir Thomas Tuddenham, who was executed on Tower Hill in 1462. It was the grandson of this marriage, Edmund Bedingfeld, who built the present house.

In 1482 Edward IV licensed him to 'build, make and construct walls and towers with stone, lime and sand around and below his manor of Oxburgh', and forgave him if he had anticipated the licence by fortifying his house without permission. This last clause has suggested to historians that Oxburgh was begun before 1482, but if so, it would be strange to refer to 'stone' when the main structure from the cellars upward is of brick, and the phrase may have referred to the earlier house half a mile away, or be a clerical formula, used without local knowledge. A licence to crenellate was by this time almost an anachronism, a reminder of regal authority, possibly a source of revenue to the King, and the identical words had been employed for centuries past, when control of castle-building was an essential safeguard for the State.

Edmund Bedingfeld was well aware that his new house must be defensible against armed vagabonds and covetous neighbours. Where there was so much land to spare, there were bitter quarrels over every yard of it. The fifteenth century was an age of chivalry, but there was little sign of it in the conduct of lawless veterans returned from the French wars. The Paston letters illustrate the danger of leaving a house inadequately protected. In 1449 John Paston gives this instance:

Lord Moleyns sent to the said mansion [Gresham, near Cromer] riotous people to the number of a thousand . . . arrayed in manner of war with cuirasses, body armour, leather jackets, headpieces, knives, bows, arrows, shields, guns, pans with fire and burning tinder in them, long crowbars for pulling down houses, ladders, pick-axes, with which they mined the walls, and long trees with which they broke up gates and doors . . .

Although 'guns' meant firearms, not artillery, such an arsenal would have been enough to break up most houses, as it did Gresham, and Edmund Bedingfeld was taking a calculated risk that Oxburgh would not suffer the same fate.

He deliberately sacrificed security to elegance, defence to comfort, trusting that more settled times had arrived, though he started building three years before Bosworth. He decorated his house with the trappings of a castle, without thought of putting them to serious military use. He compromised throughout. He dug a broad moat ten-feet deep and crossed it by a drawbridge, but placed no portcullis within his gates. He relied upon the height of his gatehouse, its battlements and machicolations, to induce a sense of awe, if not apprehension, in an intruder, but faced it with two large windows which could be shattered by a hail of stones. His arrow-slits, looking foolish alongside the windows, were outdated substitutes for cannon-ports, and the majority are so sited that no bowman could have shot from them with effect. Nothing could have been dropped through the northern machicolations, for they were sealed with stone. There were no parapet walks along the wings. If repelled from the gatehouse, an enemy need only bypass it to the sides of the house which had no defences except the moat, or to the rear, where the wall did not fall sheer into the water along its entire length, but left a broad ledge between the moat and the richly fenestrated hall, at which point there was later a fixed bridge for pedestrians.

The house, moreover, was built of brick. This was not unprecedented for a large semi-fortified house of the fifteenth century. Herstmonceux in Sussex, Tattershall in Lincolnshire, Middleton (only ten miles from Oxburgh) all predated it, and although Lord Cromwell in building Tattershall in 1440 compensated for the fragility of his material by making his tower twenty-two feet thick at the base, a brick curtain-wall was an impossible substitute for stone if serious resistance to cannon-fire was foreseen. The thinner walls of Oxburgh would have been pulverised by a few rounds. So friable is Tudor brick that when in 1952 a contractor wanted to buy the house, it was with the intention of reducing the brickwork to powder for surfacing hard tennis-courts.

Edmund had several motives in choosing brick. It was cheaper because it could be made from clay dug from the moat or in the park. It was easier than stone to transport, and to build with. In smoke-free air it was very resistant to weather, as is readily seen 500 years later from the crisp condition of the most delicate brickwork on the turret-tops. It is non-combustible, even better than stone for chimneys. As a cladding it is cool in summer and comforting in winter. Aesthetically it is an attractive material when used in large expanses and with variation of cut and patterning. Every shape devised by stone-masons can be reproduced by moulding and chipping bricks. The best example at Oxburgh of the brick-layers' skill is the spiral staircase which mounts one of the rear turrets of the gatehouse, where bricks are used with astonishing virtuosity to create a smooth winding ceiling above the steps, so ingeniously contrived that you wonder, even with the evidence before you, how it can hold together. As in many other parts of the house, the rose-pink colour of the brick is its own decoration.

The planning of the house is as domesticated as its material and architecture. It was built almost square round a large central courtyard, the great hall lying opposite the gatehouse with lower ranges on either side, in the manner of a college. This courtyard plan derived from later castles like Bodiam, architecturally satisfying because the house could be given eight outside elevations instead of the four of a keep, and domestically convenient

Oxburgh Hall, the spiral staircase in the rear turret of the gatehouse.

by the separation of the main living-rooms from the service-quarters. It is possible that Edmund Bedingfeld took as his model Shelton Hall, south of Norwich, for his first wife was the daughter of its builder, Sir Ralph Shelton. Though it has long since been demolished, we have a drawing of it dated 1782, and it shows just such a house as Oxburgh, moated, with gatehouse, side-wings and great hall in the same relative positions, but more elaborately defended with outer curtain-walls and a drum-tower at each corner.

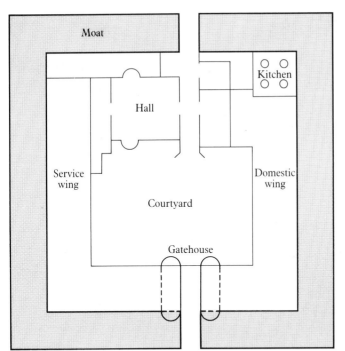

Ground plan of Oxburgh Hall as originally built (late fifteenth century).

We have no picture of the great hall at Oxburgh, but an account of it in 1769, a few years before it was destroyed, describes it as fifty-four feet long and high, and thirty-four broad, with a vast timber roof like Westminster's and a great bowed window on each side of the dais end. A ground-plan of about the same date also survives, showing the usual offices behind the hall-screen and a large kitchen with four central pillars to support the roof. It is difficult to recover from this plan the original arrangement and uses of the other rooms as they had been much altered since medieval times, and two fine seventeenth-century staircases (which survive) replaced the spiral stairs in the wings. It appears from examining the existing structure that the eastern range was two-storey between cellars and attics and used for the servicing of the house, while the west wing, always on two floors, contained apartments for the family and guests. Apart from the great hall, the main rooms were in the gatehouse, one above the other, and they remain exactly as they were built, with plain whitewashed or mottle-brick walls, fireplaces with four-centred arches, window embrasures as capacious as small oratories formed from the turrets on each side, high timber ceilings and floors of tile or wood. The lower and larger of them is called the King's Room, the upper one the Queen's Room, after Henry VII and his wife Elizabeth of York who slept there in 1487. They came accompanied by the Duke of Buckingham, the Earls of Oxford, Suffolk, Essex, Devonshire and Northumberland, with their retinues. It is hard to imagine how so large and distinguished a company could have been accommodated unless there were other buildings outside the moat, and stabling for which there was no provision within it.

Oxburgh Hall, the King's Room.

However, it is possible by analogy with contemporary houses to visualise the sort of life led by the early Bedingfelds. Sir Edmund (he was knighted by Richard III) served successive kings with a judicious trimming of his loyalties as one succeeded another, fought for Henry VII at the Battle of Stoke, and died with many honours in 1496. In his lifetime, and until the Civil War, Oxburgh's puny defences were never seriously tested, justifying his optimism. He held an annual fair there and was granted certain rights of local jurisdiction. A man of medium distinction, but in Norfolk a considerable figure, he would have made use of his house in a manner which the architecture symbolised and its arrangements encouraged, for parading his status, entertaining lavishly and raising a large family. It cannot have been very comfortable. Daily life was still medieval, and England was culturally backward and xenophobe. No art except third-rate wall-paintings and coloured cloths, no upholstery except cushions, no coaches for travel, and the master would eat his food with greasy fingers. One must imagine the stench of garlic mingling with gases from the foetid moat into which the garderobes discharged. But privacy of a sort could be found in its ample buildings, and the house would lend itself well to spurts of extravagant conviviality. The only element which it apparently lacked was a chapel, for which the parish church, with its famous Bedingfeld tombs, did duty.

For nearly 200 years Oxburgh remained intact. The Bedingfelds were relatively poor, Catholic and royalist, a combination of circumstances that discouraged major enterprises after the Reformation. They kept the house in repair and no doubt fashioned more comfortable, smaller, rooms from the gaunt chambers they inherited. In the Civil War Cromwell's soldiers attacked and seized the house, pillaged it, and set fire to the south-east corner (documents and charred timbers in the attics are evidence of it), and temporarily the property was sequestrated. At the Restoration the Bedingfelds regained possession, and slowly repaired and refurnished it. The major changes began in the eighteenth century. The roof was reclad by pantiles, and the narrower windows enlarged. In the 1780s the huge medieval kitchen was rebuilt into a Georgian saloon, and the great hall was demolished, inexcusably, for it had recently been repaired, leaving the south side of the quadrangle open to the moat.

The nineteenth century saw extensive rebuilding, for the old house, apart from the gatehouse which was never touched, was again in poor repair. In 1830 a Bedingfeld addressed a letter to his brother from 'The Ruin', signifying despair. But having married a Paston heiress, he rebuilt the south-east corner in a monumental style and with matching bricks which do no discredit to the whole, altered the windows again and raised twisting chimneys, added arcades to the three inner sides of the court, and squared off the garden by a splendid turreted wall. Almost the last change was made in 1865 when the gap left by the destruction of the hall was closed by a long low corridor of inferior design.

Thus we have a house which the Victorian Bedingfelds did much to preserve and modernise. Their rooms in the west wing are delightfully compact and welcoming, and while some of the exterior detail, like the raw brick of the Gothicised windows, is regrettable, the general effect of three of the four sides is much what Sir Edmund intended in the 1480s; and one of them, the gatehouse front, is an enduring monument to his imaginative enterprise and to the skill of craftsmen in a crude and brutal age.

Oxburgh Hall from the south-east.

He noble and myȝty Prince excellent
My lord the Prince · o my lord gracious
I humble seruant and obedient
On to ȝour estate hȝe and glorious
Of whiche I am ful tendre and ful ȝelous
Me recommande vnto ȝour worthynesse
With herte entier and spirit of meeknesse

Thomas Hoccleve and Henry Prince of Wales, from the fifteenth-century Arundel Manuscript.

3 Literature and Drama

STEPHEN MEDCALF

Introduction

From 1100 to 1500 is all but as long a period as from 1500 till today: and the more one reads in its literature the more one finds that the majestic unchangingness one first saw is exaggerated by distance, that the difference between St Godric (c.1065–1170) and John Skelton (c.1460–1529) is as marked as the difference between Skelton and ourselves. This chapter therefore is divided among five ages whose divisions, though they are not meant to be taken quite seriously, serve to remind of the passing of time: 'Literature under the Angevin Empire' (c.1100–1220), 'Images of spring', named from some images in its poetry (c.1220–c.1340), 'The Ricardian Age' (c.1340–c.1400) named for Richard II, who reigned during its most glorious decades (1377–1400), 'The flowering of ritual: towards the personal', named after characteristics not confined to but intense during the years c.1400–c.1460, and 'Malory and the waning of the Middle Ages' for the last generation (c.1450–c.1500).

But the majestic unchangingness is not altogether an illusion: it derives partly from relations between person, community, art and creed different from our own. In Skelton's lifetime, Richard Methley (1451–?1528) recommended for personal use a verse which the Virgin Mary taught to St Godric in a vision in his chapel at Finchale near Durham, with its music:

> Sainte Marye Virgine
> Moder Jesu Christes Nazarene,   *Mother of Christ*
> Onfo, schild, help thin Godric,   *Receive, shield*
> Onfang, bring heyilich with thee in Godes riche   *Having received*
>   *On high, God's Kingdom*

Methley says you may substitute your own name for Godric's, although much of the verse's point is in the pun 'Godric', 'Godes riche'.

This verse, then, has three characteristics which we do not always associate with high art:

(i)   it is not self-sufficient as a work of art, but is designed for use;
(ii) although it represents an original personal encounter, it is in no way self-expression, and may be used for personal encounters by any and everyone;
(iii) it is directed to an everlasting object.

Because it has these characteristics, it was naturally still in use after three and more centuries: many people today use prayers, for example the Lord's Prayer, in the diction of the sixteenth century. But much medieval literature besides prayer shares these characteristics, with modifications that we shall explore. The boundary between subjective and objective was less marked in those centuries and it was more natural to presume that external objects are symbols, to treat internal activities allegorically and to see visions. It was less natural to suppose that one's personality exists independently, more natural to construct it in relation to God or to one's superiors or beloveds, and so very common for it to have literary expression in prayers and petitions. The artist was less likely to be thought of as driven by emotion or inspiration, more to be considered as a craftsman with techniques that had to be learnt. All literature is necessarily involved with commonplaces – situations, relations, places and other things which are familiar to the audience; but the modern writer tends to be embarrassed if this use of commonplaces is too obvious, whereas the medieval took it for granted as a technique. Geoffrey of Vinsauf (c.1200) whose *Nova Poetria* was a recognised handbook till after Chaucer's time, thought that one of the writer's principal choices was whether to amplify his subject matter or to abbreviate it. On the whole, medieval writers tended to amplify and to rely on traditional commonplaces.

These are no more than useful presumptions for the modern reader; every one of them is subject to variation, and most, as we shall see, to progressive modification. It is most important, too, to remember that none of them is an opposite to modern instincts: some depend on not being bothered by distinctions which obsess us, others are just different. Medieval poetry is not impersonal in the sense of being unemotional; the choice of amplification or abbreviation can represent a choice, not only of techniques but between the aesthetic values of magnificence and authenticity; technique is not opposed to feeling, and so forth. The one real opposite between their literature and ours is that in all except the last decades of our period, literature was not printed nor formally published, but was either oral or in manuscript: literature therefore floated more freely both of its makers and of unalterable forms, and presumed somewhat different kinds of attention.

Finally, most medieval literature attends to two directions, the temporal and the eternal. Where these two lines meet will be our principal enquiry.

Literature under the Angevin Empire (c.1100–1220)

To read a piece of literature is to inhabit it, to cross the gap between what one would normally say and feel and what one would have to feel to use the particular words which it offers: somewhat as one understands other people by imagining what it would be like to inhabit their features. There is to speakers of modern English a special form of pleasure, the 'felt change of consciousness', in discovering after a while that Anglo-Saxon is the language they were brought up in after all. It is a pleasure which is symbolised in the further discovery that the last datable Anglo-Saxon poem, the *Praise of Durham* written some forty years after the Conquest, is about a building that still exists. In reading of the city set on steep slopes above a weir, and of its minster.

> ðaermonia windrum gewurðað ðes ðe writ seggeð
> mid ðene Drihnes wer domes bideð.
>
> (20–1)
>
> (*where many miracles happen, as books tell us, while there God's servant waits for the judgement*)

one enters, beyond expectation, into an apparently alien language, an alien aesthetic form, and an unfamiliar sense of time and humanity, in the tension of the buried saint expecting the last day.

Half a century or so later there was a collection of proverbs which are still part of the mature wisdom of our language: for example, apart from the one phrase 'than arewe' (*to the enemy/weakling*):

> If thu havest seorewe, ne sege thu hit nouht than arewe –   *say it not*
> Seye hit thine sadelbowe and ryd the singinde forth.   *ride singing*

The collection is ascribed to King Alfred – fittingly, first because Alfred ought to stand at the beginning of English literature; secondly because the wisdom of this proverb and of others in the collection is like the courageous wisdom of his own translation of Boethius' *Consolation of Philosophy*, the wisdom which sustained him against the Danes; and thirdly because it would seem that to be English in the face of Norman rule may still have needed the wisdom of 'Englene derling' (*the darling of the English*) as the book calls him.

The same kind of courage is found in the one poem of that time which can claim to be an epic, the history of Britain by the priest Layamon (c.1200) of Areley Kings in Worcestershire, called the *Historia Brutonum*, abbreviated to *Brut*. A large part of the poem describes Arthur's struggles against the invading Saxons: and Layamon (as an Anglo-Saxon) seems to transfer his own feelings of hostility against the Normans to the inhabitants of Roman Britain who were defending the country against his own invading ancestors. For he ends his account of Arthur's life with Merlin's prophecy, 'That an Arthur shulde yete cum Anglen to fulste' (*to help the English*). For Arthur and Arthur's British ancestors, Layamon expresses himself in a loose version of the alliterative metre and the heroic temper of Anglo-Saxon poetry. But his particular genius is for describing sight and colour, as when he shows us Merlin's mother dreaming before she conceived him of a fair tall knight in gold:

> This thing glad me bivoren and glitened on golde;
> ofte hit me custe, ofte hit me clupte;
> ofte hit me to baeh, and eode me swithe neh.
>
> (7842–4)
>
> (*this thing glided before me and shone in gold; often it kissed me, often it embraced me, often it bowed to me and came close upon me.*)

He is attracted too by the supernatural; it was he who added that Arthur dwells in Avalon with the elven-queen Argante (presumably the Morgan of later stories) to the story of Arthur's future return, which he took with much else from the French *Roman de Brut* of Wace (1155).

But the history of Arthur goes back long before the twelfth century. The oldest part may be his sleep in Avalon, if this is the same as what Plutarch reported in the first century, that in the Britons' belief Cronos, the god of the primitive world, lies sleeping on an island in the ocean. From the sixth century comes whatever is historic in the story of Arthur. By the early twelfth century his fame had mysteriously spread over Europe, for he was carved on a porch in Italy at Modena Cathedral before 1120, while the chronicler William of Malmesbury wrote in the 1120s that Arthur was worthy of something better than to be dreamed of in lying tales such as the Bretons tell, 'for he long preserved his dying country'.

It may be that it was this comment that roused Geoffrey of Monmouth to write his Latin *History of the Kings of England* (1138), though it did not prevent him from adding a great deal of romance to whatever his sources were. His book belongs to the new Europe of developing institutions – of the university of which there were the first anticipations in Oxford where Geoffrey wrote, and of the court of Henry I which he probably reflects when he says that in Arthur's time Britain

excelled all other kingdoms in general affluence, the richness of its decorations, and the courteous behaviour of its inhabitants. Every knight . . . famed for his bravery wore livery and arms showing his own distinctive colour; and women of fashion often displayed the same colours. They scorned to give their love to any man who had not proved himself three times in battle. In this way the womenfolk became chaste and virtuous and for their love the knights were ever more daring.

(Book IX ch. 13)

Geoffrey seems to be describing heraldry, though a heraldry in which each individual has a unique device. At about the time of his writing, in the 1120s and 1130s, we first find evidence for families passing on armorial bearings. The ritualisation of colour and courage which is heraldry was part of the same celebration of chivalry and the king's court as Geoffrey's own book.

Every culture probably adopts some of the experiences common to humanity and makes its own forms of them into nodal points or visions of glory caught in the network of ideas which help that culture to make sense of the world. A magnificent king who keeps the peace, knights who regard courage as a part of virtue and of service, and a court which is a centre of civilisation, make up one of the medieval visions embodied in the story of Arthur. The typical magnificent king of the twelfth century, Richard Coeur de Lion, gives his self-portrait in the Provençal lament – which he wrote in prison in the Holy Roman Empire – perhaps the noblest piece of writing by any king of England. He reveals how he, the magnanimous, the great-souled person, endures the deprivation of the kingdom, the power and the glory which are the proper concomitants of magnanimity.

Richard's father Henry II had already adopted the Arthurian story as a symbol of his rule: in 1187 his grandson was named Arthur and he probably encouraged the monks of Glastonbury to look for the body of Arthur, which they claimed to have found in 1191.

In the literature of the court of Henry and of his queen Eleanor a second medieval vision appears in the Anglo-Norman romances of Tristan, which became absorbed in the Arthurian cycle. This is the quasi-religious devotion of a knight to his lady which we know as courtly love. In other cultures (in ancient Egypt, for example) people have felt their beloved divine in power and beauty: the courtly lover felt this and sometimes went further, seeing the beloved as the source or the pattern of moral good. Perhaps that is peculiar to Christian civilisation haunted by the intuition of a loving God, although the very deification of the beloved opens the way to conflict between love and religion.

The third, and austerely religious vision of the Arthurian story entered it by the end of the twelfth century, but not at the Angevin court. Chrétien de Troyes and Robert de Borron (both late twelfth century) began to write stories of the Grail. Celtic legends of life-giving vessels probably found their own renewed life in the Grail: but what the French and later the English writers associate it with is the tremendous miracle of transubstantiation, and its presentation in the Mass. That Arthur's knights should divide their values between loyalty to their king, love for their lady and the quest of the Grail was a heightened version of the actual motives, as well as of the potential conflict of motives, of good medieval people.

Neither courtly love nor the legend of the Grail took shape in English. But there was a renaissance of the twelfth century in England as throughout Western Europe, and much that was written in England in Latin and Norman-French laid the foundations of what would later be written in English. We should instance the Breton lays of Marie de France, which were Breton in setting and folk-motifs, but written in England in Norman-French, and which were to influence English romances for at least two centuries: Geoffrey of Vinsauf's *Poetria Nova*, whose name – *The New Poetry* – witnesses to a real sense of renaissance, and whose pompous model of an elegy for Richard I is burlesqued by Chaucer in the *Nun's Priest Tale*, when it was perhaps beginning to be out of fashion: the Anglo-Norman play of *Adam* (c.1140) in which the Fall of the Angels is spoken about as the betrayal of a feudal seigneur, and the Fall of Humanity seen as the relation between an everyday husband and wife (which will be how the English mystery plays treat it in the fourteenth century and later, though we do not know what development there may have been from one to the other), and the chronicle of the Abbey of Bury St Edmunds and its Abbot Sampson by Jocelyn of Brakelond (c.1160–after 1212) which witnesses to the skill and vividness of biography in Latin at that time, and entered English literature in the nineteenth century by inspiring Thomas Carlyle's *Past and Present*.

Only one poem in English is really part of the twelfth-century renaissance, the *Dispute of the Owl and the Nightingale*, written probably in the 1190s and set in a valley in the south of England. The birds who dispute propose as their umpire Nicholas of Guildford. It is characteristic of the poem that its readers disagree as to whether Nicholas is the poet, someone whom this poet is complimenting, or someone at whose expense he is joking. It is a debate between beings who are in some sense opposites, a form popular throughout the medieval period, and probably intended to provoke discussion as part of the entertainment. Unlike its numerous unread fellows, *The Owl and the Nightingale* provokes discussion to this day. There have been many attempts to find some simple opposition as its subject. However, it is no allegory, but a dispute between two birds who have – with dumbfounding ingenuity on the poet's part – the opinions an owl and a nightingale would have if they thought in human terms. As birds they are well observed. The owl, for example, says accusingly:

> Wan ich flo nightes after muse   *When I fly; after mice*
> I mai the vinde ate rumhouse   *find; at the privy*
> Among the wode, among the netle   *weeds*
> Thu sittest and singst bihinde the setle.
>
>   (591–4)

The nettles are the master-touch, for nightingales do have what seems in such a beautiful singer an odd predilection for scruffy waste land. The nightingale responds:

> Wostu to wan man was ibore?   *Do you know why; born*
> To thare blisse of hovene riche   *To the; the kingdom of heaven*
> Thar ever is song and murghthe iliche   *Where; mirth continually*
>   (715–17)

That is why monks sing at midnight in church:

> An ich hom helpe wat I mai   *And I help them*
> Ich singe mid hom night and dai   *I, with them*
> . . .
> An bidde that hi moten iseche   *And pray; they may seek*
> Than ilke song that ever is eche   *That same; eternal*
>   (735–6, 741–2)

The owl's answer is that it is not so easy to reach heaven; men need to weep for their sins, and 'Tharto ich helpe – God hit wot'. And anyway if the nightingale's song is so important to humanity, why doesn't he sing up in Ireland or Norway?

It may well be that there is an allusion to the contrast of plainchant and polyphony, as there certainly is to that of a religion of awe and fear, and a religion of love and sentiment, of which the first was dominant throughout the Romanesque period, and the second began to dominate during the 1200s, the century after the birds disputed. Play and work are involved too, and love as courtship against love as a wife longing for her husband's return from travel, for the nightingale consoles one and the owl the other. One is at times tempted to call the Owl Roundhead, and the Nightingale Cavalier, and adjudge them, as in *1066 and All That*, Right but Repulsive, and Wrong but Wromantic. But the poet is subtler than that. Neither bird is simply right or wrong, and particular judgements between them reveal, as is probably the original intention of the Debate form, more about the reader than what is read. If one can find one opposition to describe them it is that of something as basic to humanity as immediate response in contrast with responsibility.

Yet the predominant things in their minds are diet and season, geographical distribution and song, the concerns of their species, although they are uncommonly concerned with the uses of their species to humanity.

The poem is in some ways of the country – but all medieval people by our standards, even in the cities, lived close to the sound of the nightingale – and Anglo-Saxon. Both birds appeal to the memory and proverbs of King Alfred, and some of the interest in them might go back to the Anglo-Saxon riddles. More widely, there is something about a world in which proverbs are a familiar part of the structure of one's consciousness, and in which one makes one's problems and doubts objective in beast fables, which goes with a peasant community where individuality is less stressed than in our experience, and one is not entirely remote from the cultures which classify experience by totems.

But the poem is also urbane. It is not wrong to be reminded by the couplet

> Among the wode, among the netle
> Thu sittest and singst behind the setle

of Pope's lines in the *Epistle to Arbuthnot*:

> Yet let me flap this bug with gilded wings
> This painted child of dirt, that stinks and stings.

The handling of nasal, sibilant and plosive to express venom, even in so unlikely a phrase as 'sit and sing', the indulgence in dirt to insult, and the disarming suggestion of play are common to both poets. But the medieval poet is more humorous, uncommitted, and urbane than Pope.

The most likely context for the poem is the world of the witty scholar–poet, the goliard, from the Latin-speaking intermixture of nations in the old cathedral schools and the new universities at Paris and Oxford. But its wit and its skill with rhyme and metre – octosyllables are the hardest metre to write in English without monotony – witness to a habit of writing good English. The humour, the irony, and the naturalist's observation make one think of a later England, whose tradition but for this poem one would have thought began with Chaucer. Perhaps the tolerant irony is not only a way to reconcile Owl and Nightingale, but the means by which in an age of proverbs and traditional wisdom one establishes individuality. The poem reminds one of the argument of Alan Macfarlane's *Origins of English Individualism* that English law bears witness to an English withdrawal from the *collective* life of traditional peasant community at least as far back as 1200. One might think of it as the first work of that centre of English culture, the country parson.

What else we can gather of English literature in the twelfth century tends to divide between the Owl and the Nightingale. The very voice of the Owl is heard in the sombre musical settings and compassionate words of the hymns heard in visions by St Godric of Finchale, one of which I have already quoted. But Giraldus Cambrensis (c.1145–1223) although himself of the Owl's party, as he makes clear when in his *Topography of Ireland* he makes a similar, one-sided comparison of Hawks and Falcons, still tells of the nightingale, in the person of revellers who danced all night in a churchyard in Worcestershire, singing a song with the refrain 'Swete lamman, dhin are' – 'Sweet mistress, thy pity' – so that the priest who had been kept awake by them began the service next day not 'Dominus vobiscum' but 'Swete lamman, dhin are'. In this, we presumably hear for the first time what the ordinary person and the peasant sang, the dancing songs called 'carols' (see p. 240).

Images of spring (c.1220–c.1340)

We meet again a union of popular and urbane in the poem of c.1230 from Reading Abbey with which some would begin English poetry:

> Sumer is icumen in – lhude sing, cuccu,   *loudly*
> Groweth sed and bloweth med, and springth the wude nu.
> Sing cuccu!
>
> Awe bleteth after lomb, lhouth after calve cu;   *loweth*
> Bulluc sterteth, bucke verteth – murie sing, cuccu!
> Cuccu, Cuccu!
>
> Wel thu singest, cuccu; Ne swik thu naver nu.   *Don't fail*
> Sing cuccu nu! Sing cuccu! Sing cuccu! Sing cuccu nu!

The musical setting is a complex canon (see pp. 224, 235), creating gaiety by a gabble of rising voices, all commenting excitedly, like birds in a wood, on the seasonable accompaniments of the cuckoo's song. Even without the setting, the words exploit to the full the capacity of English to echo sense in sound: the capacity which makes French speakers like Gide feel that English is not a proper language, being like a currency that is still at the swapping stage, almost having the weight and concreteness of objects. *Cuccu, bleteth, Ihouth* and *verteth* are straightforwardly onomatopoeic, *bloweth, sterteth* and the whole movement of the words echo the sense too, though less exactly.

In some poems the complexity of voice is much more perplexing. What, for example, do we make of

> Maiden in the mor lay, in the mor lay
> Sevenighte fulle, sevenighte fulle,
> Maiden in the mor lay, in the mor lay
> Sevenightes fulle, ant a day.
>
> Wel was hire mete. Wat was hire mete?   *food*
> The primerole, ant the – the primerole, ant the –   *primrose*
> Wel was hire mete. Wat was hire mete?
> The primerole, ant the violet.
>
> Wel was hire dring. Wat was hire dring?
> The chelde water of the – the chelde water of the –   *cold*
> Wel was hire dring. Wat was hire dring /
> The chelde water of the welle-spring.
>
> Wel was hire bour. Wat was hire bour?   *bower*
> The rede rose, ant the – the rede rose, ant the –
> Wel was hire bour. Wat was hire bour?
> The red rose ant the lilie flour.

It seems to have been widely popular; it is apparently a dancing song, with perhaps some appropriate mime. But what does it mean?

For the Owl's party, D.W. Robertson can bring forward much medieval opinion that the function of literature is to exemplify the moral and theological structure of the universe. He thinks that the seven nights and the wilderness mean the world before Christ, the one day Christ himself, the primrose fleshly beauty, the violet humility, the water God's grace, the roses charity and the lilies purity, making a bower for the Maiden Mary. This interpretation would have amazed the Bishop of Ossory, Richard de Ledrede, himself of the Owl's kind, who mentions the poem c.1340 as a shameful song, for which he composed a Latin lyric which actually is about the Virgin Mary.

Does the song then belong to the Nightingale? The Bishop's lyric has six verses, which might suggest that there were two more English verses: perhaps the maiden stays on the moor to meet her lover, and the mention of the 'bour' presages two verses in which their love-making and the birth of their child was described. Such a song might be romantic or it might have the anarchic carnivalesque humour which wells up round whatever the medievals took most seriously. The difficulty with either of these explanations is the air of faery that blows across the poem, and is strongest in the maiden's finding good food in the primrose and the violet. It is most likely then that the maiden is like the moor-maidens told of in Germany who may be spirits of well springs and who come to village dances to fascinate the young men.

All four elements, however, the religious, the amorous, the anarchically humorous and the faery are part of medieval life and poetry. The faery is the least common in surviving lyric: it does not appear for example in the Harley Manuscript 2253, which contains nearly all the English love-lyrics that survive from before c.1330, when it was compiled in Herefordshire. Yet that is an astonishingly wide miscellany; it contains poetry in French and English, as well as Latin and French prose, English love-verse influenced by goliardic and by French troubadour traditions and perhaps by the intricacy and exuberant eroticism of Welsh poetry, proverbs like those of Alfred, a song voicing the complaints of husbandmen, a brilliant comic poem spoken in a husbandman's voice, but concerned to persuade the man in the moon to come down and steal back the fine which (the speaker presumes) he paid for cutting his thornbush, the *Song of Lewes* ribaldly mocking Richard King of the Romans for hiding in a windmill after the Battle of Lewes (1264) and poems meditating on Christ's passion and our Lady. A harsh intense longing is the commonest mood in the book, whether religious, amorous or social–political, and the season specified by its most famous lyric, *Alysoun* – 'Betwene March and Averil / When spray beginneth to springe' – is just right.

It is possible that the compiler was a Franciscan friar: Franciscans had sympathy both with the poor and with Simon de Montfort at the Battle of Lewes, and the piety is their piety. The Franciscans arrived in England in 1224 and three of their characteristics, popular preaching, affective piety and the turning of popular songs and turns to religious ends, intensified the tendencies in poetry and piety of which the Nightingale approved. Affective piety is expressed and created by meditation on religious events, specially those in the lives of Christ and Mary that are most humanly moving, so that visualisation begets emotion, and emotion moral change. Affective poems were written in great numbers, often actually by Franciscans, in devotion to Christ, and in grief and wonder at His passion. Oddly enough, the Nativity, which is equally natural for affective piety, and to which St Francis himself had a special devotion, scarcely appears in surviving English lyric until the song book collected by a Franciscan called John Grimeston in 1372: and even there the words tend to be sombre. The poignant happiness of Christmas only finds expression before 1400 in two pieces: first a song of the Annunciation, translated from Latin as 'Gabriel from heven-king' (even then the happiness is largely that of the tune, the gay *Angelus ad virginem* which Nicholas sings in Chaucer's *Miller's Tale*): secondly a Franciscan piece 'Hond by hond we schul us take', the first of very many in which the secular carol already mentioned as distracting a thirteenth-century priest in Worcestershire, became for the fifteenth century and thereafter a religious form.

Perhaps after the awe characteristic of the Romanesque period, personal religious sentiment had to be learnt through grief before it could trust itself to happiness: or perhaps the instinct for poetry was too bound up with the love of man and woman to allow into religious poetry the other model of mother and baby. Mary and Jesus at the cross, Christ and the soul can be and are shewn as lovers. For example, St Edmund Rich of Abingdon (c.1170–1240) advises us to contemplate the grief of Mary at the crucifixion, how she could say with Naomi in the book of Ruth: 'Do not call me beautiful, but call me henceforth bitter: for the Almightly has filled me with bitterness and great grief', and how she says herself in the Song of Songs (which St Edmund takes to be a song of love between Mary and Jesus), 'Marvel not at me that I am dark: for the sun has discoloured me.' 'And an Englishman', St Edmund goes on, 'says in pity

> Now goth sonne under wod:
> Me reweth, Marye, thy faire rode.   *I pity; face*
> Now goth sonne under tre:
> Me reweth, Marye, thy sone and the.

Since both the Biblical texts which he quotes are implicit in the verse, it seems likely that St Edmund is the Englishman who wrote it. This joining of texts and events from far parts of the Bible and distilling them into apparently simple words often happens in meditative lyric. So too does the unity of a moment in Christ's passion with the moment now: the vivid sensuous awareness here of the light of the setting sun darkening on Mary's face: the conceptual and verbal punning, since the wood and the tree suggest both the horizon and the Cross, and Christ is both the spiritual sun and God's and Mary's son: and the making Calvary present by identifying oneself with Mary in her grief. Other models for intense love occur: John Pecham (d.1292) both a Franciscan and an Archbishop of Canterbury, in his Latin poem *Philomela* presents the nightingale, dying by bursting its body with song, as a type of Christ and a model for the Christian.

A more romantic devotion appears in the *Ancren Riwle*, the rule for anchoresses, written probably by an Augustinian Canon from Herefordshire called Brian of Lingen in the 1220s: he tells them to think of our souls as a lady for whom Christ jousted in a tournament, and of His body, broad above where His arms were spread, narrow beneath where His feet were nailed one on the other, as His shield. The nailing of Christ's feet together was new in art, and part of the new sense of Christ's agony.

This conjoined romance, realism and love is characteristic of the book. The style is part of the message: an inner life, comprehended in dramatic images and pervaded by love, lived in a loving community, described in a language conversational, easy, affectionate, but also memorably vivid and elegant – the sort of written style which, sounding easy, is one of the last achievements of manners. The rule of an anchoress, or a monk, had in common with the chivalric code of a knight a certain removal from economic pressures, which enabled one to concentrate on expressing in oneself the perfection of one's values. But all Christians had had the quest for inner perfection pressed on them in 1215 when the Lateran Council made private confession of sins obligatory at least once a year. A quarter of the *Ancren Riwle* is directly concerned with confession and penance: and the whole self-consciousness of the Middle Ages is thereafter related to this deliberate introspection.

Private confession and the quest for perfection obligatory for everybody: what this meant, not for monks and nuns, but for wealthy London tradesmen can perhaps be seen in the Auchinleck Manuscript (c.1330), a bulky collection, which Chaucer may have used, of didactic and devotional religious material and romances. Of the romances, *Sir Orfeo* is of special beauty, and also of special interest, because it embodies one of the most haunting and enduring myths, that of Orpheus and Eurydice, which like all myths provides a standard whose modifications are revealing of the special cultural situations which produce them. Orpheus the harper losing his wife Eurydice goes into the kingdom of death to find her, and regains her by the power of his music. In the most familiar form of the myth, although not it seems in the oldest, he regains her on condition that he does not look back at her till she has come into the light: and looking back when he but not she is free, loses her for ever. In this, which is Virgil's form, the story seems to be about love, art and myth itself: about the elusiveness of truth and fulfilment in these three things, and about their struggle, vain in the end, with death. *Sir Orfeo* differs in four ways:

(i)   Sir Orfeo's wife Heurodis does not die: she falls asleep on May day under a certain tree, a time and place which gives the King of Faery power to carry her to his kingdom. The poem is a Breton lay like those of Marie de France, a Celtic tale of love and enchantment, in feel not unlike Coleridge's *Ancient Mariner*: as in that, the eerily unaccountable world into which we might stray becomes part of our world in virtue of the truth of the responses which it evokes in the participants;

(ii)   In *Sir Orfeo* the important responses are to do with the quest for perfection in relation to fidelity – Orfeo's fidelity to Heurodis, the King of Faery's fidelity to the promise he makes Orfeo, and the fidelity of the steward to whom Orfeo entrusts his kingdom while he goes into the wilderness to mourn his wife. The fidelity of the steward and Orfeo's return suggest several of Christ's parables, so that the story perhaps has three of the four elements which intepreters search for in *Maiden in the mor lay*: faery, love and the Christian story;

(iii)   There is moreover a strong suggestion of Christ's harrowing of hell in Orfeo's recovery of Heurodis. There is no explicit allegory: it is rather that, as J.R.R. Tolkien has pointed out, there is in fairy story a natural leaning to Christianity in the distinctive feature of the unexpected happy ending, the unhoped-for conquest of death or evil;

(iv)   Orfeo's role as archetypal artist, a little extruded from the main story by the Christian values and the suggestion of Christian story, takes a new form in the stress that the story is itself a harper's tale, that Orfeo loved harpers, being a harper himself, and that when he pushes his way into the King of Faery's castle he acts in

> the maner of ous
> To seche many a lordes hous.
> Thei we nought welcome no be   *though*
> Yet we mote profery forth our glee.

The audience is clearly being asked to laugh and reward the teller as handsomely as did the king of Faery Orfeo. Though Orfeo may be a king, even the most enchanting of harpers is only a craftsman, not an inspired genius.

A prouder version of the poet's position in society can be found in truly Celtic poetry, in the poetry of courtly and aristocratic bards in Welsh, a poetry which ended with the wild lamentation intricately patterned for the death of Llewellyn, the last native king of Wales, in 1282. Another sense of his position again, which perhaps goes back to the Anglo-Saxon or Norse poets, is given in 1352 by the author of *Winner and Waster*, one of the first poems after Layamon's *Brut* that survive in the alliterative metre: the poet's right is to give wisdom: his poem is a debate, more stylised than *The Owl and the Nightingale*, but almost equally capable of producing further debate among readers. Are Winner and Waster equally necessary, the producer and the consumer? or equally bad, the Aristotelean opposites of meanness and prodigality, whose judges are to be Edward III and the Black Prince – naturally, if the Black Prince is thought of, as he was by the author of a famous Anglo-Norman life of him, as the pattern of the mean between these vices, which is largesse. But there is no certainty, nor was meant to be. And the poet believes that the age of largesse is past. Lords no longer love wise makers, but only beardless jokers. If there was beginning an alliterative revival, this poet admits no knowledge of it: and he has no premonition of the almost classical status of the poet which Chaucer was about to introduce.

The Ricardian Age (c.1340–c.1400)

Langland

When it was about ten years old, *Winner and Waster* may have been the jumping off point for William Langland's *Piers Plowman*. The diction, metre and intelligence about society are similar. And like the narrator of *Winner and Waster*, Langland (?c.1330–c.1390) at his beginning falls asleep, lulled by a stream, to find himself he knows not where. Perhaps because of this very similarity he is quick to establish that he is not writing a debate, but a judgement: the first people he sees are ploughmen who won what 'thise was-tours with glotonye destroieth'. The tradition he seems closest to is that of denunciatory prophecy, represented in his age by verse such as the husbandman's complaint of Harley 2253 and by many vivid and powerful sermons.

But even the first score of lines bear witness to a temperament that, if it is a prophet's, is also a poet's. He tells us, what would have been quite alien to the author of *Winner and Waster*, that his vision seemed to come from faery, and confirms this by localising it in time on a May morning, which (as Heurodis found) is a time to encounter faery, and in space, on Malvern hills; and no one who knows those hills doubts that he does something characteristic of visionaries in making their landscape show through his vision. The stream indeed which local feeling has connected him with, the principal fountain of Malvern water on the west slope of the Herefordshire Beacon under the site of a Norman castle, makes perfect sense of what is otherwise puzzling topography, with 'a fair field full of folk' below him, while above him 'into the Est, an heigh to the sonne', is a tower from which a lady comes directly down to him. But in his vision the castle is that of truth, the lady is Holy church, the field is the world, and beyond it is the castle of wrong.

We have then a prophet and poet who writes the poem, including what Holy church presently authoritatively declares. He presents himself as a narrator, who has seen things that had to be explained to him. The contrast, of a prophet saying 'This is', and a narrator saying 'It seemed to me that I saw', is present in a contrast of languages – Latin from the Vulgate Bible and the liturgy, which is firm and authoritative, and an English which is both full of perplexing symbols and uncommonly fluid in its syntax. Langland, as A. V. C. Schmidt puts it, seems to be 'exploring experience through language' in his English and this exploratory quality seems to be so much present not only in the narrator as a character, but in the grain of the poem, in the diction and the story, that one can hardly resist thinking that the poet shares it, for all his access an authoritative Latin and a teaching church.

This sense of the poem is supported by its history. For it exists in three forms, commonly called the A-text (written in the 1360s), the B-text (1377–9) and the C-text (perhaps c.1385): one manuscript may preserve an earlier draft than all – the Z-text. And the way in which language is an instrument of exploration for Langland can be seen in the development of the B- from the A-text, although it can be intuited from the beginning.

Thus in the A-text Holy church calls love 'the plante of pees'. Plants grow from earth: love comes down from heaven to be made flesh in Jesus: perhaps with aid from Jesus' own parable of the mustard seed becoming a great tree the contrast seems to generate the idea that when the plant had drawn nourishment from earth it would grow unstoppably, the heavy become light:

For hevene myghte nat holden it, so was it hevy of hymself	
Til it hadde of the erth eten his fille.	
And whan it hadde of this fold flesh and blood taken	*earth*
Was nevere leef upon lynde lighter therafter,	*linden tree*
And portatif and persaunt as the point of a nedle,	*mobile; piercing*
That myghte noon armure it lette ne none heighe walles.	*armour; hold back*

Here, in the B-text, Langland the poet uses alliteration, with an auditory imagination of which he is normally careless, to make the linden leaf lighter and the needle point more piercing, and concentrates both sound and sense, so that the passage prefigures what Langland the narrator is to explore at length.

But the development from A- to B-text was itself an exploration, and similar exploration can be traced between A and B at the level of story. In the A-text the fairfield develops through vigorous transformations to a point where the people, now vividly present to us through satiric portraiture, have become aware of the castle of truth, and are to be led to it by Piers the ploughman who alone knows the way. But first they must help him plough. The whole of society becomes what it ought to be by following the instructions of Piers Ploughman, the ordinary decent man, so that Truth sends a pardon remitting the need to go to His castle. The gospel of the A-text seems to be a social, even secular, Christianity, prophetic against abuses, but secure in the conviction that proper uses and duties can be regenerated without need of any help outside this world. For a moment this seems to be confirmed when at a priest's insistence the pardon is opened – the narrator in his excitement thrusts himself further into his dream than before, and stands behind Piers and the priest to read it – and it says 'Do well and God shall have thy soul: do evil and go to hell.'

But this sounds like bare justice, not a pardon: Piers in rage and grief tears it in two, and says that he will give up the work of the ploughman, and live in penitence and prayer. He is seen no more, and the narrator is thrown back to his beginning, wandering on Malvern hills 'al a somer sesoun for to seke dowel'. So the A-text ends on a problem – if to do well is enough, how does one do it? – which Langland not only meant to be read as difficult, but himself found more difficult than he meant.

What he has thrust himself into is expressed in his own knotty image of five interlaced difficulties in Christianity which were to be at issue in the Reformation:

(i)   the contrast between original sin, the alienation from God which is the result of the Fall, and particular sins: if the one is forgiven, does it follow that we shall cease to commit the others?

(ii)   the contrast between the forgiveness which Truth sends, and the this-worldly signs of it which the Catholic Church handles, of which the documentary pardons which began Martin Luther's attack on the Church are the most corruptible. Do the signs effectually express their meaning, and are they necessary?

(iii)   the contrast between two ways of life, work and prayer, action and contemplation. Is one better than the other?

(iv) the associated general problem of ethics, that there seems no end to the quest for perfection: if one contrives to fulfil one ideal, another appears behind it. It seems, as George MacDonald said, that 'God is easy to please, but hard to satisfy'. Is it enough to please Him, or must one satisfy Him?

(v) the problem of justice and mercy. Both are good: both are God's. But mercy taken to its limit annihilates justice, and when justice ceases to exist, mercy is meaningless. How are the two reconciled either in society (in the treatment of criminals and wilful idlers) or in eternity?

Langland either now realised, or had designed from the start, that all he had written was an Old Testament, a rule of Law. Piers in the A-text is like Moses, and the tearing of the pardon seems, though not explicitly, to be like Moses' breaking the tables of the Law, not because Piers or Moses is disgusted with the Law, but because their people cannot receive it, cannot *do well*.

Langland must now write a New Testament, a reconciliation of Law and Mercy. His narrator in the B-text searches for not only Do well, but also Do better and Do best: after many explanations and encounters, varying from the grotesque to the sublime, he sees law and mercy reconciled in Christ's passion and resurrection, happening both at their historic moment and, with the intervening time in some sense annihilated, in the present moment – in their memorials in the daily Mass and in the Christian year between Palm Sunday and Easter Day. From prophet, Langland has become simple liturgical and sacramental Christian, and it is not only Christ's passion that he sees, but that of Piers. Piers cannot be perfect humanity unless he is also the capacity of humanity to receive and become Christ. Like any knight who wishes to fight anonymously, Christ borrowed Piers' armour so that Death and the devil will be willing to joust with him for man's soul. Hidden within Piers' compassion for the rejected in the first part of the poem – 'They are my blody bretheren, quod Piers, for God boughte us alle' – is Christ's prophecy that at the last judgement – 'my mercy shall be shewed to many of my bretheren / For blood may suffre blood both hungry and akale [*cold*]'. 'Ac [*But*] blood may nought see blood blede, but him rewe'. As He enters Hell in triumph, Christ in this speech goes to the limits of time and of the conflict of justice and mercy in seeming to promise universal salvation. (How this should happen, Langland leaves a mystery: he may have inspired by this the dramatic treatment of the themes in an early fifteenth-century morality play. It is called *The Castle of Perseverance* from its first half, a simple and romantic allegory of the relation of Man to his virtues and vices. But when Man is lured in the last stage of his life by Avarice, the characteristic vice of insecure old age, out of the Castle, the second half achieves high drama on the abstract issue of justice and mercy, as Man dies shrieking for mercy whilst devils carry him off, and the chill that follows is marvellously invaded by the entry of Mercy herself and her appeal to God.)

Langland in his own poem returns to the crisis of his own time when Conscience returns, like the narrator at the end of the A-text, to the beginning of the poem, to 'walken as wide as the worlde lasteth', but now with the knowledge that the search is for Piers and through him for Christ.

In the B-text, in language and thought alike, Langland (as in his own image of love) feeds on the earth of social thought and satire until his poem grows up to heaven. As Schmidt again puts it, his aim 'seems to be to appeal to common experience in order to make ordinary people *feel* what the working of God's spirit in the soul is like'. His own work as a poet Langland rates low and the idea of *poetic* inspiration is therefore alien to him: but his mode of composition and his doctrines of the knowledge of God constantly imply *divine* inspiration.

It was, however, natural to understand his poem partially. The leaders of the Peasants' Revolt, probably basing themselves on the first part with its exaltation of the ploughman as reformer of society and stress on the equality of everyone before death and God, took *Piers Plowman* as a source of reference, and sent out messages bidding 'Piers Plowman to go to work' and the peasants to 'do well and do better'. After the revolt Langland revised the poem, excluding any hint that he recommended transference of political power to the peasants. Nevertheless, the compassion of the poem is not diminished: in this, the C-text, is added the most piteous of Langland's descriptions of the labour and hunger of the needy. And although he changes

> For oure joye and our juele, Jesu Crist of hevene
> In a pouere mannes apparaile pursueth us ever

to

> For God, as the gospel saith, goth ay as the pore

his universe is not less Christ-haunted. There is a not uncommon wall-painting of the century after *Piers Plowman*: it depicts a wounded Christ surrounded by tools which suggest the tools of His passion as they appear in earlier types, but are the tools and even the gaming devices of everyday life. It seems, as Caiger-Smith puts it, to have signified 'the daily repetition of the Passion which Christ suffers at every man's hand', in sinning, in Sabbath-breaking, in exploiting the poor. At Fingringhoe in Essex it is accompanied by the inscription '*In omni opere memento finis*' – 'in all your work remember its end', whom I take to be Christ. Its sense of the implication of Christ in our experience is part of the same piety that made *Piers Plowman* the most popular of English literary texts in the fifteenth century after *The Canterbury Tales*.

Chaucer

It is possible to prefer Langland to Chaucer (c.1343–1400) even as a poet. David Jones, who among modern poets has most studied *Piers Plowman*, says that it makes Chaucer, on the whole, lacking in *depth*, neither as 'earthy' nor as 'celestial'. But Chaucer, although he seldom inhabits either of Langland's extremes, holds earthy and celestial together with an apparent smoothness where in Langland they jar. As Schmidt again says, under Langland's 'often plain surface, all is agitation and life'. For example, Langland's 'fairfield' at the beginning of his poem could mean either the lovely landscape or place of carnival: it is impossible to decide which, and it seems likely he meant the word to carry both meanings. But there is a continual jarring in one's mind as one passes from one meaning to the other, with their different stresses (fair fie′ld, fa′ir field). But Chaucer at the end of *Troilus and Criseyde* tells his audience

> thinketh al nis but a faire
> This worlde, that passeth soone as floures faire

and the repetition carries something courtly and poignant. In Chaucer in fact we find again the urbane profundity of *The Owl and the Nightingale*, together with the subtlety and irony which Derek Pearsall describes, 'a delicious and disconcerting awareness that the poet is cleverer than we are, that each joke is part of a larger joke and that if only we have the wit to follow it will all add up . . .' (*Old English and Middle English Poetry p. 94*).

But Chaucer smiles at us out of medieval poetry not just as one who knows that he has made his final opinions elusive, but as someone who knows that this is unavoidable between centuries and cultures. He was the first person so to digest the notion of cultural difference, which had been a commonplace in the ancient world and had been relatively recently commented on again by Dante (1265–1321) and Petrarch (1304–74), as to add that what is expressed in custom and language need not change though they do, and that differences in epochs need not be fundamentally different from the differences which one can observe between friends and contemporaries:

> Ye knowe ek that in forme of speche is chaunge
> Withinne a thousand yeer, and wordes tho   *then*
> That hadden pris, now wonder nyce and straunge
> Us thinketh hem, and yet thei spake hem so,
> And spedde as wel in love as men now do;
> Ek for to wynnen love in sondry ages
> In sondry londes, sondry ben usages
>
> . . .
>
> Ek scarsly ben ther in this place thre
> That have in love seid lik, and don, in al.
>
> (*Troilus and Criseyde*, II 22–8, 43–4)

This awareness of diversity in unity may be connected with Chaucer's anomalous though not unparalleled upbringing, a London wine merchant's son made page to the Royal Duke of Clarence, a wit at Court earning his living in the Customs House at Billingsgate. More probably he was affected by his diplomatic missions to Italy, especially that of December 1372–May 1373. It was then that he seems to have made acquaintance with the writings of Dante, Petrarch and Boccaccio, an acquaintance that, amounting to meeting the shock of another culture, the Italian Renaissance, made more complex his thought about love, extended his intentions in using a *vernacular* language, and in effect gave him the ideas of *poet* and *literature*. His first ambitious poems, *The Book of the Duchess* (1369–70), written before this journey, began in an ironic but common medieval way, modelled on the French of Guillaume Machaut and Froissart, presenting the writer as sad, at a loss and sleepless. His first poem after the journey, *The House of Fame* (c.1380), similarly begins with wondering about the causes of dreams, but in its second book introduces something quite new in English, modelled on Dante, an invocation of the Muses:

> And ye, me to endite and ryme
> Helpeth, that on Parnaso dwelle
> Be Elicon, the clere welle.

And exalted poetic diction, musical and Latinate, modelled again on Dante, seems to begin in English with the invocation of another of Chaucer's poems of the same time, *Anelida and Arcita*, to the muse Polyhynnia that 'with thy sustres glade . . .'

> Singest with vois memorial in the shade
> Under the lawrer which that may not fade.   *laurel*

In *The House of Fame* Chaucer both exalts the poet as he has not been exalted before in English, and mocks him: for he seems to parody Dante's ascent to heaven and instruction by Beatrice in the *Paradiso*, and connect the instruction with the medieval writer's characteristic reliance on authority rather than nature, when he portrays an eagle carrying him up to heaven and offering to shew him the stars and himself refusing to look at such bright things: 'Hyt shulde shenden [*destroy*] al my syghte / To looke on hem.' But he looks too on the world as he ascends and; '"O god", quod I "that made Adam /Moche is thy myght and thy noblesse"'.

This wonder at God's creation is as important as irony and the Muses in Chaucer's sense of his vocation. It is at its height in *The Parliament of Fowls* (c.1382) which one might think of, as its name implies, as a debate, indeed another debate between birds, with the participants much multiplied in number but as much as in *The Owl and the Nightingale* speaking with the voices of their various kinds. There are four groups who stand also for four human attitudes to love. The birds of prey stand for the devoted service of courtly love, the seedfowls support them but with a gentler voice, the waterfowl believe in choosing mates but not in remaining faithful to a lady who remains indifferent (a notion to which the duck says 'Ye quek'!), and the wormfowl recommend solitary life and promiscuity. Nature, who judges, tells the three male eagles who dispute for the female to serve her unrequited for a year, and gives to every other bird a mate. The birds sing, as birds seem to do, a welcome to summer, and one is almost left with the same sense as John Dryden had of the *Canterbury Tales*, 'Here is God's plenty'. Yet a sense of something undecided remains, as at the end of Shakespeare's *Love's Labour's Lost*.

If Chaucer had written no more, he might still have been counted the father of English literature, as his contemporary Dafydd ap Gwilym is thought of as the father of Welsh literature. They have something in common beyond their genius for language, specially the comic inclination to portray themselves as unsuccessful lovers, as Dafydd writes of the girls in Llanbadarn church. But we know him mainly as the author of what we have lost from Chaucer, 'many a song and lecherous lay' and as a poet of nature, especially wild nature, whose inspiration is not paralleled in England before the romantics, unless in some lines of *Sir Gawain and the Green Knight*.

On the other hand in the early 1380s the battle for English as a literary language was by no means won, and it is equally possible that had he written no more Chaucer might have sunk from sight and with him the incipient Renaissance poetic which even with the aid of his greatest poems, yet to be written, would be confined to hints and guesses after him for much more than a hundred years.

In these later poems, at any rate in *Troilus and Criseyde* (c.1386) and in *The Canterbury Tales* there is something sharper, more philosophically profound even than in *The Parliament of Fowls*. It is perhaps the peculiar appearance of having first created a satisfying personal sense of the universe, and then having triumphantly fought through a crisis in which everything seems destined to destroy that personal sense, which seems common to the greatest poets – to Shakespeare, Milton, Wordsworth, T.S. Eliot. The same sharpness appears in Chaucer's later short poems, and perhaps is only missing in *The Legend of Good Women*, which claims to have been written to recompense Love for the slanders of *Troilus and Criseyde*, and one might hazard was read by those to whom *Troilus and Criseyde* was too strange.

Chaucer might well be troubled in those years. As well as the social troubles centred on the peasants' revolt, which he mentions only twice, but with chilling horror in *The Knight's Tale* and violent black humour in *The Nun's Priest's Tale*, there were the religious troubles associated with John Wycliffe, with whom Chaucer possibly, and some of his friends certainly, had sympathy. There was a wide theological and philosophical scepticism expressed with the greatest power and melancholy in some anonymous poems collected about 1390 in the Vernon manuscript, of which two in particular, *Think on Yesterday* and *This World Fares as a Fantasy* have a diction of almost Johnsonian moral weight. They may express the emphasis on the absolute and therefore incomprehensible power of God over His creation of either or both of William of Ockham (c.1290–1349) and Archbishop Thomas Bradwardine (c.1285–1347).

It is not clear how much direct acquaintance Chaucer had with Ockham or Bradwardine. Bradwardine, however, he mentions along with St Augustine (354–430) and Boethius (c.480–c.524), in another passage in *The Nun's Priest's Tale* of uncomfortable humour, as able to sift the problem of predestination. Of these Boethius is the philosopher he turned to, whose *Consolation of Philosophy* he translated and paraphrased in the 1380s, when he made its doctrine the sense of *Troilus and Criseyde* and *The Knight's Tale*.

The *Consolation*, although its final vision, the eternity of God, primarily deals with what the Chaucer of *The House of Fame* and *The Parliament of Fowls* would have found attractive, puts forward the paradox that in the worst as in the best of fortune we should recognise God's creation as good. Charles Williams treats it as the typical book of the permanent dilemma of an age in Europe when everyone presumed themselves Christian. It can, he says be

read as the work of a man teaching himself to *believe* . . . What is he? 'I know that I belong to living men, intelligent, yet doomed to die.' He confesses also that he knows that 'Everything comes from God.' These two sentences, however, represent, one might say, two different *kinds* of knowledge; the great question is whether the second answer can be known as the first is – 'felt in the blood and felt along the heart'.

(The Descent of the Dove, 1939)

This, which might in one way serve as a description of Langland's mixture of prophecy and exploration, describes also what Chaucer was probably trying to do in *Troilus and Criseyde*. When Troilus has won Criseyde, Chaucer translates a song for him with great beauty out of Boethius, expressing the manifestation of God in the love that keeps the world, which tends to leap asunder, in being and movement.

Criseyde presently deserts Troilus: but the world continues. In a passage which, although Chaucer probably wrote it late in the composition of his poem, grows naturally from the text, he shows Troilus after death recognising the harmony of the spheres and the felicity of heaven. In two following verses (which were probably not late in composition) a wonderful rising movement shews us, first, love that grows up with their age in 'yonge fresshe folkes', secondly the visage of their hearts, that they should cast up to God, and finally that they should love Christ who, for love, upon a cross, 'First starf, [*died*] and roos, and sit in hevene above'. Meanwhile, the world, in converse movement to this up-growing love, passes, as Chaucer puts it with the courtliness which we noticed 'soone as floures fair'.

Boethius said, and the Boethian hymn follows him, that every good thing – the love of Troilus and Criseyde for example – participates in the ultimate good, the love of God. If the lesser good ends, the ultimate good is not affected. But in these last verses the two draw apart, and Chaucer leaves a gap. Troilus leaves both his love and his suffering behind and instead perceives the love of God: but the later state is only a compensation for, not a consequence of, the earlier. Chaucer promised us at the beginning to tell 'the double sorrow of Troilus', and the first sorrow, Troilus' unrequited love, is satisfyingly felt as the unavoidable first stage of what is naturally rewarded by the consummation of love. The second sorrow is with equal aesthetic satisfaction seen proceeding from this first joy. Troilus is a courtly lover, he is therefore a servant and Criseyde his lady. They commit themselves to what medieval canon law would, almost but not quite certainly, deem a marriage – for they exchange rings, pledge themselves to permanence, and consummate their love. It is all that is necessary – except that they were 'pleyinge', Chaucer says, when they changed rings. But while in medieval love the 'lady' was 'mistress' (both words retain their courtly flavour), in medieval marriage the husband should be lord. But Troilus cannot at any stage dominate Criseyde: the subtly comic figure of Pandarus was needed to put him into bed with her, and so long as the code of courtly love is carried to Troilus' extreme, Troilus cannot do without Pandarus. In, at any rate, the peculiar situation of Troy at war, that humility proves disastrous. The reader is shown the result, Criseyde's desertion, as the realisation of it hour by hour and day by day eats its way into Troilus. But it is only the knowledge of the loss of his earthly heaven, Criseyde's love, not a preparation for the knowledge of heaven itself.

The reader is admitted by empathy into Troilus' mind in this passage, and into Criseyde's mind earlier when she wonders whether to accept Troilus as a lover. In these and other passages Chaucer draws us into the moment by moment decisions, the present moments of the lovers, while constantly he stresses that this was long ago, that the story has been told before him and cannot now be altered. The passage already quoted about the difference and likeness of love in different ages is part of this double strategy of nearing and distancing. By it Chaucer keeps in our hands both Boethius' problem of free will and predestination, and Boethius' teaching that if we could see the world whole, as it can only be seen from eternity, we should see that every fortune, whether it be harsh or pleasant, is good. But the two different kinds of knowledge, as Charles Williams calls them, are not assimilated, and the knowledge of time predominates over the eternal knowledge. Although we live through the fortunes of Troilus and Criseyde, we do not quite feel that their story reaches a satisfactory conclusion: the sequence of verses near the end in which Chaucer seems to announce the ending of the poem and then defers it confirms this feeling. His gentle irony delays reaching conclusions to which nevertheless it points. It is the same when he sums up Criseyde's character. Compassion urges him to excuse her: the actuality of her behaviour forbids it:

> And if I myghte excuse hire any wise,
> For she so sory was for hire untrouthe
> I wis, I wolde excuse hire yet for routhe.

But this incompleteness is the realism and the greatness of the poem. Within its own epoch, it provoked opposite judgements: just after it was written, Thomas Usk in his *Testament of Love* (1387–8) praised it for teaching that erotic love is symbolic of and continuous with the love of God: perhaps a hundred years later a nun advised that it should be read as an example of erotic love as the sweet poison which impedes our love of God.

The realism and greatness of *The Canterbury Tales* (c.1387–1400) is similar. Chaucer creates a character, himself as one of the pilgrims, who is invariably taken in by appearance, and whose naive style generates the irony in response to which the reader continually wonders, as in response to a Debate, 'Ought I really to approve of this?' Among the pilgrims whom he describes, the Knight and the Parson have traditionally been taken as the standards and leaders, and it can scarcely be a coincidence that the stories which they tell begin and end the tales, nor that the *Parson's Tale* merges with the author's apologia for his writing. The author's voice also punctuates the book both at the beginning of the *Parson's Tale* and at the beginning of *The Man of Law's Tale* with elaborate indications of the passing of time, and implied warnings against losing time in negligence and idleness. Just as in *Troilus and Criseyde* there is a framework which implies the approach of judgement and eternity, and it may be that the Knight and the Parson fit with that.

Yet modern readings have carried the irony with which most of the pilgrims are regarded so far that the Knight and the Parson too are affected, the Knight coming under suspicion of being a bloody mercenary, the Parson of being an unforgiving Pharisee. Yet more, the Pardoner, who has been called 'the one damned soul on the pilgrimage', is (it is now suggested) only evil because he manifests honesty in the presence of a corrupt religion.

Even though one concludes that the twentieth-century shrinking from the Knight's martial and the Parson's judgemental qualities, and the twentieth-century attraction to the Pardoner's self-reflexiveness, are inappropriate responses, unlikely to be true to any possible fourteenth-century feeling, and that Chaucer, had he meant these abstruse ironies, would have signalled them as clearly as he normally does, the mode of reading in question is not wholly alien from his intentions. By supplying his naive persona, Chaucer has gone as far as possible towards abdicating from the authority which from time to time he accords to other authors.

What Chaucer actually does with his characters is illuminated by comparing it with what critics have found it possible to say of Shakespeare's methods. Shakespeare, says Emile Legouis,

did not assemble and set in motion the springs of their nature after the manner of a patient watchmaker who knows all the secrets of his machine. They are not the products of pure logic, the only faculty able to produce such creations as can endure being put together and taken to pieces . . . He does not claim to be able to co-ordinate all the suggestions that they make to his observation. In a sense, Shakespeare himself does not comprehend Hamlet in his entirety. Just like us, he sometimes listens to him thinking, watches him in motion. So it comes about that a character can cut himself free of him.

Now, in the first instance, scholarship has taken Chaucer's characters to pieces with great success, showing that most details can be accounted for, if not by events and signs like the Knight's chivalric biography and clothing which retain their meaning today, then by the luxuriant languages of medieval psychophysiology (e.g. the Franklin whose 'complexioun' was 'sangwyn', which means at once 'Blood dominated over the other humours in him', 'His character was sanguine' and 'His complexion was ruddy'), physiognomy (e.g. the Pardoner, whose glaring eyes suggest that he is a eunuch from birth), astrology ('Gat-tothed I was, and that bicam me weel; / I hadde the prente of seint Venus seel', says the Wife of Bath) and iconography (the Prioress's feeding her little dogs with rich food recalls a story depicted in the church at Chaldon in Surrey of a lady who, having done just that in her life, was fetched at death by a dog-headed demon, for she neglected the poor).

Secondly, however, Chaucer deliberately does not co-ordinate the suggestions of these details. Thus the iconography of the Prioress is not pointed, only implicit, and is followed by 'And al was conscience and tendre herte.' Again, the list of the Knight's battles is delivered in such a way that one cannot be sure if the main effect is that he was a Christian and a crusader who held it wrong to fight his fellow Christians, or a mercenary who found it best to take service with infidel lords (for all his battles are outside Christendom), courageous, or simply bloody (one of his battles, the taking of Alexandria, notoriously might involve either quality), or just that he attracted the narrator by the romance of his calling and the names of the places where he had been, which rise to a Miltonic music

> In Gernade at the seege eek hadde he be
> Of Algezir, and riden in Belmarye.

In *Troilus and Criseyde* and *The Canterbury Tales* alike, Chaucer overtly disclaims knowing all the secrets of his characters.

Thirdly, he does use the technique of listening to his characters thinking, or rather telling their stories. In this, probably increasingly as he developed his scheme, his characters do cut free of him, especially the three – the Pardoner, the Wife of Bath and the Canon's Yeoman – who are given confessional narratives. It is striking that the only one of his pilgrims on whom Chaucer has given a judgement outside the *Canterbury Tales* is the very one on whom readers have felt most strongly, and commonly have liked better than that judgement. In a wry poem written to his friend Bukton towards the end of his life (probably 1396) which begins by proclaiming the universal unreliability of humanity, including himself, he offers the Wife of Bath's account of marriage as proving the slavery of husbands.

Either to observe the pilgrims and other characters of *The Canterbury Tales* without recognising that there is a judgement to be passed on them, or to be hasty in passing judgement, is to miss the Boethian crisis in Chaucer, the attempt to feel in the blood both the judgement of time, what people are, and the judgement of eternity, what they ought to be.

In the most Boethian story of *The Canterbury Tales*, the *Knight's Tale*, we need to be aware of this crisis even to respond to the language. Theseus gives a moral to the story:

> Thanne it is wysdom, as it thynketh me
> To maken vertu of necessitee.

The degree of ambiguity in the couplet is just the controlled ambiguity of Chaucer's portrayal of the Knight himself. Some take it to be the invocation by a mercenary knight and his mouthpiece, a tyrant, typical of those who would have employed him, of 'Necessity, the tyrant's plea'. Chaucer does elsewhere use the proverb 'make virtue of necessity' to suggest 'say and try to feel that a thing is good when we know it is bad', which would fit this interpretation. But in fact Theseus uses it in an active, not a passive sense, to recommend following the rhythm of the universe: specifically to marry when the due time of several years of mourning for a dead betrothed and friend is fulfilled. *Vertu* makes sense if it means, as in the description of the growth of flowers in April in the *Prologue* to the *Canterbury Tales*, what Dylan Thomas called 'the force that through the green fuse drives the flower': Theseus' recommendation then is that that force be not choked back from driving the green age of Palamoun and Emelye. Instead of its flat everyday meaning the proverb takes on the Boethian sense 'create life from understanding the eternal law'.

The point where the Knight is most conclusively seen as standard and peace-maker is at the end of the *Pardoner's Tale*, where Host and Pardoner fall out, and the Knight reconciles them. But the events immediately before entangle our sympathies so inextricably that only a reconciliation, not a judgement, can resolve them.

The Pardoner, who has in his confessional narrative exposed his motives and tricks, and then told what to him is just such a tale as normally he uses to extort money for his pardons, ends it by recommending the pilgrims to Jesus Christ's pardon: 'For that is best: I wol you nat deceyve.' But immediately he proceeds to attempt after all to sell them his pardons. Is he joking? or confident of the power of his rhetoric even after he has exposed it?

or drunk? The Host answers with a joke about the Pardoner's testicles or lack of them – a fair counter or an unfair hit? The Pardoner is too angry to answer and the Host refuses any longer to 'pleye / With thee, ne with noon other angry man'. The Knight persuades them to go on with the game, which from one view is what the *Tales* compose, a game in fact proposed by the Host, whose defection is therefore alarming. But who lost his temper first? Who should have our sympathy?

The only reasonable answer is that the author has explained all that he wishes to and left us at the end of a Debate; his information and our response to it will tell us no more about the pilgrims, but perhaps something about our relations to them and even about our capacities for resembling them. Blake may well be right about the pilgrims: no child can 'be born who is not one of these charactors of Chaucer' and among them we may recognise ourselves. *The Canterbury Tales* is, as was said in a contemporary text, *The Cloud of Unknowing*, about the Bible, a mirror.

But where in his mirror might Chaucer see himself? Perhaps as their Creator, in all the pilgrims: but one might suggest four in particular, who also illustrate his genius as a narrator.

First, the Nun's Priest. A.E. Housman thought this the tale in which Chaucer as a poet was most at home, and perhaps it is the one of which Virginia Woolf's remark is truest, that Chaucer shows us 'common things so arranged that they affect us as poetry affects us, and are yet bright, sober, precise as we see them out of doors'. He puts into it many of the concerns which one might guess were intimate with him – the love of dreams, predestination, the violence of the peasants' revolt, and the question of whether stories should have morals:

> But ye that holden this tale a folye,
> As of a fox, or of a cok and hen,
> Taketh the moralite, goode men,
> For seint Paul seith that al that writen is,
> To oure doctrine it is ywrite, y wis:
> Taketh the fruyt, and lat the chaf be stille.

> (*Nun's Priest's Tale* 3438–43)

Some have taken this as Chaucer's serious doctrine of story: in this context, I suppose, it rather means, 'if you can't enjoy a good story, content yourself with the moral'.

Secondly, the Pardoner. He is the pattern tale-teller: he uses his story to suggest the teller's reward, but so did the teller of *Sir Orfeo* and so in various ways does Chaucer. And the puzzle of meaning grows deepest in his tale. The Pardoner himself has the doctrine ironically offered in the *Nun's Priest's Tale*, and thinks the morality of his story is 'The love of money is the root of evil'; but the story is transformed by the figure of the old man who tells the young men where to find Death – which they think someone whom they could destroy, but find in a heap of money. The model for the old man seems to be a hermit in a popular medieval collection of brief moralised stories, the *Gesta Romanorum*, who finds a treasure, at which he cries out 'Death!' and leaves it to be discovered by the equivalents of Chaucer's young men. But the hermit did not, as Chaucer's old man does, direct the young men to death, nor talk in the riddling manner that half suggests Chaucer's old man might be Sin, or Death, or the Wandering Jew or Cain. Because of the old man, the story becomes a different kind of tale, which tells as much by atmosphere as by plot that 'The wages of sin is death'. It ought to have on its narrator as on its readers the effect which Collingwood attributes to pure art: to purge a consciousness which (being too corrupt to know how it distorts what it sees) can only receive correction unawares.

A consciousness can be as corrupt in refusing happiness as in not recognising wickedness. The corrective for that might be the *Franklin's Tale,* the happiest tale as the Pardoner's is the most sinister. It stands with the novels of Sir Walter Scott, as demonstrating by its very warmth that there is enough virtue in humanity – if you know how to evoke it – to resolve all dilemmas, and by a kind of infection to persuade everyone, even the reader, to be happy. Troilus' and Criseyde's dilemma between courtly love and marriage is resolved in the Knight Arviragus, 'servant in love and lord in marriage' whose 'gentilesse', when this happy co-inherence is put to the test, knows how to come through triumphant.

But 'gentilesse' is a double-edged word. The Franklin, Sir Walter Scott and Chaucer, occupied analogous positions in society, not so gentle by birth as by acquired rank and character. One of Chaucer's most enduring and endearing comments on English society is the fading of the compliment of the Franklin (gentle as representing his county in Parliament and so a 'knight of the shire' but not, it seems, of the rank of the Knight himself) to the Squire (the Knight's son), into a complaint about the Franklin's own son, who would rather play dice and talk with pages than 'lerne gentilesse', which is immediately snubbed by the Host – 'Strawe for your gentilesse!' – presumably because like the actual Harry Bailly whose name he bears, an inn-keeper who represented Southwark in Parliament, he can regard the Franklin as his equal, and is vexed at the assumption of equality with the Squire and Knight, to whom he himself is willing to defer. Yet after all, the Franklin, like Chaucer, has 'gentilesse' by virtue.

Finally, there is Chaucer the pilgrim, the teller first of the one impossibly bad story, the romance of *Sir Thopas,* then of the *Tale of Melibee,* which is solidly improving, but scarcely a tale at all, the pure opposite of the *Nun's Priest's Tale. Sir Thopas* parodies such romances as those of the Auchinleck manuscript: but it is full of diction which Chaucer employs elsewhere without mockery. It is himself whom he mocks in both the stories he tells: the teller of all the stories cannot when he comes among the characters he created tell a true story or create a rounded character. In *A Midsummer Night's Dream,* which Shakespeare built on *The Knight's Tale,* and in the middle of the mechanicals' play of *Pyramus and Thisbe,* which is parallel to *Sir Thopas,* Theseus says 'The best in this kind are but shadows; and the worst are no worse, if imagination amend them.' But Chaucer makes himself the shadow, and rightly, for to this day his characters live more vividly than he. In this recognition there is something like Troilus' laughter in heaven, the humour of the sublime that flickers over all *The Canterbury Tales.*

In the *Retraction* at the end of the *Tales,* however, Chaucer abandons all these subtle accommodations of story and meaning together with all his work that could be regarded as 'worldly vanitees' and asserts without irony the opinion of the end of the *Nun's Priest's Tale*, 'Al that is writen is writen for our doctrine'. It may be that in the prospect of death he found no need to continue the task of holding together time and eternity, but only to resign himself to the end of time, in the hope 'that I may been oon of hem at the day of doome that shulle be saved'.

In accepting these doctrines of story and experience he was returning to the ordinary doctrine of his day, and notably of his friend John Gower (c.1330–1408). The attractiveness of Gower's *Confessio Amantis* lies in the balance in him of two poetic temperaments, the Proverb-maker, who has a taste for expressing general reflection in quaint and memorable specific detail, and someone else with a sense of the shared deep pathos of humanity, the longing and the suffering. Gower has found a perfect expression for the latter in the confession of Amans, the lover grieving to know why he is unsuccessful in love, and for the Proverb-maker in Genius, Venus' priest, who expounds to Amans the models of love in stories which are moralities all elegantly 'written for our doctrine'. There is a grave balance between the two: Amans' individuality is built up, in a real echo of what must often have happened in the confessional, very delicately in relation to the code offered him, and expressed with the Proverb-maker's gift for detail, while Genius' tale-telling rises to heartrending sympathy when the stories are appropriate. The couple parallel the Owl and the Nightingale, but the doubleness of the *Confessio* provides the exploration of a given moral structure rather than a debate, and its octosyllables do not have the tearing high spirits of the earlier poem. Fortunately, however, Gower balances his softer style by a taste for wild romantic stories of wandering, like the tale of Apollonius, whom Shakespeare called Pericles Prince of Tyre, or that of Constance the Empress, in the telling of which Gower and Chaucer (in *The Man of Law's Tale*) vie without either having the advantage, or above all that of Medea and Jason. His gliding verse wonderfully embodies Medea as she prepares for sorcery,

> Al specheles and on the gras
> She glod forth as an addre doth

in which context the word *glod* acquires a greater eeriness even than it had in Layamon's emphatic alliteration, 'This thing glad me bivoren and glitened on golde' (above, p. 99). The combination in Gower's understanding of Medea of maidenly, and ultimately betrayed innocence with witchcraft, raises great power – simple, sensuous and passionate – when she waits to hear if Jason has won the golden fleece:

> She preide and seide, 'O, God him spede,
> The Knight which hath mi maiden hiede,'
> And ay sche loketh toward thyle
> Bot whan sche sih withinne a while
> The flees glistrende ayein the Sonne
> She saide, 'Ha lord, now al is wonne,
> Mi Knight the field hath overcome.'

(V 3739–45)

The fleece when it is seen through Medea's eyes transcends Gower's ordinary visual effects, which to a modern eye are like the illuminations of his contemporary Herman Scheere – neat, bright, small, ancient and fitting the Proverb-maker –

> . . . as a bussh which is besnewed
> Here berdes woren hore and white

or

> The beaute of hire face schon
> Wel bryhtere than the Cristall ston

which latter however Gower revised to something more haunting:

> The beaute of here faye face
> Ther may non erthly thing deface.

The world to Gower is *faye*, beautiful but dangerous and unaccountable: God removes the Empress Constance 'fro this worldes faierie' (II 1593) to His own company. Though he does not display the profound disquiet with experience of *Troilus and Criseyde*, Gower shares with Chaucer the intent to show the world 'cleansed of its stiff and stubborn manlocked set' (Wallace Stevens, *Angels Surrounded by Paysans*).

The Gawain poet

The same intention dictates the very shape of *Pearl*, one of the most intricate in English poetry, the work of the third (with Chaucer and Langland) of the supreme Ricardian poets. It embodies an interrogation, like the interrogation of Boethius in the *Consolation* by Lady Philosophy, who comes with that alien understanding which, as figure in the dialogue, Boethius learns, and which, as author, he teaches himself to believe. But the narrator of *Pearl* is taught by a sharp young girl (who is by a natural affinity in the poems, or possibly by actual acquaintance, rather like the Beatrice of Dante's *Divine Comedy*) and the dialogue takes place in a marvellously alien world of bright colours, where the dust is pearls.

The pain of longing is embodied in the poem too. It begins

> Perle plesaunte to princes paye   *delightful for a prince's pleasure*
> To clanly clos in golde so gaye . .   *to set cleanly*

The pearl was lost in a garden like the garden of love in the *Parliament of Fowls* and before that in the *Roman de la Rose*: it is described in the language of love-longing

> So smal, so smothe her sydis were   *slender*

which becomes grief for the dead. The love-longing remains, although presently it appears that the maiden who is the pearl died before she was two years old. The age suggests the innocents of Bethlehem whom Herod killed, all those from two years old and under, in an attempt to kill Christ, the Lamb Himself, and she has joined them to follow the Lamb like the little boy to whom Chaucer's Prioress cries 'O martir souded to virginitee'. (*enlisted in/welded to*). But we feel this narrator's grief and adoration, we see with his eyes and stand within him as we never do with the Prioress's sentiment and piety.

His feelings are in a measure reformed, in a measure ours are too, and this above all is reflected in the poem's form. It ends with almost the lines with which it begins, but the form is not circular. For the opening expresses the longing of the man for the Pearl, and the end of the longing felt, from outside our man-locked set, for the man and for ourselves, by Christ:

> he gef us to be his homly hyne   *may he give; household servants*
> And precious perles unto his paye.

Another echo from beginning to end is as complex as one of Langland's. In the garden at the beginning the lost pearl is compared to the seed in Christ's parable which abides alone unless it dies, but if it dies brings forth much grain, and the narrator falls asleep there

> In Auguste, in a high sesoun
> When corn is corven with crokes kene

that is August I, called Lammas, Loaf-mass because the first sheaf was then cut and the first loaf baked from it. At the end the commendation is to Christ, 'That in the forme of bred and wyne
The prest us schewes uch a daye . . .' The seed become grain become bread has become Christ's body, experience totally transformed.

In his *Testament of Love*, to which I have already appealed for an orthodox response to *Troilus and Criseyde*, Thomas Usk has a beloved who is a literal woman and a pearl and besides, he says, 'grace, learning, or wisdom of God, or else holy Church': and he appeals both to the bread's becoming Christ's body and to the orthodox acceptance that the manna of the Old Testament which fed the Israelites in the desert signified the same Bread, to justify his many levelled meaning. Quite probably he has *Pearl* itself in mind: certainly the symbolism of the poem is comparably many-levelled. The maiden is a pearl, and the pearl is also that of another of Christ's parables, the pearl for which one would be ready to give everything else, which signifies the kingdom of heaven. But the grief of the poem is not diminished in force by this meaning: and it is essential to its theology that Pearl primarily is a dead child. For the point is that the child is exalted in heaven to enjoy all heaven, where every innocent is a queen: and yet she never did anything to deserve it. This specific point, illustrated by a third of Christ's parables, that of the labourers in the vineyard, is part of the larger point which the whole transformation of the poem suggests: that what we do is nothing, what is overwhelmingly important is the love for us of Him whom we adore daily in the lifted Host. As often in Ricardian literature the subject is the absoluteness of the grace of God which Archbishop Bradwardine emphasised for fourteenth-century theology in his book *De Causa Dei* (finished 1344).

The transformation of experience, and the employment of dramatic empathy to reveal it are essential to the other great poem in the *Pearl* manuscript, written in a diction and with a sharp, bright, visual sense which only the doubts proper to scholarship could deny to the same poet. But the kind of story is different. It is a later fourteenth-century romance of Arthur's time, *Sir Gawain and the Green Knight*, and although, as if to enforce their common authorship, it has the same number of verses as *Pearl* – 101 – and the same device of ending with an echo of the first line, the purposes are different. The stanza is the old alliterative line, employed in heroic narrative, but divided into verses to break the monotony into which that line is apt to fall, by a recurrent set of short lines. The echo of

> Sithen the sege and the assaut was sesed at Troye
> The borg brittened and brent to brondes and askes

(1–2)

at the end, by

> After the sege and the assaut was sesed at Troye
> I wysse,
> Mony auntrez here beforne
> Haf fallen, such er this.

(2525–8)

marks no progress in feeling, but rather an enclosure of the story's immersion in the present moment by vast historic distance, as in *Troilus and Criseyde*. The diction of *Pearl* expressed grief controlled and articulated, that of *Sir Gawain and the Green Knight* a juxtaposition, again like *Troilus and Criseyde*, of the chivalric code with something more immediate. The first line, *siege, assault, ceased, Troy* has

> the sharp little brightness, as of a window pane flashing just after sunset, which belongs to the ancient technical language of heraldry [and] to more common Norman words – *banner, hauberk, lance, pennon, . . . arms, assault, battle, fortress, harness, siege, standard, tower,* and *war.*
>
> (Owen Barfield, *History in English Words*)

The second line *borg, brittened, brent, brondes, askes,* all Anglo-Saxon and Norse, conveys the bitter, destructive underside of war. But the two languages do not pull apart: together they express a fullness of experience which is part of a larger empathy.

Gawain is given the fullest heroic perfection from the moment when the elvish Green Knight rides into Arthur's court on New Year's Day and challenges Arthur's knights to deal him one blow now on condition that the striker bears a blow in exchange a year later. Only Arthur himself and Gawain are courageous enough to take up the challenge: and for the king it would be at once too frivolous and too dangerous. But Gawain strikes off the knight's head, and when the red blood glitters on the green body, and the body lifts up the head and the head tells Gawain to meet him at the Green Chapel on New Year's morning, still both Arthur and Gawain laugh undismayed. There follow two great verses in which the passing of the year is briefly but most graphically described: Gawain's realisation of what 'stern work' he has committed himself to by 'those games in hall' is set against the seasons, themselves increasingly felt as a contest in which the colour green is disturbingly involved.

Wrothe wynde of the welkyn wrastles with the sunne   *heaven*
The leaves lancen fro the lynde and lighten on the ground,   *linden trees*
And al grayes the gres that grene was ere;   *grass turns brown*
Thenne al rypes and rotes that ros upon fyrst . . .   *ripens, rots*

Green is the colour of vegetation: it is also – as in the Green Knight's case – the colour of faery. In this quintessentially medieval environment interwoven of natural and magical forces Christianity is also given a part, by the mention of Christmas, Lent and Michaelmas. Against the background of the green world and the winter world that follows, Gawain keeps his resolve, and on All Saints Day sets out to meet the Green Knight, carrying a red shield. On its inner side Mary is painted, and on the outside a pentangle signifying the interdependence of virtues in a man of 'trawthe', honour: 'fraunchyse', the nobility of a leader, 'felawship' which a leader also needs, 'clannes', chastity, which in Gawain was never 'croked' with 'cortaysye', although in the world of courts and the game of love it might well be, and 'pite', which some have translated pity, but in a shield which carries the image of Mary rather should be piety. This is the ideal of a knight: but as J. Jusserand says, when we compare the men and women in *Sir Gawain and the Green Knight* with the puppets of ordinary romances we feel as if the 'Knights and ladies in their well-fitting armour or their tight dresses, whom we see stretched in churches on their fourteenth-century tombs, have come back to life once more; and now they move, they gaze on each other, they love again'. (*A Literary History of the English People*) The poet interweaves with our sense of Gawain's perfection a sense of his feelings, notably through his physical discomfort on his journey through Wales in winter:

Ner slayn with the slete he sleped in his irnes
Mo nyghtes than inogh in naked rokkes . . .   *enough*

In *Sir Gawain and the Green Knight* the odd union of admiration and self-identification which the techniques of the opening create in us is brought into action when, in the days before Gawain meets the Green Knight again, the lady of the castle tests his 'cortaysye' and 'clannes', as the challenge has tested his 'fraunchyse' and 'felawshipe'. With too simple delight we applaud him as, in tense and polished conversation, he evades her seductions, while outside her husband hunts down boar, deer and fox. Each day in pursuance of another Christmas game, apparently but not actually less dangerous than the beheading game, the husband gives Gawain what he has killed, and Gawain, without revealing their source, gives the husband the kisses he has allowed the wife to give him. From the worst fall Gawain's 'pite' and his Lady the Virgin Mary's care save him. But successful tempters concentrate the subject's defence and attention elsewhere than the real point. Gawain falls, and does not know he has fallen.

The reader does not yet recognise it either, and some devout Catholics, notably J.R.R. Tolkien, deny to the end that he does seriously fall: for if he does, then before he goes out to face death he makes a confession which, as the poet does not explicitly reveal, must be a bad one, compounding his offence. But this, in an age when self-knowledge is bound up with the confessional, and in a poem which exploits our degree of knowledge of and self-identification with Gawain's inner self, is a natural device.

The transformation of our experience comes when the Green Knight, whom hitherto we have seen only as external threat, becomes our eye in the poem, and, with a jarring, we see Gawain from the outside. The Knight approves him, and gives him a roughly humorous penance with his axe for his fall. But in the shock of self-revelation, Gawain's own sense of his integrity is shattered, and momentarily his interdependent virtues fall altogether: he, who, like all 'cortays' knights, has hitherto spoken of ladies with reverence, rails against the lady of the castle, as conventionally clerks were thought to do. He recovers his sense of honour in abject penitence. One possible moral to the story is that the code of chivalry is (as for different reasons Troilus found it) too high-strained to live by. Another, more compelling, is that the highest is our legitimate aim, but falling short of it something to be received either (as Arthur receives Gawain) with fellow-feeling, or (in ourselves) as the broken heart through which Christ enters: the turn at the end from closing the book of history to

> Now that bare the croun of thorne,
> He bring vus to His blysse. Amen   (2529–30)

is perhaps, in a poem where all conventions are put to use, not only a conventionally pious ending.

As in *Sir Gawain and the Green Knight*, so in his other poems the poet is concerned to bring together the two sets of ideals by which late medieval society was led, chivalric courtesy and Christian piety. In *Pearl*, a transformed 'cortaysye' is said to be the mark of the unearthly society in which every woman is a queen: in a third poem, *Clannes*, he constructs through a series of stories a cleanness, a delicacy of feeling which will unite good manners at table, good manners towards God and good manners in bed – of which God Himself says that 'the play of paramorez I portrayed Myselven' than which 'welnyghe pure paradys moght preve no better'. *Clan* is even the word he uses himself (as in the second line of *Pearl* already quoted 'To clanly clos . . .') for the sharp, articulated form and bright colour which he likes.

But (aside from *Piers Plowman*, different alike in theme and language), the only one of the considerable body of fourteenth- and fifteenth-century alliterative poetry to have passed into the main tradition of English literature is the alliterative *Morte Arthure*, rendered into prose and ruthlessly cropped by Malory and Caxton in the fifth book of the prose *Morte D'Arthur*. The cause of this neglect is that alliterative poetry is written mainly in the dialect of the north. Yet during its flourishing this poetry was not confined to the north, though possibly written only by people born there. The one poem in this style whose author can plausibly be identified, a charming, recently discovered piece, *The Bird in Bishop's Wood*, was drafted in London on the accounts of St Paul's Cathedral, probably by the canon responsible for them, John Tickhill. And *Saint Erkenwald*, which has been not implausibly attributed to the Gawain poet, is set in St Paul's and concerns a saint particularly honoured there.

Whether or not by the Gawain poet, *Saint Erkenwald* shares with his poems a sense of combined extremity and loneliness which is not common in Ricardian, perhaps not in late medieval poetry. A man is seen alone with his soul or God, throwing himself upon God: apart from him, whether present in the scene portrayed or not, is the crowd, the community in relation to which most medieval lives were lived – privacy was a rare thing – and most medieval stories told. It is a common modern, a rare medieval sentiment that religion is what one does with one's solitude. Langland, for all his individuality, does not have it, nor does Gower. Gower avoids it even in the story of the Empress Constance which seems to cry for it, for she is twice set adrift in an open boat, once alone, once with her child, and miraculously preserved in it on both occasions for several years. It is only in his telling of this story that Chaucer has it, and it seems the stranger there for being associated with the common visual symbol of a community, the church, protected in its ark from the stormy sea of the world. But the subject of the whole of the Gawain poet's fourth poem, *Patience*, the story of Jonah, and of much of *Sir Gawain and the Green Knight*, is a man who had 'no gome but God bi gate with to karp' (*no-one but God to talk with on his journey*). And Erkenwald goes through a helpless crowd to his fearful task of confronting a dead man, saying that *when overthrown* – 'quen matyd is mannes myght and his mynde passyd / And al his resons are torent, and redeles he stondes', then is the moment when God reveals His power.

This sense of individuality before God appears most clearly in the two great Ricardian mystics, the author of the *Cloud of Unknowing* and Julian of Norwich (1342–after 1416). They have been read with more attention in this century than in any since the fifteenth, and are perhaps the only writers of their time, not even excepting Chaucer, who are easily read without sense of period. They are also the only writers of their time to have achieved good English prose. W.P. Ker remarked of Chaucer's *Tale of Melibee* that it 'is beyond rivalry for its enjoyment of the rankest commonplaces . . .'. Fourteenth-century English prose – besides *Melibee*, Chaucer's *Parson's Tale* and translation of Boethius, Sir John Mandeville's *Travels*, Usk's *Testament of Love*, the Wycliffite translations of the Bible, even, though they are more sharply written, the great wealth of sermons, and Sir John Clanvowe's *Two Ways* – tends to be at best undistinguished in form though often entertaining in matter, and to achieve original thought only at the cost of clumsiness. Only Julian and the author of the *Cloud* can think in English prose.

These two share certain further things: first, the promise of satisfaction for an immense longing, as in the phrases T.S. Eliot picks from them in *Little Gidding*: 'All shall be well, and all shall be well, and all manner of thing shall be well' – 'I am ground of thy beseeching' – 'What weary wretched soul and sleeping in sloth is that which is not wakened with the drawing of this love and the voice of this calling?'

Secondly, both put an immense complexity of meaning into terse visual images as in Julian's 'he showed a little thing, the quantity of a hazelnut, lying in the palm of my hand, as meseemed, and it was as round as a ball', which is 'all that is made': or in the *Cloud* 'smite upon that thick cloud of unknowing with a sharp dart of longing love . . .'

Thirdly, they share a sharp sceptical awareness of their experiences. Julian carefully classifies her shewings as they are spiritual, physical or by 'word formed in my understanding': the author of the *Cloud* comparably classifies the ways in which mystical experience may be deceptive so that his reader will realise, as J.A. Burrow puts it, 'that the physical world has its own necessary and proper integrity as well as the spiritual world, and that to conceive either in terms of the other imperils the integrity of both'.

In all other ways, they differ. Each represents one of the two mystic ways, the negative and the affirmative. In a letter to a friend choosing between the two, the author of the *Cloud* reorders some of the elements in Langland's Dowell, Dobetter and Dobest:

silence, it is not God, ne speaking, it is not God, ne company, it is not God; ne yet any of all the other two such contraries. He is hid betwixt them, and may not be found by any work of thy soul, but all only by love of thine heart.

In another letter he makes clear the loneliness of a soul making such a choice, for 'no man knoweth which ben the privy dispositions of man but the spirit of the same man which is in himself'. The uncompromisingness of the *Cloud* is terrible: and for all its beauty and intelligence, which are consequent upon its author's fixing his attention on a point outside experience, it cannot be read without a sinking of the spirit by anyone who is not called to its task. Walter Hilton (d.1395/6) may have written his *Ladder of Perfection* to counterbalance the effect it might have on beginners in contemplation.

Hilton shares with Langland and Julian the conviction that Jesus is to be found in our souls. Whatever Julian means by this, it was for her a matter of experience. Her first book was a report of visions which she saw in the middle of May 1373 (in the same week that Chaucer returned back in England from Italy) and was probably written shortly afterwards: her second was enlarged from it over twenty years. Whatever happened to her, although it appeared at first in the piety of her age, in the blood of Christ's passion and the humility of Mary, presently conveyed thoughts to her unparalleled in her age, as of the motherhood of Christ. Her writing has an authenticity about it such that the Christian may well believe she talked with Christ, and the non-Christian wish to put the same conviction in other terms, as Iris Murdoch has done in her novel *Nuns and Soldiers*.

In Julian's *Showings* and in the *Cloud* the wish which haunts the great Ricardians to hold together two kinds of awareness of the universe finds its best harmony.

The flowering of ritual: towards the personal (c.1400–c.1460)

When, as we are apt to do, we go to the Middle Ages for a balance to hyperconsciousness, fragmentation and individualism, we look for an art which is anonymous and grand, representing an uncompromised and unselfconscious moral and theological structure, harmonious, impersonal, untroubled by the fissure between subjective and objective, instinct with awe, timeless, the ritual self-expression of an organic community achieving its effects without the need to resort to originality, dominated by the voice of whatever section of the community the reader finds congenial or (if one's taste in reading runs to the adversarial) peculiarly detests. This is a quest which distorts much medieval and most Ricardian literature: but it is more nearly achieved in the mystery plays.

The mystery plays

Three great cycles of these plays survive in forms which, although many times in part rewritten, still might be recognised by the audience of the 1370s, when probably they first appeared at York and Chester. The third, the Wakefield cycle, seems to have a common origin with that of York and may preserve some plays in a form closer to that original. Who exactly wrote the plays we have little notion but most of them are, as language, just as good or bad as one would expect if literature were really generated by a community or a language without any important intervention of individual genius: that is, in simplicity they can be noble, but when they aim at grandeur they lapse into a hollow booming. Their scheme is noble; it begins with the Creation and ends with Judgement Day: so it represents all time, and this at York was given its image by performance from dawn and the appearance of light to dusk illuminated by the supernatural light and flames of heaven and hell artificially produced. Within time the important action was that of the fall of man and its consequences, first the sequence of sin and justice, the first murder (of Abel by Cain), the corruption of humanity, its destruction by the flood and Noah's salvation: secondly the sequence of mercy and redemption, the nativity, passion, resurrection, and ascension of Christ; and finally the return of justice at Judgement Day.

For the dramatic time of the plays is not only the whole of worldly time, nor even the whole of wordly time as a parenthesis in eternity, but the present moment seen as the moment of choice, and therefore of judgement or salvation. How long that moment will last no one knows: it will be closed for the individual either at death or earlier, for the world at Judgement Day. But the offer of salvation is before you, and every play is an attempt, by explanation or example, by raising your terror of death and judgement, your gratitude or compassion at the death of Christ, and your exultation and gratitude at His victory, to make you accept it. The whole drama is corporate affective contemplation.

A further influence on the atmosphere and dramatic time of the plays is the day on which they were commonly performed, and after which they were called: Corpus Christi, the feast of the Body of Christ, the first Thursday after the seasons of Easter and Pentecost, on a Thursday because Christ instituted the sacrament of His Body on Maundy Thursday, and on that particular one because it was the first Thursday after the celebration of Christ's natural life in the Christian year was over. In 1317 Corpus Christi became a principal feast in the diocese of Canterbury and in the same year processions began in which the Sacrament itself was carried. It may be that the processions which were one means of staging the plays, pageant wagons – one for each play, proceeding through the streets and stopping at set stations for performances – began as processions of pageants before or behind the Host.

However that may be, the ultimate root of the plays is in the Last Supper: Christ's act of breaking bread and pouring wine as a symbol of His coming death was already dramatic, and its representation in memory of His death in the Mass is a sacramental drama. In the Christian year the Mass had long been celebrated with readings and ritual following through Christ's life, and from the tenth century dramatic actions (the earliest being the women meeting the angels at Christ's tomb) were introduced into it. On the principal feasts, plays (such as the *Mystery of Adam* which I have mentioned) were performed, bearing on the event of that day: it is not certain in what connection with the Mass. The *Mystery of Adam* was a Christmas play in which the Fall was portrayed as the occasion of Christ's birth, so that the principle of the representation of all time was already there. But the celebration on Corpus Christi, a day honouring no particular event nor associated with any particular emotion in response to Christ's natural life, but instead adoring with jubilation the perpetual implicit presence in the Body of Christ of the whole act of redemption, points to eternity.

Commonly the plays set the Biblical events in the present, and their complex sense of time is like Langland's. Like Langland's, it represents life lived within a Christian community. The drama does appear to have involved the whole community: in towns all over the country each play was the responsibility of one of the guilds of the trades and occupations, sometimes practically appropriate or representing a special devotion – as the Bakers for the Last Supper, the Goldsmiths to supply gifts or adorn a crib for the Nativity, or (at Chester, and the only case not involving a guild) the 'worshipful wives' for the Assumption of the Mother of God – but largely as sharing the plays among as many as possible.

As well as the implicit metaphor of one day for all time, in some towns, instead of the procession, a special place marked out an area to represent the world. The removal of the plays from direct association with the liturgy encouraged a greater freedom of treatment, suggested by the adoption of the metaphor of *play* for what is otherwise called the *thing done* (Greek *drama*, Latin *agere*, act): it is liturgy for the medievals that is the thing done, a sacred event mystically made present, but this is a *play*. Further subjects were added, some sacred and tending to stress the pattern of history, as in the version in Cornish where all the plays are bound together by the legend that the Cross was grown from seed of the Tree of the Fall. But new characters appeared too, modelled partly on secular interludes of which fragments about courtship (*De Clerico et Puella*) and family struggle (*Dux Moraud*) alone survive. They are mostly characters implied but not developed in the Bible and represent the inadequacy or perversity of people confronted with the supernatural, people lovably or hatefully funny – Noah's wife who will not enter the Ark because she will not leave her friends or because she thinks her husband a fool, Joseph lamenting the fate of old husbands, the shepherds at the nativity imitating the angels' song, Herod raging insanely outside the acting space, Simeon refusing to believe the prophecy that a virgin should conceive.

The principal legacies of the mystery plays to the Elizabethan theatre are, first, these characters mediating between a sublime event and common life: secondly, the sense of the stage as the whole world, to any part of which the action may move, and in which the audience may be included: and thirdly the sense of a period of time unlimited in length but ending in judgement. In these respects the plays are conspicuously at odds with the Elizabethans' other inheritance from Roman drama, Seneca, Plautus and Terence, of a spatially and temporally limited dramatic form set in a chaotic universe.

The density of the representation of reality which the Elizabethans derive from this double inheritance is to some extent already present in the work of two notable individuals among the revisers of the plays, who can be identified by their linguistic and dramatic genius. Both worked about 1420: the York Realist, who adds black comedy to the executioners at the Crucifixion, great religious power in the contrast of their unfeeling gabble with two short noble speeches by Christ, and a painful muscular empathy as they tug and stretch His body; and the Wakefield Master, who adds social satire and a jesting with the conventions of the mystery. In the second of his nativity plays, the shepherds use local placenames which place Bethlehem in Wakefield, yet one of them remarks mazily that in a dream 'I thought that we had laid us full nere Yngland.' In the same play the sub-plot of Mak the sheepstealer makes a merry parody of the nativity in which a stolen horned ram, a devilish-looking thing, is laid in a cradle to deceive its owners: yet the adoration of the shepherds at the true nativity is the most moving in any play.

The plays of these two individuals bear witness to a familiar ripeness in the use of ritual and symbolic acts and of the language of Biblical symbol and type, which enables people who are not mystics to say complex things with simplicity through an intense concentration, as we have found Julian and the author of the *Cloud* doing. Ritual and symbol moreover intensify everyday experience and its natural magic, which becomes the vehicle of religious truth. The possibilities of using this rich language together with the fact that the second quarter of the fifteenth century was one of the great ages of English music, whose tunes give shape and concision to song, are among the conditions of the great fifteenth-century flourishing of religious lyric and carol.

The best example of these qualities is the most gracious of English poems:

I sing of a maiden that is makeles:	*without peer/mate*
King of alle kinges to here sone she ches	*chose*
He cam also stille, ther his moder was,	*where*
As dew in Aprille that falleth on the gras.	
He cam also stille, to his moderes bour,	
As dew in Aprille, that falleth on the flour.	
He cam also stille, ther his moder lay,	
As dew in Aprille, that falleth on the spray.	
Moder and maiden was never non but she:	
Well may swich a lady Godes moder be	

It is based on a longer thirteenth-century lyric on the Annunciation:

Nu this fules singet and maket hure blisse	*these birds*
And that gres up thringet and leved the ris	*grass thrusts up;*
Of on ic wille singen that is makeles,	*branch puts forth leaves*
The King of alle Kinges to moder he hire ches . . .	
Maiden and moder nas never non wimon boten he,	*was; she*
Wel mitte he berigge of Godes sune be . . .	*bearer*

The later poet concentrates 'ic wille singe' into 'I sing', as if there is nothing else that the singer does or is, and removes the complexities of Christ's choice 'to moder he hire ches' and the presence of God the father 'berigge of Godes sune', leaving simply Mary's choice of the lonely miracle, to be mother and maiden, and the coming of Christ in response, something supernatural expressed in terms of the natural but wonderful appearance of dew from the air. The natural wonderfulness in the earlier poem of 'gres up thringet and leved the ris' is intensified by the later poet, as it calls to his mind the stem of Jesse that flowered, and with it the whole language both of Old Testament types of Mary, the lily and enclosed garden of the Song of Songs, Gideon's fleece in Judges on which the dew lay while the ground about was dry, and again of types of Christ, dew falling from heaven in Isaiah, Wisdom descending in the silence of the night in the book of *Wisdom*; perhaps too from the language of medieval beast lore, the pearl in the shellfish that was thought to have been formed from dew and to be a symbol of the virgin birth. The catalyst might have been the feast of the Annunciation, Lady Day itself, 25 March, but dated according to the Roman calendar the eighth day of the kalends of April. All this intertextual complex in the poem is no more than latent. It does not so much help us to understand, rather we are helped to understand it by the almost-sacrament which the poem offers, the meeting of God and lady in and through the expectant fullness of an early morning in April. Quite incidentally the poem also draws in and interprets for later ages the wealth of feeling which medieval piety and secular love gave the word 'lady'.

This concentration should perhaps be classified among medieval poetic techniques as *abbreviatio*. Another poet might have used *amplificatio* and set the symbols side by side, as John Lydgate (c.1370–1449), a monk of Bury St Edmunds, does in his *Life of our Lady*:

> She was the castell of the cristall wall
> That never man myght yet unclose
> Which the King that made and causyth all
> His dwellyng chefe by grace gan dispose,   *did*
> And like as dewe descendeth on the rose
> With silver dropes, upon the leves fayre
> The fressche beaute ne may not apayre,
>
> Ne as the rayne in Apryll or in May
> Causyng the vertu to renne oute of the rote,
> The grete fayrenesse nought apayre may
> On violetes and on erbes soote:
> Right so this grace, of al oure greves bote,   *grief's bettering*
> The grace of God, amydde the lyly white
> The beaute causyth to be of more delyte.

(II 546–59)

This is only a fraction even of the passage on the Annunciation: Lydgate's style is, though lovely, lengthy. It can be a great pleasure to read, but one must arrange one's mind to receive it: it does not strike one's mind unawares like *I sing of a maiden*. Perhaps apart from single lines and couplets, only two whole poems in Lydgate's huge body of work achieve this power. One is his *Dance of Death*, perhaps partly because it was written to accompany a set of pictures in the cloisters of St Paul's, so that his prolixity was under control, but more because mutability is a subject which always tends to raise him above his normal level. It is the theme of his greatest poem, whose refrain 'Al stant on chaung like a midsomyr rose' concentrates a beautiful catalogue of mutabilities.

This rich language, as in drama in the work of the Wakefield Master and the York Realist, so in the lyric sometimes encounters a personal twist. John Audelay, who in 1426 transcribed a fine collection of religious poems at his monastery of Haughmond, some of them by himself, includes Christmas carols with a warmth of sentiment which appears in another poem on childhood:

> And God wold graunt me my preyere   *If*
> A child alone I wold I were

in which of the two medieval attitudes to childhood he adopts not the penitential one which goes back to St Augustine, but a genial one that is associated with St Gregory and appears in *Pearl*. Characteristically in another poem again he claims, as the expression of personal experience, a proverb which goes back at least to *The Owl and the Nightingale*: 'Lerne this lesson of blind Awdlay: | When bale is highest, then bot may be.'

In the same decade a similar personal twist appears at length in secular love poetry: in the *Kingis Quair*, the imprisonment of James I of Scotland in England from 1406 to 1424, and his love affair there with Joan Beaufort are narrated, probably by the King himself, in a beautiful transposition of the language of *The Parliament of Fowls* and *The Knight's Tale* to an individual's experience. And another prisoner, Charles d'Orléans, between the battle of Agincourt in 1415 and 1440, wrote a *Livre de prison* of love poetry in French, of which there exists an elegant English version, part translation and part original, probably by Charles himself. 'Long before Wyatt', as Derek Pearsall puts it, 'he introduces the intimate, passionate speaking voice into English courtly lyric' in poems which are also at will allegorical, formal, humorous, polite and, indeed, French.

Lydgate, James I and Charles d'Orléans were all admirers and followers of Chaucer. But his closest pupil was Thomas Hoccleve (1368/9–1426), who not only claimed personal acquaintance with him, but preserved a miniature of him, the first English portrait other than of royalty which looks like an individual. This is characteristic of Hoccleve: for although in his own time his most popular work by far was his didactic *Regement of Princes*, he lives now because through an oddly various array of literary forms which shows how abnormal the task was, he presents his own life as a clerk in the privy Seal office, and his experience of a nervous breakdown. It was perhaps his need to control and understand his mental disorder that made him write so unmedieval a thing as autobiography, and it is not only his occupation but his temperament that makes one think, with affection towards both, of Charles Lamb.

Affection is the right emotion for a contemporary of Hoccleve's who also turned a traditional form to autobiography, Margery Kempe (c.1373–after 1439), although irritation, devout reverence and possessive defensiveness have also been felt for her in her own time and in ours. The difficulty about her is that she wishes to be judged as a mystic like Julian of Norwich, with whom she talked, and St Bridget of Sweden whose *Revelations* she took as a model. Her visions and her uncontrollable weeping impress some and not others then and now. They were more normal then: a Carthusian monk annotating her book remarks that Richard Methley, the spiritual guide whom I mentioned as recommending Saint Godric's hymns, behaved similarly. Her devotion to Christ was powerful and deep: but in what she believed Christ to have said to her there is more of her own time and indeed of herself than there is in Julian. Nor has she Julian's analytic self-understanding, nor any uncommon intuitions like the Motherhood of Christ. There is the affective piety for which Jesus 'deeth is as fressh to me as he had deed this same day', and the contemplative piety which allows her, when she is reminded by a mother and child at Rome of Mary and Jesus, to hear Christ saying 'This place is holy.'

The pieties are those of her time. She would not have written the book without them: but what is individual to her is the vigorous and vivid description of her dealings with people, from beggar to archbishop, from her long-suffering husband to the friend who deserted her at Paris, and the prose in which she describes them, which makes mock of attempts to derive telling narrative from tradition and literacy, for, she being illiterate, it was taken down from her conversation.

Malory and the waning of the Middle Ages (c.1450–c.1500)

The world of Margery Kempe was also that of Sir Thomas Malory (d.1469/70?): a world of visions and meetings with wise religious people, of emotion immediately and physically expressed, of a passionate devotion, religious or secular, which subsumes ethics and is made as concrete as possible, of wandering in search of the supernatural apparent in local and visible form, whether it was the blood which was believed to have flowed from a consecrated host at Wilsnak in Poland, to which Margery made pilgrimage, or the holy Grail. It is the world that can be sensed today in the chapel of the blood of Christ at the heart of the highly commercial city of Bruges, and in the van Eycks' *Adoration of the Lamb* at Ghent, where the felicity of Paradise is seen in jewels, fur, grass, light and the blood pouring from the Lamb's side – curiously unlike the alien and unearthly beauty of the same scene in *Pearl*.

In Malory's *Morte Darthur* it is the world where Guenever's love for Lancelot is measured by 'It hath cost my lady the Queen twenty thousand pounds the seeking of you': where when the Grail was seen, all the hall was 'fulfilled with good odours, and every knight had such meats and drinks as he best loved in this world'.

But in Malory, as not in Margery Kempe, we are aware of a literary context. Geoffrey of Monmouth's chronicle of royal, martial and developing chivalric feeling has drawn into itself during three hundred years the changing traditions of love, piety and honour, together with such ancient myth as the sleep of Arthur, or the three women, maiden, matron and crone, probably once a Celtic traid of goddesses, who guide knights errant to adventure.

But Malory most fully interweaves, now at their most mature development, the four strains we detected in interpretations of *Maiden in the Mor Lay*, the faery, the Christian, the comic and the amorous, and makes them part of his history of honour. The whole tapestry even accepts the genial presence of Sir Dinadan, a good knight, loved by all knights, who nevertheless finds a rich humour in the knight-errantry of Sir Tristram or his own defeat at the hands of 'the old shrew Sir Lancelot'.

Humour as a way of mediating the world of chivalry to ordinary humanity is balanced by what C.S. Lewis called 'the iron in Malory, the tragedy of contrition'. Lancelot's son Galahad takes his father's place as the best of knights for the reason which he implies in his farewell: 'salute me unto my Lord Sir Lancelot my father, and bid him remember of this world unstable'. Over against Galahad, the maiden knight who achieves the Grail, Lancelot the lover of Guenever is unstable. But against the present-day world of which Malory laments that lovers are not stable now as they were in Arthur's time, and that neither now nor then could Englishmen remain loyal to a good king, Lancelot is not unstable. He is only trying to carry stability into a compromise with a situation in which, being in love with his Lord's wife, he can only be faithful in either love or chivalry by unfaithfulness. There is in him the struggle to unite the knowledge of time and the knowledge of eternity which we have seen throughout medieval literature: but compared with the Gawain of *Sir Gawain and the Green Knight* he has been put in an impossible situation, which bears witness to a despair of the reconciliation of the two worlds which the Gawain-poet did not feel. Lancelot and Guenever by their own choice live their last days apart and in penance.

Fifty years after Malory ceased work on the *Morte Darthur*, the Reformation was sparked off by Martin Luther's reaction against the embodiment of contrition in the confessional, whose concrete side of penance had become so quantifiable that it could be reduced by payment to pardoners. With this reaction, which most reflective medieval writers like Chaucer or Langland already felt, went a reaction against the whole notion of forgiveness being offered for anything less than a complete spiritual rebirth. In Langland's terms, Dowell was no longer to be regarded as enough: it was to be drawn up into Dobetter.

Langland himself would remain acceptable to Protestants: Margery Kempe's book disappeared: but Malory was a debatable case. Sir Philip Sidney admired him, but in the 1560s Ascham in his *Scholemaster* wrote that the *Morte Darthur* is a book whose whole pleasure

standeth in two special points, in open manslaughter and bold bawdry: in which book those he counted the noblest knights, that do kill most men without any quarrel, and committed foulest adulteries by subtlest shifts.

This is unfair to Malory, against whom the worst that could truly be said on such points is embodied in Sir Ector's lament over Lancelot '. . . thou were the truest lover of a sinful man that ever loved woman. and thou were the kindest man that ever struck with sword . . .' which is moving because it is the voice of a simple man who can, through the complexity of the religious and ethical system against which Ascham had reacted, express the paradoxical nature of the struggle for goodness.

For Ascham, a story which represents sin sympathetically even ending in contrition, does not do what it is literature's duty to do. He is beginning, as Derek Brewer puts it, to feel 'that demand for naturalistic plausibility and didactic morality that Malory does not show, but is as strong in D.H. Lawrence as in Ben Jonson'. The *Morte Darthur* is not a novel: nor does it respect other, non-religious, canons of Ascham's generation, notably of decorum. There has been much debate as to whether it is a unity or simply an accumulation of Arthurian romances. It is rather a pointless debate: for Malory makes it clear that not all parts of the book have reached a final state – 'who that will make any more, let him seek other books of King Arthur, or of Sir Lancelot or Sir Tristram. For this was drawn by a knight prisoner, Sir Thomas Malory, that God send him recover. Amen'. It is the most economical supposition that the last phrase means that he was not only in prison but he was also sick; and that the reason why the book of Sir Tristram is unfinished is that he died.

But indeed the *Morte Darthur* stands at the boundary of the book as we understand it, the printed book with a defined text, author and date of publication. Of unity Malory is careless. Yet in other respects his book is of the kind that printing would make normal. For several centuries the art of the romance writer had been to interlace his stories, in the manner of a present day television serial and for the same reason, because the whole book was told in episodes, and each strain of the story was to be kept going in each episode. Malory is writing for private reading; as normally with technological innovation, printing did not create an appetite and a taste, but responded to it. So he already does what a writer for the printing press would do: undoes the old-fashioned interlacing, quickens the pace, and tells the various strains of his romance in larger blocks.

The growth of a reading public is evidenced in other works of Malory's time: in the development, by Reginald Pecock (c.1395–c.1460) and Sir John Fortescue (1394?–1477/9) of an English prose which accurately expresses theological and political thought: in the writing of letters, by the Pastons (in the third quarter of the fifteenth century) and others, which at least in odd sentences, try to entertain as well as inform correspondents and perhaps by the fourth surviving cycle of mystery plays, the *N-town* (mid-fifteenth century), which was attached to no town and therefore not preserved in written form by civic pride: it has a more definitely theological concern than the other three had, evinced in the introduction of allegorical figures, and in places has stage directions long enough to amount to brief narratives. In short, although as actable as the rest, in the form it takes in our manuscript, it may have been designed for private reading.

When, therefore, about 1470, William Caxton (c.1421–91) began translating the *History of Troy* from the French, he was part of an existing movement for providing reading matter in an already traditional context. And it is of great importance that his tastes and practices remained traditional when, having learnt printing in Cologne, he published his *History of Troy* in Bruges in 1473/4 – the first book printed in English: and when he set up his press in the precincts of Westminster Abbey in 1476. His first large printing enterprise was *The Canterbury Tales*, and he continued to mingle free translation and redaction in the medieval manner in producing such books as his translation of the endlessly fascinating *Golden Legend* of the lives of the saints, and his redaction of the *Morte Darthur*, in which, as we have already mentioned in dealing with alliterative verse, he halved Malory's version of the alliterative *Morte Arthure*. To a large extent he must have confirmed or created a taste that would, at least in imagination, fulfil the appeal he makes in the preface to the *Morte Darthur*, and the epilogue to *The Order of Chivalry* (1484): 'Then let every man that is come of noble blood and entendeth to come to the noble order of chivalry read this little book and do thereafter in keeping the lore and commandments therein composed'. He laid the foundations for *The Faerie Queene* and much else in the English tradition.

Whether there was such a continuity in the Scottish tradition is a question which goes beyond our period. One might think so in considering how exactly Byron's description of Robert Burns fits William Dunbar (?1460–after 1513),

What an antithetical mind! – tenderness, roughness – delicacy, coarseness – sentiment, sensuality – soaring and grovelling, dirt and deity – all mixed up in that one compound of inspired clay.

Tenderness is the only one of these qualities which it is hard to find in Dunbar. It is characteristic of Dunbar's extremity whether in lamentation, abuse, obscenity or celebration that he should in his *The Golden Targe* praise Chaucer for his 'fresch anamalit termes celicall', for fresh, enamelled and celestial are the qualities of his own high style much more than of Chaucer's.

Robert Henryson, somewhat earlier, with equally characteristic sobriety describes Chaucer's 'terms' only as 'gudelie', yet he drew at least as much from Chaucer as Dunbar did, and specially in the poem from which this phrase comes, *The Testament of Cresseid*. There he fulfils the need which many readers of *Troilus and Criseyde* feel, when Criseyde has faded from the immediate scene and we are left in painful identification with Troilus, to know something more of her from within. But Henryson's world is in some ways much more extreme than Chaucer's (as is Dunbar's): in place of Chaucer's gentle 'I wolde excuse hire yet for routhe', there is for Criseyde an infinitely pathetic last sight of Troilus, and a bitter suffering, concerning which readers debate whether it is punitive, or perhaps, with an uncompromising mercy, purgatorial.

The extremity and energy of Scots medievalism means that it encounters the Renaissance on level terms. Gavin Douglas's translation of Virgil's *Aeneid* is what the *Aeneid* never received before from all its medieval admirers, a scholarly translation bearing witness to the conviction of the Renaissance that the classical world is long dead and can only be resurrected. Yet Douglas naturalises his translation as Chaucer or any other medieval writer would have done in the conviction that they were simply continuing the life of

Virgil and of Rome. And his prologues to the books of the *Aeneid* give such a richness to the conventions of natural description as rivals the Gawain-poet and has no real parallel in English before the nineteenth century.

Despite the continuity that established itself with the Elizabethans, contemporary English poetry has neither the extremity nor the assurance of the Scots. In Stephen Hawes' verse (c.1474–c.1523) Renaissance allegory piles itself on medieval fine pictures and wholly inadequate words and metre. The superabundance of material in his mixture of chivalric romance and various allegory would have to wait till Spenser's poetic diction for a language. John Skelton (c.1464–1529) has abundant life: but the admiration which in the twentieth century he has received as 'helter-skelter John' from Robert Graves and W.H. Auden perhaps witnesses to the need he shares with them to take drastic measures in releasing himself from a proliferating growth of traditions: in his case, of allegory and morality, clerkly wit and courtly praise. In the mixture of nursery and *eros*, charm and impudence of *Philip Sparrow*, perhaps one might not be wrong in finding the similarly drastic measures of Betjemanic irony.

But there are also achievements of simplicity in England at this time; there are the border ballads, there is the play *Everyman* (c.1500), the austerity of whose vision of death as a stripping off of everything but good deeds finds an appropriate medium in a verse more nervous and terse than anything earlier surviving from English drama: and there are such verses as

> Western wind, when wilt thou blow
> The small rain down can rain.
> Christ if my love were in my arms
> And I in my bed again.

The last beautifully implies both a story (a voyager or soldier waiting, perhaps in hardship, for the right wind to take him home) and an analogy (drought, waiting for rain) with something of the same way of implication as 'Now goth sonne under wod' 250 years earlier: but the effect is more internalised, both physically and emotionally: there is nothing visual, rather it works in the stomach and the muscles. In the earlier poem too, the story was known and religious, here it is obscure and private. Something was appearing which the metaphysicals will develop.

But both little poems set one longing: both in their various ways exemplify the dominant philosophy of the whole Middle Ages as we have seen them – summed up in 1484 by Richard Methley, whom I have already quoted for something enduringly medieval, his recommendation of St Godric's hymns, and for something late medieval, the violent physicality of his piety,

The final concern of everything that is made is to love and be loved.

Misericords from St Lawrence's Church, Ludlow, Shropshire.
Top Some form of street entertainment: a grotesque harridan and her attendants.
Centre A dishonest ale-wife being cast into Hell, while the Devil reads a list of her misdemeanours.
Bottom The antelope gorged and chained, and the Green Man.

4 Festive Culture in Country and Town

RICHARD AXTON

An account of the popular culture of medieval England – of the games and the traditional ceremonies of the illiterate majority – can be pieced together only with difficulty. Fortunately, a framework to which the miscellaneous shreds of evidence can be attached survives in the Church calendar of holy days. For most people these were times of recreation. By King Alfred's ecclesiastical laws (AD 876) men were protected from work obligations on the twelve days of Christmas, on seven days each side of Easter, for a week at the Assumption of the Virgin and on All Saints Day. In the time of Edward I (c.1274) labourers enjoyed also eight days at Pentecost (Whitsun). These periods of sacred emphasis were times of concentrated social activity – processions, feasting, dancing and game-playing. They were also times of licence. Freedom from arrest for debt and trespass was granted to citizens of Grimsby in 1481 between Christmas Eve and Plough Day, at Candlemas, from Shrove Tuesday to Easter, on three days at Pentecost, at Corpus Christi and Midsummer. Licence to pursue 'honest mirth and game sports' was – to judge from the stream of ecclesiastical condemnations of drunkenness, obscene songs, 'filthy shows', wild dancing in churchyards, and 'diabolic' practices – often (perhaps usually) overleaped.

Bishops' decrees, penitential manuals, and parish sermons offer an unsympathetic and often maddeningly unexplicit viewpoint on this twilight world. But condemnations are not the only evidence. Civic guild records, chronicles, court rolls, churchwarden's accounts show that professional entertainers – minstrels, dancers, mimic performers – were busy from Anglo-Saxon times to the Reformation. Payments for their services tend to cluster around the major festivals. Some popular seasonal practices can be surmised from the idealisations in courtly romances and from motifs in the earliest English and Anglo-Norman play texts. The scenarios of some of the scurrilous *choreae* (chain-dances or ring-dances) may be reconstructed from surviving song refrains. Visual evidence, painting or carving, is often casual or concealed – the playful marginalia in a manuscript or a misericord beneath the lip of a choir stall – and is difficult to interpret. Cult objects, like Maypoles, dragons and giants, as well as masks and carnival costumes, have generally not survived wear and tear and the hostility of a Reformed Church. Like the painted crucifixes, gilded saints' shrines, the Easter Sepulchres and mechanical doves found in pre-Reformation parish churches, such properties could provide a kind of 'script', a rationale and focus for a ceremony or play.

The hobby horse is an interesting example. It survives as a child's toy, and in the Mari Lwyd (?grey mare) of twentieth-century Glamorganshire Christmas customs; less innocently, in the Padstow (Cornwall) 'Teaser' of May Day. Hobby horses were a favourite medieval amusement for all seasons and are found capering in most walks of medieval life. But, although the hobby horse is recognisably a single festive idea – a plan for a performance – its social and seasonal manifestations are very various. Appearing first in fourteenth-century Wales, the medieval hobby horse could assume various forms: a stick horse, or a mock-tournament horse worn by the rider with a hooped skirt concealing his own legs, or a ghastly decorated horse-skull whose moveable jaws were activated by a sheeted performer. All three versions required 'riding' and exacted money from bystanders. An early Tudor hobby horse painted in a Staffordshire manor window (1509–36) consorts with Morris dancers, Maid Marion and Friar Tuck, and holds a collecting ladle in his mouth. Before the Reformation many parish churches kept a hobby horse and the money it raised was often spent to buy candles to burn at Christmas or Easter vigils. The horse cloth, brightly painted with flower and butterfly designs, was probably in the same style of decoration as the hangings round the Easter Sepulchre. Itinerant professionals, virtuosi acrobats, sometimes had live 'hobby horses'. In city Midsummer shows, such as those of Coventry, Chester and London, hobby horses went in procession with dragons, camels, and pole-borne man-and-wife giants. A sixteenth-century London pageant showed twelve, ridden by boys with pasteboard helmets and little flashing swords, prancing in combat, six against six.

In contrast to these orderly civic 'shows', summer festivals in country parishes could be occasions of misrule, when hobby horses ran amok. An Elizabethan Puritan observes how the 'wild heads' of the parish, after crowning their 'king of misrule' and being invested by him in green and yellow spring colours, with ribbons, laces, rings and bells,

then marche these heathen company towards the Church and Church-yard, their pipers pipeing, their drummers thundring, their stumps dancing, their bells jyngling, their handkerchefs swinging about their heds like madmen, their hobby horses and other monsters skirmishing amongst the route.

(Phillip Stubbes, *The Anatomie of Abuses*, 1583)

Like 'devils incarnate' they dance and mock their way through sermon and prayers before banqueting in the churchyard in their 'sommer-haules' or 'bowers'. Sunday was not yet the Sabbath.

The variations noted here of practice, of seasonal timing, and of scale between cathedral city and country parish complicate the notion of a festive calendar observed throughout Britain. Regional differences of practice might relate to the chief means of livelihood: return to work after New Year,

Morris dancers, from a window in the house of George Tollet at Bettley, Staffordshire (c.1509–36).

celebrated on Plough Monday in an East Midland agricultural village, might take the form of women's spinning ceremonies on Rock (i.e. distaff) Monday in wool-raising Suffolk; while in a fishing port such as Hull the 'plough' was a wheeled pageant-ship. Processions and work-songs in a Welsh cemetery, described by Gerald of Wales at the end of the twelfth century, mimed the driving of oxen to plough, shoe-making, and spinning. Village festivals centred on church and churchyard, on parish boundaries with their special trees, stones or wells; the practices were primarily participatory, often 'magical', performed to bring good luck or avert bad. Cathedral cities, with multiple public square and churches, having civic officers and trade guilds as well as religious bodies, and being used to catering for visitors, developed large-scale spectacular and processional forms; city festivals were occasions of display and expense.

The Middle English words 'game' and 'play' include a wide range of pleasurable social activity, from amorous dances and children's amusements to sacred dramas. Many of these forms have an ambivalent aspect, for festivals both sacred and profane.

The Church calendar itself was the result of long negotiation with the pagan world, with solstices and equinoxes, the farming seasons of the Celtic grazing and Anglo-Saxon agricultural years, local cults, to produce a regular rhythm of festivity. There seem to have been seven periods of special excitement and distinct social activity: Christmas–New Year, Shrovetide, Easter, May, Midsummer, Harvest, Winter. The periods of 'cycles' varied from a day or two to a few weeks' duration. Each had distinct aspects in itself and in relation to other times of festival.

The twelve days of Christmas, stretching over the pagan midwinter festival of Yule and the New Year Saturnalia revels, focused renewal on the figure of the holy child: Nativity (25 December), Holy Innocents (28 December), Circumcision (1 January), and Epiphany (6 January). Plays of the Shepherds and of the Three Kings were traditional by the thirteenth century at York Minster. Gift-giving was echoed in courtly society, while the theme of child king was parodied in the revels courts of Lords of Misrule, Christmas Princes and Boy Bishops. The customs of different social groups could readily combine: in 1415 Winchester College paid men from Ropley village for singing and dancing before the Boy Bishop on Innocents' Day. Widespread practices, in which 'children being strangely decked and apparelled to counterfeit priests, bishops and women, and so to be led with songs and dances from house to house blessing the people and gathering money, and boys do sing mass and preach in the pulpit', were suppressed at the Reformation.

Christmas was principally an indoor time of feasting in common. The idealised courtly world described in *Sir Gawain and the Green Knight* (c.1400) with its mirth and minstrelsy, its toasts of 'Nowel' and 'New Year', its ritual exchanges of gifts, had a counterpart in humbler life. A shepherd or labourer in service usually had Christmas rights of feast (*gestum*) and drink (*medale*) at his lord's expense. Like William Brygge of Wells diocese in 1314, he would have to bring his own cloth and wooden trencher, but might take

Stilt walking.   *Boys riding hobby horses.*

from the feasting for himself and his neighbours 'one wastel [cake] cut in three for the ancient Christmas game to be played with the said wastel'.

Other, darker customs survived from pagan practice: the wearing of beast skins and animal heads in nocturnal visits forbidden by eighth- and ninth-century bishops, persisted in the fourteenth century (colour plate 4). Wearing masks (visors) and false heads was thought particularly devilish. A century of prohibitions culminates in a London order of 1418:

No manere persone, of what astate, degre, or condicioun that ever he be, duryng this holy tyme of Christemes be so hardy in eny wyse to walke by nyght in eny manere mommyng, pleyes, enterludes, or eny other disguisynges with eny feynyd berdis, peyntid visers, diffourmyd or colourid visages in eny wise.

Such practices may have concerned the 'expulsion of winter', a custom referred to in Bury St Edmunds (1369/70) and as old as the ninth century. The element of uncouth violence in actual Christmas feasts can surprise us. At the Inner Temple during one sixteenth-century St Stephen's Day feast (26 December) a huntsman in green entered the hall with 'nine or ten couple of hounds', which chased and devoured a cat and a fox tied to each end of a pole. The Christmas challenge of the Green Knight in the Middle English romance, his beheading and survival in a Christmas 'game' or 'enterlude', has been interpreted as evidence for a medieval tradition of mumming plays. In the Victorian rural folk-plays (which may be survivals of that tradition) the action usually begins with the formula, 'In comes I, a champion bold' and included combat, death, and miraculous revival. Possibly the preferred Middle English spelling *enterlude* indicates as association of such plays with *entering* a hall from outside, the invasion of cosy indoor space by demonic creatures from the dark outdoor world.

Mummers' plays may have originated in the games of medieval labourers
'offered' to their lords or at church at season feasts, in return for reward,
usually food and drink. Villagers drawing the plough about the fire and into
church at Epiphany were rewarded by Durham Priory (1378, 1413) for a
practice condemned as superstitious by the moral fifteenth-century author of
Dives et Pauper. A Scots 'Song of the Pleugh', surviving in three-part music
from about 1500, describes an intriguing dance ceremony performed by
plough 'hinds' for their 'laird', to whom they offer service in return for
pasturage rights. In the action of this drama a tired 'old ox', impersonated by
the leader of the revels, is 'broded' to death by the sticks of a circle of
dancers. The ox-head is removed from the man and set on a 'new ox';
members of the team, called by rustic or heroic names, are renamed as oxen
and are bound together before the plough. The company is blessed and the
team moves off. Here the play is an 'offering', its archaic action expressing
the death of the old, the blessing of the new, as the participants affirm their
social bonds, their obligations and rights. For labouring men such ceremonies
marked the end of Christmas holidays, while at court and the universities the
leisurely festive season for plays extended till Candlemas (2 February) or
even Shrove Tuesday.

Shrovetide, the second period of festival, corresponded to *carnevale* (putting
away of the flesh) in the Latin countries. Food was important, but not, as at
Christmas, in sociable indoor feasts; rather it was a theme for public display
and aggression. Shrove Tuesday, back to back with Ash Wednesday,
epitomised the conflict of youth with authority, the notion of a 'last fling'
before Lent. In twelfth-century London, boys staged cock-fights or threw
cocks at each other during the morning and played football in the afternoon.
In schools the custom of 'barring out' the schoolmaster is thought to go back
at least to the fifteenth century. The morality play *Mankind*, written for
touring in East Anglia, preaches a Lenten theme, enlivened by youthful
gymnastics, parodies of prayer and shrift, digging and dunging, antic
mockery of ecclesiastical authority, scatological obscenities.

Cock-throwing with a stick.

Civic pageants were, as usual, more decorous. Norwich city records describe a show of 1443 and say that such 'disporte is customary in any city or burough thrugh all this realm on Fastyngong Tuesday'. There, a certain John Gladman

made a disporte with his neighburghs having his hors trapped with tyneseyle and otherwyse dysgysyn things, crowned as King of Kristmesse in token that all merthe shuld end with the twelve monethes of the yer, afore hym eche moneth disgysed after the seson therof, and Lenten cladde in white with redde herrings skinnes and his hors trapped with oyster shelles after him in token that sadnesse and abstinence of merth shuld followe and an holy tyme.

Compared to the battles of Lent and Carnival, the burning of straw effigies, ritual humiliation of cuckold husbands, and scatological excesses of *Fastnachtspiele* documented in continental Europe, English Shrovetides seem to have been very restrained.

Holy Week, the third festive cycle, included the climax and turning point of Christian celebrations in a spring feast of renewal. In the eighth century the venerable Bede derived 'Easter' from Eostre, the Anglo-Saxon goddess of Spring. (It needs to be remembered that the medieval calendar was thirteen days ahead of ours, so that spring and greenery would have been more advanced.) Homilist John Mirk, Augustinian canon in Shropshire (c.1400), interprets Astyr-day with reference to hearth (*astyr*) customs: cleaning out winter ashes and arraying the hearth 'with green rushes and sweet flowers strawed all about' symbolises spring-cleaning of the soul. Branches of green were sanctified and carried in procession about church and precincts on Palm Sunday, a liturgical observance accompanied by singing, bell-ringing and sermons. A friar's verse monologue survives from about 1300, connected with Palm Sunday procession at a southern cathedral; he preaches in the person of 'Bishop Caiaphas', recommending shrift and begging money. In remoter parts celebrations could be more primitive. A thirteenth-century priest at Lanercost (Cumbria) joined his Easter to rites of Priapus,

compelling the young girls of the village to engage in *choreae* in honour of Father Bacchus, while he bore aloft on a pole before the dancers a representation of the human organs of reproduction. Dancing himself, he stirred the spectators to wantonness by mimic action and shameless speech.

The sexual aspect of the festival, acknowledged in the remarkable Sarum Easter Vigil rite for blessing of the Paschal Candle at the font, is apparent in popular and courtly games. Court ladies 'caught' Edward I in bed one Easter morning and exacted an unspecified forfeit. Early fifteenth-century prohibitions of 'contests and struggles of men and women' and of 'boys and girls, with cakes and kisses as prizes' are illuminated by the fifteenth-century Coventry practice of 'hocking'. On Hock Monday (a week after Easter) the women roamed about in gangs to catch and bind with ropes any man they found, exacting a forfeit for his release. On Hock Tuesday the men retaliated and 'hocked' the women. Love games and the motifs of capture, choice of mates, binding and release, recur through the spring customs that stretch through May Day to Midsummer.

May Day, unlike Easter, proved resistant to consecration. Popular practices marked the 'coming in' of medieval summer by focusing on the return of green to the earth and on choosing sexual partners. In 1244 the Bishop of Lincoln complained of clergy who put on 'games called inductions of May or of Autumn'. The wooing song, 'Colle to me [?embrace me with] the rysshys grene', gave offence to clergy worried about the safety of girls whose hands were tied with rush rings. Robert Mannyng, English author of *Handlyng Synne* (1303), complains of beauty contests and the garlanding of young women in 'gatherings for lechery'. Game-songs allowed a soloist 'bele Aelis' to deck herself with garlands and choose a lover from the circle of dancers, who are urged in one version to protect her from a jealous husband, 'that old man'. Preachers' tales of unwary dancers, as at Kolbeck seized in churchyards by the devil or Death, may have given rise to the fourteenth-century Dance of Death.

Later in the Middle Ages, priests allowed 'Mays' – arbours of green leaves – to be built against church walls in return for money collected by performers, who might bring 'their May' from a neighbouring village. Plays and 'vulgar comedies' of Robin Hood are recorded in Scotland (1437) and in Devon from 1426 onwards. A fragmentary text from about 1475, possibly from Norfolk, contains simple, formulaic dialogue of a play concerning Robin's killing of Sir Guy, and the Sheriff of Nottingham's capture and binding of Robin's men. Robin and Guy compete at bow-shooting, casting stones, heaving the axletree, at wrestling and sword-fight. After killing his opponent Robin dresses in Guy's clothes, cuts off his head and carries it in his hood. A post-Reformation text 'very proper to be played at May games' makes much of Friar Tuck's sexual prowess in winning Robin's 'lady'. In the nine men's morris (plus hobby horse) depicted in the Staffordshire window (p. 143), the Lady wears a crown and holds a flower, while the wanton friar dances, a (rush?) garland in his hand.

The Midsummer cycle may be thought of as stretching from Rogation-tide (Monday, Tuesday, and Wednesday before Ascension), through Pentecost to St John the Baptist's Day on Midsummer Eve (24 June). Rogation or Gang (going) week was marked by public processions with bells, branches, and garlands of milkwort, around parish and field boundaries, to protect the new crops and confirm territories. Rogations, originally supplications 'against earth shaking', had anciently been occasions for games, horse races and feasting. 'Beating the bounds' had a strong magical element, too. John Mirk explains in his *Festial* that 'the fiends that fluttereth in the air' are the cause of human disasters and 'bloweth down houses, steeples and trees'. Ringing bells, carrying banners and crucifixes scare the fiends from the crops. In Wells diocese in 1400 a Rogation Dragon was carried for the same purpose. In thirteenth-century Devon processions round the corn with firebrands belonged to Midsummer Eve.

At the solstice itself it seems to have been the shortness of night rather than the length of day which was celebrated in popular customs, all of them outdoors. The liturgical motifs of Pentecostal fire and Baptismal water were echoed in the popular season rituals. Nocturnal wakes and bonfires, dancing, bathing, and feasting were traditional at Barnwell in London in 1295. At Winchelscombe, leaping over fires and rolling flame wheels – perhaps to 'keep the sun up' – were said in the fifteenth century to be 'very ancient'. John Mirk explains in his *Festial* of homilies that Midsummer heat causes aerial dragons to couple, and that 'the froth of their kind' falling into ponds causes sickness in men and cattle; St John's fires are made of wood and bones (bones-fires) and their stench averts the danger. The practice was hazardous, and the Lanercost chronicle records in 1288 that the Ascension fires got out of control and burned down the church. In the cities, doorways were shaded with green birch and flowers, and lamps burned all night. Standing watches in every ward and street wore 'bright harness' (armour); marching watches paraded through principal streets with huge lanterns (cressets) slung on long poles from their shoulders.

During the daytime, a biographer of Becket's records, twelfth-century London organised sports, javelin and stone-throwing, archery, wrestling and fighting with bucklers. Church-men thought some of the activities unsuitable for clerical participation: Robert Mannyng (1303) disapproved of clerics playing summer 'miracles' 'by ways and groves'. In 1250 Oxford University forbade its students from wearing masks and garlands of greenery and flowers in summer processions. But there was also some clerical compromise. Performance of a play of the Resurrection, c.1220 in the churchyard at St John's Beverley at Ascension, mentions that the actors were 'masked as usual' and that performance was 'on the *north* side of the church' (often thought of as 'the devil's side').

The playing of 'king and queen' games, condemned by the Bishop of Worcester in 1240, and the garlanding of a 'summer king', known from the fourteenth century in Scotland, were apparently unruly and may have had a subversive, parodic element. Actual 'coronations' usually took place at Pentecost and some medieval kings (Edgar, William I and II, Henry I, Edward III) made public crown-wearings almost an annual event.

Wrestling for the prize of a cock.

The outdoor nature of Midsummer rites is emphasised by records of leafy bowers, play 'houses' and 'castles'. These could be tents or pavilions such as the guilds of York, Ripon and Beverley set up for their members. Emulation of royal pageantry, the sort of spectacular which set the scene for Richard II's or Henry V's French marriage treaties, may have been a significant bourgeois motive here. 'Castles' were sometimes carried in guilds' summer processions; they might form the central property for a tournament or wooing game ('maydens castle') or an outdoor devotional play (*The Castle of Perseverance, Mary Magdalene*, both fifteenth-century).

Institution of Corpus Christi (1311), to fall at its latest on 24 June, introduced into the Midsummer period a major Christian observance centred on worship of the bodily presence of Christ in the mass bread. Processions between churches to display the host in city streets and squares before returning it to the altar for mass were expanded by newly formed Corpus Christi guilds, who carried crosses and banners (Ipswich 1325). Scarlet-robed and chain-bearing civic officials rode or marched with liveried guildsmen, who carried emblems of their trade or pulled tableaux vivants of sacred history. Some towns had only processions, others cycles of play 'pageants' of sacred history, divided up for separate guilds to perform at stations along a processional route during the long daylight hours. This was the characteristic form of Corpus Christi play at Chester, Coventry and York. Smaller scale Corpus Christi interludes toured in East Anglia. A fifteenth-century play from Croxton (Norfolk) demonstrates the miraculous properties of the host by spectacular stage tricks, and combines the folk-play antics of a quack doctor and his servant with a solemn Corpus Christi procession.

Abolition of Corpus Christi at the Reformation and civic reorganisation of the plays at Whitsun (Pentecost) may have freed some secular elements to join the old Midsummer shows. At Chester, the 'Midsummer Watch' and fair at St Werburgh's were very ancient and included a dragon called 'Graull', 'naked boys' and a feathered devil riding horseback. There was exchange between the sacred and secular festivals: the tableau of 'a man in womans apparell, with devils attending there, called "cups and cans"' turns up as a scene in the Cooks' and Tapsters' play of the *Harrowing of Hell*. The Chester Alewife, shouldered off to hell by lascivious demons for watering the beer and selling short measure with her 'cups and cans', is preserved in a misericord carving of 1447 at St Lawrence's Church, Ludlow (p. 140).

In remote western Cornwall, the great three-day fifteenth-century play, *Ordinalia*, seems never to have been attached to Corpus Christi, but to have been played in summer in an ancient earthen 'round' (*plen an gwary*: the place of the play). Here, a poetic, Cornish-language treatment of Old and New Testament history was enlivened by comic torturers who were expert in Cornish wrestling and by minstrels who invited the audience to dance for the Resurrection.

Harvest. The crowded half-year of liturgical observances ended by Midsummer, leaving the second half free from major Christian feasts. It may be that a lack of tension, an absence of intense feeling for the sacredness of feast days in late summer and autumn, explains the relative paucity of clerical

Comic Devils fetch away Pilate's body in the Cornish play Resurrexio *(fifteenth century).*
(Modern performance University of Bristol Drama Department.)

condemnations at these times of year. 'Harvest', the August period of modern
summer holidays, passed in leisurely manner with a scattering of saints' days,
markets and fairs, grouped about the feast of the Assumption (15 August). 1
August, Lammas (loaf mass, with bread baked from the first new grain)
marked the beginning of the cycle which ran till Michaelmas (29 September)
with parish feasts, the renewing of labour and land tenures, and the drawing
up of accounts. It was a period of harvest suppers, church 'ales' and vigils on
the eves of local saints' days. Vigils particularly attracted the familiar
episcopal condemnations: Worcester (1240) forbade dancing in cemeteries;
York (1367), games at saints' vigils; London (1308) tried to incorporate
cemeteries to prevent women's unruly *choreae* and obsequies of the dead;
Hereford (1385) uprooted a tree by a spring with a bird's nest to which
people had been bringing offerings. Weddings and funeral wakes incurred
similar admonitions against bawdy songs and round-dances and (Worcester
1229) against 'throwing about of the corpse'.

en fruie el ual de iofafaille er oment al re tyr le refferduré
r en a   la fure gentui nonrier le uofift a altranore.

Dancers with beast heads.

Winter. The dead were the theme of the seventh and final period of the festival year. The double church feast of All Hallows and All Souls (1 and 2 November) fell upon the Celtic *Samhain* or New Year and, with prayers for the souls of the departed, attempted to consecrate the older pagan practices: putting out food for dead ancestors, wakes in cemeteries, bonfires, torch bearing, mask-wearing to frighten off spirits, the burning of effigies (as at Guy Fawkes). Slaughter of cattle brought in from grazing provided beef for Martinmas feasts (11 November) with their associated apple-roasting. And so the process of wasting the year's winnings began in earnest at this darkest time of year. Advent, at the beginning of December, marked the renewal of the liturgical calendar with ambivalent anticipation. St Nicolas (6 December) patron of schoolboys was celebrated with gifts, plays (an English verse prologue to a miracle-play of St Nicolas survives from the thirteenth century), and boy bishops. The child-centred cycle of indoor winter festival began again.

Correspondence between the cycle of the year and the 'seven ages of man' is only one of the sorts of pattern cherished by medieval calendar makers. Students of folk drama have seen the surviving mummers' plays as fragments of an ancient and coherent 'life-cycle drama'. From a different perspective we can note two halves of the year: a 'sacred half', from Advent to Pentecost, a time of anxiety, of output, sowing or spending food; and a 'secular half', from Pentecost to Advent, when living was easier, a time of gathering and storing, when the church had little of urgency to impart. Who remembers how many Sundays are in Trinity?

Aided by clocks, artificial lighting, television, newspapers, and weekends, we experience time differently, more regularly than medieval people; they were more dependent on the seasons and lived variable periods of time 'in memory of one festival and in anticipation of the next'. The medieval calendar, somewhat reformed, remains with the Church of England. Vestiges of folk custom cling to the feasts and festive periods, nourished by the church-and-pub culture of English village life by antiquarian societies, and by school children. Until the Reformation, when the Church began to be ashamed of the ruder parts of its body of customs, there seems to have existed a complex system of seasonal practices. The rhythms of this popular cultural activity came in and out of phase with the Church's liturgical preoccupations, sometimes reinforcing, sometimes opposing the sacred with the superstitious, the unruly and profane. The calendar maps the common ground on which were constructed the 'higher' art forms: sophisticated part-songs ('Sumer is icumen in'), Pentecostal tournaments or Mayings at court; courtly poems for Christmas (*Sir Gawain and the Green Knight*) or St Valentine's (Chaucer's *Parliament of Fowls*) or Midsummer (Dunbar's scurrilous *Two Married Women*); the massive and teeming structures of urban Corpus Christi plays. But this common ground is also important for itself, for it carries the traces of a popular culture which gave meaning and rhythm to everyday life by shaping it into traditional and expressive forms.

The Virgin Mary, sculptured figure in the spandrels of the Chapter House, Westminster Abbey (c.1253).

5 The Visual Arts and Crafts

T. A. HESLOP

Introduction: artists, critics, patrons and audience

'Almighty God, save thy people from erring in images.' Thus begins one of
several surviving later medieval English tracts dealing with the dangers
attendant on the use of pictures, sculpture and indeed any other sort of
elaboration in the furnishing or decoration of churches. For many reasons,
what we would now call art had more detractors than defenders in the
Middle Ages and the particular abuses that were identified at the time help to
explain much about medieval attitudes. Perhaps the most commonly cited
danger was idolatry. In the orthodox view a painting or sculpture of Christ
or one of the saints was merely a symbol. But for many of those accustomed
to praying before such an image it was too easy to forget that this was no
more than a stimulus to and channel for devotion. If the Virgin Mary
answered prayers offered before one statue of her but not another surely it
was because of some magical quality inherent in the object. As our late
fourteenth-century author put it, those of rude wit forget 'the marvellous and
precious works done by Thee and by Thy holy saints, fully believing that
images have done the works of grace and not Thee'. Some people even 'cling
firmly, stroking and kissing the old stones and pieces of wood, laying down
their great offerings and making vows right there to these dead images to
come again next year'!

Another cause of disquiet among commentators was the sheer expense
involved in making and embellishing ecclesiastical buildings and their
contents. A crucifix was obviously a worthy focus for meditation on Christ's
passion, but there was no need to 'paint it with great cost, and hang much
silver and gold and precious clothes and stones thereon . . . and suffer poor
men . . . to be thereby left naked, hungry and thirsty'. Reformers from early
Christian times (such as St Jerome) and among the new monastic orders
(notably the Cistercians in the twelfth century) made the point that money
given to the church was properly meant to help the needy and not to delight
the senses.

Against these recurrent indications of excess there was only one regularly admitted justification for imagery. It was that, for those who were unable to read, visual narratives were a valuable method of learning sacred legends and, having learnt them, keeping them fresh in the mind. Many stories were so widely known that the symbol of a wheel, for example, served not only to identify a figure as St Catherine, but would also remind the viewer of her martyrdom and the ways in which God intervened to protect her and confound her tormentors. However such representations might also mislead by telling the story incorrectly, or so that it might be misinterpreted. A common error was to show 'poor apostles of Christ, and other saints that lived in great poverty and great penance and despised in word and in deed the foul pride and vanity of this careful life . . . painted as though they had lived in wealth of this world and lusts of their flesh as large as ever did earthly man'.

Nor is it just that artists were being inadequately supervised by their religious patrons. Late fourteenth-century Lollard critics, such as the one quoted above, suggest that many of the clergy connived at these questionable uses of art because people were thereby attracted into the churches to see the results and to leave offerings: 'for to the gayest and most richly arranged images will the people offer, and not any poor image standing in a simple church or chapel, but only if it stands royally tabernacled with carving and painted with gold and precious jewels and also within a minster or great abbey'.

It is ironic that the opinion of 'heretics' like the Lollards agreed so closely with the writings of Fathers, such as St Jerome, and with the inclination of accepted reformers such as the early Cistercians. The fact that reformers and 'revolutionaries' found it worthwhile espousing these apparently unexceptionable views is evidence that, no matter what the clergy approved in writing, it was common to behave in quite a different way. Many of our more elaborate churches are filled with needless embellishment that is dogmatically irrelevant and occasionally lewd as well. One English cleric in about 1200 'struck with grief that in the sanctuary of God there should be foolish pictures, and what are rather misshapen monstrosities than ornaments' was moved to write a short treatise suggesting more appropriate subject matter. He attributed the follies he was attacking to 'the criminal presumption of painters which has gradually introduced these sports of fantasy', and adds 'which the church ought not to have countenanced . . . for it has certainly seemed to countenance what it has not ceased to support with reprehensible succour'. If it was not only against orthodox dogma but also cost money, then why did so many churchmen, great and small, act so differently in deeds than word?

Writers who favoured church embellishment were prone to quote Psalm 26 (XXV in the Vulgate): 'Lord, I have loved the beauty of thy house' (*dilexi decorem domus tuae*), without explaining why beauty meant embellishment, and to refer to the Biblical descriptions of divinely ordained ornaments in the Tabernacle and in Solomon's Temple. But the real reasons for approving 'art' seems to have been that it delighted and fascinated them.

Pure sensual pleasure was even less intellectually and theologically respectable then than it is now. As a result there is no fully developed *apologia* for it in English medieval writing. On the other hand, descriptions of buildings, rich cloth, of gold, silver and gems make clear that the appeal to the sense of sight was a major, if not the principal reason behind the creations of what we now call 'art'. William, the monk and librarian of Malmesbury, writing in the early twelfth century described an ancient treasure:

a vast palace with golden walls, golden roofs, everything of gold; . . . vessels of great weight and value, where sculpture surpassed nature herself. In the inmost part of the mansion a ruby of the first quality, though small in appearance, drove off the darkness of night [by its brilliance] . . . the exquisite art of everything ravished the eyes of the spectator.

But this did not apply just to the ancient, secular world.

We think it not enough in our holy vessels unless the heavy metal [i.e. gold] is eclipsed by precious stones; by the flame of the topaz, the violet of the amethyst, the green of the emerald; unless the priestly vestments frolic with gold [*ludent auro*] and unless the walls glisten with multicoloured paintings and throw the reflections of the sun's rays up to the ceiling.

Thus he was able to write of the 'glistening marble', the painting and stained-glass windows of the new eastern arm of Canterbury Cathedral begun in the time of Archbishop Anselm (1093–1109) – and this too 'ravished the eyes'. It is noteworthy that much of the tremendous appeal of art, as manifest in these passages, seems to depend on effects of light and colour.

With one or two exceptions, which are notable for their rarity, individual artists are not lauded in medieval texts. The quality of the material is important, but the material is seen as controlled by the abstract concept 'art'. It was sculpture itself and not the sculptor that surpassed nature on William's 'vessels of great weight', and it was 'art' not the artist that was responsible for the assault on the eye. This attitude is summed up in inscription on a mid twelfth-century enamel made for the Bishop of Winchester: 'Art comes before gold and gems'. It continues by saying that above both of these come the Author, that is God. Thus art, which is skill of any kind, descends from God, through the worker and into the object. While it was felt that a craft could be perfected by diligence, the praise ought properly to go to the Author of all things, the only true Creator. Although this attitude is never given full independent treatment by writers, it is fairly explicit in many medieval inscriptions and descriptions. It also receives Biblical support from those texts concerning the works of Bezaleel (Exodus 31, 1 ff.) and Hiram of Tyre (1 Kings 7, 13 ff.).

Another more practical reason why an individual artist's role as innovator or original genius was of little interest was simply that so much was produced by collaboration. Some objects required the participation of workers with different trades but more important than this was the role of patron. Confusion has been caused to historians by the medieval habit of giving the patron's name as the maker of something; hence 'Abbot so-and-so made me'. An alternative, which avoids ambiguity but still stresses the patron's role is 'Abbot so-and-so ordered me to be made' (inscriptions at this period nearly always refer to objects in the first person). But all in all, the important act of will was seen as coming from the moneyed customer and not from the rude mechanical who translated the commission into a finished product. Few contracts survive indicating what was asked for. Nonetheless we do occasionally hear the patron's voice. Henry III (1216–72) sent his carpenter, John of St Omer, to St Albans because he wanted the new lectern being made for Westminster Chapter House to be like the one at St Albans, or even better. This last phrase, which occurs in other contexts, is all the scope for invention the artist has to introduce an element of personal taste or originality. Other instructions are in the same vein; something is to be like a specified model, with particular modifications mentioned. It may sometimes, of course, have been an artist who prompted the patron to a certain decision. Henry III, the greatest patron of the visual arts ever to occupy the English throne, was persuaded by his artistic adviser, Edward of Westminster, to have two lions made for his throne from bronze rather than marble 'because bronze is more magnificent'. Usually, though, the person ordering work must have had the first and last say. In the contract for the tomb of Sir Ralph Greene, a fortuitous survival from the early fifteenth century, his widow stipulates among other things that the two alabaster carvers in Derbyshire should show the effigies of herself and her late husband holding hands. And so indeed they appear on their monument at Lowick in Northamptonshire. It is hard to imagine any circumstances under which the sculptors would unilaterally have taken the decision to include such a feature.

If talent was God's doing and the will and guidance were the patron's, it left very little with which to credit the artist. Furthermore, if a work was particularly startling or complex in its form, or if it had magic powers, more direct heavenly (or satanic) intervention might be suggested. Thus an early Irish Gospel Book which Gerald of Wales saw on his trip to Ireland (with Prince John) in 1185 was so subtle and beautiful that it seemed the work of angels. And in another story he tells how an impious soldier knocked the arm off a sculpture of the Christchild seated in the lap of the Virgin Mary, only to be driven insane by the sight of the real blood which poured forth. Such potency was not the work of any human agency.

The existence of these attitudes and the degree of logic we may still find in them, make it doubly difficult for us to gain an entry to the mind of 'the medieval artist', but there are perhaps two areas useful for exploration. One is seeing in what ways two closely related images differ from each other and how and why this comes about. The other is considering things which would seem to be of peripheral interest to a patron where the maker might give free rein to his own invention.

It is often said that medieval art is about copying. In fact, although there are some famous cases in England and elsewhere where a prototype is reproduced quite closely, these instances constitute a small percentage of the total output. More usually we are presented with variations on a theme. A case we can profitably examine concerns a manuscript which was painted by an artist who had a particular model in front of him. This can be demonstrated by all kinds of technical details, but suffice it to say that the sizes of the two works correspond exactly and so does the subject matter of the vast majority of the long and complex series of pictures. A few of the

Infancy scenes from an English psalter (c.1155).

scenes in the 'copy', made in about 1190 probably in Canterbury, are near replicas of the layout of their exemplar. One instance is the quite rare subject of the 'Suicide of Herod'. It is easy to suppose that here an unoriginal artist is relying on what would now be considered base plagiarism. However it is nothing so simple since in the majority of cases he behaves quite otherwise. There are two other approaches which he more commonly takes in devising this cycle. One is to substitute a new composition which nonetheless depicts the same Biblical story. Another is to take over the basic form, or a few of its constituent parts, from his model, but then to vary the rest. A case in point is the scene of the 'Massacre of the Innocents' adjacent to Herod's suicide. Although Herod still sits to the left, directing the mass-murder, the groups of mothers, infants and soldiers depart radically from the prototype. The result was, no doubt, regarded by the artist as an improvement on or modernisation of the original, which was incidentally only about thirty years old when he was asked to make a new version.

But by what means and with what purpose was this variation achieved? Although no direct answer is available in this case, so many medieval artists behaved in a comparable way that we can, by examining their more personal productions, reconstruct something the process involved. Few 'sketchbooks'

Infancy scenes from an English psalter (c.1190).

survive from the Middle Ages, but they are remarkable documents. Unquestionably the finest English example is now in Magdalene College, Cambridge, and, by virtue of its having belonged to Samuel Pepys, it is known as the Pepysian Sketchbook. In its earliest and best parts, drawn around 1400, the artist owner has noted down figures 'invented' by other masters. Some of these were already over 100 years old, whereas others were in the latest style. The thirteenth-century images that our late fourteenth-century draftsman chose to record were the product of an original genius (and genius is not too strong a word) who had worked for the English court at the end of Henry III's reign. The postures, head and hair styles,

Page of drawings from the Pepysian Sketchbook (c.1400).

gesticulating fingers reminiscent of oriental dance, are unmistakably those of a painter who illuminated an Apocalypse manuscript for the future King Edward I, c.1270. It is not however the Apocalypse that the Pepysian artist saw. In fact, we do not know from what subject he was making excerpts precisely because he only took a figure here and a pair of figures there. He was not apparently interested in whole scenes but in certain poses or groups that appealed to him either because they might be useful in other contexts or, quite simply, out of admiration and a desire to learn by imitation. His behaviour in this regard is typical of that attested by other sketchbooks, from all over Europe, from the eleventh to the fifteenth centuries.

There are analogues for this too in medieval literature, where an episode or quotation is borrowed from one context for use in another. This was occasionally explained by means of the metaphor: as a bee collects from various flowers to make sweet honey, so I /we have sought the best parts from various works to make a new composition. With this literary analogy in mind we can see what the artist of our late twelfth-century picture cycle is doing; as it were re-using some sections and 'phrases' from an earlier version while adding or inventing others. The end result expresses the narrative in an idiom better suited to the more dramatic tastes of the time.

A healthy respect for tradition combined with a love of novelty was not unique to the medieval West. Nonetheless it needs to be stressed to a modern audience because we have been persuaded over the last two centuries or so that innovation and the *personality* of the creative artist are more important than skill in retelling an old story. However it would be a mistake to imply that simple storytelling, and the production of cult images, was all that the visual arts of the Middle Ages involved. Many, more fanciful creations were, as we have seen, attributed to 'the criminal presumption of painters' and condemned as meaningless. Modern writers have tended to agree that much of the apparently decorative invention on medieval luxury products is no more than jeu d'esprit on the artists' part. But this is an oversimplification.

A dragon initial, such as that at the beginning of the Book of Job in a Bible probably made at Winchester in the 1160s, is certainly decorative but is also more than an elaborate doodle. It compares interestingly with the description of the dragon in the Bestiary, a book popular in England in the late twelfth and thirteenth centuries.

Dragon initial from the Book of Job, from a Bible made at Winchester (c.1160).

He is said to have a crest or crown because he is the King of Pride, and his strength is not in his teeth but in his tail because he beguiles those whom he draws to him by deceit, their strength being destroyed. He lies hidden round the paths on which they saunter because their way to Heaven is encumbered by the knots of their sins, and he strangles them to death. For if anybody is ensnared by the toils of crime he dies and no doubt goes to Hell.

It takes a moment to realise that all the foliage in our initial stems from the dragon's tail, and it is this which, as in the passage just quoted, traps the unwary soul like a beast. It is the particular irony of this painter's version that it is the victim who confirms the dragon's status as King, by placing on his head the crown of vice. So the unseeing soul rewards the Arch-deceiver. This contrasts with the prophet Job himself, whose humility and trust in the Lord enabled him to defeat Satan.

There are countless compositions of this type in which scrollwork ensnares the unwary. They exist as much in ivory, metalwork and stonework as they do in painting and drawing. For example, the splendid sandstone font from Eardisley in Herefordshire shows two soldiers fighting while entwined in scrollwork (demonstrating the futility of striving in the body while ignoring the soul). As if to make clear that entanglement is darkness of soul, the adjacent scene of the Harrowing of Hell shows Christ pulling a figure out of interlace instead of from the more normally shown dragon's mouth. A self-contained visual language, which makes the meaning of its own vocabulary explicit, is being devised and exploited by artists for moral as well as decorative purposes. If some critics regarded such moralising as 'meaningless' or 'criminal presumption' it may be because people generally were inclined to view such inventions as delightful and curious rather than improving and cautionary or that clerics felt that their own role as moral and spiritual guides was being usurped by a bunch of unlearned quacks.

The widespread refusal among medieval literati to give due credit to the cerebral as well as the mechanical skills of their visual artists has endured. We can still choose to see those craftsmen and women as simple-minded, subservient or merely imitative. But in doing so we fall into the trap of believing what was written rather than what was made, or allowing words to speak louder than deeds. This is not merely unrealistic but it confuses our understanding of the period and the thought processes involved in the commissioning, making and viewing of medieval art. The surest access to those thoughts is to be gained through the art itself, provided that our looking is tempered by as much socio-historical and cultural information as may be helpful in revealing the causes of the people's actions.

English Romanesque illumination

The making of a medieval manuscript of any pretensions was an undertaking of considerable expense which relied on access to a wide range of materials and skills. The preparation of animal skins for the pages was in itself a quasi-industrial process, but apart from that there was ink to be made, pigments to be acquired and then the whole business of binding, which at its most lavish

The Harrowing of Hell, from a sandstone font in Eardisley Church, Herefordshire.

involved not only thread, leather, wooden boards and all the associated tools, but in certain cases precious metals, gems, and enamel. The illuminated books which have concerned the art historian presuppose an economic and technical environment of some complexity.

It is generally assumed that books were produced by monks in monasteries, and there is probably some truth in this. However, by the 1340s, Richard d'Aungerville, the bibliophile Bishop of Durham, could write that monks had grown lazy and no longer devoted themselves to copying. Clearly, by this date the work was in other hands. But there is evidence even as early as the fifty years following the Norman Conquest that scribes were frequently secular. The Abbey of Abingdon had six paid scribes producing books for the library in the early twelfth century, and at St Albans, even earlier, money was set aside for those who worked in the scriptorium. Thus at this period, one of the greatest in terms of the quantity and quality of manuscripts written, although a monastery, or probably any large ecclesiastical establishment, might be a centre of production, it employed at least some outsiders who were specialists.

Christina of Markyate's Psalter

While the majority of the books copied in these circumstances were no
doubt intended for the use of the Church itself, some were made for the laity.
Among these none can have been more popular then the psalter – that is the
book of psalms. Not only was it the primary devotional text favoured by the
pious person in secular life, it also seems to have been used as a pre-school
educational reader. We are told in one of the biographies of Thomas Becket
that he went to school after he had learned his psalter. These two uses,
educational and devotional, explain much about the content of the English
manuscripts of this text made between about 1050 and 1170. On the one
hand a gloss, or crib, might be provided (in Old English early in the period
and French later on) to help the lay to understand the meaning of the Latin.
On the other, various additional devotional texts can be found accompanying
the psalms. These range from the canticles and a few prayers to lengthy
works such as the Hours of the Virgin or the Prayers of St Anselm.
Manuscripts could, however, promote other forms of devotional meditation
which relied not so much on words as on images. These pictorial stimuli
could show single iconic figures, or narratives from the Bible or saints' lives,
or more allegorical inventions alluding to the battle between Good and Evil.
One of the earliest books of this kind contains over 200 images, including 42
full-page paintings. It also quotes in Latin and in French translation, part of
Pope Gregory's famous letter explaining that the proper use of Christian
representational art is to help one 'to learn more [addiscere] what one should
adore'. This manuscript, variously called The Albani or The St Albans
Psalter, was written for a remarkable person, Christina of Markyate, a female
hermit who was renowned for her beauty and her spirituality.

Fortunately Christina made such an impact on contemporaries that
substantial information survives about her life, notably in a biography written
by a monk of St Albans. In the work we learn of her background, that she
came from a well-to-do family in Huntingdon, and of her decision after a
visit to St Albans to devote her life to Christ. This ambition was all but
thwarted by the malevolent Ralph Flambard, Bishop of Durham, who having
failed to seduce the girl himself persuaded her parents to marry her off to a
young man of the locality. After much misery and ill-treatment Christina
escaped from home and remained in hiding for six years, suffering more
privations for the sake of her vow. Eventually by virtue of her powerful and
attractive personality she overcame opposition and became an anchoress at
Markyate near St Albans, where she remained with a small group of
companions for the rest of her life. Her private psalter, now in Hildesheim,
enriches the view that we have of her and allows us a unique opportunity to
see the ways in which such a book was tailor-made for a particular individual
in the twelfth century.

One of the standard features of a psalter was a calendar. In it were
recorded those names of people and occasionally events which the owner
wished to commemorate on various days of the year. The majority of saints
noticed in Christina's book are those venerated at the nearby abbey. There
are additions, though, and these help to indicate her own particular interests.

Christ's deposition from the cross, from Christina's Psalter (c.1120).

A clear case is the feast of the discovery of the relics of St Ives at Ramsey, only 8 or 9 miles from Christina's family home. Also included are the obituaries of friends and relatives, added under the days of their deaths. One particular addition, for Roger the Hermit, is especially significant. For he had received and sheltered the runaway Christina during her many adventures, and it was his hermitage that she inherited. Although living the life of a hermit, he was a monk of St Albans where, we are told, the psalter was made. As well as its written entries, each calendar page carries an illustration of an appropriate 'labour' for the month in question, and a zodiac sign. For August we are shown a man with a sheaf of corn and 'Virgo'. The constellation is personified as a winged, haloed woman holding a stick with a curious spear-shaped top. In its outline this is very like the distaff which Eve carries in the nearby illustration of the Expulsion from Paradise. The relevance of this is that Christina was a needlewoman who 'embroidered three mitres and sandles of wonderful workmanship' which the Abbot of St Albans presented to Nicholas Brakespeare, the son of one of his monks, upon his elevation to the papacy as Adrian IV. The reason for the attributes of this constellation as well as for its greater size and more elaborate colour washes when compared with those of other months, seems to be that there was an assimilation between 'Virgo' and the owner of the manuscript.

Another indication of relevance to Christina's life among the original illustrations is the small picture prefacing the litany. It shows a monk with two groups of kneeling women before the Trinity. Not only was her cell at Markyate under the guidance of the monks of St Albans, but it was dedicated to the Holy Trinity.

While a calendar and a litany were commonly joined to a psalter, whether made for private or institutional use, one element of Christina's book is unique, the French prose life of St Alexis. No doubt this was included because of its parallels with her own experience. Alexis too had been betrothed, but had left his bride on their wedding night, renouncing wealth and family for the life of a pilgrim. The picture which is chosen to illustrate the story in the manuscript shows the parting of the couple, and the central caption states that 'the ultimate gifts are given to the chaste bride'. It is noteworthy that the reference here is to the woman and not to Alexis. She indeed is shown centrally and larger than the hero. Thus the picture and its main caption make patent the relevance of the Life of Alexis to Christina's vow of chastity upheld in the face of impending marriage.

Intriguing and revealing as these details are, the principal glory and interest of the manuscript lies elsewhere, in the initials to the psalms and the forty full-page miniatures which precede the text. In common with the later Copenhagen and Winchester Psalters of the 1160s, Christina's Psalter concentrates on paintings of scenes from the life of Christ. There is thus an apparent lack of relationship between the main text of the book and the main illustrations. Furthermore, the very fact that the pictures are collected together at the front, rather than being interleaved throughout the manuscript shows that particular images were not seen as counterparts to passages from the psalms themselves. In effect we have a collection of sacred poetry and prayers with no link to the pictures other than a common contemplative function.

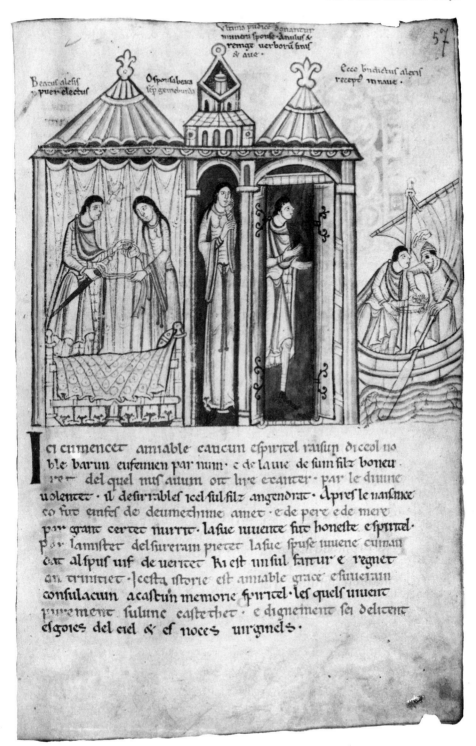

St Alexis leaving his bride to take up the life of a pilgrim, from Christina's Psalter (added c.1130).

The choice of scenes indicates something of this purpose. The first two show the 'Fall of Man' and the 'Expulsion from Paradise'. In other words we are told briefly in pictures why the Incarnation was necessary. Then comes the main subject, which is the life of Christ. There are thirteen infancy scenes followed by the Baptism, the Temptations of Christ and, more unusually, Mary (Magdalen) washing Christ's feet. Then eighteen pictures are devoted to the Passion and Resurrection. While the majority of subjects chosen are central to the theme, there are some rarities, for example, 'Mary Magdalen telling the Disciples of the Resurrection'. It is tempting to suppose that both the Mary Magdalen scenes were included because she was the prototype of the later 'handmaids of Christ' and Christina would naturally have been interested in her.

There is confirmation of this from a fascinating source. St Aelred, the Cistercian abbot of Rievaulx in Yorkshire, wrote a guide for his sister who, like Christina, had decided to become a recluse. Although this work, written some twenty or thirty years after Christina's Psalter, follows Cistercian practice in repudiating visual imagery, it lays similar stress on particular episodes from Christ's life, such as Mary washing His feet. Aelred takes his reader through select moments of the gospel story indicating the kinds of thoughts they might stimulate. In the Resurrection sequence he enjoins her to go with Mary Magdalen to buy spices. And in the garden after the visit to the tomb

thou shalt see and hear how Our Lord spoke to Mary, calling her by name 'Mary'. Oh this was a sweet voice . . . at this voice all the veins of her body dissolved and spilled out tears of sweet devotion.

It is obvious that the stress both Aelred and Christina's Psalter lay on the career of the Magdalen results from the vocation of the audience for which they were designed. In the Psalter it is possible that artistic style has been similarly adapted. The Passion scenes reveal the artist's purpose most clearly, and the Deposition (see p. 165), standing at the culmination of Christ's suffering, is perhaps the most instructive. Again there is a parallel with St Aelred who advises his sister:

if women wept beside his passion, thou must weep . . . fall down to His feet and beseech Him that His blessed passion might commend thee to His Father. . . . Seest thou not how Our Lady weepeth? Creep into that blessed side where blood and water came forth and hide you there among the rocks [cf. Song of Songs 2, 14] well liking the drops of his sweet blood till that thy lips be made red like a scarlet ribbon [cf. Song of Songs 4, 3]. Abide a while, seest thou where that noble officer cometh, Joseph of Arimethea. Stand still and see what the blessed man will do. As soon as he comes, he undoes the nails of his feet and clasps that sweet body in his blessed arms.

The weeping, swooning intimacy of these meditations finds its counterpart in the Psalter miniature. The gently undulating body and limbs of Christ and of Joseph who receives Him have an almost languorous poignancy. The holy women, tears welling in their eyes, gaze on the wounds of His body. The range of expression is limited, but serves its purpose very well. The picture's composition achieves a slow enough tempo in its structure to encourage the viewer to consider the reactions of each participant in the scene. For by preserving a degree of neutrality in expression and action the picture allows its viewer to project a wider range of thoughts onto it. If the image were too positive it could restrict precisely that type of audience participation it was hoping to encourage.

Rather different in style and purpose from the set-piece narratives are the initials which precede every psalm and prayer in the body of the book. Their visual content is related to the words which follow, and their exhortatory nature is evident from the excited gesturing of the figures and from the text labels which they sometimes hold. In one of the initials (L) to Psalm 119 (CXVIII in the Vulgate) is a man attempting to buy the affections of a woman (as Flambard had by bringing Christina silk dresses from London). Another man points down to this scene and holds a book with the words 'turn away mine eyes from beholding vanity'. Above them all, God raises His right hand in a speaking gesture presumably in order to fulfil the first request in this section of the psalm: 'teach me, O Lord, the way of Thy statutes'. The emphasis in many of these initials, as here, is on the proper use of the senses, which are not for delight, but for seeing and hearing divine intention and transmitting this to others. Open-mouthed, brandishing forefingers at ears, eyes, tongue or forehead, or pointing at salient words in the adjacent text, these figures, often in contemporary dress, stress the continuing relevance of the psalms as guides to right-minded thought and action.

The initial L to Psalm 119, from Christina's Psalter (c.1120).

We have in these initials the work of an artist of a very different temper from the one who designed and executed the full-page narratives. There is no doubting that both kinds of work could have acted as suitable stimuli to Christina's fervour, but it is a salutary reminder that the persuasion of two artistic personalities might be poles apart, even when they were working together on a single project.

We have no means of knowing how exceptional this psalter was in the degree of its adaptation to the taste and circumstances of its owner. At the very least some of the symptoms just analysed alert us to ways in which such books could be tailored for an individual. But the importance of this manuscript is far more wide-reaching. The artistic standard of the paintings and drawings, their innovatory and influential styles, and the insistence they place, by implication, on visual stimuli for devotional practices are striking departures from or extensions of earlier English tradition. Indeed the illumination has been seen as initiating attitudes which persisted for the rest of the Middle Ages. It is easy to be seduced by the 'masterpiece mentality' which claims such as these imply. To achieve a balanced view of the place of the book in an environment which was, after all, scarcely revolutionary in any sense that we understand, it is helpful to consider another very different work which is more or less contemporary

The Bury Bible

The rebuilding of the Benedictine Abbey of St Edmund at Bury had begun about 1082. By the 1120s it was nearing completion and the Abbot, Prior and Sacrist were free to turn their attentions to supplying those embellishments with which wealthy religious houses made their environment more beautiful and awe-inspiring. One of their most daring and costly enterprises must have been the bronze doors for the west front of the church. Although there are isolated instances of bronze doors being made before 1050, the Romanesque fashion for them seems to have spread from Italy where Byzantine doors had become a popular luxury import. There can have been few craftsmen in the north of Europe with the experience, or failing that the confidence, to undertake casting on this scale. However the community of St Edmund procured the services of an artist with the requisite skill. His name was Hugo. Needless to say, the doors which he made have long since been melted down, but of them we are told that as in all his works he outstripped his fellows, so in these doors he surpassed even himself.

But Hugo was not just a metalworker. The *Gesta Sacristarum*, a book of the achievements of the sacrists of Bury, tells us that he carved images of the Crucifix, the Virgin Mary and St John for the choir of the Abbey – these were presumably large figures suspended as a group above the screen – and he illuminated a Bible. The first part of this latter work survives and fully justifies the comment in the record that it was 'incomparably painted'. The Bury Bible was commissioned by the Prior, Talbot, but paid for out of the revenues of the Sacrist's office, occupied at the time by his brother Hervey. Fortunately their tenures of office can be dated, from about 1125 to 1137 or 8. Thus we know within reasonable bounds when the project was undertaken.

The initial E, from the Bury Bible (c.1125–37).

Something of the tenor of Hugo's professionalism is also apparent from the documents. For when he could not get vellum to his liking in the vicinity, he procured some from Scotland. This hint that Hugo was technically fastidious is more than borne out by his work on the Bible itself. The pigments are of a previously unrivalled purity and refinement and the paint is applied with such evenness and subtlety of blending that brushmarks are practically invisible. Colour was a great concern, for rather than modelling forms strongly in highlight and shadow, which would have broken up and obscured the intense hues of his palette, Hugo tended to use only a small amount of muted lighting and shading. To compensate for the loss of relief that might have resulted, he employed a device for disposing the folds of the garments which was becoming familiar in western Europe at the time. This trick, known as damp-fold drapery, was of Byzantine derivation and involved representing cloth as though it was clinging smoothly to the body in some areas while forming angled or curving folds elsewhere. With skill these folds, which in Hugo's case are rather like bent pipes, could be drawn so that they seemed to disappear round the backs of forms (legs, shoulders and so on) and thus create an illusion of three-dimensionality. However, while Byzantine artists usually combined 'damp-fold' with a full tonal range from dark to light, Hugo was concerned to leave his colour as rich and pure as possible.

In the twelfth century the use of a particular combination of colours might be unique to one artist, who probably 'invented' one or more of the pigments himself. With the exception of an artist who worked on The Winchester Bible, and who may have been his pupil, this is true of Hugo. This argues that quite apart from the care he obviously took in the mundane chores of grinding and mixing ingredients, he devoted some time to what might be called research and development.

Apart from the quality of his materials and the fluent minuteness of his technique there are other hints in his work on the Bible which demonstrate Hugo's artistic priorities. One of these is a love of variety. Among the group of Israelites before Moses we see not only different poses, but a particularity about, for example, complexion which is unparalleled in its period (colour pl. 5). Whereas the painters of Christina's Psalter were quite happy to use the same profile and the same flesh colour for ninety per cent of their figures, indicating age merely by hair-colour and gender by hairstyle or clothing, Hugo had a far more developed sense of human types. Thus his red-head has pale skin but rosy cheeks while his dark-haired man has a swarthy complexion.

The concept of *varietas* is an important constituent of the Romanesque aesthetic and finds other expression in The Bury Bible, notably in the foliage painting. The inventiveness that is applied to developing new types of 'blossoms' in the borders of pictures but more especially in the decorated initials is remarkable (p. 171). It is difficult to find precise parallels for these forms elsewhere, and since it thus seems that Hugo did not copy them one is forced to the conclusion that he is deliberately ringing the changes so that the existing stock is hybridised into a hundred new flowers.

Hugo was an artist with priorities quite distinct from those which are found in Christina's Psalter's. One is tempted to say that he was concerned more with the medium than with the message, or even that the medium is the message. But this is perhaps not quite fair, for the subjects which he represented (a choice that was probably out of his hands) lack the emotional appeal of, for example, narratives of Christ's passion. Nonetheless, none of the Psalter's figures has the assured, almost balletic, elegance of Hugo's Moses and Aaron who walk one way and turn to face the other, inducing a fashionable curve to the hips, waist and torso. This courtly refinement, evident both in the style and the mechanics of the painting, would doubtless have been apparent no matter what image Hugo was rendering.

No comparison of the Psalter and The Bury Bible can ignore the very different purposes for which they were intended. In all likelihood the Bible was always meant for public reading in the monastic refectory where, no doubt, it would occasionally be shown to visitors eminent enough to dine there rather than in the guests' accommodation. Thus, unlike the private and very personal nature of Christina's Psalter, this book needed to be instantly stunning and self-evidently sumptuous. Its audience was more likely to spend a short time wondering at the artifice than pondering sacred mysteries prompted by its imagery.

The stained glass windows of Canterbury Cathedral, 1175–1225

Fires figure largely in the history of medieval art and architecture, and no medieval fire has become more famous than that which destroyed the east end of Canterbury Cathedral in 1174. This fire is particularly remembered because of the description of it and of the subsequent rebuilding of the choir written by the Canterbury monk Gervase. He goes into far greater detail about the progress and technical aspects of building work and the layout of the liturgical features than any other medieval writer. This considered, it is remarkable what he fails to record. Among the many lacunae is mention of what was perhaps the most ambitious glazing programme undertaken in Europe up to that date.

Gervase makes only a single reference to windows, the three that were placed in the temporary wooden screen which divided the finished part, the choir and presbytery, from the building site outside, where work on the Trinity Chapel was still in progress. It has been plausibly argued that such a concern with niceties in a temporary wall is only credible if the rest of the building which it terminated was already glazed. There is indeed the evidence of style to indicate that the monks' choir contains the earliest of the surviving glass, and although a date prior to 1180 would make it very precocious it is not unlikely that the metropolitan see of Britain would acquire the services of the best glaziers available. But before considering the artistic personalities of these designers and painters it is useful to form an overall impression of the scheme which they were to undertake.

Common sense dictated that whereas windows that were close to the ground, and thus to the viewer's eye level, could contain many complex scenes with figures on a small scale, those high up needed simpler, larger forms if they were to be read successfully from a distance. Thus in the clerestory, immediately below the vault, pairs of large figures were placed, one above the other, representing the ancestors of Christ. This sequence began at the north west extremity of the choir with Adam and proceeded via the eastern apse to the south west ending, presumably, with the Virgin and Child. At ground level in the choir aisle and in the eastern transept, New Testament subjects were shown. In many cases they were juxtaposed to thematically related episodes from the Old Testament. This paralleling of events in Old and New Testaments was not merely a way of filling a vast acreage of window space. It embodied one of the main tenets of medieval thought and had a clear message which went back to the Bible itself. This was that the intentions which had been implicit in God's guiding of the course of history before the Incarnation, became explicit in Christ's own life and teaching. Thus, to take examples from the Canterbury windows, the Ascension of Christ was paralleled with Elijah's ascent to heaven in a chariot, and the Adoration of the Magi with the visit of the Queen of Sheba to the court of Solomon. That episodes from the age of Grace were prefigured by older events encouraged two conclusions. One was that the revelation by Christ of the true meaning of these ancient mysteries confirmed that he was the Messiah, for he was seen to fulfil and expound prophecy. The other consequence of this mode of thought was that events and sayings, especially

Jared and Joanna, windows in Canterbury Cathedral. Jared by the Methuselah Master (c.1178); Joanna by the Joanna Master (c.1180).

if of direct divine origin, were thought to have an import that went beyond their superficial content.

Because of the complexity and rarity of some of the ideas expressed in the typological windows, they were supplied with quite long inscriptions. The combination of literacy and relatively esoteric learning required to make sense of this scheme indicates that the audience envisaged was the monastic community itself, and not primarily the laity. The latter would indeed rarely have been allowed to visit the liturgically exclusive east end. What would have been perfectly visible to them from the nave were the ancestors of Christ, high up in the clerestory windows, and although they too are provided with inscriptions, these are limited to the person's name, writ large so as to be legible.

Beyond the temporary screen to the east, in the Trinity Chapel, there is a subtle shift in the programme for the clerestory glazing. Whereas to the west, the ancestors of Christ selected for representation were all taken from St Luke's Gospel, the appearance to the east of additional figures from St Matthew's genealogy of Christ suggests that the scheme was being expanded.

One reason for this might have been that the building itself was assuming a greater length than at first envisaged, which would imply the desire to provide a more spacious area behind the high altar where the shrine of St Thomas was to stand.

Thomas Becket, Archbishop of Canterbury from 1163, had been murdered in the Cathedral late in 1170. The sacriligious infamy of this deed, its political motivation and the fact that miracles were soon being worked in the presence of the martyr's body meant that his canonisation in 1173 was more or less a formality. In normal circumstances the promotion of the saint's cult at Canterbury would have proceeded apace. But because of the politically sensitive stance which Becket had taken not everyone was in favour of fostering devotion to his memory. Furthermore there was some doubt whether decisions about the future of his remains were in the hands of his successor or of the monks. This is pertinent to the glazing because the windows at aisle level in the Trinity Chapel were filled with scenes of Becket's life and, more particularly, miracles.

The quantity of glazing and the speed with which it was apparently wanted encouraged the community to employ at least six different glass painters and designers in the first phase of the work. This estimate is based on stylistic analysis of the surviving glass and, since virtually all that from the south side is now lost, it is possible that twice this number of masters was used. We do not know the nationality or previous career of any of the artists involved but, whatever their origins, their skill was consummate. The Methuselah Master, named after one of the ancestor panels in the clerestory, had a remarkable capacity to create massively grand figures. His Jared employs various linear techniques (for example cross-hatching on the cloak to the right of Jared's chest) and shading to model the forms. But it is the drawing itself which makes the three-dimensionality so compelling. A huge swag of cloth encircles Jared's torso and emphasises his bulk. The weight of the material itself is shown by the way his left hand, large as it is, only just encompasses the folds in his lap. The angling and implied foreshortening of arms and hands and the turn of the head all add to the sense of latent power and controlled dynamism which is typical of this master's large figures.

In his smaller scale narratives the drawing is necessarily more delicate, but even so the energy remains. The 'Flight of Lot from Sodom' (colour pl. 7) is a masterpiece of drama and didacticism. The contrast between the tumbling towers and leaping flames of the city's destruction at the right and the petrified, pivotal upright of Lot's wife, transformed into a pillar of salt, is total. As her gaze takes us to the city, so her hands point in the direction of the salvation of her husband and daughters as, guided by angels, they scramble earnestly into the hills. Although the means used to describe space are minimal, Sodom is clearly in the background, Lot's wife in the foreground, and the flight is effected upwards and slightly into the depth of the picture. Landscape is shown not merely by a groundline, but by an undulating surface with herbs and trees, and although the father stands in front of his children, their dress and feet are made to reappear at strategic intervals to show that they are complete, volumetrically discrete entities.

Faced with such artistry, it is easy for us to forget the technical complexity of the processes involved in making these panels. Once the molten glass, a mixture of ash and sand, had been coloured by the addition of metal salts it had to be transformed into panes. This was done by blowing a large bubble, the ends of which were opened to make a cylinder. When cut up the side and reheated this could be flattened into a sheet. Meanwhile the designer would draw out on a whitened table the cartoon for a figure or decorative pattern. This drawing would include the major divisions between pieces of glass, where ultimately the leads would be placed to hold the pieces together, and much of the details of drapery folds, facial features, etc. Panes shaped to correspond with the gaps between lead-lines would be cut from the coloured glass sheets and put in their correct position on the cartoon. When the jigsaw was complete, the painter would take black paint, made with copper and ground glass, and brush all the lines showing through from the cartoon onto the surface of the glass. By using the black paint thinly a deepening of tone could be effected which did not totally obscure the colour when light was shining through the glass.

Of these various operations the most difficult must have been cutting the glass, and yet in some areas, particularly where decoration is involved, the complexity of the designs seems deliberately chosen to show off the virtuosity of the work. In one window is a blossom which contains an array of small pieces of glass with outlines whose shaping must have required the greatest skill if the thin slivers were not to break. And yet such decoration was not occasional, but repeated in quantity in the borders and between scenes in virtually every window.

It will be clear from the above that there was plenty of scope for artists' predilections to manifest themselves. One or two factors were prescribed, such as the iconographic scheme and perhaps the general range of colour available. Others, the drawing, including the positions of lead lines, the choice of overall colour balance and juxtaposition, and the types of surround, were all in the hands of the designer. Thus a comparison between the figure of Joanna, by the eponymously named master, and that of Jared can be made in largely formal terms. Beside the robust work of the Methuselah Master, Joanna (see p. 174) appears attenuated and elegant. Even at the level of the shapes of the pieces of glass from which he is constructed there is a sense of repose. While the third dimension is not ignored, there is far more concern with a refined outline, and there is no more telling contrast than that between the powerfully articulated fingers of Jared's hands and the gentle curving relaxation of Joanna's.

Throughout the progress of the glazing at Canterbury there is a steady movement away from the strongly characterised, stocky figure types with which the work began, towards a style that relies on linear grace. While it may lack the monumentality of the earliest work, the later glass retains dramatic intensity, and arguably gains in narrative clarity. In the 'Curing of Matilda, the madwoman of Cologne' at St Thomas' shrine, the difference between time before and time after is expressed largely in terms of the patterns made by the figures. The superimposition of violently bending forms on top of the rectilinear grid of the building convincingly represents the mental and physical disruption of the first scene.

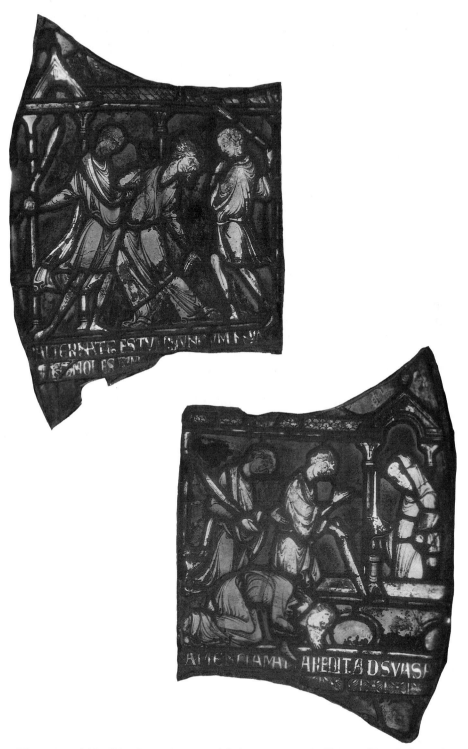

The curing of Matilda, the madwoman of Cologne, window in Trinity Chapel, Canterbury Cathedral (c.1200).

The tranquillity of the subsequent episode, where heads and bodies are gently bowed but are otherwise largely in line with the architecture, self-evidently portrays the calm after the storm. Even if one does not know the story, the basic message is clear. Every effort is made to reduce the visual accoutrements to their bare essentials. There is no sense here, as there was in the 'Flight of Lot', that spatial depth is an important element, and there are no details equivalent to the trees on the hillside, which might distract the viewer's attention. A deliberate economy of means has replaced the element of artistic licence which was apparent in many of the earlier, Biblical narratives.

The changes that occur in the Canterbury glass are not restricted to this country or to that medium. In metalwork, manuscript painting and stone sculpture across much of northern Europe there are similar shifts of emphasis. No satisfactory explanations have ever been put forward to account for the relative speed with which the transformations took place, or how it was that artists practising different crafts hundreds of miles apart could seem to be so acutely aware of the latest developments in each other's work. No matter quite how this state of affairs came about, there is no greater monument to this seminal move towards the Gothic in the figurative arts than the glazing of the east end of Canterbury Cathedral.

The sculpture of Westminster Abbey, 1245–1272

A small marshy island called Thorney, in the Thames, was transformed during the eleventh century. A great abbey, built by King Edward the Confessor, and a royal palace grew up in place of the original small monastery. The abbey church became the Confessor's burial place, and his canonisation and the increasing presence of subsequent kings at their neighbouring residence ensured that some measure of patronage would always be forthcoming. It was not, however, until 200 years later that a royal benefactor appeared to match and even to exceed St Edward himself. Henry III counted among his major passions both devotion to his saintly predecessor and a love of art and architecture. It must have seemed natural to him to combine these enthusiasms and finance the completion of the expensive new Lady Chapel at the east end of the Confessor's building. Rather more surprising was the decision to destroy the venerable structure of the main church and its chapterhouse and replace them with something that was as self-evidently modern as it was sumptuous.

Architecturally the new scheme adopted several features of recent French High Gothic cathedrals. Of French inspiration was the layout of the presbytery with an ambulatory and radiating chapels. French too was the use of bar-tracery in the windows and its simulation in blind openings. Although not a large building by Continental standards, the rebuilt abbey was clearly intended to appear tall to the English, and the general proportions of the elevation call to mind those, for example, of Amiens Cathedral, begun a quarter of a century earlier in 1220. The overall scale of the work was limited by the site and it may have been for this reason, as much as for love of

The main arcade and gallery, north presbytery, Westminster Abbey (c.1250).

surface embellishment for its own sake, that so much attention was paid to the decoration and furnishing. The ultimate effect, as has often been remarked, was a building whose resonances were with the works of the goldsmith rather than of the mason. But how was this achieved? The short answer is, through the texturing of the surfaces with detailed carving which was then painted and gilt.

One of the most striking and original features of the new work is the use of diaper patterns in the spandrels of the main arcade and gallery (see p. 179). The squared rosettes are carefully carved on each stone, a process that must have been time-consuming and therefore costly. The source of this idea is usually said to be a thin band of diaper low on the west facade of Amiens Cathedral, but there is really no comparison. It is far more likely that the Westminster walls were intended to bring to mind the stamped or enamelled metal sheeting in the spandrels and behind the figures on contemporary saints' shrines. Although we know that many of these large house-shaped caskets of precious material were made in medieval Britain, none has survived. However, Continental examples from the late twelfth and thirteenth centuries, such as the Shrine of the Three Kings, at Cologne, have squared or diamond shaped rosettes stamped into the gilt metal backgrounds. At the same time as rebuilding the Abbey, Henry III was paying for the making of a new shrine for St Edward. It is not unlikely that it had diaper detailing of this kind and, if it had, that the walls of the church were echoing, reflecting as it were, the glory of this focal point of the east end.

To this richness of surface is added a complexity and variety of arch moulding which further enlivens the overall effect. The depth of the rolls and hollows on the main arcade adds a play of light and shade to the thickness of the wall, but it is the equally 'unclassical' alternation of arches in the gallery

Shrine of St Edward the Confessor, from a manuscript (c.1260).

which is most surprising. The sequence of three types, stiff-leaf frond, diaper and moulded, is unlike anything in French 'cathedral Gothic'. Furthermore, the fact that there are two openings in each bay means that, given strict sequencing such as that in the eastern arm, repetition of a bay design can occur only after three bays: bay 1, patterns A and B; bay 2, patterns C and A; bay 3, patterns B and C, and only then back to A and B.

It is, of course, open to question whether such things as diaper and mouldings should be regarded as 'sculpture' rather than as architecture. But it is perhaps not stressed often enough the degree to which 'art' in a medieval building was intended to contribute to an integrated whole. In this regard the use of paint over the interior surfaces is just as instructive as the use of carving. According to one source, in the last century there was still evidence that the 'diaper work of the triforium was gilt on a red ground; the sculptured bosses were gilt and coloured'. Nor was the painting necessarily just in pure, flat colour. It was often carefully modelled in darker and lighter tones to enhance the real three-dimensionality of mouldings and sculpture with fictive light and shade. Thus in the overall effect it was difficult to distinguish what was building and what was sculpture, what was real depth and what was painted imitation.

The integration of carving into the architectural scheme has another facet to it. A basic differentiation seems to be made between the more sacred and the more secular parts of the church. In the spandrels of the nave aisles is a splendid series of stone shields, carved as though they were hanging on their straps from dainty little heads. The shields are arranged in order of importance from east to west. The Holy Roman Emperor and the kings of England and France appear adjacent to the monks' choir by the crossing, whereas away from the holy area, towards the west front, are those of lesser nobility and gentry. In the transept and around the eastern chapels we move from the secular world of heraldry to the realms of Nature and the saints. The chapels contain what is almost certainly the earliest naturalistic foliage carving in England. In St John the Baptist's chapel little birds sit among recognisable vine, and alongside can be found oak and ivy which are quite distinct from the generalised stiff-leaf otherwise used at Westminster and in earlier thirteenth-century English buildings. The representation of particular plant species had occurred about two decades earlier in France, and it is no doubt from that quarter that the innovation came to the English court circle. Foliage in this context may well have been intended to convey the general sense of the verdance of Paradise, for interspersed among these spandrels are others with figures of angels and saints but not shown as part of any recognisable narrative sequence. None the less, the distinction between the secular heraldry in the nave and the sacred and natural subjects in the transepts and eastern arm is consistent, and presumably intended to convey the different character and function of these two parts of the building.

The same phenomenon is apparent in the vaulting of the various aisles of the church. Immediately above the blind arcading in the west aisle of the north transept are bosses which show figures and scenes: David harping, the Annunciation and, probably, Moses and Aaron. This area of the church is showing sacred events which occurred on earth, and further to the east and in the south transept are other religious subjects, again interspersed with foliage. But if we return to the nave aisles, the bosses above the heraldic spandrels carrying the shields of the English nobility, instead of biblical characters, develop a series of grotesques. In one, a centaur, galloping hard, aims his bow at some quarry, in another, a man's head is savaged by lions.

The best preserved bosses, in that they retain original paint as well as a crisp surface, are those at the south end of the west gallery of the south transept, in the so-called muniment room (colour pl. 7). As it is now a rather obscure part of the church the sculptural richness of the whole area may at first appear surprising. However, closer examination reveals that it was originally provided with its own access of staircases and passageways. For these and other reasons it is likely that this gallery was set aside for important people, such as members of the royal family, to view the sanctuary. This is borne out by the fact that until the sixteenth century there was no monument or other tall furnishing in the wall enclosing the choir which might have obstructed the view of the high altar from this vantage point. But, at best, this can only have been an occasional box seat. The main processional entrance for public ceremonial seems to have been the north transept facade, and this would have led visitors into the choir or ambulatory.

There is virtually nothing left of the thirteenth-century sculpture on the north front. Indeed the architecture itself has been mauled by time and misrepresented by subsequent 'restorations'. Early drawings and engravings show something of its original form, and that it was covered with sculpture. Not only were the doorways themselves elaborately worked but the major buttresses between them were adorned with large figures set on corbels. Of the subject matter of the sculpture we know little, but its disposition suggests that here, if anywhere, was where the French High Gothic facade found its closest English follower. But although the general scheme is reminiscent of those on the cathedrals of Amiens and Rheims there are striking differences too. The independence of thought at Westminster is stressed when one enters the building through the north portal. The triple tiers of windows on the facing, south transept elevation presumably once carried stained glass. Of this nothing remains, but immediately below the rose window are substantial traces of a large-scale sculptural composition in which two angels cense a group known as St Edward and the Pilgrim. In legend St Edward's generosity to the pilgrim, who turned out to be a disguised rematerialisation of St John the Evangelist, was a manifestation of his sanctity. The ring which Edward gave to John was returned to him as a token of his impending death and passage to Paradise. It was towards this didactically central ensemble that those entering the main north entrance processed. The arrangement on the south was mirrored on the north interior wall. Now only the censing angels remain there; the central figures are lost without trace. The intention must have been, though, to remind people leaving the building, or the monks in their choir enclosure under the crossing gazing up at the walls, of the devotional magnificence of the whole structure. Below the censing angels in the north transept, a 'choir' of angels is shown in the soffits (or under-surfaces) of the narrow lancet arches. This suggests that the upper parts of the building too, like the eastern end, were regarded as more heavenly than the western parts at a lower level. Thus one can see a hierarchy being established throughout the building which expresses the greater religious significance of east, as against west, and heavenly, as against earthly.

In addition to the work on the main church, Henry III funded the rebuilding of the chapterhouse. This not only served the abbot and convent, but also, on various state occasions, for receptions and meetings. As a result, it too was carefully elaborated. Although now only an abraded shadow, the main doorway from the cloister to the vestibule was clearly very fine. Set against carved foliage on the tympanum above the doors, the Virgin and Child were censed by angels, while around on the voussoirs (the wedge-shaped stones of the arch) was shown, apparently, a Tree of Jesse to demonstrate Christ's ancestry and His Incarnation as the fulfilment of prophecy. Beyond the vestibule, stairs lead into the raised octagonal room which was the chapter's meeting place. Flanking the doorway are more figures in foliage and on the inside, in the spandrels, two large freestanding figures of the Archangel Gabriel and the Virgin Mary, censed by small angels in relief (see p. 154). Representations of the Annunciation in two spandrels either side of an arched opening are not uncommon. Perhaps the void between messenger and Annunciate was intended to call to mind the passage of the Holy Spirit to Mary through the air. (Sadly, this effect has been ruined by the unwarranted interpolation of a nineteenth-century figure of God enthroned.) But though the idea is common, its appearance as a sculptured group, rather than in painting or mosaic, is rare.

It is quite likely that Mary and Gabriel are the two figures for which William Yxeworth was paid 53/4 in 1253. In the same account we see Warin the painter receiving 11/- 'for painting two images with colour [*cum colore*]'. This last phrase was included, I think, because medieval sculpture was often painted in just black and white with perhaps a little gold, or one other colour. It was not so at Westminster. The figure and foliage carvings which retain original paint usually show a full range of expensive pigments. On the figures, paint is invariably used naturalistically: the cheeks heightened with red, the pupils and iris of the eye distinguished. The effect of life-size, naturalistically painted carving of such sophistication and elegance as the Annunciation group must have encouraged those in the room to suspend their disbelief, to see not a composite of artistic skill but sacred history as it were truly present before them. The immanence of profound religious events is a notion disquieting to the post-Reformation mind. To the medieval viewer it was simply fact.

An inscription on the contemporary floor of the chapterhouse boasts 'As the rose is the flower of flowers, this is the house of houses'. In the hierarchy of the decoration the rose takes on yet another role. While the spandrels of most of the bays bear the now familiar varieties of diaper, that by the centre of the easternmost bay contains a naturalistic rose bush in a trellis. It was here that the abbot of Westminster had his seat. The implications are clear enough; that as the rose is a cut above other flowers, the abbot is superior to the ordinary monks.

Within the overall schemes for church and chapterhouse, the basic principles of which must have been established by someone in authority, it is quite likely that individual carvers were allowed to exercise some freedom. Matters such as composition, how to fit a figure or scene onto a spandrel or a boss, required practised ingenuity. Yet it is not certain that this sculpture was done by specialists. The large quantity of documentation for Westminster, including commissions and accounts of wages, reveals only one individual certainly paid for sculpture, William Yxeworth. Whereas people designated smith, carpenter, mason, painter, glazier, are common, there is only a single craftsman called sculptor. The relevant mention, coming from the Close Roll for December 1257, refers to John 'sculptor of the king's images'. This may be regarded as a quasi-official position since he received a robe of office, but the only work he can be shown to have undertaken was a candelabrum, and that was quite possibly made of wood or metal. Whatever materials John habitually worked, the quantities of stone sculpture used in the Abbey suggest that several carvers must have been at work even if one allows that mouldings, diaper and foliage could be carved by those simply called 'mason'. It is tempting to use modern ideas about the relative quality of some of the carvings in deciding what may be the work of a specialist and what the efforts of a talented shaper of stone blocks. Among the many corbels (load-carrying projections on a wall) and head-stops in the eastern parts of the church can be found both the elegantly refined and the gawkily expressive. But the distinction might be as much the result of the genre employed or the type of character being represented as the skill of the artist.

We may speculate about how the work was divided up, but in the final analysis we do not know. There is little evidence that the later distinction between masons and sculptors applied rigorously, or even at all, as early as the mid-thirteenth century. And yet among the carvings at the Abbey are many that are rightly regarded as considerable artistic achievements. No doubt Henry III and his contemporaries also singled out individual pieces for admiration. But in the building (as opposed to isolated on the plates of an art history book) what is surely most remarkable are the ways in which the sculpture was used ubiquitously to enrich the architectural structure as a whole and to indicate the 'meaning' and differences in function of the various parts. At Westminster the painted sculpture helped to create the almost magical environment in which the king and his court, the abbot and his monks could stage the various rituals which were part of the ceremonial continuum of their lives.

The goldsmiths' craft

Painting has long been at the top of the notional hierarchy of Western art, but it was not always the case. In England as in most of northern Europe in the Middle Ages goldsmithing once had far more prestige. On one basic level this is not surprising since raw materials were such a highly-regarded component of medieval art and, of course, precious stones, gold and silver conferred their own kudos on those who worked them. But there were other factors reinforcing the status of goldsmiths. Several saints had reputations for this craft, notably St Eloi (Eligius) on the Continent and, in Britain, St

Dunstan (c.909–88). As friend and adviser to King Edgar, as a reforming abbot, and ultimately as Archbishop of Canterbury, the imprimatur of Dunstan was such that it comes as no surprise to find him adopted as patron saint by the Goldsmiths' Company on its foundation in 1327. Indeed it seems that he had been considered as the English goldsmiths' special saint long before the guild proper was formed.

Several other senior ecclesiastics in the pre-Conquest England worked in metal but, following the Norman invasion, the situation changed. In part this may be a result of the conquerors' attitude of mind and an increasing feudalisation of society, which emphasised the divide between the menial and the aristocratic. It must also have been the result, though, of the rapidly increasing urbanisation and industrialisation in the mid- and late eleventh century. Before that time the expertise necessary for making elaborate, ritual objects for church use was scarce, and the bishop's or abbot's direct participation was not unusual. By the twelfth century, however, a buoyant economy and the dissemination of technical skills in city-based workshops was obviating the need for high-ranking churchmen to roll up their sleeves and 'do it themselves'.

While it may no longer have been acceptable or necessary for the land-managing class in the church to practise a 'mechanical' art, goldsmithing maintained much of its prestige in the cities. The oligarchies that ruled in many of Europe's largest urban centres included goldsmiths among their number. London was a prime example of this. From the thirteenth century to the end of the period covered by this book, upwards of a dozen of London's mayors were goldsmiths, whereas no painter or sculptor ever was. The wealth

Seal of Henry III (detail) by Walter de Ripa, goldsmith (1218).

and organisation of this group at an earlier date is evident from the huge fine, £30, levied in 1179–80 on the unlicensed goldsmiths' guild. The sum is far larger than that imposed on any of the other 'adulterine' guilds of the city and represents the equivalent of one master's wages for about four years.

The internal workings of this independent craft association are obscure, and equally shadowy is the institution known as the King's Goldsmiths of London. There were, apparently, eight men so designated at any one time and they received from the crown an annual stipend. This may have operated as a kind of retainer. Certainly the kings were major patrons and such payments were a way of ensuring that skilled craftsmen were on hand who were beholden to them. Nearly all the plate, the jewellery, the regalia and the chapel furnishings that were produced for the Norman and Plantagenet monarchs is lost. But evidence for the quality of work undertaken at royal behest can still be found among the Great Seals. From the late twelfth century onwards there are occasional references in royal rolls to goldsmiths being paid for such work. A Great Seal was made for Richard the Lionheart in 1195 by William Aurifaber (goldsmith), who received a robe, and Master Walter de Ripa, goldsmith of London, was paid the large sum of 40/- for making Henry III's seal in 1218 (see p. 185). Interestingly these men were not provided with the raw material, in this case silver, for their work. They were expected to provide that themselves in the first instance and then to claim reimbursement when the finished object was delivered. The weight of silver needed for a large two-sided seal-die was five marks, the equivalent of about four months' wages. To afford this outlay, even temporarily, the craftsman had to be a person of substance. Equally obviously he needed considerable artistic skill. Master Walter's beautifully proportioned image of the young king enthroned has a poise and natural elegance which, as has been remarked before of English art of this period, is comparable with classical Greek sculpture. To succeed at the highest level, mastery of figure drawing and modelling as well as technical skills such as casting and gem setting were essential.

The range of work a goldsmith might normally undertake is indicated by the recorded misdemeanour in the fourteenth century of one Henry Lyrpool, who used a bar of false metal for making 'plates for two small cups, a seal and the harness of a girdle'. Such objects as cups and buckles are, indeed, often shown on the seals which goldsmiths used and which they probably made for themselves (see p. 188) and ultimately became part of the arms of the Company. There is no obvious reason why a man who could make these things should not also produce church plate, particularly as many of the objects made for ecclesiastical use were very similar in design and construction to those used by the laity. The only difference might be the degree of elaboration with which a chalice, for example, was worked for a wealthy church so as to distinguish it from a secular drinking cup. But in some cases we are in doubt about the function of a surviving object because its design comes from this common stock. The splendid silver stemmed-bowl and cover, now in St Maurice d'Agaune in Switzerland, is a case in point.

Silver cup and cover, from the Abbey of St Maurice D'Agaune (c.1200).

The seal of Thomas Brundish, goldsmith (c.1350).

Made in England around 1200, it resembles the form of contemporary *ciboria* made to contain the bread for the Mass. *Ciboria*, however, with their emphasis on the re-enactment at the altar of Christ's sacrifice, if they have narrative scenes, include appropriate episodes from the Passion. On the St Maurice cup the subjects range from the Annunciation only as far as the Baptism and are thus concerned with infancy. On the lid is a splendidly classicising group of the boy Achilles with the centaur Chiron, which is a corresponding subject from ancient mythology of the nurturing, and in this case the education, of youth. Female figures around the stem may well be personifications of virtues, perhaps associated with learning since they hold books. The whole tenor of the subject matter is such that it would be more appropriate as a christening present to a child of noble descent or as a container of chrism than as a container for the body of Our Lord, and it may well be a secular commission.

The desire almost automatically to regard such an object as ecclesiastical stems from two causes. The first is the belief that the Middle Ages lavished the bulk of its efforts on works to glorify God. The second, which also partly causes the first, is that the written record, particularly in the period before about 1300, is largely the work of monks or clerics who, not unnaturally, are expressing their own view of the world. Thus the goldsmiths whose biographies we know most about are those who worked for a church where there was a writer who chose to record the information. There is no better case of this than St. Albans where the mid-thirteenth-century chronicler Matthew Paris was himself an artist of no little ability. He makes it clear that those goldsmiths who worked for the Abbey were, at least to begin with, secular craftsmen brought in from outside. In several cases, though, they subsequently became monks.

It was of clear benefit to an abbey to have unsalaried, skilled labour readily to hand. On the craftsman's side, the prospect of security and some comfort in old age, quite apart from the spiritual advantages, must have been an equal attraction. Anketil, who worked as a layman on the shrine of St Alban in Abbot Geoffrey's time (1119–46), subsequently joined the community, and in the early thirteenth century there was a real coup when Master Walter of Colchester, his brother and his nephew, all artists, were 'signed up'. Matthew Paris tells us of the work which Walter did for the abbey; the frontal for the high altar and two silver gilt book covers, one with the crucified Christ between the Virgin Mary and St John, the other showing Christ in Majesty with the symbols of the four evangelists. But undoubtedly his most prestigious commission was for a new shrine, finished by 1220, for the translation of the remains of St Thomas Becket on which he collaborated with Master Elias of Dereham. Nothing remains now of their work except generalised medieval representations of it, descriptions by visitors of its richness and the account of the staggering quantity of precious metal and gems taken from it at the Dissolution. Walter thus remains known, like his predecessors at St Albans, through surviving information but not from his own output, all of which is destroyed. But even if we cannot reconstruct his chef d'oeuvre in detail, its basic form is clear enough.

The stained glass windows which surrounded it (see above) carry two images of the shrine, either as it appeared, or as it was intended to appear. Essentially it was a wooden chest about six feet long and one foot wide, with gabled ends about two feet high supporting a pitched roof. The whole house-shaped container stood on a platform which was raised on stone columns so that it could be seen over the top of the high altar of the church. Entirely encasing the wooden structure were layers of gold and silver sheets, encrusted with gems, filigree and probably enamelling. It is highly likely that there were figures worked in relief on the flat surfaces. Surviving contemporary shrines on the Continent make it clear that this was normal, and in England we have drawings, for example of the shrine of Edward the Confessor, which show similar details (see p. 180). Undertakings such as these involved a vast expenditure in time and money. The Confessor's shrine was in the making, albeit fitfully, for nearly thirty years and is estimated to have cost King Henry III about £5,000. It would be surprising if the Canterbury shrine, which was far more popular with pilgrims and which consequently attracted greater donations, was much, if at all inferior to Edward's at Westminster.

By the mid-thirteenth century considerable efforts were being made in England, as elsewhere in Europe, to secure the fineness of precious materials. From 1238, six wardens were being appointed by the city authorities from among the goldsmiths, and it was their responsibility to see that silver was of sterling quality or better – that is, at least as pure as the coinage. A statute of 1300 introduced the idea of the 'hallmark', in the form of a leopard's head. The fact that this symbol derived from the royal arms shows the concern of the king himself to guarantee that his realm did not deal in debased metal. The royal charter which granted official status to the Goldsmiths' Company in 1327 initiated an organisation which legislated for itself and kept records thereafter. It is from the Company's ordinances that we learn about such things as length of terms of apprenticeship (reduced from ten to seven years in 1394) and the controls over goldsmiths who are strangers, either from another city in England or from overseas, working in London. The existence of such regulations encourages us to believe that the organisation of the craft had itself become more rigid. Indeed, patterns of behaviour do seem to have changed. Whereas in the twelfth and thirteenth centuries there were, as we have seen, goldsmiths who entered monasteries in later life, and goldsmiths who practised other arts as well (Walter of Colchester was a painter), in the later Middle Ages this mobility appears much rarer. The increased specialisation may have been the result of increasing commercial complexity, and with the formation of the guilds, which were in part charitable and could help to maintain members who had fallen on hard times, the security offered in the past by the monastic life was no longer so compelling.

English goldsmiths' work was renowned. In the immediately post-Conquest period Bishop Hildebert of Le Mans writing to King William II commented that whereas his region of France was bereft of goldsmiths who could undertake work such as the making of a shrine, England was full of wonderful craftsmen and their work. At the end of the Middle Ages an Italian visitor to London saw in Cheapside '52 goldsmiths shops so rich and full of silver vessels great and small, that in all the shops in Milan, Rome, Venice and Florence put together, I do not think there would be found so many of the magnificence that are to be seen in London'. As all but a handful of their works have long since been melted down, we rely on the relatively few pieces that do remain and the written evidence of what there once was to confirm the importance, both social and artistic, of the goldsmiths' craft in medieval England.

Embroidery *Opus Anglicanum*

The Middle Ages did not recognise the progression of styles we now refer to by the blanket terms Romanesque and Gothic. When an object was classified more subtly than by use or by such simple descriptions as 'old' or 'new', it was usually in terms of an association with a place where it was fashionable or where there was a major centre of production. Thus an armlet can be 'more danico', in the Danish manner, or a piece of enamel 'opus Lemovicense', Limoges work. The use of such terms implies enough fame for the designation to have meaning, if not cachet, at least for an informed audience, and it is significant that the work to which the appellation 'English' was attached was fine, silk embroidery. Until the large scale production of alabaster carvings in the fifteenth century, it was England's most famous luxury export.

The Papacy in particular seems to have admired the skill and beauty of these vestments, and the Vatican inventory of 1295 lists over a hundred items of *Opus Anglicanum*. In 1288 Pope Nicholas IV gave a beautiful cope to his native town of Ascoli, where it is still preserved. It is likely that he commissioned the work personally since the subject matter of the embroideries is largely concerned with his predecessors; in the upper row sainted popes, and below other thirteenth-century popes who were the fourth of their name, culminating in Clement IV (1265–8). One of the others so represented, Innocent IV (1243–54), had made the remark on seeing examples of *Opus Anglicanum*, 'truly England is for us a garden of delights' and let it be known that he wanted as much of the work as possible. As the chronicler Matthew Paris commented, this 'did not displease the London merchants who traded in embroideries and sold them at their own price'. Perhaps it was an inflation in their cost that caused Urban IV (1261–4) to retain his own English embroiderer, Gregory of London.

The qualities which made these products so desirable were, as usual, beauty of colour and texture, the value of the materials, and the exquisitely careful execution. The latter two factors meant that very large sums of money were expended. In 1317, Queen Isabella paid Rose, wife of John Bureford, half the 100 marks (nearly £70) owing for a cope, and sums of £30 or £40 seem to have been quite normal for such vestments. To give some indication of their value, such prices were equivalent to about fifteen years wages for the people involved in their manufacture. The sheer labour involved in their stitching meant that complex embroideries were indeed several years work. Four women were paid a total of £36 for the nearly four years it took them to make an altar frontal for Westminster Abbey, but that was out of a total cost of over £250. While the cloth and silk thread itself was a relatively small expense, the gold (both for thread and for setting stones), the gems and the pearls and other attachments accounted for over eighty per cent of the total.

The reputation of English needlewomen was not exclusively a later medieval phenomenon. The art was widely practised in the Anglo-Saxon period and was praised by the Norman apologist, William of Poitiers, soon after the Conquest. At this early date nearly all the references we have are to the embroideries of aristocratic and even royal ladies. St Dunstan himself (see previous chapter) designed a stole to be worked by a certain noble matron called Aethelwynn. The Confessor's queen Edith, King Henry I's first wife Matilda and Christina of Markyate (herself of noble birth) are a few among many recorded as skilled with the needle and, it is important to note, they are all of English rather than French descent. Women of the Norman aristocracy do not seem to have shared this enthusiasm: perhaps it was regarded as mechanical and menial, perhaps too, as noted in the case of goldsmithy, production was already developing an altogether more commercial basis. Certainly by the time we encounter fuller records, such as the thirteenth-century ones just mentioned, the organisation is businesslike and professional, involving contracts, rates of pay and the specifications of the materials to be used.

Among the various shadowy figures whose names feature in documents, one stands out by virtue of the quantity of information we have about her. Mabel of Bury St Edmunds fulfilled two large commissions for King Henry III, first (1239–41) making a chasuble and, two years later, a red samite (silk) banner embroidered with figures of the Virgin and St John. In the latter instance, although the subject was the King's choice, the design was left to Mabel herself. Throughout the periods of work the King supplied funds for materials, for labour, and ex gratia payments as a sign of his approval. We hear no more until 1256, when the King, visiting Bury, ordered her to be given cloth and fur for a robe in recognition of her long service to himself and his queen in the making of ecclesiastical vestments. Such records show him to have been as generous as we know he was discerning as a patron. Clearly, Mabel was the best artist available.

The technical and aesthetic character of English embroidery was not static. Particularly during the thirteenth century, various broad developments occurred, the most immediately visible being in colour. Early in the century the majority of the threads used were of precious metal wound round a silk core, but by the end a wide range of coloured threads was in use which might occupy as much as half of the embroidered surface. The method of stitching metal threads remained constant. It is known as underside couching and involves a linen thread coming from the reverse of the background cloth through to the front where it encircles the main thread and pulls a tiny loop of it back through to the reverse. This technique has two main advantages: firstly it conceals the couching thread, which cannot be seen on the surface,

Embroidered altarpiece (detail) (c.1350).

and secondly it creates the equivalent of a row of fine hinges in the metal thread which make the whole fabric more pliable and adds a texture which fragments the diffusion of light. Coloured silks, on the other hand, were sewn with split stitch. Although the stitch was intricate, it ensured an even spread of dense colour which seems to have been regarded as particularly important for embroidering in the flesh areas of figures (colour pl. 1).

The size of stitch used on faces and hands was, by the later thirteenth century, minutely fine whereas both the thread and stitch length used on draperies was a little coarser. The fineness of the threads used on hands and faces has usually led to their being the most worn, but on well-preserved embroideries it is still possible to see the subtlety that was intended. For example on larger figures, where two tones were used for the flesh, the stitch direction reinforces the forms in much the same way as the laying of tesserae (small squares of glass or marble) does in mosaics. Thus the cheeks are worked as a spiral and the darker threads across the forehead follow the gently curving lines of the wrinkles. The use of colour also allowed the introduction of modelling. This is most obvious on draperies where it is common to find three tones ranging from dark to light used to depict highlights and shadows. Nothing so pictorially naturalistic had been produced in earlier needlework.

The vast majority of *Opus Anglicanum* to have been preserved is ecclesiastical, but we know from medieval sources that secular commissions were also undertaken. Because more subject to the vagaries of fashion and to heavy use, almost none of this has survived, but one magnificent exception is the heraldic 'Leopards of England' now in the Musée de Cluny in Paris (colour plate 1). There are several fragments of this embroidery which may have formed matching cloths for a horse and its rider. Whatever its precise original form, the value of its gold thread and pearls is such to suggest that the user was either royal, or acting as a royal agent at the highest level. The dramatically elongated 'lions passant' show heraldry transformed. The level of complexity in the drawing of the curling fur of the mane, tail and body is purely aesthetic, and no doubt the material was meant to impress by its sheer artistry as well as its opulence. To make them flash the more the beasts' eyes are covered by cabochon (polished rather than cut) crystal and, to increase the sense of the scale and power of these royal beasts, beautifully designed and worked little figures are shown sitting among the fronds of foliage which bestrew the red velvet of the background.

The high quality and technical homogeneity of most of the surviving English embroidery of the period c.1270–1350 suggests a uniform, probably even a quasi-industrial system of training and production. To judge from the surviving contracts and other references, the people in charge of the workshops were, by this date, often male, and there has been some debate about the composition of the workforce. We do not have enough information to give a reliable answer, but it is clear that both men and women were involved. Paradoxically, given the apparent developments in the trade's organisation, after only a few decades at its height, the quality, quantity and complexity of *Opus Anglicanum* declined. But for about one hundred years it had been responsible for the best, as well as the most famous embroidery in medieval Europe.

The construction and furnishing of the parish church of Salle, Norfolk

Visitors to Salle (pronounced to rhyme with Paul, the dedicatory saint of the church), half-way between Norwich and the north Norfolk coast, find a community so small and scattered that they could scarcely consider it a village. And yet there stands in its midst one of the grandest parish churches in England; remarkable alike for the scale and quality of its building and for the survival of a significant part of its medieval furnishings. As an ensemble, it was clearly the product of a patronage that had wealth and taste, and yet it is doubtful whether even at the height of its prosperity the parish of Salle contained more than about 300 people. Furthermore, even the wealthier inhabitants, occupants of the farms and manors, seem not to have been particularly rich by contemporary standards. That so much money was found for the church can perhaps best be explained by inordinate piety, by a sense of rivalry between this parish and some of its neighbours, and by an equivalent competition for status among the residents of Salle itself.

We are fortunate that enough information survives in inscriptions and heraldry (whether extant, or destroyed but recorded by antiquaries) and in wills and other documents for us to know at least some of the ways various parishioners contributed to the work. The shields of arms above the west door which include those of two local families, the Mautebys and the Brewes, suggest that the building was begun soon after 1400. This is borne out by other evidence. Geoffrey Melman, who died in 1404, left money for the north porch. And the court roll for the manor of Kirkhall (one of the four manors in the parish) records that in 1408 'William Melman and his brother John, Thomas Rose, Geoffrey Boleyn, and Giles Bishop, with other commoners of the church of Salle . . . occupied a close of the said manor with timber of the church of Salle'. The precise implications of this misdemeanour for the construction are unclear, but making provision for roofing or scaffolding are possible explanations. More relevantly, the names of the locals held responsible recur in the documentation for years to come, and it is difficult to avoid the conclusion that they were prime movers in the whole project. Interestingly, none is from the wealthiest class. William and John Melman were the sons of the Geoffrey who paid for the porch. But while Geoffrey himself was a free man, his wife, Agatha, had been of villein status. Thomas Rose, the next on the list, seems to have been involved in the wool and cloth business, since he and his wife, Katherine, both belonged to the Coventry Cloth Guild. Some years later, in 1425, Thomas was fined for keeping as many as 500 sheep on Cawston Common, where he ought not to have had more than 200. A measure of his ultimate financial success was his ability to fund at least part of the north transept at Salle, which seems to have been complete by his death in 1441.

One gets such contradictory impressions of the people living in Salle, and indeed many other English towns and villages, in the later Middle Ages. On the one hand they usually get into the official record only when they have done something 'wrong', and this suggests that they are shifty characters. On the other, their wills indicate that they are models of piety, and surviving

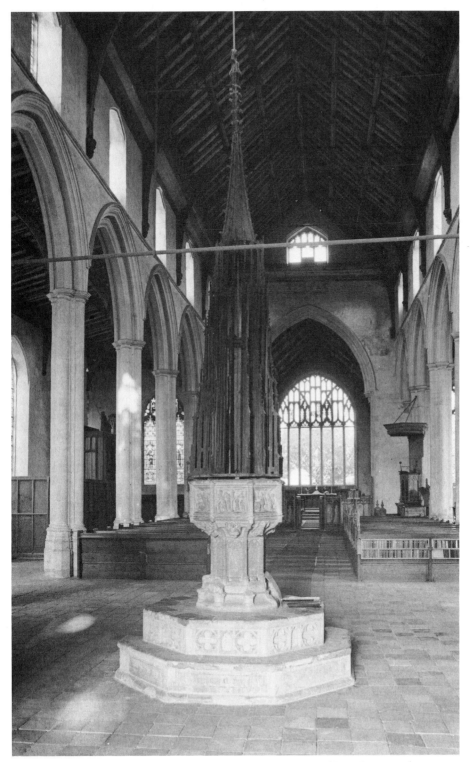

Salle Church, interior looking east, with font and cover (early fifteenth century).

Salle Church, brass of Thomas and Katherine Rose (c.1445).

memorials that they are the epitome of respectability. The beautiful and distinctive fragment of Thomas and Katherine Roses' brass shows well dressed burghers with a large family. It is the finest of the early brasses made in Norwich to have survived. When complete on the floor of the transept it must have been even more impressive. The thought which went into the choice of the design is still evident in the 'rose' window which alludes to their name, and the engraving is refined and delicately executed. The Roses must also have paid for the roof above their resting place since its ceiling has wooden bosses in the form of roses encircled by the letter T, for Thomas. He may even have paid for the walls and windows since, in his will of 1454, Robert Luce, chaplain of Salle, left among other bequests a chalice and a cloth for the altar of St Mary in what he calls 'the chapel of Thomas Rose'. Of the altar itself nothing now remains save the shallow niche, in the wall between the windows, which once accommodated the altarpiece. But in the windows is preserved enough of the old glass to show that their subjects both referred to the Virgin Mary. They were her Coronation (now turned into an Annunciation!) and, probably, a Tree of Jesse.

Wherever enough of the glazing survives in the body of the church, or where there are records of it, it seems that the windows were paid for by individuals or families. The easternmost glass of the south aisle contained an inscription asking the viewer to 'pray for the soul of John Holwey, once rector of this church'. John had died in 1401 at which point the new building may not have been begun, but doubtless the project was already under discussion and he left money knowing that it was soon to be undertaken. Another asked 'pray for the souls of Thomas Boleyn [and his wife Agnes] who gave this window'. Thomas was a small farmer working a few rented acres. He died in 1411. His son Geoffrey, mentioned in the case of 1408, carried on his father's profession. The Boleyns had not apparently been rich enough to fund their own chapel (as the Roses were able to) and Geoffrey and his wife, Alice, are buried under a brass of simple form and London manufacture in the main body of the church. Geoffrey Boleyn died in 1440 and thus failed to see the major upturn in his family's fortune. His son, also Geoffrey, having become a hatter and mercer in London ended up as Lord Mayor of that city, married into the nobility and bought the manor of Blickling, not far from Salle. His great granddaughter, Anne, was the luckless second wife of Henry VIII and mother of Elizabeth I.

The other glass remaining in the church whose donors are certain is in the Briggs' chapel of St James in the south transept. Thomas Briggs and his two wives, both called Margaret, are shown kneeling in prayer. Other figures, notably St Thomas Becket, Briggs' patron, are clearly from the same scheme. This glass is not however in its original window, or at least not in the tracery for which it was first designed. But it very probably came from this part of the building as the fine wooden ceiling above their heads has bosses bearing the initials T.B. The Briggs family interest in the church, and most particularly in their own chapel, was maintained into the early sixteenth century, and the donor portraits must have been reset following a general modernisation of the south transept. This may have been undertaken by Thomas's son, John, since his heraldry and that of his two wives, Eleanor Beaupre and Margaret Rokewood are found on the exterior parapet of the chapel. More probably, however, it was his son, Thomas who was responsible since a crowned T (again for St Thomas Becket) appears beside the shields and the name BRIG.

It will be apparent from what has been said thus far that gifts to the fabric and the commemoration of individuals and families by such means as inscriptions and heraldry were an essential part of the process in which the people of Salle were engaged. The fine 'seven sacraments' font at the west end of the nave (see p. 195) has engraved into the stone base 'Pray for the souls of Thomas Luce and [Agnes] his wife and Robert their son, chaplain, and for those for whom they are bound to pray, who caused this font to be made'. Such fonts, named because they show sacraments, for example baptism, marriage, unction, confirmation, etc. carved in high relief around the bowl, are almost certainly of quite local origin since all but two of the forty or so surviving are to be found in Norfolk and Suffolk. The example at Salle retains both its tall, elegant font cover and the large and handsome moulded and cusped bracket and beam from which it is suspended.

Although there is no information pertaining to the other surviving furnishings in the main body of the church, the pulpit and the screen, it is quite possible, on analogy with other documented examples in Norfolk, that they too were paid for privately rather than out of a common fund. For example the very similar fifteenth-century pulpit at Burnham Norton retains paintings of the four Doctors of the Church and the donors kneeling in prayer, showing that it was a personal gift to the church. Similarly, evidence relating to the construction of screens in the rest of the county suggests that it is quite likely that one large benefaction would have paid for the carpentry and a series of smaller donations for painting the panels along the dado (the lower section). Such screen paintings were done after the woodwork had been set in place, sometimes many years later. At Salle, as elsewhere, the task of filling up the panels had not been completed by the time of the Reformation, but what was executed, the four Doctors and four of the Apostles, stems from a single campaign around 1500 and shows the fine decorative sense of the best local work of the period. By Norfolk standards even the figure painting is good. As we see it now, the screen has lost both the tall uprights and intervening vaulting which would have supported the loft across the chancel arch and the great rood, or cross. This must have been in place by 1437, since the will of John Northland, chaplain, made in that year left 2/- for the light on the perch before the High Crucifix.

It is likely that screen and rood were only quite recently finished by this date, and with them probably the transept chapels. The final work required for the completion of the new fabric was the rebuilding of the chancel itself. An inscription formerly to be found along the base of the chancel windows stated that Master William Wode, rector, built this building from the foundations and finished it in 1440. It was the rule in the construction and upkeep of parish churches that while the parish itself was responsible for the nave, everything east of the chancel arch was the incumbent's concern. Wode had become rector in 1428 having, apparently, studied law. We may none the less doubt whether he was wealthy enough himself to fund this substantial structure, let alone to pay for its embellishment. Very probably the patrons of the living, the Brewes family of Stinton Manor, helped with donations. Their heraldry certainly figured largely in the east window, along with shields of such nationally important families as the Delapoles and the Beauforts.

The glazing of the chancel, even in its present fragmentary state is one of the glories of the church. The Nine Orders of Angels in the east window are painted on glass which is largely red, blue and clear. With the black paint and areas of pale golden yellow-stain this strikes a perfect balance between richness of colour and translucency. The execution as well as the materials are as good as the best that can still be found from mid-fifteenth-century England. Equally good in terms of drawing are the figures of prophets and patriarchs in the side windows. A range of techniques is used for modelling and highlighting heads and draperies. These include hatching and cross-hatching, wash shading and also a subtractive process in which an area of dark paint is applied and then selectively scraped away using the pointed handle of the brush. By this means parts of Elijah's hair, beard, moustache and bushy eyebrows are indicated. None of the other glass surviving in Norfolk, which has preserved much from this period, can be compared with the chancel at Salle. This fact and the high quality of the painting suggest either that it was produced by a travelling workshop of national reputation, or that it was commissioned from some major centre, perhaps London.

The other remarkable feature of the chancel is the stalls, twenty-six of them. Normally stalls are found in churches served by communities of monks or a secular college. As there is no evidence that Salle was ever intended to become collegiate, we may well wonder how the seats could have been filled. There is no obvious answer. But Salle cannot be seen in isolation. Among the grander parish churches of eastern England it had become fashionable to

Salle Church, Elijah and Noah, windows (c.1440).

include stalls, though only one or two have the number found at Salle, and none the restrained and refined design and execution. Again, there is no parallel in the county and one is drawn to suggest that the work was done by itinerant craftsmen brought in specially, or that it was sent prefabricated from elsewhere.

The glass and the seating of the east end indicate the pretensions and the taste and wealth of the rector, William Wode, or his patrons. Only on the attractive wooden roof bosses, showing scenes from Christ's life and passion, do local artists seem to have been used, and as they are placed high up one might argue that the best was not necessary. They are, none the less, very good by local standards.

While it is not possible to claim that Salle is a typical parish church of its period, it shows very well the ways in which a community might put money and effort into the creation of what was simultaneously an object of local pride and an expression of piety. It also shows that the aspiring middle-class patron of the fifteenth century was not necessarily content to go to the nearest painter, sculptor or carpenter, but would often seek out the best local artist he or she could find, or better still look outside the region. Parish churches were not only built on a larger scale towards the end of the Middle Ages, but they contained more furniture and memorials and bigger windows than they had before. This gave ample scope to a community of increasingly successful entrepreneurs and farmers for a display of individual and family wealth, and, without reflecting adversely on the genuine religious feeling of the people, it had the added advantage that it could claim to be for the glory of God.

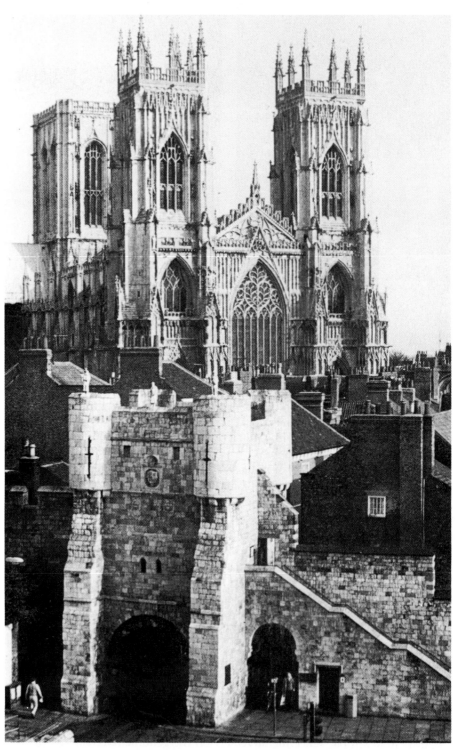

Bootham Bar, one of the four medieval gateways into York, and the west front of York Minster.

6   The City of York

R. B. DOBSON

On the last day of May in 1982 Pope John Paul II descended from the sky
by helicopter to address – on Knavesmire racecourse – the largest multitude
of human beings who can ever have been assembled in or near the city of
York during the course of the latter's almost two thousand year-long history.
By opening his speech with an expression of personal pleasure at being the
first pope ever to visit England's most 'historic city', John Paul II was
thereby endorsing modern York's recent astonishing success in becoming this
country's single most popular memorial to times past, and especially to the
medieval past.

Throughout, and ever since, the Middle Ages, York has always been a
much visited town; and for its first historian, Sir Thomas Widdrington,
writing in the 1660s, it was already axiomatic that 'the dial of the city hath a
long time turned backwards'. But nothing, one supposes, would have
surprised the clergy and burgesses of medieval York more than that the
battered remnants of their own city should have now become a primary
objective of the massive pilgrimages of modern tourism. Such popularity has
its own very special dangers for the student of the arts in Britain; and it is,
for example, only too easy to forget that the survival of so many medieval
buildings in late twentieth-century York owes as much to the inability of the
impoverished inhabitants of the post-Reformation city to replace them as it
does to the achievements of their predecessors in creating them. It might be
even more hazardous still to assume that because York is now so regularly
publicised as a uniquely medieval city it was similarly *sui generis* in medieval
England itself. All allowances made for the very distinctive features of its
history between 1100 and 1500, this metropolis of the north and self-
designated '*secounde citee du Roialme*' deserves our attention most because of
the way in which it so often exemplifies – no doubt under exceptional
pressures – the universal aspirations and preoccupations of medieval English
townsfolk everywhere.

Nor, despite the difficulties of interpreting the remaining evidence, can the
historian of York justifiably complain of a lack of resources with which to
recapture the rhythms of life and the patterns of artistic patronage in the

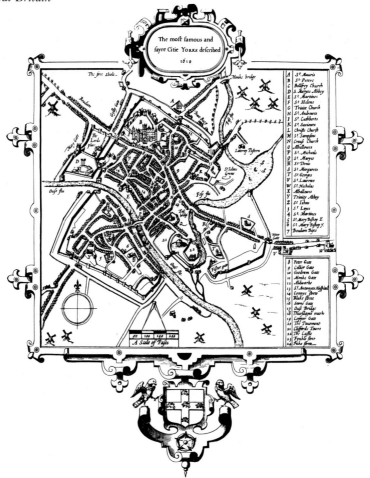

John Speed's plan of the city of York (1610); nearly all the parish churches survive, but not the religious houses.

medieval city. The survival of substantial civic and abundant ecclesiastical archives within walking distance of the architectural remains of the pre-Reformation city has stimulated much recent research into various aspects of York's history; and to that archival research has been added the even more spectacular boom of intensive archaeological investigation, especially after the creation of the York Archaeological Trust in 1971.

Nevertheless a documentary historian can be forgiven the belief that during the period between the Norman Conquest and the Reformation it is the written sources which still remain the most secure guide to the often confusing development of the medieval city. As always, it is the strengths and limitations of those records which shape our knowledge and perceptions of the life and artistic activity conducted within the walls of York. From 1086 (when a lengthy entry in Domesday Book provides us with our first specific clues to patterns of lordship in the city) until the visitation of the Black Death in the summer of 1349, the historian of York is usually condemned to see the activities of its inhabitants through the eyes of outsiders – most obviously, perhaps, the writers of monastic charters and the administrative agents of the English crown. However, from the middle years of the fourteenth century onwards, the citizens of York increasingly speak to us directly, not only through the records of their own city's administration and council meetings but through their copious surviving wills, now preserved in a long sequence of Probate Registers at the University of York's Borthwick Institute of Historical Research.

For this reason above all it will always be easier to recapture the tenor of urban life in late fourteenth- and fifteenth-century York with more detail and immediacy than is attainable in the case of the Norman and Plantagenet city. Fortunately there are good grounds for believing that it was precisely during this later medieval period that York experienced its most notable and distinctive artistic and cultural efflorescence; for it was in the hundred or so years after c.1350 that most of the features of the city which are now thought of as York's most characteristic legacies from the medieval past were originally achieved. This was the century, for example, when the city's most individual contribution to English drama and literature, its annual production of a lengthy cycle of Corpus Christi plays, not only emerged but acquired its final form; the century when York's already renowned walls reached their perfected stage; and the century when the most substantial works of secular architecture in the city – the halls of the fraternities of mercers (later Merchant Adventurers), of St John the Baptist (later Merchant Taylors) and of the city itself (the Common or Guild Hall) – were all conceived and built.

It was in the late fourteenth and fifteenth centuries too that many of medieval York's forty parish churches were either thoroughly reconstructed or, as in the case of Holy Trinity, Goodramgate, or All Saints, North Street, remodelled, refurbished and redecorated in conformity with the latest Perpendicular architectural fashions. This was the period too – 18 May 1396 is the exact date – when the city of York received from King Richard II a royal charter elevating it to county status, an urban privilege previously only enjoyed by London and Bristol. Not only did this emancipate the citizens of York from the jurisdiction of the sheriff of Yorkshire by enabling them to elect their own two city sheriffs but it also greatly enhanced the powers of their annually elected mayor, an office which had first emerged – as in so many of the larger English provincial towns – at the beginning of the previous century. All in all, Richard II's charter of 1396 can be said to mark the highest point in the citizens' corporate confidence that they could themselves manage the affairs of their own city, a confidence already beginning to be eroded by 1500.

It was also in the century after the Black Death that one of the major enterprises in the history of medieval British architecture, the gradual rebuilding of the metropolitan cathedral church of St Peter in the Gothic style, finally neared completion. When, in July 1472, the dean and chapter held a special service of solemn consecration and rededication of York Minster, they were celebrating the final achievement of a long and intermittent series of building campaigns inaugurated by the construction of Archbishop Thomas of Bayeux's great Norman cathedral church in the years immediately before 1100. The building of this, the largest medieval English

York Minster and chapter house from the south-east.

cathedral, was supervised by a succession of famous, and often royal, master masons; and it is also abundantly clear that the revenues which built and sustained what John Ruskin once called 'the Acropolis of English Gothic' were derived primarily from the landed estates and tithes of the church of York in the northern countryside rather than from the industrial and commercial wealth of the city itself. Nor would the medieval archbishops of York themselves, heavily committed as they normally were to administrative responsibilities on behalf of the English kings to whom they owed their promotion, have been at all familiar figures to the citizens of York. Its early thirteenth-century chapel, used as the Minster Library since 1810, still bears witness to the vanished splendours of the archiepiscopal palace north of the cathedral, but this was a palace rarely visited by the pontiffs themselves after 1200. Although capable of contributing handsomely towards building works at York Minster and – even more – at their own favourite country residences of Bishopthorpe, Southwell, Cawood and elsewhere, the medieval archbishops of York (from Thurstan to Wolsey) are not usually to be regarded as important founts of artistic and educational patronage within the city of York itself.

Much more significant for artistic activity as well as literary sponsorship in medieval York were the dean, dignitaries and secular canons who made up the chapter of the cathedral. Admittedly only a tiny minority of this chapter, which attained its final complement of thirty-six prebends in 1294, were actually resident in the cathedral close: for York Minster has to be interpreted not only as the most magnificent house of God in medieval Yorkshire but as the most important economic instrument in the north for diverting the wealth of the church of York into the hands of those careerist ecclesiastics who actually operated the twin engines of the late medieval English state and church. Nevertheless the four or five residentiary canons who did live in York to conduct diocesan affairs from the great Minster chapter house and from their own prebendal houses in the cathedral close probably deserve to be remembered as the most influential as well as the most wealthy individuals who regularly walked the streets of the medieval city. Despite occasional contributions from neighbouring noble and burgess families, most famously perhaps the York goldsmith Richard Tunnoc who donated the so-called 'bell-founders' window' in the north aisle of the cathedral nave soon after 1328, the construction and adornment of York Minster was essentially their own achievement. Usually graduates of canon law from the universities of Oxford and Cambridge, these residentiary canons not only owned the largest private libraries in the north but also acted as the most assiduous patrons of young scholars as well as artistic craftsmen in the city and its region. Even the comparatively undistinguished Canon Thomas Parker could afford to finance the complete rebuilding of the local church of Bolton Percy in the most advanced Perpendicular architectural style shortly before his death in 1423.

Not surprisingly, the lay citizens of York usually treated the canons of their Minster with a respect they often denied the many other clergy in the city, even those who were members of religious orders. For in York, as in many of medieval England's largest provincial towns, the authority of the mayor and council over their city was always limited by the existence in their vicinity of a remarkable conglomeration of now vanished or almost totally ruined monastic and mendicant houses. Of these much the most formidable was the great Benedictine monastery of St Mary's Abbey in the suburb of Bootham; founded in the 1080s, this Abbey rapidly became the richest monastery in the north of England and still housed at least fifty monks at the time of its suppression in 1539. The wealth of the abbot of St Mary's was sufficiently proverbial to earn him a place as the personification of monastic cupidity in the *Lytell Geste of Robyn Hode* and sufficiently real to provide him with living quarters so spacious that they became the headquarters of the Council of the North at York in the Tudor and Stuart periods.

Much more modest, but by no means untypical of the small religious houses which adorned the urban and suburban landscapes of medieval England, were the two Benedictine priories of Holy Trinity, Micklegate, and All Saints, Fishergate as well as the Gilbertine priory of St Andrew's and the nunnery of St Clement's, not one of which can have been inhabited by more than a dozen religious after the Black Death of 1349. Although recent archaeological excavation suggests that it would be unwise to underestimate the size of their buildings and precincts, all four of these religious houses failed to live up to the high monastic expectations of the twelfth century.

By contrast, the thirteenth century belonged to the disciples of St Francis and St Dominic, to such an extent that by the 1270s York had become one of the thirteen towns in England which housed priories of each of the four main orders of mendicant friars, Carmelites and Austin Friars as well as Franciscans and Dominicans. The religious and social role played by the friars – of whom there were still fifty-nine living in the four York convents at the time of their suppression in November 1538 – is notoriously difficult to assess with any precision; but in a late medieval city where comparatively few could write at all and those who did so largely confined themselves to the spheres of law and administration, it is highly probable that the mendicants continued to be the town's most productive authors as they were certainly its most influential preachers until the Reformation swept them all into oblivion.

The subsequent destruction of all four of medieval York's mendicant convents is in many ways the most serious disaster in the architectural history of the city; but it is almost as grave a misfortune that of the forty parish churches of the medieval town only a half still survive, and even those usually in a sadly truncated and diminished form. Already in the later Middle Ages it might well have been argued that the city was 'over-churched'; and certainly few of the city's rectories and vicarages were well enough endowed to attract the interest of particularly distinguished parish priests. Nevertheless the complex building history of these churches, much of it yet to be fully revealed by archaeological investigation, can leave no doubt that it was within their *ecclesiae parochiales* that the inhabitants of the medieval city gave fullest expression to their deepest religious loyalties. Few testators of the late medieval city failed to leave bequests for the fabric or adornment of the parish churches in which they almost universally desired burial; and it was within those churches too that the richest citizens could best hope to influence and at times control the practice of the religious life.

The choir screen, York Minster, portraying the kings of England (fifteenth century).

Visiting the Sick, window in the Church of All Saints, North Street, York.

For the most wealthy citizens of all a perpetual chantry, at which a priest celebrated masses for their souls, had by the early fourteenth century become the most desirable means of attempting to ensure both their salvation and the survival of their memory after death. When Edward VI's commissioners visited the city in 1548 to suppress these chantries, they discovered thirty-eight perpetual chantries in the Minster (almost all founded by canons of the cathedral) and thirty-nine chantries established by the citizens of York within the parish churches of the town. Nowhere in modern York can one more readily visualise a citizen of the medieval city as he would have wished to be remembered than in the east window of All Saints, North Street, where Nicholas Blackburn Junior (mayor in 1429–30) and his father (mayor in 1412–13) kneel as donors at the foot of the stained glass window they had financed to adorn their perpetual chantry in their parish church. For the vast majority of the lay inhabitants of medieval York at all times it was the parish clergy of the city (numbering at least 300 in the 1430s) whom they knew more intimately than they knew the canons of the Minster and the inmates of the religious houses. Whatever their inadequacies, it was from those parish clergy too that the citizens of York normally received the most influential schooling as well as religious instruction to come their way.

In the last resort, however, the political power, social status and self-esteem of those citizens depended absolutely upon the economic and commercial fortunes of their town rather than upon York's role as the ecclesiastical metropolis of the north. As early as the beginning of the eleventh century, an anonymous author of a life of St Oswald had described York as a town with a 'huge population . . . crammed with the merchandise – too rich to describe – of traders who come from all parts, but especially the Danish people'. Like the population, so the commercial activities of the city underwent many vicissitudes in the subsequent five centuries; but there was apparently never a period during that half millennium when York was in serious danger of losing its all-important economic position as the most significant entrepôt for the distribution of imported, and often luxury, goods to the denizens of Yorkshire.

A city which probably numbered at least 10,000 men, women and children at the time of the Domesday Book survey in 1086 is revealed by the national Poll Tax returns of 1377 (which record 7,248 adult lay tax-payers in the city) as then the most populous provincial town in the kingdom. By 1377, a generation after the Black Death of 1349 inaugurated a series of chronic outbreaks of bubonic plague, the population of York was admittedly already in decline. In the late fifteenth century depopulation was to inhibit the industrial and commercial energies of the city because (in the words of a petition addressed to Henry VII by the aldermen of York in 1487) 'ther is not half the nombre of good men within your said citie as ther hath beene in tymes past'. However, in the century immediately after the Black Death, recurrent attacks of plague seem – by a familiar paradox – to have positively enhanced the prosperity of the survivors.

It is in this period too, from c.1350 to c.1450, that surviving tax returns and the city's own freemen's register at last provide the basis for an accurate impression of how the inhabitants of York actually earned their livings.

Admittedly little will ever be known about the large groups of non-citizens or 'foreigns' resident in the town; and only now is recent research beginning to throw much light on the important economic roles, especially as domestic servants, played by the women of medieval York. On the other hand, the main categories of occupational specialisation on the part of the male adult citizens of York can be analysed in considerable detail. As in the great majority of Europe's medieval towns, the largest group of York's inhabitants was engaged in the woollen industry; and amidst a very wide range of more specialised textile crafts, there never seems to be any doubt that the weavers and the tailors formed the most numerous of the city's eighty or so separate crafts or mysteries. A substantial section of the town's population also worked in the leather industry, mainly as skinners, tanners, saddlers and cordwainers. Other important elements of York's urban society were involved in metal-working, ranging from bell-founders to pin-makers, as well as in the highly variegated provisioning or victualling businesses of the city. Yet another large group of York burgesses found employment in the building trades, within which the triumvirate of stonemasons, carpenters and tilers were always the most numerous. More distinctive to York's status as an outstanding regional centre was a minority of more specialised craftsmen, among whom the most famous now are the city's workers in stained glass, even if there were rarely more than five or six master glaziers working in the late medieval town at any one time. More interesting still, and positively increasing in numbers towards the end of the fifteenth century, were the inhabitants of the city best interpreted as the progenitors of the modern urban professions. By 1500 York was comparatively thickly populated with various types of medical practitioner, by attorneys, notaries and lawyers, by schoolmasters and book-binders and even (in 1497) by a printer of its own in the person of the German immigrant, Frederick Freez.

At the apex of York's civic society was a more wealthy and influential group still – those inhabitants of the town engaged in local and, more especially, overseas trade. The merchant class of medieval York traded not only in the city's own manufactured cloth, leather and other goods but in all the commodities of international commerce; and for that reason among others these were the only burgesses of York whose mental horizons ranged continuously wider than the walls of their city. Never an absolutely large group within the city's lay population, of which they probably formed less than five per cent, they had been the dominant one since at least the late twelfth century. However, it was in the century after the Black Death that mercantile families like the Graas, Holmes, Thrisks and Blackburns moved into especially dramatic prominence. No less than sixty of the sixty-five different mayors of York during that hundred years proudly styled themselves 'merchaunts' or mercers of the city in their wills and epitaphs. Never since has the city of York played so significant a role in English overseas trade; and it can be no coincidence that the comparatively informal fourteenth-century fraternity of mercers not only built themselves one of the greatest surviving guild halls of medieval England but in 1430 became a chartered mercers' company, receiving their later title of 'Company of

Old Ouse Bridge, York, (built 1565); wash drawing by Joseph Farington.

Merchant Adventurers' only after the years of its members' most profitable ventures came to an end shortly after 1450.

York's merchant class, a genuine if not excessively rigid oligarchy, must have been all the more formidable because it dominated not only the commercial but the political organisation of the city. Whether those merchants also evolved a distinctively bourgeois attitude to literary and artistic patronage is a less certain matter; for in many ways the merchants of medieval York always tended to imitate the behavioural patterns and social mores of the minor Yorkshire gentry families to which they sometimes owed their own origins and to which their descendants were so frequently to return. Among the most valued possessions of the late medieval mayors of York were suits of fashionable plate-armour which they can never have worn in battle at all.

There can however be no doubt of the York merchants' complete dedication to the welfare of their city and of their central role too in directing that city's vigorous ceremonial and festive life. Ironically enough indeed, it is only when the popular culture of the illiterate majority of the town's inhabitants was shaped, controlled and supervised by the mayor and aldermen in the civic Council Chamber on Ouse Bridge that we are afforded a few tantalising glimpses into the ceaseless round of communal celebration and ritual which actually constituted social life in medieval York. Most carefully rehearsed, and therefore best documented, of civic spectacles came to be the elaborate 'shews' prepared by the city government for the visits of ruling sovereigns. When the recently crowned Henry VII made his first entry into the city in the spring of 1486 he immediately encountered 'a place craftily conceived in manner of a heaven, of great joy and angelical harmony', before riding down Micklegate under 'a rain of rose water' to the accompaniment of a long alliterative poem vaunting the achievements of his supposed ancestor and legendary founder of York, King Ebraucus.

Such spectacular pageants were of course exceptional, primarily designed to impress a monarch rather than to entertain a city. At a much more humble level, and despite the absence at York of the churchwardens' accounts which do so much to reveal the prevalence of folk plays, church ales and other more or less informal diversions in southern England at the close of the Middle Ages, enough evidence survives to suggest that the craft and parish fraternity was the single most influential agency for promoting conviviality amongst the lesser ranks of urban society. Not surprisingly in a city so dominated by the institutions of the church, the most dramatic manifestations of this conviviality tended to focus around the major festivals in the Christian calendar, above all when they were celebrated at the Minster itself. No crowds in medieval York can have rivalled in size those which thronged into the cathedral nave to witness the enthronement of a new archbishop, to celebrate the latest English victory over the French in the Hundred Years' War and to commemorate the major saints of the Christian, and especially northern, church.

Whatever the origins of the city of York's most distinctive contribution to the history of English literature and drama – the annual production of a cycle of plays at Corpus Christi – by the date of the first surviving ordinance *ludi Corporis Christi* of 1399 it is clear that they had already come to represent an intoxicating fusion of all the most dominant elements – clerical, civic, craft and plebeian – in late medieval urban culture as a whole. Until 1580, when the commons of the city made their last recorded but unavailing plea 'that Corpus Christi play might be played this yere', the cycle normally comprised fifty or so separate plays each performed by different York crafts or 'mysteries', the obligation upon whose members 'to sustain and maintain their pageant' was crucial to their continuous success and popularity.

Each play was mounted on a pageant wagon, itself hauled from Micklegate through the centre of the city and past the Minster to its terminus at Pavement. Performances were given at twelve fixed points or 'stations' along the route; and this whole semi-processional dramatic spectacle, which must have lasted from before dawn until after dusk, attracted a multitude of visitors to the city, from royalty to the hordes of countrymen whose unruly behaviour so often alarmed the mayor and aldermen. In 1417, for example, it was ordained that no one in York at Corpus Christi should be armed with sword, Carlisle axe or any other weapon. In a late medieval city which fostered all manner of other religious plays, including the obscure *ludi* of St James the Apostle, of St Denys and of sloth (*accidie*), the processions and plays of Corpus Christi always held undisputed pride of place as the most popular and highly organised events in the civic year.

It has sometimes been argued that the words spoken by the actors of the Corpus Christi pageants – fortunately preserved in a single manuscript of the text, one of the civic 'prompter's copies' of the plays – reveal little real individuality of literary taste and religious belief on the part of the citizens of York. Perhaps so; but then that is hardly surprising in the case of an ideology no less strongly held because it was that of traditional medieval Christianity and of a series of dramatic performances possibly designed to exercise a conservative social control over the inhabitants of the city in the interests of its civic rulers. If so, what more appropriate than that the final and most elaborate pageant in the entire Corpus Christi cycle was performed by the mercers' fraternity itself on the grandest and most sombre of themes – the 'Day of Judgement' itself?

As on Judgement Day perhaps, so in York 500 and more years ago, we would certainly be in the presence of an unashamedly hierarchical society. There is no doubt that the co-existence within the characteristic medieval York household of a master craftsman, his own family and his servants and apprentices helped to promote a more closely-knit series of personal relationships than in post-industrial towns. Similarly, the many craft and other guilds which honeycombed late medieval York provided agencies for co-operative fraternity, conviviality and charity often lacking in a twentieth-century city. For these and other reasons – most obviously the illiteracy of all but a minority of the urban population – medieval provincial towns like York have sometimes been seen as havens of a supposedly communal and largely visual culture, only to be transformed into a more competitive world of separatist and individualistic mentalities under the impact of the Reformation. In view of the revelations afforded by York's own city chamberlains' accounts of the mid-fifteenth century that the town was visited every year by hundreds of strangers, ranging from magnates to bishops, and from professional players to itinerant minstrels, it might be unwise to make too much of the self-sufficiency of the late medieval English city. Its artistic achievements, from architecture to sculpture and from communal drama to private letter-writing, were by no means exclusively self-generated and always reflected changes in national fashions at remarkable speed. But that medieval York was a genuine 'world we have lost', a town of intense civic pride in which 'good fellowship' was the most highly regarded of social and public virtues, there can be no reasonable doubt at all.

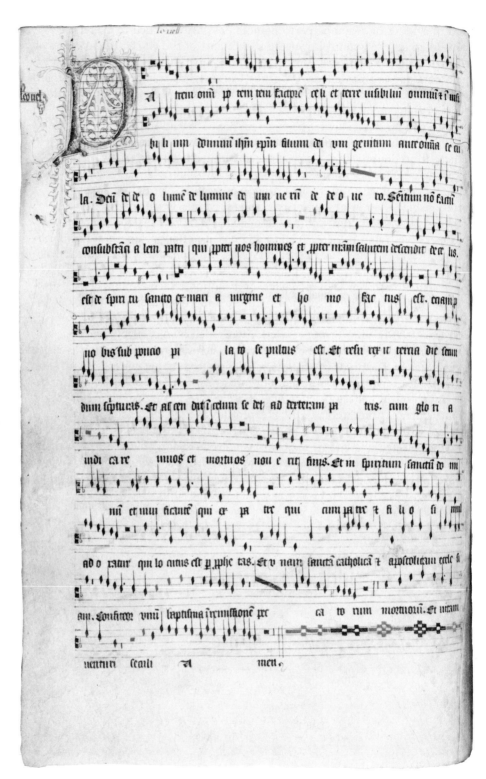

Page from a credo by Lionel Power, the Old Hall Manuscript (early fifteenth century).

7 Music

NICK SANDON and CHRISTOPHER PAGE

Introduction: the nature of medieval music (*Nick Sandon*)

In approaching the music of medieval Britain we must begin not with Britain in isolation but with western Europe as a whole. The culture of medieval Latin Christendom was essentially homogeneous, and music was as international as any other art or creative activity. In the church, the same repertory of plainchant (with regional variants and additions) was sung from southern Italy to Scandinavia and from Ireland to Poland. Polyphonic music, too, was born and nurtured in the church, and even when it spread into secular society and acquired new functions and styles it retained a great deal of technical and philosophical common ground. The church was not the only force for cultural cohesion; the courtly and chivalric culture of the secular aristocracy transcended political and geographical boundaries. Music in Britain did not always take precisely the same paths of development that it took elsewhere, and it did not always evolve at the same speed, but even at its most insular it still had much in common with Continental music.

We differ greatly from our medieval predecessors in our conception of the relationship between music and other aspects of life. We tend to treat music as a means of distraction or withdrawal from the reality of the present; for example, we use recorded music to make a repetitive task less tedious, and we relax by retreating into what we regard as the timeless and absolute art of a great composer. In the Middle Ages, however, music of all kinds was far more closely related to contemporary needs and experience. It not only grew out of and reflected this experience, but also played an essential or highly desirable role in many aspects of day-to-day living.

The religious preoccupations of the Middle Ages created an enormous demand for church music, because the liturgy and the ever-increasing fashion for extra-liturgical devotion required a great deal of singing and chanting. At first sacred music was fostered almost entirely by the church itself, but in the fourteenth century music began to figure with increasing prominence in lay religious patronage. Such patronage might contribute to the remuneration of the choir, or pay for the provision of music, or finance special services.

Aristocratic patrons maintained private chapels in their own households, engaging the best available singers to perform church music in the current fashion. They also employed secular musicians, just as they cultivated artists and scholars, in order to advertise their wealth, taste and intellectual acumen. Ceremonies such as a meeting between princes, a royal marriage or the signing of a treaty were often marked by the performance of music composed specially for the occasion. The texts of some medieval compositions contain so much political allusion and topical comment as to suggest that they were designed to announce a ruler's or a faction's intentions or to influence their decisions. On the battlefield and in the hunt, commands and information were relayed by trumpet and horn calls. Tradesmen and peddlars could be recognised by their typical cries, some of which have survived because they were quoted in art-music of the period. The craftsman in his shop and the labourer on the land had a repertory of work-songs designed to speed the performance of particular tasks; these too could become stylised and turn into art.

This is not to say that the recreative and restorative powers of music were unappreciated or ignored. Contemporary writers discussed the spiritual and psychological effects of music, and medieval literature abounds in references to many varied kinds of musical entertainment. Often, however, in contexts where we would ascribe to music an essentially diversionary role, a medieval observer would have credited it with a more complex function: not only to entertain and give pleasure, but also to inform, edify and influence. Members of religious communities included in their recreation the singing of devotional songs indistinguishable in content and character from some of the plainchant sung during formal worship. Evangelistic religious orders such as the Franciscan friars made up didactic or devotional poems in the vernacular to fit the melodies of popular secular songs. The Latin texts of some plainchant items and devotional songs were translated into the vernacular in such a way that they could still be sung to the tunes associated with them. The courtly songs of the later Middle Ages grew out of, discussed and recommended as an ideal the elaborate and sophisticated pattern of formal behaviour that the members of every aristocratic ménage endeavoured to observe. The epic and the romance, both of which seem sometimes to have been chanted or declaimed to musical accompaniment, served not only to entertain a military aristocracy but also to encourage observance of the same code of values. The oral song tradition of humbler people was, as it remained almost until our own time, a blend of the timeless and the immediate: of myth, magic and archetypal situations seen through the eye of contemporary experience.

Medieval music was, then, functional and contemporary; it was not part of a museum-culture. At virtually every level of medieval society musical entertainment was, or at any rate could be, home-made. For ordinary people it would usually have to be, but even among aristocrats, who could and did employ professional musicians, there seems to have been a widespread belief that competence in singing and playing the harp, lute and medieval fiddle was a socially desirable accomplishment: an attribute of a rounded and, cultivated man. Religious foundations were fortunate in having inmates whose musical abilities could be put to recreational use. Professional musicians were regarded, and must have regarded themselves, as craftsmen supplying immediate needs, not as creative artists responding consciously to an inner compulsion. The vast majority of them spent their working lives, or at least aspired to spend them, in the service of a religious institution or aristocratic employer. Only a very small number of medieval musicians ever rose into the higher ranks of society; those who did rise owed their success not so much to their musical talents as to their achievements in other spheres of activity, such as ecclesiastical and civil administration, diplomacy, literature and learning.

In the medieval scale of values the theory of music was more highly esteemed than its practice. The most respected type of musician, who alone merited the title *musicus*, was the theorist and philosopher, the scholar whose province extended from speculation about the nature of music and its place in the created cosmos to more mundane matters such as musical style and notation. Practical music began to figure in university education only in the later fifteenth century; even then, most professional musicians must have continued to learn their trade simply by practising it. Executant musicians were graded according to their function, so that those working for the Church were (theoretically at least) more highly regarded than those working in secular society. Lowest came instrumentalists, partly because they were usually uneducated and illiterate and partly because instruments were considered to be greatly inferior to the human voice. A medieval connoisseur of music would be perplexed by the heavily instrumental bias of the current revival of interest in early music.

In the Middle Ages the specialist composer scarcely existed. Most composers were primarily choir-masters, singers or instrumentalists who found it necessary to provide themselves with a repertory. For most of the period very little significance was attached to the authorship of compositions; practically all music in manuscripts copied before about 1400 is anonymous, and thereafter the practice of ascribing works to composers spread only slowly. For a long time it was only within the church, where an extensive and ever-expanding repertory of plainchant and polyphony had to be kept under control and preserved in reliable versions, and where mistakes in the course of a service would have been considered most unseemly, that music was habitually written down. Until the thirteenth century secular music was rarely notated, because its simplicity and its secure place in a living oral tradition made notation irrelevant; notation became necessary only when secular music began to rival sacred music in complexity, and when a few enthusiasts became interested in conserving repertories (such as that of troubadour song) in danger of oblivion.

Although notated music is today the most palpable evidence of medieval musical activity, in the majority of situations music must have existed solely as an aural phenomenon. It was created when and where it was needed, by drawing on a stock of material which the performers had learnt by ear and memorised, or by improvisation, or by a combination of the two. Medieval musicians' retentive capacity would probably strike us as prodigious. Most secular performers must have carried in their heads all the material that they ever needed. In the church, the clergy were required to memorise the most frequently-occurring items of the liturgy, which constituted a fair proportion of an enormous repertory of words and music. Medieval performers also made much use of improvisation; this was particularly true of secular musicians, especially instrumentalists (who probably rang the changes on basic patterns and procedures rather as jazz musicians do now), but even in church, competent singers were allowed to improvise harmonisations of plainchant melodies by applying comprehensive rules for doing so. Improvisation and composition were, in fact, closely linked; most of the stages in inventing a musical work seem usually to have been carried out in the composer's head; only when he was satisfied was the piece written out. The evolution of a musical work did not necessarily cease with its notation; compositions were frequently revised and adapted to suit changing circumstances and requirements, sometimes by substituting new words for the original ones, or by altering or replacing some of the musical material. Music not kept up to date in such ways tended to fall out of use within a generation or two.

Medieval society regarded music more as a commodity than as an art-form. Like any commodity, it was heavily influenced by the use to which it was to be put: by the function of a liturgical item, for example, or by the choreography of a particular dance, or by the form and purpose of the text. This does not mean that purely aesthetic considerations were totally irrelevant; if some compositions circulated more widely than others, it must have been at least partly because people simply enjoyed them more. Nevertheless, medieval music criticism tended to concern itself much more with such issues as technical propriety, stylistic polish and intellectual ingenuity than modern criticism does. The concept of the significance or profundity of the experience offered by the composer took a correspondingly lower place in the scale of musical values. A medieval commentator would not, in any case, have shared our modern notion of music as an autonomous mode of communication: an absolute medium. On the contrary, he would have regarded music as a means of persuading in a uniquely powerful manner: as a system of rhetoric. Music gave words a greater vividness and sense of presence than they had when simply spoken; it could by its aptness and beauty increase the listener's receptivity to the words; it could enhance its effect by utilising the devices of literary rhetoric, such as repetition, antithesis, climax and metaphor; and it could incorporate many of the qualities, such as symmetry, proportion and symbolism, which medieval artists used to inform their work with the greatest possible significance and virtue.

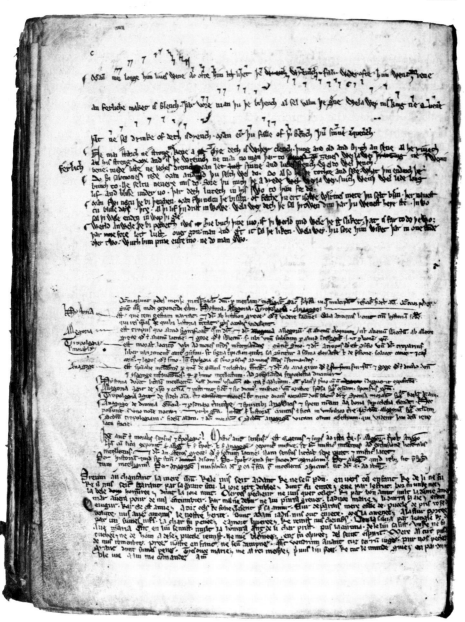

This informal, even untidy, presentation of a fifteenth-century English poem with its music testifies to the relatively low esteem in which English song was held by scribes of this period.

Religious music (*Nick Sandon*)

Words and the language of music

The relationship between words and music in the Middle Ages cannot easily be summarised. Relatively few medieval compositions show an obvious concern to reflect the emotional character of a text or to reinforce its meaning in an immediately audible way. Such features are perhaps most common in plainchant, where the melody may enhance the intelligibility of the words and even provide a discrete gloss upon them, illustrated in the Offertory *Stetit angelus* from Mass on St Michael's Day (see p. 250, Example 1). The close relation between the phrases of text and melody is very clear: several important words are set melismatically (with many notes to individual syllables); the melodic similarity between 'in manu sua', 'incensa multa' and 'in conspectu dei' underscores the purposeful connection between the incense, the angel, and the deity; and the enormous swirling melisma on 'ascendit' illustrates the fumes of the incense rising into the presence of God.

In monophonic secular song the melody is usually neutral in character, at least partly because it often has to carry several stanzas of varied emotional content. In polyphonic music, whether sacred or secular, a medieval composer tended to treat his text in an essentially abstract fashion. What most influenced word-setting in polyphony was the formal character of the text: the line-by-line structure and rhyme-scheme of a poem, for example, or the division of prose into sentences and paragraphs, or even the total number of words or syllables. In some types of polyphony the immediate intelligibility of the words was apparently not considered important; it was enough that the words were present. In the medieval motet, for instance, two or even three complicated texts may be sung simultaneously, and in the chansons of Guillaume de Machaut (c.1300–77) the syllables sometimes seem to be treated more as individual sensuous objects than as components of words.

The major difference between the language of medieval music and that of more recent music concerns the relative priority of melody, rhythm, harmony and tonality. Medieval music was conceived primarily melodically and rhythmically. Much of it – plainchant and devotional song, practically all instrumental music, and (until well into the fourteenth century) most secular song – consisted of a single melodic line: it was monophonic. Having no need to accommodate itself to the requirements of harmony or tonality, it was free to develop on its own terms, creating for itself a very wide stylistic range whose nuances are extremely subtle. Various types of monophony continued to be cultivated throughout the Middle Ages, but from the thirteenth century onwards composers devoted more and more of their time to polyphonic music, in which two or more lines were heard at once. Polyphony was, in fact, really an offshoot of monophony, being conceived as the art of combining melodies with each other so that when sounded simultaneously they made a pleasing effect. Today we pay more attention to medieval polyphony than to the monophony of the period, but we should remember that monophony must always have been the staple musical diet of the medieval listener; polyphony was something special, not encountered every day. Rhythm played an extremely important role in many kinds of medieval music; it worked on a variety of musical levels, from large-scale structure to small-scale ornamentation. In more recent music the primacy of melody and rhythm has been replaced by that of harmony and tonality; this, in essence, is why medieval music sounds so different from, say, that of the classical and romantic periods.

Plainchant

The modern revival of interest in early music has tended to ignore plainchant. Yet the church exerted an unrivalled influence on the development of medieval music, and plainchant formed the staple musical diet of the church. In the broadest sense, the term 'plainchant' embraces all of the monophonic music sung in church. Most items of text in medieval services were in fact sung, because singing made words audible in large and resonant buildings and also enhanced the sense of solemnity and occasion. The stylistic range of plainchant was very wide, and included decorated monotones to which prayers and readings were chanted, melodic formulae used for singing psalms and canticles; simple melodies for items sung by the whole choir; and lengthy and elaborate melodies for items sung by soloists. Here we should remember the passive role played by the lay congregation; some of the laity probably would have been able to join in the more familiar chants and make the customary responses, but formal worship was essentially something carried out by professionals on behalf of society as a whole. A church choir itself was not primarily a musical body; it was simply the whole professional community attached to the church. Its main duty was to perform the liturgy, which did indeed include a great deal of singing, but this does not mean that the singing would necessarily have been particularly expert. This explains why when new kinds of music such as polyphony were introduced into church services they were often entrusted to a small group of skilled soloists rather than to the whole choir.

The plainchant repertory and liturgical customs of western Europe were mainly those of Rome, with local additions and substitutions. The plainchant and liturgy of an individual church was known as its Use or Rite; some Uses (such as that of Salisbury Cathedral) were particularly admired and observed by other churches locally or farther afield. The essential core of the liturgy had been formed by about 650, and at least a small nucleus of plainchant may date from the pre-medieval period. The repertory seems, however, to have expanded greatly during the next three centuries; this must have been connected with the invention of plainchant notation in about 800. Plainchant composition continued throughout the Middle Ages, not only through the creation of new pieces in traditional forms but also through the expansion of existing pieces (a technique known as troping) and the devising of new forms. The most successful of the new forms was the Sequence, invented in the mid-9th century; in the Sequence newly written poems were set to melodies composed specially for them, an innovation which introduced new opportunities for literary and musical collaboration. Plainchant also influenced other types of music: elements of its melodic style have been detected in various types of secular song, and plainchant melodies were also incorporated into many kinds of medieval polyphony.

Polyphony

Polyphony as a calculated art probably began in the Frankish Empire in the ninth century as a means of enhancing the solemnity of a church service by making the performance of plainchant sound more impressive. To this end the church seems to have taken over and regularised improvisatory practices then current in secular music. The new art spread rapidly, particularly through France and into England. As with learning and art in general, Benedictine and Cluniac monasteries played a major and at times virtually solitary role in the creation and dissemination of early polyphony; these monasteries were also largely responsible for the continued composition of plainchant and for developments in music theory and notation.

The earliest use of polyphony in the church was to adorn the singing of texts which would otherwise have been sung in plainchant. We call this kind of polyphony liturgical because it was utilised to perform texts which formed an obligatory component of the liturgy. The earliest methods of creating liturgical polyphony (methods known today as organum) entailed either singing the plainchant melody in parallel intervals (usually fourths, fifths or octaves), or inventing a second and different melodic line that would combine with the plainchant to produce a pleasing succession of mainly consonant intervals when the two lines were sung simultaneously. In polyphony based on a plainchant, the chant melody itself was known as a cantus firmus, meaning a fixed or 'decided' melody acting as the foundation of the music. The voice singing the cantus firmus came to be called the tenor, literally the 'holding voice', implying that it held the most important element in the piece: the 'tenor' of the musical argument, in fact. This name described the voice's function, not its pitch; 'tenor' came to mean the highest natural male voice only in the sixteenth century.

The rest of the polyphonic texture was created by adding other lines of melody above, below or around the cantus firmus. Until the late twelfth century all notated polyphony consisted of two melodic lines (otherwise called parts or voices): the tenor and the duplum. By about 1100 it had become normal for the duplum to be higher than the tenor, so that the latter really did serve as an audible foundation to the texture. Between about 1100 and 1400 France led the way in the development of polyphony. Shortly before 1200, Parisian composers expanded the polyphonic texture by adding a third part or triplum, usually giving it a slightly higher range than the duplum. They also began to make the duplum move more rapidly than the tenor, and the triplum move a little faster than the duplum. This type of three-part texture soon spread to England, and it remained fairly standard throughout the thirteenth, fourteenth and early fifteenth centuries, although two-part pieces continued to be composed and some composers experimented with writing in four parts, generally by adding a part called a contratenor moving in the same range and at the same speed as the tenor.

Polyphony was, however, only one means by which the liturgy could be embellished. Music figured in at least three other methods of doing so: methods which pre-dated the introduction of polyphony and then co-existed with it. The first involved the composition of plainchant for new feasts added to the church calendar from time to time. The second involved interpolating into existing plainchant items passages of new text and music expanding and commenting on the content of the original words; this was a rhetorical procedure, and it took its name (troping) from rhetoric; it was particularly popular in France and England between about 900 and 1200. The third involved the production of new and non-liturgical pieces to be inserted into services as need or fancy dictated, rather as Anglican anthems and hymns have traditionally been used. This seems first to have happened around 1000 in south-western France where such items were called versus; by the mid-twelfth century they had spread to northern France and Britain where they were called conductus. Polyphony, the trope, and the versus/conductus were essentially three different ways of achieving the same end, the decoration of the liturgy, and they came to be very intimately linked. They were often reserved for performance by skilled solo singers, and very soon after their introduction they were being set polyphonically. These as yet modest polyphonic works were highly significant for the future, because they were the earliest composed and notated polyphony to dispense with a plainchant cantus firmus; composers could now create polyphony free from the constraint of incorporating pre-existing melodies.

By the late twelfth century polyphonic music was beginning to acquire secular roles and functions. The stages by which it did so seem to have been fairly gradual. The process probably began with professional church singers performing for their own diversion some of the music that they usually sang in services. The earliest major type of secular polyphony, the motet, was created in Paris around 1180 by extracting sections from long liturgical compositions and adding words to the duplum and triplum: by a judicious mixture of selection, abbreviation and troping. The motet was the chief polyphonic form in France between about 1225 and 1425, a period when French composers largely abandoned the production of liturgical music; it failed, however, to achieve similar dominance in England, where composers continued to cultivate liturgical and devotional polyphony. Although not itself liturgical, the motet retained evidence of its liturgical origin in that it was customarily based on a cantus firmus, usually a quotation from a plainchant whose text could be interpreted as an allusion to the subject of the texts in the upper voices. The first motets actually had sacred Latin texts and it is possible that they may sometimes have been sung during a service. By the early thirteenth century, however, many motets had French texts, and frequently the subject was non-religious. In fourteenth-century France the motet became a type of vocal chamber music with distinctly intellectual connotations; its texts tended to be self-consciously 'literary', characterised by ornate language, fanciful imagery and recondite allusions. Incomprehensibility was, in fact, virtually guaranteed because the triplum and duplum (in motets the duplum is sometimes called a motetus) usually had different texts. Musically the motet also tended to be complicated and demanding, using ingenious structural schemes and a detailed and often dissonant style. As the largest and most impressive type of secular polyphony, it came also to acquire ceremonial functions; many examples from the fourteenth and fifteenth centuries were apparently written with a particular event in mind.

The only other significant type of secular polyphony in the Middle Ages was the polyphonic song, which emerged in France and Italy in the second quarter of the fourteenth century (there are a few earlier French examples of a very primitive kind). These songs tended to be less awe-inspiring and more approachable than the motet, setting courtly love lyrics to music that was obviously intended to captivate. Such songs almost never used a cantus firmus, but they still tended to treat the tenor line as a structural foundation. Although the polyphonic song quickly became very popular in aristocratic circles on the Continent, it seems to have played a minor role in Britain until the early fifteenth century.

The survival of notated music in Britain

Most of the points made so far apply generally to medieval music throughout western Europe. Some of them must now be modified in connection with British music. As far as the survival of notated music is concerned, we are necessarily almost entirely limited to the music of England. Although there are musical remains from Ireland, Scotland and Wales, they are not of the music indigenous to those countries. Most of them consist instead of plainchant belonging to the fairly standardised repertory of the Roman church, or of polyphony imported from England or France. Celtic music itself seems to have been entirely unwritten until antiquaries began to conserve it in the eighteenth century. We have no sure means of dating anything that they or their successors preserved, or anything still current among traditional performers.

The written remains of English music also pose problems. What has survived has withstood not only the vicissitudes of time but also the destruction wrought by religious fanatics. Leaving aside books of plainchant (which survive in large numbers but duplicate a standard repertory) we have today a mere handful of manuscripts of pre-Reformation English music in anything like a complete state. Our knowledge is based primarily on fragmentary sources: remnants of several hundred individual English manuscripts, some of which (to judge from surviving folio numbers) must have been very large indeed. Such incomplete evidence creates considerable difficulties. For example, a great deal of scholarly attention has been devoted to what is sometimes described as the 'problem' of 'Sumer is icumen in'. To state this briefly: how is it possible to account for the solitary existence of this late thirteenth-century canon, technically so much more sophisticated than any other English-texted polyphony surviving from before about 1420? If we had more evidence, the problem might turn out to be illusory; in terms of style and technique nothing occurs in this work which cannot also be found in English sacred music of the time. The peculiarity of 'Sumer is icumen in' is the musical artifice with which it sets a vernacular text, but the unique source of the piece does give it a Latin sacred text (*Perspice Christicola*) as well. Which text came first, the English or the Latin? Was the work a 'sport', or were there others like it? As so often with medieval English music, the surviving evidence will not support a firm conclusion.

The musical culture of medieval England was naturally influenced by that of her Continental neighbours. The links were strongest with France, the artistic and intellectual leader of western Europe from the twelfth century to the fourteenth. Music participated in the general cultural awakening which occurred in England during the monastic revival of the tenth century, a revival heavily dependant on the example and expertise of the great abbeys of northern France. As far as music is concerned, the monastic revival established a pattern for the next 400 years, during which the larger Benedictine and Cluniac abbeys and the major Benedictine cathedrals played a central role in English musical culture. This role embraced all aspects of religious music: plainchant, polyphony, music theory, composition, performance and notation. Before 1300 the contribution of non-monastic churches and secular patrons appears to have been relatively minor. Most music manuscripts surviving from before 1400 seem to have come from monasteries (such as Bury St Edmunds) or monastic cathedrals (such as Worcester and Durham). The monastic foundations lost their musical primacy during the fourteenth century for two main reasons. First, Edward III, his sons and their peers began to emulate their continental counterparts in the conspicuous consumption and patronage that constituted a major feature of late medieval court culture. Second, royal and aristocratic patrons showed increasing interest in creating chantries in order to have services perpetually sung for the salvation of their souls. Early chantries made little or no specific provision for music, but later ones did, sometimes most generously.

The production of religious music in medieval England appears to have been fairly localised. The basic repertory of plainchant was, of course, universal, but it was grouped into local Uses such as those of Salisbury, York and the various monastic orders. There are few signs of a common polyphonic repertory; instead, each institution probably manufactured most of what it needed, honouring its own saints and making the most effective use of its own resources. Music certainly could travel, however, and surviving concordances (copies of the same piece in different manuscripts) prove that it did. Links between religious houses belonging to the same order could have encouraged the spread of music along particular lines of transmission, as could the travels of monarchs and nobles accompanied by their chapel singers. Nevertheless, most compositions survive in only a single source and seem not to have circulated outside the institution for which they were created.

This pattern may have begun to change as aristocratic patronage of religious music increased during the fourteenth century. The monarch in particular had to provide not only for his own household chapel but also for the growing number of permanent chapels in royal palaces; such establishments may well have shared their musical resources. Ties of blood and marriage must also have stimulated the circulation of music, as they undoubtedly stimulated that of literature. For example, the Old Hall manuscript, the largest surviving English source of early fifteenth-century church music, testifies to the musical interests of the House of Lancaster. It was probably compiled for Thomas, Duke of Clarence, when he became heir-presumptive to the throne on the accession of his bachelor elder brother, Henry V, in 1413. Old Hall contains works by at least twenty-five composers, many of whom are known to have been associated with members of the ruling dynasty, from Clarence's grandfather John of Gaunt to his nephew Henry VI. We also have fragments of at least two very similar manuscripts containing some of the same pieces; perhaps these are the remains of a 'super-league' of inter-related musical sources from the highest households in the land.

Although we have very little notated secular music from medieval England, the prolonged persistence of regional dialects, combined with the very late emergence in England of a widely dispersed aristocratic literary culture, suggests that in the oral tradition localism must also have prevailed. The fact that large-scale secular patronage of the arts began so late in England shows the aristocracy only gradually extending their range of interests from that proper to a landowning military elite. The lack of a tradition of courtly lyric poetry and music had important consequences. In fourteenth-century France and Italy secular patronage resulted in music which reflected the worldly activities and values of the patrons, whereas in fourteenth-century England it stimulated even greater production of religious music. Conditions encouraging the creation of a notated repertory of secular song seem not to have operated in England before the later fourteenth century. The crucial factors in bringing about such conditions were probably the increased contact between English aristocrats and their French, Italian and Spanish counterparts, and the twenty-five-year captivity in England of Charles, Duke of Orléans, taken prisoner at Agincourt in 1415. Charles was a poet, and during these years he wrote in both French and English; some of the anonymous musical settings of his poetry could well be by English composers. Secular songs begin to appear in English manuscripts around the middle of the fourteenth century, but they constitute a minute proportion of the surviving polyphonic repertory until the later sixteenth century.

The early fifteenth century: Power and Dunstable

In the early fifteenth century English music went through a period of intense activity and rapid and significant stylistic development, during which the composers succeeded in revitalising their musical language without forfeiting its individuality and traditional virtues. English music also became widely popular abroad, and it seems to have helped some major continental composers, such as Guillaume Dufay (c.1400–74) and Gilles Binchois (c.1400–60) to renovate their own style. In this way, English composers made a telling contribution to the musical lingua franca of the Renaissance, a language that was to reach its zenith in the works of Josquin des Pres (c.1440–1521) and remain unchallenged until the end of the sixteenth century. Our survey of these crucial years will centre on the careers and music of two outstanding English composers: Lionel Power (c.1380–1445) and John Dunstable (c.1390–1453). At first sight Power and Dunstable may seem to have had so much in common as to be virtually indistinguishable, but closer examination reveals quite significant differences between them: differences in their professional lives, the diffusion of their works, the kinds of music that they wrote, the techniques and styles that they employed, and their posthumous reputations.

As far as we know, both Power and Dunstable spent the major part of their careers in royal service, though not in that of the king himself. The earliest reference to Power (December 1419) describes him as instructor of the choristers in the household chapel of Thomas, Duke of Clarence, and lists him second among the clerks of the chapel. To have attained such a position in what was, after the royal household chapel itself, probably the most prestigious aristocratic establishment in the country suggests that Power must already have been a senior musician with a high reputation. If the Old Hall manuscript really was compiled for Clarence's chapel, Power's prominence among its contributors makes good sense; he may even have been responsible for its preparation. What happened to him on Clarence's death in 1421 is unknown; it is perhaps most likely that he was taken over by one of the Duke's younger brothers, John, Duke of Bedford, or Humphrey, Duke of Gloucester. During his later years at least Power maintained some kind of association with Canterbury Cathedral; in 1438 he seems to have become master of a choir of eight boys singing polyphony in the Lady chapel there. In the late fourteenth century, the wealthier monasteries had begun to employ special choirs of skilled lay musicians to sing services in the Lady chapel of the monastic church; these services included up-to-date polyphony, thereby allowing the institution a degree of vicarious participation in current musical developments which would otherwise have been beyond it. Far from being a sinecure provided for an elderly musician living in retirement, looking after such a Lady chapel choir could have been quite a demanding job; as the contemporary chronicle of John Stone (a monk of Canterbury) reveals, the cathedral took its music very seriously.

The details of John Dunstable's career are no less obscure, although its general pattern seems clear. The available information suggests that for twenty years or more he served some of the highest nobility in the kingdom. By 1427/8 he was sufficiently closely associated with Joan of Navarre, widow of Henry IV, to receive a substantial New Year's Day gift from her; his association with the dowager queen was later marked by a generous annuity. A document of July 1438 refers to Dunstable as 'a servant and household familiar of Humphrey, Duke of Gloucester'; it is probable that after Queen Joan died in 1436 Dunstable passed straight from her service into Gloucester's. Precisely what form that service took has yet to be established. The substantial nature of the payments and grants made to him (including estates in English-occupied France) suggests a rather higher reputation and status than those of a mere chapel musician. An epitaph on Dunstable by John of Wheathampstead, Abbot of St Albans, mentions his unusual skill in music, mathematics and astronomy. If a seventeenth-century transcript of another rather fulsome epitaph (perhaps also by Wheathampstead) on his now vanished tomb in St Stephen's Walbrook is to be trusted, the composer died on Christmas Eve 1453,

tua laus tua lux tibi musica princeps *thy glory, thy light, thy leader, O music*

Virtually all of Power's and Dunstable's known compositions set sacred Latin texts. Even though they may also have written some of the few anonymous secular songs surviving from this period, and some of the rather more numerous carols (devotional or celebratory songs written in a mixture of Latin and English and having a refrain, as in the well known 'Agincourt , Song' *Deo gratius anglia*), this would not materially alter the very heavy religious bias of their work. In this respect they show the same preoccupation with sacred themes evident in the work of most creative artists in medieval England. Their sacred music can be divided into two main categories: liturgical and non-liturgical. Liturgical music set texts which were an obligatory constituent of a service such as Mass or Vespers, whereas non-liturgical music set texts intended to be performed as an optional addition to a formal service or as a separate devotional or ceremonial act outside the normal scheme of daily worship. Most of Power's music (except for a few very late works) falls into the former category, and most of Dunstable's into the latter; this may reflect changing fashions in musical patronage.

The largest single source for Power's music is the Old Hall manuscript; essentially this is a collection of polyphonic music to be sung during Mass. In early fifteenth-century England Mass was the act of worship most likely to receive ambitious musical adornment. For Power and his contemporaries, this adornment seems mainly to have involved setting in polyphony those plainchant items whose texts remained the same from one day to another: these items (in Mass they were the Kyrie, Gloria, Credo, Sanctus and Agnus Dei) were known as the Ordinary because their texts were common to (nearly) all Masses (see p. 214). English composers had been setting these texts at least since the early thirteenth century and they continued to do so until the Reformation.

In one important respect, however, Old Hall shows a modification of this tradition of setting individual Mass movements. There are signs that Power and some of his contemporaries such as Thomas Damett (c.1390–1436 /7) were beginning to experiment with ways of interrelating settings of individual items so as to form pairs of Mass movements consisting of either Gloria and Credo or Sanctus and Agnus Dei; there are several such pairs in Old Hall, including a Gloria and Credo by Power. It was probably this interest in pairing movements that led Power and other composers to the idea of making musically interrelated settings of all five items of the Mass Ordinary, thereby creating what has come to be known as the cyclic Mass. There are no complete cyclic Masses in Old Hall itself, but the earliest surviving examples were probably written very soon after work on the manuscript ceased, in the early 1420s. The methods of interrelating movements devised by Power and his fellow-countrymen became the standard means of doing so both in England and abroad for the next hundred years.

The basic procedure which the English devised to relate the movements of a cyclic Mass to each other was a brilliantly simple but effective one, powerful and yet capable of enough variation to satisfy the most imaginative and resourceful composer. It was an extension of the practice, evident in many of the Old Hall pieces, of setting a Mass movement as though it were a motet, with a plainchant cantus firmus laid out in long notes in the tenor.

The breakthrough to the cyclic Mass came when it occurred to somebody (perhaps to Power himself, perhaps to Dunstable, who may already have written many of his motets) to base settings of all five items of the Ordinary on the *same* cantus firmus, thus creating a unifying thread strong enough to bind the cycle together while allowing the music to develop freely and without irksome repetition in other ways. The first known cyclic Masses, ascribed to Power and Dunstable themselves, show varied applications of this idea. The cantus firmus may be quoted in an identical melodic and rhythmic version in every movement, as in Dunstable's Mass *Da gaudiorum premia*; it may be ornamented melodically and / or varied rhythmically, as in Power's or Dunstable's Mass *Rex saeculorum*; it may be treated so freely as to disappear completely for a few bars or for whole stretches of music, as in the Mass *Sine nomine* attributed variously to Power, Dunstable and John Benet.

We may speculate that the cyclic Mass evolved at least partly to satisfy a widespread and strongly felt desire to create extended and imposing compositions whose constituent parts were related to each other in an organic, harmonious and satisfying way: the same desire that informed the planning of, for example, Salisbury or Florence Cathedral. On a more practical level it was a perfectly logical solution to the problem of combining liturgy and music to mark a special day. Most scholars now believe that such works were probably written for performance to mark a major state occasion such as a coronation, a royal wedding or visit, or the signing of a treaty. It has, for instance, been suggested that *Da gaudiorum premia*, based on a plainchant cantus firmus from Trinity Sunday ('Give the prizes of joy, give the gifts of grace, loose the bonds of strife, bind the bonds of peace'), was first sung in the nuptial Mass of Henry V and Catherine of Valois on Trinity Sunday 1420.

The cyclic Mass seems to have become the normal type of large-scale liturgical composition for Power's and Dunstable's English successors, such as Walter Frye (c.1420–c.1475), John Plummer (c.1410–84) and Robert Fayrfax (1464–1521), and examples continued to be written until the final disappearance of the Latin rite in 1559. At the same time, however, there is evidence of a growing interest in providing polyphony for other services. One of the first services to receive such attention appears to have been Vespers, notably with the composition of polyphonic settings of the Magnificat, the Vespers canticle. Dunstable's only surviving Magnificat is the earliest English setting by a named composer, and it bridges the gap between the few anonymous fourteenth-century examples (most of which are so rudimentary as to resemble lightly decorated improvised harmonisations) and the enormous and luxuriant settings by Fayrfax, William Cornysh (c.1460–1523) and other early Tudor composers.

In addition to the Mass movements that form its main contents, the Old Hall manuscript includes two types of non-liturgical composition. One of these, the isorhythmic motet, seems to have been a fairly recent arrival in England, and it was soon to disappear after a brief blaze of glory apparently kindled largely by Dunstable. The other, the votive antiphon, had a longer history and was to continue to prosper until the Reformation, inspiring some of the finest music ever written by Englishmen. An isorhythmic motet was essentially similar to any other medieval motet: it was written on a cantus firmus (often chosen to allude to the occasion or function for which the work was intended) set out in the tenor in long notes. Above the tenor an animated duplum and an even more lively triplum declaimed prose or poetry in rather flowery Latin or French, offering two different and usually complementary views of the matter in hand. Sometimes there was also a fourth voice, a contra-tenor, sharing the tenor's range, pace and supporting function. Isorhythm itself (literally 'same rhythm') was basically a very simple idea, involving the construction of a composition as a series of sections whose rhythmic patterns were related to each other by exact or proportional repetition. Virtually all late medieval motets were, in fact, isorhythmic; the rigour and sophistication with which composers were interpreting the principle by the late fourteenth century were the ultimate development of potential already present in the motet at its birth some two centuries earlier.

As we have already seen, the medieval motet was born in the late twelfth century in France. It always remained a characteristically French genre; its literary content, its counterpoint, and its emphasis upon rhythmic structure and ornamentation have been recurrent features of French music ever since, through Machaut, Couperin, Berlioz, and Messaien. Perhaps predictably, English composers took some time to warm to the motet, and when they did accept it (in the later thirteenth and fourteenth centuries) they developed it along different lines reflecting their own traditions and taste, particularly their love of sonorous homogeneous textures and smoothly flowing lines. They tended, in fact, to blend the features of the motet with those of the polyphonic conductus, a genre which had gone out of use in France around 1250. The resulting contrast in sound will be immediately evident on hearing in quick succession a French motet and an English one of roughly the same date (1330): for example, Philippe de Vitry's *Vos qui admiramini*/*Gratissima virginis species* (PMFC I p. 76) and the anonymous *Ave miles caelestis curiae* (PMFC XV 20, TECM I 15) from Bury St Edmunds (see p. 250–1, Examples 2a, 2b).

In the later fourteenth century, however, English composers appear to have made an effort to master the isorhythmic motet as it was being cultivated by their French contemporaries. This seems to have been part of a larger process of renewal, stimulated perhaps by experience of French and Italian music gained when accompanying English royalty and nobility on their continental travels in the decades after Crecy (1346) and Poitiers (1356). One of the earliest and most intricate English examples, John Aleyn's *Sub arcturo plebs* / *Fons citharizanthium*, may have been written around 1360 to demonstrate the skill of native musicians. English interest in isorhythm continues to be evident in the Old Hall music, not only in its motets but also and much more extensively in Mass movements written on isorhythmic principles. Here again we see English composers assimilating a Continental technique into a native tradition.

The great majority of known English isorhythmic motets are by John Dunstable; we have eleven by him, and only three by the next most prolific Englishman, John Benet (c.1400–c.1450). All English motets are clearly sacred in character and function, even though some of them could also have been put to political and ceremonial use. Each of Dunstable's was apparently intended for a specific feast day. Particular state occasions have been

proposed for performances of some of them: Henry V's marriage in 1420 to
Catherine of Valois for the Catherine-motet *Salve schema sanctitatis*,
for example. We have already noted that the artifice and intricacy of the late
medieval motet led to it being regarded as a special, solemn and intellectually
demanding kind of music. A work like Dunstable's *Preco preheminencie /
Precursor premittitur*, with its ponderously alliterative triplum
and duplum texts ricocheting against each other above the sustained
notes of the tenor and contratenor, must surely have been meant to impress
and edify rather than to charm. Its gravity and reserve are certainly
impressive, and the way in which its gradually increasing tension achieves
eventual release in the final cadence is supremely satisfying. There is quite
strong evidence that this motet was sung before Henry V and the Emperor
Sigismund in Canterbury Cathedral during the summer of 1416. It is
possible that most or all of Dunstable's motets were early works, and it may
be that English composers abandoned the motet in favour of the cyclic Mass,
seeing in the latter an even better vehicle for ceremonial composition and
large-scale musical architecture.

A votive antiphon was a Latin poem or (more rarely) prose text intended to
be recited or sung in honour of a particular saint or object of religious
devotion such as the Holy Cross, addressed in Dunstable's *O crux gloriosa*,
or the Seven Joys of Our Lady, which form the subject of *Gaude
flore virginali*, a frequently set poem attributed to St Thomas of Canterbury.
It is impossible to say precisely when votive antiphons began to be composed
polyphonically in England, because they seem to have emerged imperceptibly
out of an older English tradition of setting devotional Latin poems as
polyphonic conductus. The polyphonic votive antiphon diverged from this
earlier tradition in three main ways: it was cultivated chiefly in secular
institutions (aristocratic chapels, cathedrals and collegiate churches, choirs of
lay singers employed by monasteries); it was associated with the practice of
aristocratic benefaction to religious houses; and it reflected a growing interest
in personal devotion evident also in the increasing demand for Books of
Hours. By the reign of Henry VII (1485–1509) the votive antiphon had
joined the cyclic Mass and the Magnificat as one of the main forms of
polyphonic church music. It had also grown in scale and splendour, from the
intimate and concise settings of Dunstable such as *Beata mater* to the
monumental and spectacular works of Fayrfax and his contemporaries.

As far as we can tell, most of these votive antiphons were composed for
performance as part of a religious community's evening devotion. From the
late fourteenth century onwards the founders and benefactors of chantries
often required the members of the community to perform a special act of
devotion every evening, and they sometimes specified one or more antiphons
that should be sung during its course. In his foundation statutes for Eton
College, for instance, Henry VI stipulated that a votive antiphon should be
sung by the choir every evening before the image of Our Lady: *Salve regina*
during Lent, and any other antiphon on feast days in Lent and during the
remainder of the year. This accounts for the large number of polyphonic
settings of *Salve regina* in the Eton choirbook, a large collection of
magnificent polyphony copied in about 1500. With its emphasis on devotion
to the saints and to religious objects (such as the instruments of the Passion

and the Five Wounds of Our Lord) the votive antiphon exemplified an approach to worship that could, like the cult of relics, lapse all too easily into idolatry and superstition. The degeneration of religion into art had already been a major complaint of John Wycliffe and his followers, and the theme was taken up again, perhaps with even greater justification, by reformers in the early sixteenth century.

Lionel Power and John Dunstable are the only English composers of their period whose work survives in sufficient quantity to permit an appraisal of their creative personality and achievement. We have some fifty compositions which can be fairly safely ascribed to Power; these survive in about thirteen manuscripts, all but two of which were written outside England (mainly in northern Italy, Savoy, Burgundy and Flanders). Equivalent figures for Dunstable are approximately seventy-three compositions in about forty-three manuscripts of which some twenty-five are not of English origin. The next most generously represented English composers of the period, John Bedyngham (c.1420–59/60) and John Benet, come a long way behind with about twenty compositions each. Such figures cannot, of course, be precise or definitive, because new discoveries are constantly being made.

Musical links and contrasts with the Continent

The high proportion of non-English manuscripts attests the popularity that English music enjoyed on the Continent in the mid-fifteenth century. Power and Dunstable are by no means the only English composers to be represented. These Continental sources contain well over a hundred works by other named Englishmen, and an even larger number of anonymous pieces with English stylistic features; some of the anonymous pieces are designated *Anglicanus* or *de Anglia* ('English' or 'from England'). Contemporary commentators had no doubt about the reasons for this sudden popularity of and demand for English music. An often quoted passage in Martin le Franc's poem 'Le Champion des dames' (c.1440) describes how Dufay and Binchois copied the English style from Dunstable. In the mid-1470s the theorist Johannes Tinctoris also named Dunstable as the most eminent practitioner of a new musical art invented by the English. It is interesting that the commentators of the time singled out Dunstable for praise, and that Dunstable's music survives in approximately thrice as many sources as Power's, when the quality of their music would suggest that Power did not have significantly less to offer. Perhaps the most likely explanations are that Dunstable's long association with members of the English royal dynasty made his music peculiarly influential, and that Power's heyday slightly pre-dated the awakening of continental interest in English music. Whatever the reasons, the uniquely high reputation that Dunstable enjoys today is the direct consequence of this early fame. Power, on the other hand, has been left in the shadows. Yet Power's music is in no sense inferior to Dunstable's (some would say that it is actually rather more characterful and less bland), and Dunstable's own music is stylistically indebted to Power's.

It seems clear that the mainstream Continental musical style of the 1430s and 1440s, exemplified in the early work of Dufay and Binchois, was in need of renovation, and that English music provided one source (not necessarily the only source) of renewal. The opportunity for such an influence to operate must have been provided largely by political circumstances, in particular by the contacts (diplomatic, dynastic and cultural) between the major English nobility and their Continental peers. English music had something to offer partly because of the peculiar way in which it had evolved during the previous two centuries, and partly because it had itself recently undergone renovation. To understand this we must retrace our steps.

During the thirteenth and fourteenth centuries English and French music developed along different lines; between about 1250 and 1350 the flow of music between England and France seems almost to have ceased. The stylistic divergence between English and French music became very marked, and its aural consequences extremely distinctive. French composers concentrated upon secular music and developed a texture in which the individual lines are strongly differentiated from each other. They approached musical construction in rather an abstract way, and the sound of their music is somewhat meagre and cool, with short phrases, jagged and metrically irregular melodies, syncopated (off-beat) rhythms, a high level of dissonance, an emphasis on the empty-sounding intervals of the fifth and the octave, and a fairly arbitrary juxtaposition of chords. English composers, on the other hand, continued to concentrate upon sacred music and developed a texture in which the voices resemble each other and blend together. Their structures tend to arise from the musical material, and the sound of their music is predominantly rather generous and warm, with long phrases, smooth and metrically regular melodies, a lack of syncopation, a high level of consonance, an emphasis on the full-sounding intervals of the third and the sixth, and an instinct for satisfying chord-progressions that sometimes sound remarkably up-to-date. For a modern audience, English music is undeniably easier on the ear.

Nevertheless, English polyphony of the thirteenth and fourteenth centuries generally lacks variety: it flows easily, usually in trochaic metre, with very few rhythmic or melodic surprises; it has a clear and symmetrical placing of cadences and a consistently sonorous and well-blended texture; its texts are simple and straightforward and its formal schemes are fairly limited. There are signs that in the later fourteenth century renewed exposure to Continental music (not only French but also Italian) may have made English composers feel rather old-fashioned, and have encouraged them to be more experimental in their music. The Old Hall manuscript itself shows English composers responding with apparent enthusiasm and impressive competence to Continental musical influences. While it contains some pieces in a thoroughly insular style that would not have been out of place half a century earlier (such as Power's *Beata progenies*), it also includes many works successfully assimilating contemporary French and Italian musical elements. Among the former are textural and structural concepts from the isorhythmic motet, and stylistic elements from the polyphonic chanson, particularly its concentration of melodic and rhythmic interest in the highest part, as in Roy Henry's (Henry V's?) Gloria and Sanctus. The Italian influence is harder to isolate, but some of the Old Hall compositions (such as an anonymous Gloria) share with Italian works a melodically dominant top line that works more smoothly, in longer phrases and with less syncopation than one generally finds in the French song style. While they were experimenting with non-insular techniques and idioms the Old Hall composers did not, however, forsake their own musical inheritance. Even the most extravagant and adventurous pieces, such as Power's rhythmically extremely complicated Credo have a warmth, a stability and an immediate melodic appeal that set them apart from their French equivalents.

The mature style of Power, Dunstable and their fellows, the style that helped to liberate Dufay and his contemporaries, grew out of this harmonious integration of native and foreign idioms. Because it successfully merged so many disparate elements, it was a style of extraordinary richness and versatility. It complemented the typically English qualities of sonority, consonance, and vocal blending with increased rhythmic variety, a more distinctive and characterful top line, and an interest in large-scale musical architecture. Dunstable's little votive antiphon *Beata mater* sums up the results very well: the highest voice has the lion's share of the melodic interest, moving mainly by step and tending to outline chords; rhythmically it does very little that is obviously unpredictable, yet it never becomes repetitive; and its cadences are carefully timed and subtly varied. The lower voices have a supporting role but move nearly as rapidly, and the composer has tried to make them as elegant as possible. There are hardly any dissonances, and the harmony sounds perfectly logical and carefully directed. Formally the piece consists of an opening trio in triple metre ninety beats long, a central duet in triple metre sixty beats long, and a concluding trio in duple metre forty beats long, producing a short yet varied piece whose constituent sections make the pleasing proportions 9:6:4 or $3 \times 3 : 3 \times 2 : 2 \times 2$. For all its modesty this is a perfectly-wrought work.

The English withdrawal from France in the 1450s and the dynastic struggle between the houses of Lancaster and York seem to have inhibited the continuance of musical liaison with the Continent, and it cannot be denied that never since has England been part of the musical mainstream of Europe, let alone a leading current in it. But by creating a fertile new musical style out of diverse insular and Continental idioms Lionel Power, John Dunstable and their fellows had made a significant contribution to the development of the musical language of the Renaissance. Perhaps just as important as the question of style was the fact that they were, as their English predecessors had always been, musicians in the service of the church. Centuries of uninterrupted concentration and experiment had made them completely conversant with the liturgy and its plainchant, and thoroughly adept and resourceful in devising ways in which polyphony could be integrated into worship. To Continental composers of Dufay's generation, whose immediate heritage was largely one of secular music but who, as fashion changed, now found themselves once again required to write for the church, these Englishmen could offer experience available perhaps from no other source. The church music of Dufay, Ockeghem, Josquin, Morales and Lassus would simply not have been possible without them.

Secular music *(Christopher Page)*

Introduction

When the Saxon rebel Hereward the Wake was a young man 'the women and girls used to sing of him in their dances'. So says Richard of Ely, whose *Deeds of Hereward* was written in time to catch the last reminiscences of men who had served under the famous warrior in his struggle against William the Conqueror. Richard had probably heard some of these dance-songs and he may even have absorbed them into the *Deeds of Hereward* since his written sources amounted to little more than 'a few scattered and decayed leaves, partly rotten with damp'. If he used the songs in this way then his pages hold all that remains of them; like most of the secular lyrics sung in medieval England, the ditties about Hereward were never written down. Had a monastic antiquary not wished to celebrate a local hero, 'comely in aspect and with beautiful yellow hair', we should not even know that they had once existed.

It is odd that one of the best-known pieces of medieval music, 'Sumer is icumen in', should be an English secular poem of the thirteenth century set to sophisticated music, for this six-part composition is like a sumptuous binding around an empty book, leading us to a disappointment and a surprise. We look into medieval English song and find that only twenty lyrics in the mother tongue survive with musical notes from before c.1400, and most of these are pious hymns or pungent sermons in song ('Before you fall down off your bench /be sure the fire of sin be quenched'). There are but four secular songs in this handful of lyrics with music, one of them being the Summer canon.[1] The repertory of lyrics composed in Anglo-Norman is also a small one (perhaps some twenty items in all) although, as we shall see, it is most revealing.

Many of the forty poems with music, English and Anglo-Norman, are preserved on stray leaves in manuscripts of sermons, tracts on the Deadly Sins and other writings 'sownynge in moral vertu'; taken together, they amount to little more than Richard of Ely's wodge of scattered and decayed leaves. No doubt many sources like them have perished over the centuries (the rotten pages discovered by Richard of Ely cannot have been more than fifty years old), yet it must still seem that vernacular songs were not generally written down in England before c.1400 – at least, not in any systematic way. To this extent the history of secular music in these Islands is a history of lost music, and it is also a history of lost opportunities. Between 1300 and 1400 Britain produced little to put beside the polyphonic chanson repertory of fourteenth-century France – as represented, for example, by Guillaume de Machaut, the poet-composer whose literary works were devoured by Geoffrey Chaucer. To judge by what has survived, English composers were not generally interested in setting vernacular lyrics to sophisticated polyphonic music like that of 'Sumer is icumen in' – a curious circumstance that calls for an explanation.

The courtly lyric in twelfth- and thirteenth-century England

We begin where we must: with the Anglo-Norman aristocracy. The influx of Norman magnates into England after Hastings banished many Anglo-Saxon earls from their firesides; as a result the domestic contexts for high-class English song began to wither. Richard of Ely tells this story clearly enough in his *Deeds of Hereward*. In one episode a group of Norman knights carouse on an estate which they have snatched from a noble English family by the simple device of murdering the rightful heir. As the festivities begin to boil over the air becomes thick with jibes against the English; Hereward hears voices and instruments on the night air and makes his way to the house where he spies a minstrel 'singing to his instrument and abusing the English' while another performs ungainly antics in the middle of the room 'in imitation of English dancing'. Such was not the place for an Anglo-Saxon song.

Several generations later the situation had cooled somewhat. An Anglo-Norman aristocracy had emerged whose tower-houses and solars were graced with readings from some impressive literary works: the *Lais* of Marie de France, for example, and the *Tristan* poems of Thomas and Beroul, all dating from c.1170 and each one composed in England. Clearly, Anglo-Norman had ceased to lie fallow and was undergoing intensive cultivation. These Anglo-Norman patrons, like their Continental counterparts, had a taste for lyric as well as narrative poetry. A passage in Thomas's *Tristan* suggests that the royal court in London was crowded with music-loving courtiers just like those who saunter through Old French romance:

Then came the chamberlain. Behind him there comes a throng of knights and young men who are courteous, valiant, fair and handsome; they sing beautiful songs and pastourelles [*Chantent bels suns e pastureles*]. The young ladies follow, daughters of princes and barons who come from many lands. They sing songs and delightful melodies [*Chantent suns e chanz delitus*].

Behind this passage we glimpse the activity of Anglo-Norman trouvères – men like Denis Piramus, probably a monk of Bury St Edmunds in the 1170s, who candidly admits in *La Vie Seint Edmund le Rei*:

I have spent too much of my life like a sinner in a very foolish way . . . when I was at court amongst the courteous I made *serventeis*, *chanceunettes*, *rimes* and *saluz* . . .

A poet with these talents could expect a welcome in many Anglo-Norman households, especially if a person of influence there cared for music. Often that person was 'a woman trained in liberal knowledge and mechanical arts', to quote from the *Deeds of Hereward* once more. Queen Maud, for example, the first wife of Henry I, is reported by William of Malmesbury to have been a patron of clerks

famed in music and poetry; he who charmed the queen's ears with novelty of song considered himself lucky. She contributed payment not only to these but also to all kinds of men, especially foreigners.

These 'foreigners' were probably from France and enthusiasms like Maud's helped to bring French lyrics to England. The Anglo-Norman piece

'S'onques nus hoem par dure departie', preserved with its music in a British Library manuscript (MS Harley 3775),[2] is a version of a song attributed in continental sources to one of the most important French trouvères, the Chastelain de Couci (although not exclusively to him). 'Ben deust chanter', also in a British Library manuscript (MS Arundel 248), is a pious version of a chanson by another important trouvère, Blondel de Nesle. However, the most arresting of all these Anglo-Norman pieces has not yet been published as a song, although the poem was printed many years ago. It seems to be a prize-winning song from the London *pui*. This society, like its counterparts in Arras and Amiens, was a kind of guild for townsmen who shared an interest in the old courtly poetry. Its aim, according to statutes compiled c.1300, was to celebrate '*La bone cite de Lundres*' and to promote love-poetry in the French manner. Meetings were held, great feasts were eaten, and songs were submitted to the two 'princes' of the *pui* who crowned the best entries.

A single leaf of parchment in the Public Record Office preserves a song which these judges seem to have examined and approved (E163/22/1/2). The name of the composer, Renaus de Hoiland, is decorated with a drawing of a coronet and the last lines of the song mention the *pui* directly. There are many signs of an Anglo-Norman colouring in the language (forms such as *cascons, pur, dou* and *vus* are decisive when taken together). The musical notes are messy and seem to have been copied too soon after a feast. Fortunately, their meaning is clear and Renaus de Hoiland's 'Si tost c'amis entant a ben amer' proves to be a High Style love-song in the most elevated tradition of the trouvères; could such a song have been sung on the banks of the Thames, a generation before the birth of Chaucer, without a preceding tradition of courtly song in Anglo-Norman?

Song by Renaus de Hoilande (c.1300).

So much for songs *en francoys*. Why do so few songs survive with English words? There must be a better answer to that question than the familiar one: that English was not a 'courtly' language in post-Conquest England. The downtrodden Saxons of *Ivanhoe* – raising 'swine' in the field while their French overlords eat 'pork' in the Hall – have too much hold over our imaginations. English was the language used in low levels of society, that much is obvious, and in the *Deeds of Hereward* the hero, disguised as a potter, is mistaken for a 'rustic' by Norman women who think him ignorant of French. Yet the situation becomes more complex as we move through the twelfth century and encounter many different kinds of households inhabited by people who may have mixed English and French in many different ways.

The English treatise *Ancrene Wisse* ('Guide for Anchorites') is revealing here, for it exposes a literary milieu of c.1220 where English was being cultivated in the social context of the Anglo-Norman knightly class. The author, passionate in his desire to write a book that 'smoothens and straightens the heart', was probably a member of the Augustinian community of Wigmore Abbey in Shropshire and he wrote, in the first instance, for three sisters whom he describes as 'well-bred' women whose food was supplied from the Hall of some nearby patron (from whence it was fetched by their servants). To judge by some of the parables which the author uses, these three sisters were familiar with love-songs and romances: 'So, through his courtliness, this king was so overcome with love that he said to his lady . . .' Such things lie easily in the language of *Ancrene Wisse* and it is no surprise to learn that the three sisters could read French as well as English for the author enjoins them to read pious material in both languages. He also forbids them to sing amongst themselves and to go to public dances 'on ring' (i.e. dances where the participants held hands and moved in a chain or circle). It seems hardly conceivable that there was no tradition of high-class English song c.1220 to cater for 'gentile' women of this kind.

Some traces of this lost English tradition do survive, and they lead us almost directly to the carrels where *Ancrene Wisse* lay on the shelves of nuns and anchorites. *Ancrene Wisse* is written in a special literary form of Middle English developed in northern Herefordshire or southern Shropshire and one of the other pieces cast in this dialect is an impressive lyric in quatrains which deserves a closer look. In 'On Gode Ureisun of ure Lefdi' ('A Good prayer to Our Lady') the poet proclaims that he will 'singge' Mary's praises and that once he has sung his 'englissce lai' all his friends will be the better (Brown no. 3). In several places he adapts the conventions of secular love-lyric to his purpose and as he calls upon the Virgin we seem to hear echoes of lost songs for an English-speaking class of gentlewomen, knights and landowners: 'For love of you I toil and sigh often enough; for love of you I am brought into servitude':

> Vor thine luve i swinke
>   and sike wel ilome;
> Vor thine luve ich ham ibrouht
>   in-to theoudome.

By c.1220 the clamour of songs in circulation inspired some scribes to produce written copies of the choicest lyrics. The Bodleian library in Oxford houses a damaged page which seems to have come from just such a bilingual songbook as might have appealed to 'gentile' ladies like those invoked in *Ancrene Wisse*. Torn and detached, an autumn leaf amongst manuscripts, it bears parts of Anglo-Norman lyrics, two of which have music, and one English poem, 'Miri it is while sumer ilast', which has also been supplied with musical notes (MS Rawlinson G.22, f.1). These fragments show that the impulse to record the words and music of French lyrics was also felt by lovers of English song – but how often, and on what scale, we cannot tell.

No doubt the binders and printers of the Renaissance tore many medieval English songs to shreds when they needed something to stiffen a spine or reinforce a board. Yet the ravages of ignorance and time can only be held responsible for so much. Perhaps there never was a written tradition of 'courtly' love-song in English comparable to that of the troubadours and trouvères in France. We have already abandoned the suggestion that English was an 'uncourtly' language during the twelfth and thirteenth centuries; each manor, castle and town-house of the Anglo-Norman landscape must have given lodging to English in its own way. Let us rephrase the question: why did the English language not give rise to a High Style of love poetry before Geoffrey Chaucer?

High Style in poetry – any poetry – expresses a view of the nobility of Man. Whether the theme be courage, as in the heroic poetry of *Beowulf*, or whether it be the ennobling influence of love, as in the lyric poems of the troubadours, a High Style poetic is one that expresses its sublime subject in a special language that has been purged of all trivial associations. The French songwriters of the twelfth and thirteenth centuries, the troubadours and trouvères, believed that the experience of desiring a woman could ennoble any man whose feelings had the finesse to be spun into *fin' amor*. Such a view of Man's nobility demanded a High Style cleansed of everything extraneous and impure, concentrated like water distilled to its quintessence and placed in a sealed flask:[3]

> Las grans beutatz e.ls fis ensenhamens
> e.ls verais pretz e las bonas lauzors
> e.ls autres ditz e la fresca colors
> que vos avetz, bona dona valen,
> me donan genh de chantar e sciensa,
> mas gran paor m'o tol e gran temensa,
> qu'ieu non aus dir, dona, qu'ieu chant de vos,
> e re no sai si m'es o dans o pros.
>
> (*The great beauty, the fine discrimination, | the true worth, the fine praise | and other things said of you, the fresh colour | that is yours, good and perfect lady, | give me skill and ability to sing | –but my great fear and fright take them away from me | so that I do not dare mention, my lady, that I sing of you | and I do not know whether I will come to harm or good.*)

In England there was no High Style because poets using English did not have a view of Man's nobility to express. Many centuries earlier the situation had been different. Four hundred years before the first troubadour, the poets

of Anglo-Saxon England were using a High Style of narrative poetry to
explore the meaning of suffering 'in old age or at the sword's edge'. We meet
this High Style fully devolped in *Beowulf* (composed before c.1000) and as
late as the 990s it was still being used in *The Battle of Maldon,* the work of a
poet who knew that the ancient style was the best means of calling
Englishmen exhausted by Viking raids to the ancient values of courage and
resolve: 'Courage shall be the greater and heart the bolder, resolve shall be
the stronger as our might lessens.' This was aristocratic poetry; it celebrated
the values of a warrior elite and chose all its furnishings from life in the Hall:
gilded pillars, adorned swords and corselets of mail. As much as any
troubadour lyric, an Anglo-Saxon poem presents itself as a golden coin free
to pass at any moment into the privileged circle of some great household
where its worth will be recognised.

Measured in terms of years the distance which separates *The Battle of
Maldon* from the first troubadour lyrics is not great: a century perhaps, or
even less. Measured in terms of spirit the distance is incalculable. The
troubadour's view that love for a woman can ennoble a man is unlike
anything in Anglo-Saxon verse; there women are 'encircled with rings and
twisted gold' like the goblets they carry along the hall-benches. In 1066 the
native vocabulary of English could tell stories and proclaim (rather than
explore) the feelings of the characters in them; but the High Style poetry of
the troubadours and trouvères is about refined feeling alone; their view of
Man could not be expressed in English until self-conscious poets, recognising
the difficulty of what they wished to achieve, began to draw French words
into English and to use native words in contexts specially designed to give
them the associations required by a poet of courtly love in the French
fashion. Geoffrey Chaucer seems to have been the first to attempt the task. If,
in the fifteenth century, a composer like Walter Frye could produce
sophisticated polyphony for lines like these:

> So ys emprentid in my remembrance
> Your wommanhede, iour yowght, your gentilnesse,
> Your goodly port, your frely continance . . .

it was because Chaucer had written like this:

> So hath myn herte caught in remembraunce
> Your beaute hoole and stidefast governaunce,
> Your vertues alle and your hie noblesse . . .

Dancing songs

The search for what can still be glimpsed of English secular music begins in
the churchyards and squares of the towns. It was there, to the horror of
churchmen and to the delight of market traders, that the people of
medieval England enjoyed the entertainment which was the principal form of
secular music in these Islands: the chain-dance, or carol.

These carols (in Latin *coreae*) constantly intruded into the lives of
churchmen, keeping them awake before Mass or disturbing them in the very

act of raising the Host. The Statutes of Canterbury from 1213/14 forbid the enjoyment of *coreae* and other 'dissolute games' in churchyards, and the same prohibition was issued by Councils at Salisbury, Winchester and Worcester in subsequent years. In 1240/3 there was another blast, this time from Norwich, against '*coreae* and lascivious songs which are sung in the church-yards and the open spaces of churches'.

The writings of indignant priests and confessors offer us a gratifyingly full picture of these carols. We learn that they were usually held during the warmer months between Easter and Autumn, and that those who wished to participate in the dance prepared themselves beforehand; the dances were not spontaneous, in other words, but were planned to coincide with certain holidays (and, no doubt, with fair-days). 'Old wrinkled women, in the words of one merciless moralist, rummaged in their boxes for dancing clothes to lend the young girls who had none; maidens painted their faces and wreathed garlands of flowers for their heads, 'the very Devil's trophies, like the garlands which knights put around the necks of their chargers'.

Once prepared, the girls made their way to a local churchyard, linked hands with the men and began dancing in a line or circle moving towards the left. The sound drew so many people out of their houses that this kind of seduction was classified as a distinct 'sin of voice' by confessors, whose manuals of confession show that the luckless girls and apprentices of the villages and towns were required to do penance for their pleasure in the carol (and not just for their singing; there were 'sins of movement' and 'sins of touching' to be atoned for as well).

Many of these carols will have been sung to songs with English words and fragments of them survive here and there. Somewhat surprisingly, perhaps, these songs were sometimes 'topical' ones dealing with local heroes or events. We have already seen that Richard of Ely, author of the *Deeds of Hereward*, may have heard dance-songs composed in honour of the famous English rebel; and as late as the lifetime of Robert Fabyan (d.1513) the words of a song were still remembered that was 'sungyn, in daunces, in carolis of ye maydens and mynstrellys of Scotlande, to the reproofe and dysdayne of Englysshe men' during the Scottish wars of Edward I.

It is a remarkable coincidence that the songs in honour of Hereward have vanished but some traces of a 'topical' dance-song from the Ely region have in fact survived, albeit without their music. Four lines of English verse, attributed to King Canute (and probably of eleventh-century date), relate how Canute was so enchanted by the singing of the monks at Ely, as he listened from his boat on the Ouse, that he composed this poem on the spot:

> Merie sungen the muneches binnen Ely
>   tha Cnut cning reu ther by;
> Roweth, cnites, noer the land,
> And here wve thes muneches saeng.
>
> (*The monks sang merrily in Ely | when King Canute rowed by; | 'Row, men, near the land | and let us hear the chant of the monks.'*)

The twelfth-century chronicler Thomas of Ely, who records these verses, adds that they, and others, are sung in public dances ('in choris publice cantantur').

The custom of dancing to songs did not come to England with the Norman boats that beached at Pevensey in 1066. The Anglo-Saxons had songs for dancing. Around 1000 a monk calling himself 'Auctor B' composed a Life of the celebrated Anglo-Saxon saint and archbishop of the tenth century, Dunstan (d.988), and at one point in his narrative 'B' tells how Dunstan saw a vision of heavenly maidens dancing in a church. As they danced they sang the hymn 'Cantemus socii, Domino, cantemus honorem' by Sedulius. It seems that Dunstan particularly noticed the manner in which they sang; 'according to the custom of mortal maidens' ('more humanarum virginum'), they repeated the lines

> Cantemus socii, Domino, cantemus honorem
> Dulcis amor Christi personet ore pio.

after each *versus*. So it seems that an author writing in Anglo-Saxon England c.1000 could describe the following poetic form as characteristic of dance-songs performed by 'mortal maidens':

> *Cantemus socii, Domino, cantemus honorem;*
> *Dulcis amor Christi personet ore pio.*
>
> Primus ad ima ruit magna de luce superbus
> Sic homo cum tumuit primus ad ima ruit.
>
> *Cantemus socii, Domino, cantemus honorem;*
> *Dulcis amor Christi personet ore pio.*
>
> Unius ob meritum cuncti periere minores
> Cuncti salvantur unius ob meritum.
>
> *Cantemus socii, Domino, cantemus honorem;*
> *Dulcis amor Christi personet ore pio.* etc.

> (Stubbs, *Memorials of Dunstan*, pp. 48–9)

The human women mentioned by 'Auctor B' are presumably Anglo-Saxon maidens of c.1000 who would have sung in English. So we are led to a striking conclusion: by the end of the first millennium Anglo-Saxon poets were already familiar with a poetic form which we shall not meet again until the fourteenth century: the carol.

Songs and minstrelsy in the thirteenth and fourteenth centuries

If we widen our field of view beyond dance-song we find fragments of secular lyrics floating like driftwood in narrative poems of the fourteenth century. The refrain 'hey trollilolly', reminiscent of some well-known sixteenth-century songs, is embedded in a passage of William Langland's *Piers Plowman*, for example, where 'wasters' sing in their ale-house instead of helping Piers to plough his half-acre. Langland also preserves a line which 'diggers and delvers' sang as they set to work: 'Dew vous save, dame Emme' – perhaps a lyric about the 'wycche' Dame Emma of Shoreditch who is mentioned elsewhere in *Piers Plowman*. Chaucer's *Miller's Tale*, so full of

references to the musical life of a fourteenth-century English town,
incorporates what may be a fragment of love-lyric: 'Com pa me' ('come kiss
me').

Perhaps the most tantalising scraps of English song, however, are those
assembled in the celebrated Red Book of Ossory. This is a collection of Latin
lyrics, some of them by Richard Ledrede, Bishop of Ossory (d.1360),
designed to provide the mostly English vicars, priests and clerks at Kilkenny
with pious songs 'so that their throats and mouths, consecrated to God, may
not be polluted by poems which are lewd, secular or associated with revelry'.
In some cases the Latin hymn is preceded by a snatch of English (or Anglo-
Norman) giving the first line(s) of the vernacular item whose melody is to be
borrowed. The Latin poems are therefore X-ray photographs of lost English
lyrics where the skeleton of the poetic form is clear but the flesh of words has
gone. Here and there, however, more can be seen; these five lines, for
example, seem to be the start of a piece in the French *mal mariée* vein where
a young girl laments her marriage to a senile husband:

> Alas, hou shold y syng?
> Yloren is my playng.   *lost*
> Hou shold y with that olde man
> To-leuen and let my lemman,   *live and leave my love*
> Swettist of al thinge.

Another song is represented only by this poignant couplet; an allusion,
perhaps, to the floral garlands worn by young girls when they danced?

> Gayneth me no garlond of greene,
> Bot hit ben of wyllowes ywroght.
>
> (*No garland of green becomes me | unless it be made of willow*)

So far we have only considered lyrics, the *luxuriosa carmina* (lascivious
songs) which angered the priest in his pulpit and the confessor in his box.
There were also narrative songs, and the repertory of minstrels who sang the
deeds of princes and lives of saints was almost limitless. There were tales of
heroes from Antiquity like Alexander, Julius Caesar and Achilles; next came
Arthurian knights such as Gawain, Tristan and Lancelot. For audiences who
tired of these came tales of Charlemagne, Roland or Oliver, and behind these
great warriors a host of lesser heroes and heroines whose names sound empty
today: Regnas, Tegeu, Wyrwein, Byrne, Wylcadoun, and many more.

The minstrels who sang these narratives came in many different guises and
we should not let our view of medieval English minstrelsy be dominated by
the poorest among them. At bottom, it is true, the minstrel was often a
desperate man who had failed at some other occupation and then hurriedly
learned to juggle or show puppets before Hunger out of *Piers Plowman* beat
him 'so that he looked like a lantern all his life after'. At the other end of the
scale, however, there were the liveried minstrels in great households:

well-to-do gentlemen who, like professionals at any time, did their work and, when off
duty, lived lives comparable in every way to those of their fellow-citizens of similar
social and economic standing.

(Bullock-Davies, p. 23)

Some of these were drummers and trumpeters who provided fanfares and other ceremonial music (none of which has survived, no doubt because it was never written down). Others were 'string-men' who are usually listed as instrumentalists in account books but may also, in some cases, have been narrators (*gestours*) as well as harpists, fiddlers or whatever. Their repertory would have included tales which they declaimed or sang to their own accompaniment. Minstrelsy of this kind, conducted in English or Anglo-Norman according to a minstrel's accomplishments and the nature of his audience, may have accounted for much of the music played in noble and even royal courts in thirteenth- and fourteenth-century England.

What remains of these narrative songs? The answer must lie, in part, with the metrical romances, those narratives which survive in such bulk from the later thirteenth century onwards. These tales, which rattle along with the finesse of wooden carts down a cobbled hill, usually recount the deeds of some secular hero (perhaps a knight with Arthurian connections), often with coarse but vigorous piety. The surviving romances seem to have been intended for 'romanz-reding on the bok' for none survives with musical notation, yet some of them are undoubtedly close to standard minstrel fare and may have been written with minstrels in mind. Some such relationship between author and performer seems to be implied by Robert Mannyng's firm statement in 1338 that he *did not* write his rhymed chronicle of England for professional reciters and *harpours*. Presumably some authors did write for professional entertainers, much to Mannyng's annoyance.

When romances were delivered by 'amateurs' in chamber they were presumably declaimed, yet minstrels may sometimes have sung them. The late-fourteenth-century romance of *King Edward and the Shepherd*, for example, opens with an address to 'all those that love melody', while *Sir Cleges* (probably a minstrel-favourite to judge by its cruelty towards porters, ushers and stewards) contains what may be a barely fictionalised account of a romance being sung by a harpist:

The kynge was sett in hys parlore
Wyth myrth, solas, and onor;
  Sir Cleges thedyr went.
An harpor sange a gest be mowth
Of a knyght there be sowth   *in truth*
  Hymselffe, werrament.   *truly*
Then seyd the kynge to the harpor,
'Were ys knyght Cleges, tell me here,
  For thou hast wide ywent.
Tell me trewth, yf thou can
Knowyste thou of that man?'
  The harpor seyd, 'Yee, iwysse'.

Of all the metres used in the Middle English romances it is this one, called tail-rhyme, which may bring us close to sung romance. The basic unit is a rhyming couplet of four-stress lines followed by a 'tail' of three stresses. A large amount of the Latin liturgical poetry used in England is also cast in tail-rhyme; here is an example from the rhymed office composed soon after 1322 for 'St' Thomas of Lancaster who was executed by Edward II:

O iam Christi pietas
atque Thome caritas
   palam elucessit.
Heu! nunc languet equitas
viget et impietas,
   veritas vilessit.
Nempe Thome bonitas
eius atque sanctitas
   indies acressit,
Ad cuius tumbam sospitas
egris datur, ut veritas
   cunctis nunc claressit.

(*The loving kindness of Christ | and the charity of Thomas | have now shone forth. |
Yet, alas, it is in these same times that justice languishes, | irreligion flourishes, |
and truth is held in low esteem. |
Even so, it is a sure fact that the goodness | and saintly stature of Thomas | grow
day by day, | for such succour attends the sick | who visit his tomb that the truth |
shall now be revealed to all.*)

Many liturgical poems now preserved with their music in the bulky missals
and antiphonals of medieval England may yet provide a clue to the lost
narrative music of the minstrels.

The romances, however, were not the only kind of narrative song known in
medieval England. There was another, and one that bridged the gap between
folk music and minstrel repertory: the ballad. Many ballads have now been
collected from oral tradition in the English-speaking world and they display
an enormous variety of metrical forms and themes. Yet for all this diversity it
is possible to discern a 'classic' ballad form and style. The basic form is the
quatrain, either composed of four-stress lines, or of four-stress alternating
with three:

He struck the top mast with his hand
   the foremast with his knee;
He broke the gallant ship in twain
   and sank her in the sea.

The poetic style may involve an almost incantatory repetition of clauses
where the sense to be conveyed is smaller than the metrical form to be filled:

They had not sailed a league, a league,
   a league but barely three . . .

The narrative is sparse and enigmatic; protagonists are often anonymous;
motivations are not explained; time and place are sometimes left obscure.
This abruptness in ballad narrative is often intensified by sudden shifts to
direct speech with movement from one unidentified speaker to another:

'O peddlar, peddlar, what's in thy pack?
   Come speedily and tell to me.'
'I've several suits of grey-green cloth
And silken bowstrings by two and three.'

All of these ballad features can be found in a thirteenth-century narrative about Judas Iscariot, *The Bargain of Judas* (Brown, no. 25). The story tells how Christ gives his betrayer thirty pieces of silver so that he may go and buy food for the disciples. 'You may meet some of your kinsmen there', Jesus tells him, with grim foresight, and as Judas goes through the streets of Jerusalem he meets his wicked sister who invites him to sleep; when he wakes the thirty pieces of silver which Jesus gave him have vanished. Pilate, 'the powerful jew', suddenly appears before him and asks if he will sell his lord; 'Only for the thirty pieces of silver that Jesus gave me', replies Judas, and the poem ends with Christ announcing his betrayal to the disciples. Like so many Middle English lyrics, the metre of this one seems halting and ragged in many places, but the stress-patterns of the quatrains vary between 3–3–3–3 and the 4–3–4–3 arrangement of so many ballads:

> Iúdas gó thou ón the róc,
>   héie up-ón the stón,
> léi thin héved i my bárm,
>   slép thou thé anón.

There are ballad-like repetitions:

> Thou comest fer i the brode stret,
>   fer i the brode strete

Sometimes these repetitions are combined with abrupt changes in direct speech:

> Imette wid is soster,
>   the swikele wimon.   *wicked*
> 'Iudas, thou were wrthe   *worthy*
>   me stende the wid ston.   *to be stoned*
>
> Iudas, thou were wrthe
>   me stende the wid ston,
> for the false prophete
>   that tou bilevest upon.'
>
> 'Be stille, leve soster . . .'

The Bargain of Judas suggests that English balladry already existed in many of its essentials by the thirteenth century. We are looking into the vanished world of English narrative song so suggestively evoked by Sloth in *Piers Plowman*:

Y can rymes of Robyn Hode and of Randolf erle of Chestre.

Polyphonic secular music: improvised traditions

So far we have confined ourselves to monophonic traditions where there is only a single line of melody. No doubt this is how most secular music was performed in medieval England, yet sometimes something more elaborate seems to have occurred and polyphonic music was performed. Here we must distinguish between 'written' polyphony, which arises when a composer makes a design upon sound and records his choices to produce a 'piece', and 'unwritten' polyphony, which is produced when singers improvise part-music according to simple, traditional processes. 'Sumer is icumen in' is a fairly sophisticated piece of written polyphony applied to secular English words and nothing else like it survives. It remains as puzzling now as it has always done. Can it have been the only one of its kind? That seems unlikely, but nothing can be said for certain.

To pursue the 'unwritten' polyphony of medieval England let us retrace our steps to the early twelfth century and to Richard of Ely's *Deeds of Hereward* where we began. One of the most striking passages in Richard's narrative tells how Hereward disguises himself and goes to a marriage-feast; once there he takes a *cithara* (?harp) from a minstrel and begins to play 'most skilfully striking the strings', and singing 'now by himself and now in a three-fold way (*tripliciter*) with his associates according to the manner of the Fenmen'. Richard of Ely does not explain how Hereward and his associates sang 'in a three-fold way', but it sounds very much like some kind of improvised vocal polyphony in three-parts.

Throughout the Middle Ages various techniques for improvising two-, three- or even four-part music were employed by liturgical singers as a means of elaborating the plainchant they performed every day. The simplest method of all was to double the chant at the fifth, octave and twelfth, so that a remarkably imposing sound was produced by singers performing the same melody, each in his appointed range. This device, whose origins are lost in the prehistory of European folk-music, emerges into written record in the ninth-century treatise *Musica Enchiriadis*, and was still in use as late as 1274 when a French theorist, Elias of Salomon, described it in detail.

The technique of doubling a melody in parallel intervals is a simple one with analogues in modern folk-music all over the world. It was probably a common device in the popular music of medieval Europe. However, there seems to have been something distinctive about the impromptu folk-polyphony of the English: it showed a marked fondness for the intervals of the third and sixth, as well as the fifth, octave and twelfth. As early as the fourteenth century a continental musician noticed this feature of English folk-music. Johannes Boen studied at Oxford in the early fourteenth century and was struck by the English fondness for the imperfect consonances. He noticed that everyone used thirds and sixths with as much fondness as fifths and octaves and he was surprised that the practices of England should be so different to those of his native Holland just across the North Sea.

There may be some record of the popular singing which Johannes Boen heard in Oxford in a musical treatise entitled *Quattuor Principalia Musica*, compiled at Oxford in 1351 by a Franciscan friar. Amongst his chapters on written polyphony (*discantus*) there is one which bears this intriguing title: 'Details of a certain act by which several men may appear to be singing discant when in reality only one is discanting'. It is worth quoting at length (Coussemaker, IV, p. 294):

There is another manner of producing discant which, if it is well attempted, will appear most artistic to the ear, even though it is very easy . . .

Let there be four or five men who are good singers, and let the first begin the plainsong in the tenor (i.e. at the bottom of the texture); let the second place his voice a fifth higher [than the tenor] and the third an octave higher [than the tenor]. As for the fourth singer should there be one, let him place his voice at the twelfth.

So far this is simply a recipe for doubling a plainsong at the fifth, octave and twelfth. Yet our anonymous Franciscan introduces a refinement: let the singers who begin at the fifth, octave and twelfth ornament their parts:

Once they have all begun in perfect consonance, they will continue the plainsong until the end, and those who continuously sing the twelfth, the octave and the fifth should break and flourish their notes [*frangere debent et florere notas*], as may seem most fitting, always keeping time.

So it seems that we must imagine a dense texture of parallel intervals with the four singers elaborating their parts at will. But the true secret of this 'art' has yet to be revealed. In addition to these three or four singers there is another who 'descants'; instead of singing in parallel he must weave through the texture

rarely making the perfect consonances [of fifth, octave and twelfth] but rather making imperfect consonances such as the third, sixth and tenth. He should course up and down producing these consonances as may seem to him most convenient and pleasing to the ear.

This technique is so simple that it can be reconstructed with reasonable certainty. It produces a remarkable sound, in some ways reminiscent of the four-part written polyphony produced in fourteenth-century England, yet with a wildness all of its own.

Musical instruments

The musical instruments used in medieval England seem to have been almost limitless in number. We meet them everywhere in medieval art: drawn in the borders of manuscript pages, carved on corbels and embroidered onto copes and tapestries. Chief among them was the harp, small enough to be played in the lap, which is so often shown in the hands of King David. It could be equipped with as many as twenty-five strings, generally made of sheep-gut (although metallic substances were used by the Irish as early as the twelfth century), and plucked with the nails to produce a bright and rhythmic sound quite unlike the rich and romantic colours of the modern concert harp.

The psaltery, like the harp, was an open-stringed instrument with a string for every note. It consisted of a shallow box equipped with metallic strings that were plucked with quill plectra, one in each hand.

Among the plucked fingerboard instruments were the lute, citole and gittern. The lutes of the English Middle Ages were similar in form to their various Renaissance descendants, save that, as was the general practice throughout Europe before the last decades of the fifteenth century, they were plucked with a quill plectrum.

The citole was built in a variety of forms, most of them distinguished by their adherence to what might be crudely called a 'holly-leaf' shape. A fourteenth-century English citole survives and is now in the British Museum.[4] The customary number of strings appears to have been four.

The gittern was essentially a small lute and appears to have been closely associated with tavern brawlers and young men about town (like Chaucer's Absolon in the *Miller's Tale*). To judge by pictorial sources there were usually four strings, as on the citole, or possibly eight strings arranged in four double courses.

Among the many forms of bowed instruments pride of place goes to the fiddle, usually equipped with five strings. The body was generally hollowed out from a solid block with the soundboard glued on top, while the strings were made of gut, or possibly (in some cases) of horsehair.

In addition to these stringed instruments the minstrels of the Middle Ages had an appreciable array of winds and percussion at their disposal. For ceremonial purposes there were various forms of straight trumpet, often accompanied by the pairs of small kettledrums, called nakers, which the Crusaders brought back from the East (as suggested by their name, of Arabic origin). By the later fourteenth century this 'loud' instrumentarium had expanded to include various reed-instruments, the shawms and bombardes, capable of producing a deafening roar in a medieval hall (colour pl. 8).

For domestic music-making the choice was narrower; the ensemble of three-hole pipe and tabor (where one musician plays both instruments) was often used, both in court and street, when dance-music was needed, and sometimes the bagpipe was employed for the same purpose.

Very little is known about the music which these instruments played. Nothing recognisable as minstrel music has survived from medieval England, and in all probability very little of it was ever written down. No doubt much of it was spontaneous, impromptu and ephemeral, and closely related to dance.

The Angel Musicians Glass, Great Malvern Priory (fifteenth century).

Example 1: Plainchant Offertory Stetit angelus *from Mass on St Michael's Day*.

Translation: An angel stood by the altar of the temple having a golden censer in his hand: and much incense was given to him: and the scent of the spices went up into the presence of God, alleluia.

Example 2a: beginning of Philippe de Vitry's motet Vos qui admiramini / Gratissima virginis species *(note the repeated five-bar rhythmic patterns in the Contratenor and Tenor)*.

Translation: (Triplum) *O you who admire maidens! If we are to be more worthy than others of choosing the maiden whom we shall marry, when we are married she must be greatly loved.* (Duplum) *Most gracious species of maiden, whom bodily purity adorns through and through.* (Tenor) *Rejoice, O glorious* (a quotation from the votive antiphon *Ave regina celorum*).

Example 2b: beginning of anonymous English motet Ave miles caelestis curiae/Ave rex patrone patrie *(at bar 15 the Triplum and Duplum exchange melodies, as do the two Tenors).*

Translation: (Triplum) *Hail, O soldier of the heavenly court, whom the honour of victory adorns; you live with God enjoying repose in the manner of those who dwell in heaven.* (Duplum) *Hail, (O king, protector of the nation).* (Tenors) *Hail, O king (of the English race).*

Notes

1 For the music of 'Sumer is icumen in' and of all the songs with English words surviving from before c.1400 see E.J. Dobson and F.Ll. Harrison, *Medieval English Songs* (1979).

2 I am most grateful to Professor John Stevens of Magdalene College, Cambridge, for sharing with me his unpublished material on Anglo-Norman lyrics surviving with music.

3 This stanza is from a *canso* by the troubadour Arnaut de Maroill. For text and music see H. Van der Werf, *Extant Troubadour Melodies* (1984), p. 17*.

4 See Remnant and Marks, 'A Medieval "Gittern"', for a lavish account of this remarkable instrument.

A tunnel-like lane in Cornwall, in use for hundreds of years.

8   The Working Landscape

TOM WILLIAMSON

Artistic considerations played little part in the making of the medieval landscape. Those characteristic features which have served as images in the art of later periods, or which are now considered aesthetically appealing in their own right, were created for purely functional purposes. It is, however, important to be clear about which features in the complex palimpsest of the English countryside really are of medieval date. For in some ways, rather more survives from the medieval period than we might expect; in others, considerably less.

On the whole, relatively few buildings survive from the Middle Ages. There are, it is true, over 8,000 parish churches constructed before 1500 in England alone, an archaeological legacy so omnipresent that we tend to take it for granted. Yet in the case of domestic architecture, little survives. The half-timbered cottages which form so characteristic, if hackneyed, a feature of our countryside are seldom medieval. With but few exceptions, the only domestic buildings which survive from before the fourteenth century are the great palaces and castles of the baronial elite. Even for the later medieval period, what survives is in many ways exceptional, the homes of local gentry, merchants, and prosperous yeomen. The houses of the vast majority of the population were too flimsy to have survived, and villages like Lavenham in Suffolk which contain a wealth of late medieval timber-framed houses are atypical; Lavenham was not a farming community but a wealthy industrial centre. Outside such unusual concentrations, late medieval vernacular buildings tend to be far more common in some regions of the country than in others. They are, in particular, a feature of the south east of England, and of East Anglia. In these areas the late medieval period saw the rise of a class of wealthy yeomen, with sufficient surplus wealth to invest in the construction of dwellings which were durable enough to survive to the present. Most people in medieval England were never in this fortunate situation.

Yet although relatively few medieval buildings survive, a multitude of less obvious features of medieval or earlier origin exist in the modern landscape. The varied nature of such survivals, however, reflects important differences in the landscape of medieval England, differences which continue to determine much of regional variation in the appearance of the English countryside.

During the Middle Ages, a broad belt of country running across Midland England from Dorset to Yorkshire was farmed under the classic 'open field' system of agriculture. The farms were clustered in villages, and farmers held most of their land not in unitary, discrete blocks, but in unhedged strips or lands, each usually less than an acre in area, which were intermingled with those of their fellow villagers over the entire area farmed by the village. These strips were grouped into bundles, usually called shotts or furlongs. These in turn were grouped into vast fields, generally two, three or four in number, over which some system of communal rotation was enforced. Each year one of the fields would lie fallow, to be grazed by the village herds. The meadows, which provided hay, were also communally managed, as were the wastes or commons, the non-arable land which was primarily used for grazing. The origins of this co-operative system of agriculture are still hotly debated by historians, although it is now clear that it was not, as was once thought, introduced fully-formed by Saxon settlers in the fifth and sixth centuries. Instead it seems to have developed rather later, between the ninth and the eleventh centuries, at different times (and probably in different ways) in different places.

Today, it is difficult to gain a clear impression of the appearance of these champion landscapes, as they were called from the sixteenth century – a term ultimately derived from the Latin *campus* (a field). From the end of the Middle Ages they were being enclosed, that is, replaced by a landscape of hedged fields in individual occupancy, over which the use, access and control of the wider community were extinguished. Yet in many places traces of open field cultivation can still be seen, in the form of earthworks known to archaeologists as 'ridge and furrow': wave-like undulations in what are now grass fields. Medieval farmers created these ridges intentionally, by following a particular method of ploughing. Intended primarily as an aid to drainage, each ridge was usually, in origin, equivalent to a single land in the open fields, although by the time the earliest detailed maps were made this neat correspondence had often been obscured by some amalgamation of adjacent strips.

Not all ridge and furrow is of medieval date, for fields continued to be ploughed in this way well into the post-medieval period. Where a medieval date can be demonstrated, however, a great deal can be learnt from these earthworks. In particular it is noteworthy that in many Midland villages medieval ridge and furrow runs right to the parish boundary, meeting with the furlongs of adjacent parishes, and leaving no room for intervening waste. Such examples vividly illustrate the fallacy of the view that the medieval landscape was sparsely settled, with abundant reserves of uncleared woodland and waste. Before the early fourteenth century, when natural disasters, climatic deterioration and epidemic disease halted and then reversed a long period of demographic increase, the population of England probably exceeded five million. Areas of waste – an essential resource for the medieval farmer – were, in fact, in very short supply in many parts of lowland England.

The enclosure of the open fields was a process which continued over many

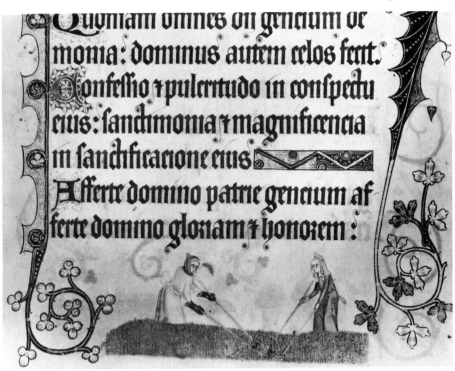

Thistle uprooters, from the Luttrell Psalter (c.1340).

Ploughmen with oxen, from the Luttrell Psalter (c.1340).

Ridge and furrow of former open field agriculture at the village of Padbury,
Buckinghamshire. The straight hedges were established after the Enclosure Act in the late
eighteenth century. The circles (lower right) mark the site of a former windmill.

centuries, and which was accomplished in a variety of ways. Some of the
present boundaries in the former champion areas were established by
piecemeal enclosure, that is, by individuals gathering together a number of
strips through purchase or exchange, surrounding them with a hedge or wall,
and taking them out of communal cultivation. Most, however, were created
by some form of general enclosure, by the proprietor or proprietors in a
village acting to remove common fields and wastes at a stroke, and to re-allot
property and rights in the form of enclosed blocks of land. General enclosure
began in the late medieval period, in places where manorial lords had gained
absolute rights of ownership over villages. Such enclosures, which continued
into the sixteenth century, were associated with the conversion of open field
arable to permanent pasture, and affected areas of north Buckinghamshire,
Northamptonshire, and Leicestershire in particular. They were often
associated with the shrinkage or desertion of villages, whose sites are now
marked by the distinctive earthworks of former house sites and roads.
Enclosure continued, with accelerating intensity, into the seventeenth
century, although now increasingly occurring in parishes under multiple
ownership, by agreement between the principle proprietors. Later sixteenth-
and seventeenth-century enclosures were often associated with improvements
in mixed farming systems, although after 1650, on the heavier soils of the
Midlands, they were often motivated once more by a desire to convert land to
pasture.

Whatever the particular motive for enclosure, however, its general social
and economic background was the long decline of the small farmer and the

amalgamation of farms into larger and larger units, a process which undermined the co-operative basis of the open-field system. The Parliamentary Enclosures of the eighteenth and nineteenth centuries removed the last areas of common fields and common grazing.

Piecemeal enclosure tended to fossilise something of the earlier layout of the landscape, in that the resultant field boundaries followed and preserved the sinuous outline of the open field strips. In contrast, general enclosure, and in particular Parliamentary Enclosure, preserved little of the earlier layout of property boundaries and also often involved a radical reorganisation of the existing pattern of roads and lanes. In most former champion areas, therefore, the medieval landscape survives largely in the form of the low ridges of the open fields, if it survives at all. In other areas of England, however, the situation is rather different.

It is still widely believed that the hedged landscapes of lowland England were entirely the creation of these late- and post-medieval enclosures of open fields and wastes, and in particular of the Parliamentary Enclosures of the eighteenth and nineteenth centuries. Yet this is certainly not the case. Large areas of lowland England never developed open field farming on the familiar Midland pattern, and in these areas the existing pattern of field boundaries and lanes is mainly of medieval or earlier origin. These woodland landscapes, as they were called from the sixteenth century, are found in two principal blocks. One lies in the area to the south and east of the Chiltern escarpment, and includes the Home Counties and much of East Anglia. The other lies in the west of England, in a broad band of country running from Lancashire and Cheshire southwards through Shropshire and Herefordshire to Somerset, Devon, and Cornwall.

Although woods did generally survive better in these areas than in the champion regions of England, the term woodland referred more to the wooded appearance of these landscapes which resulted from the numerous hedges which, by the sixteenth century, existed within them. For by this period, these were mainly areas of enclosed fields. Some open fields still existed in a few places, and moving back in time into the early medieval period it is clear that in many of the woodland areas such fields would have been a much more prominent feature of the landscape. But these had never been worked with the co-operative enthusiasm of the champion fields. They were 'irregular' field systems, in which the strips of each farmer were usually concentrated in one part of the fields, rather than being scattered across the whole area of the village. In many areas the open fields were themselves smaller, and more numerous, than in champion villages, with each containing the strips of relatively few farmers. The nature of medieval fields in woodland areas was intimately related to the pattern of settlement. This was usually more dispersed than in the champion regions, and included, besides villages, numerous hamlets and isolated farmsteads. In these regions, farmers did not all live together in large settlements, and organise their agriculture on a strongly co-operative basis.

Such areas still contain many hamlets and isolated farmsteads, the former often described as 'ends' or 'greens', the latter frequently bearing the name of some medieval owner or occupier. Yet above all they are distinguished by their irregular, ancient appearance: by their winding, high-banked lanes, and by their hedges which, containing an abundance of shrub species, present a striking visual contrast to the more flimsy and species-poor hedges of the former champion lands.

The field boundaries which existed in woodland areas by the end of the medieval period had very varied origins. Some were formed by the early piecemeal enclosure of irregular open-fields; others surrounded fields which had been enclosed direct from the wastes. Such landscapes are often considered to be characteristic of areas of relatively late settlement, but recent research suggests that many were already extensively cleared during the later prehistoric and Roman periods. Indeed, in some woodland areas many surviving field boundaries and lanes are, in fact, of Iron Age or Romano-British origin. Woodland areas were not necessarily cleared and settled at a later date than champion ones, and the underlying reasons for the differences between these two kinds of landscape in lowland England remain poorly understood. The layout of fields and lanes in woodland areas incorporates elements of many periods, and represents a complex historical document of immense importance – where it has not been damaged beyond repair by the impact of modern agriculture.

Apart from the complex pattern of lanes and hedges, other relics of the medieval landscape are more common in woodland areas than in the former champion regions. In particular, it is in such areas that our native, ancient woods tend to survive best. These, to the artist or the poet, often seem the last vestiges of natural wilderness in lowland Britain, pockets of land untouched by human interference. Yet this is not so. Ancient woods bear the marks of intensive management in the medieval period and later. The importance of wood for medieval communities, which in most of lowland England lacked any alternative source of fuel or building material, was so great that intensive management was unavoidable. But woods were not, in general, a resource directly exploited by the community as a whole. Their very survival depended on the fact that they were private property, which could be protected from indiscriminate felling and over-grazing. Most of our larger commons were at one time wooded, a fact sometimes reflected in names like 'Wood Green', but during the medieval period most of this woodland was destroyed. Medieval woods represented portions of the wastes which had been enclosed, and over which the rights of the wider community, and especially grazing rights, had been limited.

The private status of woods is physically expressed by the often substantial banks and ditches which surround them, and which protected the shoots of coppices from browsing animals. For it was coppices, rather than the more familiar full-grown standard trees, which were the characteristic feature of medieval woods. Coppiced trees were repeatedly cut down to a stump or 'stool' at irregular intervals of between five and eight years, in order to produce regular crops of straight, thin-sectioned 'poles', suitable for fuel and other everyday uses. The standard trees, which provided the more substantial timber for construction, were much more sparsely distributed within medieval woods. As a result they would have had a much lighter, more airy and more managed appearance than they usually have today. The real

Medieval woods often resembled this intensely managed woodland in the RSPB reserve of Wolves Wood, Suffolk.

atmosphere of a medeival wood can only be savoured at a few places, such as Felsham Hall Woods, Bradfield, Suffolk, where traditional forms of management have continued up to the present day. The dark, overgrown appearance of most of our ancient woodland is a relatively recent development.

Medieval England had a varied landscape, and this variety was in large part man-made. Not only the landscapes of arable fields, woods, and lowland commons, but also the more extensive areas of open grazing on the high moorlands of the north and west, were largely the product of human interference with the natural environment. The woods which once covered the upland moors were destroyed by felling and grazing in the Bronze Age, and it was the consequent waterlogging of the soil which led to the formation of the acid peat which is now their distinctive characteristic. While the medieval landscape was man-made, it was not made entirely by the hands of medieval man. It bore the scars of an immensely long history, stretching back many millennia before the coming of the Normans.

Most of the land in medieval England was under the de facto control of a multitude of small peasant farmers. We do not know what their attitudes were to those features of the landscape, such as hedges, which we now appreciate aesthetically, and which we seek to preserve in an economic and technological climate which has often rendered them redundant. These farmers were certainly, given the small size of most medieval farms, in no position to modify their environment significantly for aesthetic reasons. To varying degrees, the manorial lords and great magnates were in such a position, although to a lesser extent than those of later centuries. For, at least in the early part of the medieval period, the manors held by medieval lords were not their private property, not were the inhabitants of their estates propertyless serfs. The peasants of medieval England were not tenants in the modern sense of the word, but communities of farmers with an often underestimated power of self-determination, who bought and sold their land, and often entered into disputes with their manorial lords. Most medieval manors included a portion, the demesne, which was under the direct control of the manorial lord. Yet in many cases, and particularly in the champion areas, even this was subject to some measure of communal access, use, and regulation.

Under such conditions large scale aesthetic planting, of the kind which occurred from the late seventeenth century, would have been difficult. Aesthetic manipulation of the landscape was really only possible where extensive unitary blocks of property in absolute private ownership existed, and in many parts of the country this only came about with the progress of enclosure in the late- and post-medieval periods.

Yet contemporary concepts of ownership and property cannot have been the only factor which limited the aesthetic manipulation of the medieval landscape. For, as we have already seen in the case of medieval woods, even in the early medieval period blocks of land were taken into private ownership by manorial lords, and the customary rights of the wider community curtailed; and much of this was used to create deer parks. These, however, were very different from the landscaped parks of the eighteenth century.

Complex field pattern at Luppit, Devon.

They were not usually intended to form a setting for a great house; nor were they aesthetically designed landscapes. They were functional landscapes whose distinctive appearance was a direct consequence of their function. Parks were essentially enclosed areas within which deer were kept for hunting and food, although they had important subsidiary functions, such as the production of timber and the provision of grazing for cattle. Some parts might be occupied by coppiced woodland, from which the deer would be excluded during the early stages of the coppice rotation. The greater part, however, consisted of rough open grassland or launds, irregularly dotted with trees. The latter were generally pollarded – that is, coppiced, but with the shoots growing on a tall trunk instead of from a low stool, in order to protect them from the deer and cattle.

The deer park was a landscape as unnatural as any in medieval England, but the most private and exclusive. Its general resemblance to the developed 'informal' landscape parks of the eighteenth century, and the fact that many of Brown and Repton's parks were simply modifications of surviving deer parks, suggests that the eighteenth-century style was inspired as much by this elite and non-agricultural landscape as by Italian landscapes and Italian landscape paintings.

Yet there is no evidence that medieval parks were themselves intentionally landscaped, and it is significant that medieval gardens appear to have been both small in area, and enclosed. They were private places, from which any sight of the wider working landscape was usually excluded. The medieval landscape was, above all, a working landscape. It was not regarded as a broad canvas upon which to display taste and status. The aesthetic manipulation of the wider countryside was not to begin until after the close of the Middle Ages, as concepts of ownership, as ideas about the uses of land, and as the organisation of society itself, all gradually changed.

Part III
Appendix: Further Reading and Artists' Biographies

CAROL MEALE

Contents

Introduction

In compiling this Appendix priority has been given to citing books and other materials which are readily available, and accessible to the general reader. The listing is divided into sections which correspond with the individual chapters of the book, and after the introductory section on The Cultural and Social Setting, are arranged alphabetically. Where appropriate, sub-sections cover topics specifically dealt with in the text. Biographical information on individual artists is also given, where this is available. A number of general studies on the arts are to be found in the last part of The Cultural and Social Setting section, and these provide an essential supplement to what follows. Guides and bibliographies are listed, where possible, and fuller, more specialist references may also be found in the hardback edition of this book, published under the title *The Cambridge Guide to the Arts in Britain: The Middle Ages.*

Unless otherwise stated the place of publication is London.

1   The Cultural and Social Setting

General history

Standard reference works are those published in the *Oxford History of England* series:

> Poole, A.L., *From Doomsday Book to Magna Carta* (2nd edn, Oxford, 1958)

Powicke, F.M., *The Thirteenth Century, 1216–1307* (Oxford, 1953)

McKisack, M., *The Fourteenth Century* (1959)

Jacob, E.F., *The Fifteenth Century, 1399–1485* (Oxford, 1961)

See also vols. III and IV of the *Pelican History of England:*

Stenton, D.M., *English Society in the Earlier Middle Ages* (4th edn, Harmondsworth, 1965)

Myers, A.R., *England in the Later Middle Ages* (1952)

All these volumes contain useful, though necessarily out-of-date, bibliographies. See, in addition:

Graves, E.B. (ed.), *A Bibliography of English History to 1485*, Royal Historical Society, and others (Oxford, 1975) [annual up-date bibliographies]

Social and economic history

Bennett, H.S., *The Pastons and their England* (Cambridge, 1922; repr. 1990)

Du Boulay, F.R.H., *An Age of Ambition: English Society in the Later Middle Ages* (1970)

Dyer, C., *Standards of Living in the Late Middle Ages* (Cambridge, 1989)

Evans, J. (ed.), *The Flowering of the Middle Ages* (1966) [superbly illustrated]

Hilton, R.H., *The English Peasantry in the Later Middle Ages* (Oxford, 1975)

Keen, M., *Chivalry* (New Haven and London, 1984)

English Society in the Later Middle Ages, 1348–1500 (Harmondsworth, 1990)

Labarge, M. Wade, *Women in Medieval Life* (1986)

Lloyd, T.H., *The English Wool Trade in the Middle Ages* (Cambridge, 1977) [definitive account]

Platt, C., *The English Medieval Town* (1976)

Power, E., *Medieval Women*, M.M. Postan (ed.), (Cambridge, 1985) [illustrated]

Rickert, E., *Chaucer's World* (New York, 1948) [illustrated; contains modernised selections from contemp. documents]

Thrupp, S.L., *The Merchant Class of Medieval London 1300–1500* (Chicago, 1948; repr. Ann Arbor, 1962)

Vale, M., *War and Chivalry: Warfare and Aristocratic Culture in England, France and Burgundy at the End of the Middle Ages* (1981)

Ziegler, P., *The Black Death* (Harmondsworth, 1967)

Religion and learning

LAY PIETY AND PARISH LIFE

Hughes, J., *Pastors and Visionaries: Religion and Secular Life in Late Medieval Yorkshire* (Woodbridge, 1988)

Owst, G.R., *Literature and Pulpit in Medieval England* (Oxford, 1933; repr. 1961)

Southern, R.W., *Western Society and the Church in the Middle Ages* (Hardmondsworth, 1970)

LEARNING AND EDUCATION

Clanchy, M.T., *From Memory to Written Record: England 1066–1307* (1979)

Leff, G., *Medieval Thought: St Augustine to Ockham* (Harmondsworth, 1958)

Lewis, C.S., *The Discarded Image* (Cambridge, 1964)

Orme, N., *English Schools in the Middle Ages* (1973)

From Childhood to Chivalry: the Education of the English Kings and Aristocracy 1066–1530 (1984)

MONASTICISM, MYSTICISM AND HERESY

Colledge, E., *The Medieval Mystics of England* (1962)

Knowles, M.D., *The Religious Orders in England*, 3 vols. (2nd edn, Cambridge, 1979)

Leff, G., *Heresy in the Later Middle Ages*, 2 vols. (Manchester, 1967)

McFarlane, K.B., *Wycliffe and English Non-Conformity* (1952; repr. Harmondsworth, 1972)

Platt, C., *The Abbeys and Priories of Medieval England* (1984) [illustrated]

Power, E., *Medieval English Nunneries, c.1275–1535* (Cambridge, 1922)

Thompson, S., *Women Religious* (Oxford, 1991)

The arts

Alexander, J. and Binski, P. (eds.), *Age of Chivalry: Art in Plantagenet England 1200–1400*. Royal Academy of Arts (1987) [a visual feast]

Blake, N.F., *Caxton and his World* (1969)

Chaytor, H.J., *The Troubadours of England* (Cambridge, 1912)

From Script to Print (Cambridge, 1945; repr. 1950)

Coleman, J., *Medieval Readers and Writers 1350–1400*, English Literature in History Series (1981)

Dronke, P., *Medieval Latin and the Rise of the European Love Lyric*, 2 vols. (2nd edn, Oxford, 1968)

Green, R.F., *Poets and Princepleasers: Literature of the English Court in the Late Middle Ages* (Toronto, 1980)

Haskins, C.H., *The Renaissance of the Twelfth Century* (Cambridge, Mass.,1927)

Henderson, G., *Gothic* (Harmondsworth, 1967)

Lasko, P. and Morgan, N.J. (eds.), *Medieval Art in East Anglia 1300–1520*, (Norwich, 1973)

Legge, M.D., *Anglo Norman Literature and its Background* (Oxford, 1963)

Medcalf, S. (ed.), *The Later Middle Ages* (1981) [essays on art, architecture and literature]

Oxford History of Art series, vols. III–V:
　Boase, T.S.R., *English Art 1100–1216* (Oxford, 1953)
　Brieger, P., *English Art 1216–1307* (Oxford, 1957)
　Evans, J., *English Art 1307–1461* (Oxford, 1949)

Pearsall, D., *Old and Middle English Poetry* (1977) [excellent introduction]

Pelican History of Art series:
　Rickert, M., *Painting in Britain in the Middle Ages* (2nd edn, Harmondsworth, 1965)
　Stone, L., *Sculpture in Britain in the Middle Ages* (2nd edn, Harmondsworth, 1965)
　Webb, G., *Architecture in Britain in the Middle Ages* (2nd edn, Harmondworth, 1965)

Salter, E., *Fourteenth Century English Poetry: Contexts and Readings* (Oxford, 1983)

Scattergood, V.J. and Sherborne, J.W. (eds.), *English Court Culture in the Later Middle Ages* (1983) [essays cover architecture, literature, manuscript painting and music]

Wilson, K.M. (ed.), *Medieval Women Writers* (Manchester, 1984) [includes essays on Marie de France and the religious writings of Julian of Norwich and Margery Kempe]

Wilson, R.M., *The Lost Literature of Medieval England* (2nd edn, 1970)

2　Architecture

General

Bony, J., *The English Decorated Style: Gothic Architecture Transformed 1250–1350* (1979) [authoritative]

Clapham, A.W., *English Romanesque Architecture after the Conquest* (1934) [this remains the standard work on the early period]

Colvin, H.M. (ed.), *The History of the King's Works*, I, II, *The Middle Ages* (1963) [excellent: the standard account and reference work]

Harvey, J., *Henry Yevele: the Life of an English Architect* (1946)
　The Medieval Architect (1972)
　The Perpendicular Style 1330–1485 (1978)
　English Medieval Architects: a Biographical Dictionary down to 1540 (2nd edn, Gloucester, 1984)

Kidson, P., Murray, P. and Thompson, P., *A History of English Architecture* (Harmondsworth, 1965)

McLees, A.D., 'Henry Yevele: disposer of the King's works of masonry', *Journal of the British Archaeological Association*, **36** (1973), 52–71

Royal Commission on Historic Monuments [RCOHM] county inventories (1910–　) [in progress]

Domestic and ecclesiastical architecture

Butler, L. and Given-Wilson, C., *Medieval Monasteries of Great Britain* (1979)

Clifton-Taylor, A., *English Parish Churches as Works of Art* (1974)

Knowles, D. and St Joseph, J.K.S., *Monastic Sites from the Air* (1952)

Knowles, M.D. and Hadcock, R.N., *Medieval Religious Houses: England and Wales* (2nd edn, 1971)

Little, B., *Abbeys and Priories in England and Wales* (1979)

Mercer, E., *English Vernacular Houses, RCOHM: England* (1975)

Pevsner, N. and Metcalf, P., *The Cathedrals of England*, 2 vols.: I *Southern England*; II. *Midland, Eastern and Northern England* (Harmondsworth, 1985) [includes glossary of architectural terms and select bibliography]

Wood, M., *The English Medieval House* (1965; repr. 1981)

THE ART OF THE CARPENTER: WESTMINSTER HALL AND MILDENHALL CHURCH

Brandon, R. and Brandon, J.A., *The Open Timber Roofs of the Middle Ages* (1860) [notable for its superb drawings of church roofs]

Hewett, C.A., *English Historic Carpentry* (1980) [includes domestic and ecclesiastical carpentry of the Middle Ages]
　English Cathedral and Monastic Carpentry (1985)

Sawbridge, P.F., *Roof Carving in Mildenhall Church* (Oxford, 1938)

CASTLE-BUILDERS: HARLECH AND
CAERNARFON

Platt, C., *The Castle in Medieval England
and Wales* (1982) [illustrated]

Taylor, A.J., *Studies in Castles and
Castle-building* (1986) [includes studies
of Master James of St George, the
dating of Caernarfon Castle, the stages
of building of Harlech Castle]

Toy, S., *Castles of Great Britain* (6th edn,
1966)

THE CATHEDRALS OF DURHAM AND WELLS
AND RIEVAULX ABBEY

Colchester, L.S. (ed.), *Wells Cathedral: a
History* (Shepton Mallet, 1982)

Fergusson, P.J., *Architecture of Solitude:
Cistercian Abbeys in Twelfth Century
England* (Princeton, 1984)

*Medieval Art and Architecture at Durham
Cathedral, Transactions of the British
Archaeological Association Conference*, **3**,
(1980)

Norton, E.C. and Park, D. (eds.), *Cistercian
Art and Architecture in the British Isles*
(Cambridge, 1986)

Pantin, W.A., *Durham Cathedral* (1948)

Peers, C.R., *Rievaulx Abbey*, 'Blue Guide'
(1967)

SHRINES, TOMBS AND CHANTRIES

Cook, G.H., *Medieval Chantries and
Chantry Chapels* (1947)

Finucane, R.C., *Miracles and Pilgrims:
Popular Beliefs in Medieval England*
(1977)

Sumption, J., *Pilgrimage: an Image of
Medieval Religion* (1975) [bibliography]

Wood-Legh, K., *Perpetual Chantries in
Britain* (Cambridge, 1953)

3   The City of York

General

Aylmer, G.E. and Cant, R. (eds.), *A
History of York Minster* (Oxford, 1977;
rev. 1979) [chapters on architecture,
stained and painted glass, music and
sculpture]

Gee, E.A., 'The painted glass of All Saints,
North Street, York', *Archaeologia*, **102**
(1969), 151–202 [arguably the finest
church glass in York]

Harrison, F., *The Painted Glass of York*
(1927) [minster and parish churches]

Hutchinson, J. and Palliser, D., *York*,
Bartholomew City Guides (1980) [best
modern guide]

Pevsner, N., *The Buildings of England –
Yorkshire: York and the East Riding*
(Harmondsworth, 1972)

Drama

See also under 5

Beadle, R. (ed.), *The York Plays* (1982)

Beadle, R. and King, P.M. (eds.), *York
Mystery Plays – a Selection in Modern
Spelling* (Oxford, 1984)

4   Festive Culture in Country and Town

Axton, R., 'Popular modes in the earliest
plays', in *Medieval Drama*, N. Denny
(ed.), Stratford-upon-Avon Studies,
XVI (1972), pp. 13–37.

Cawte, E.C., *Ritual Animal Disguise*
(Cambridge and Ipswich, 1978)

Chambers, E.K., *The Medieval Stage*, 2
vols. (Oxford, 1903)

Greene, R.L. (ed.), *The Early English
Carols* (2nd edn, Oxford, 1977)

Hole, C., *A Dictionary of British Folk
Customs* (1976)

James, E.O., *Seasonal Feasts and Festivals*
(1961)

McLean, T., *The English at Play in the
Middle Ages* (Windsor, Berks., 1975;
repr: 1983)

Phythian-Adams, C., 'Ceremony and the
citizen: the communal year in
Coventry, 1450–1550', in P. Clark and
P. Slack (eds.), *Crisis and Order in
English Towns 1500–1700* (1972), 57–85

Wiles, D., *The Early Plays of Robin Hood*
(1981)

5   Literature and Drama

Bibliography and anthology

Burke Severs, J. and Hartung, A.E. (eds.),
*A Manual of the Writings in Middle
English 1050–1500* (1967–   ) [series in
progress]

Burrow, J.A., (ed.) *English Verse 1300–1500*
(1977)

Sisam, K. (ed.), *Fourteenth Century Verse
and Prose* (Oxford, 1921; repr. 1955)

Gray, D. (ed.), *The Oxford Book of Late
Medieval Verse and Prose* (Oxford,
1985) [excellent introduction]

General

Bennett, J.A.W., *Middle English Literature*
D. Gray (ed.) (Oxford, 1986)

Bolton, W.F. (ed.), *The Sphere History of English Literature*, vol. I, *The Middle Ages* (1970; rev. ed., 1986)

Brewer, D.S., *English Gothic Literature* (1983)

Burrow, J.A., *Medieval Writers and their Work* (Oxford, 1982)

Ford, B. (ed.), *The New Pelican Guide to English Literature*, I, *Medieval Literature*, Pt 1, 'Chaucer and the alliterative tradition' (2nd edn, Harmondsworth, 1982) [bibliography and anthology]

Pearsall, D., *Old English and Middle English Poetry* (1977)

Pearsall, D. and Salter, E., *Landscapes and Seasons of the Medieval World* (1973) [illustrated]

Spearing, A.C., *Medieval Dream Poetry* (Cambridge, 1976)
Medieval to Renaissance in English Poetry (Cambridge, 1985)

Alliterative and debate poetry

EDITIONS

[see also under the Gawain poet and Langland; for editions of texts other than those discussed by Medcalf in this volume, see Turville-Petre, *The Alliterative Revival*]

Conlee, J. (ed.), *Middle English Debate Poetry* (Michigan 1991)

Stanley, E.G., *The Owl and the Nightingale* (Manchester, 1960; repr. 1972)

Turville-Petre, T., *Alliterative Poetry of the Middle Ages: An Anthology* (1989)

SECONDARY READING

Hume, K., *The Owl and the Nightingale: the Poem and its Critics* (Toronto, 1975)

Lawton, D.A. (ed.), *Middle English Alliterative Poetry and its Literary Background* (Woodbridge, 1982)

Turville-Petre, T., *The Alliterative Revival* (Cambridge 1977)

Drama

[for York see **3**]

BIBLIOGRAPHY

Stratman, C.J., *Bibliography of Medieval Drama* (New York, 1972)

EDITIONS

Axton, R. and Stevens, J. (tr.), *Medieval French Plays* (Oxford, 1971)

Cawley, A.C. (ed.), *Wakefield Pageants in the Towneley Cycle* (Manchester, 1958; repr. 1975)

Happé, P. (ed.), *English Mystery Plays* (Harmondsworth, 1975)
Four Morality Plays (Harmondsworth, 1979)

Lumiansky, R.M. and Mills, D. (eds.), *The Chester Mystery Cycle*, 2 vols., *Early English Text Society Supplementary Series* **3**, **9** (1974, 1986)

SECONDARY READING

Axton, R., *European Drama of the Early Middle Ages* (1974)

Cawley, A.C. *et al.* (eds.), *The Revels History of Drama in English*, vol. I, *Medieval Drama* (1983)

Happé, P. (ed.), *Medieval English Drama*, Casebook Series (1984)

Kolve, V.A., *The Play called Corpus Christi* (Stanford, 1966)

Neuss, P. (ed.), *Aspects of Early English Drama* (Woodbridge, 1983)

Taylor, J. and Nelson, A.H. (eds.), *Medieval English Drama: Essays Critical and Contextual* (Chicago and London, 1972)

Tydeman, W., *English Medieval Theatre 1400–1500* (1986)

Woolf, R., *The English Mystery Plays* (1972)

Lyrics

[see also under **6**]

EDITIONS

Brook, G.L. (ed.), *The Harley Lyrics* (2nd edn, Manchester, 1968)

Brown, C., (ed.), *Religious Lyrics of the Fourteenth Century* (Oxford, 1924; repr. 1965) [includes the Vernon lyrics]
English Lyrics of the Thirteenth Century (Oxford, 1932)
Religious Lyrics of the Fifteenth Century (1939; repr. 1955)

Davies, R.T. (ed.), *Medieval English Lyrics: a Critical Anthology* (1963; repr. 1987)
The Early English Carols (2nd edn, Oxford, 1977)

Robbins, R.H. (ed.), *Secular Lyrics of the Fourteenth and Fifteenth Centuries* (Oxford, 1939; repr. 1955)

SECONDARY READING

Dronke, P., *The Medieval Lyric* (1968)

Fox, J., *The Lyric Poetry of Charles d'Orléans* (Oxford, 1969)

Gray, D., *Themes and Images in the Medieval English Religious Lyric* (1972)

Woolf, R., *The English Religious Lyric in the Middle Ages* (Oxford, 1968)

Prose

BIBLIOGRAPHY

Edwards, A.S.G. (ed.), *Middle English Prose: a Critical Guide to Major Authors and Genres* (Brunswick, N.J., 1984)

EDITIONS

Davis, N. (ed.), *Paston Letters and Papers of the Fifteenth Century*, 2 vols. (Oxford, 1971, 1976)
  The Paston Letters: a Selection in Modern Spelling (1975)

Gray (ed.), *The Oxford Book of Late Medieval Verse and Prose* [see V, 1]

Letts, M. (tr.), *Mandeville's Travels; Texts and Translations*, Hakluyt Society, 2nd ser. **101** (1953)

Skeat, W.W. (ed.), Thomas Usk, 'The Testament of Love', in *The Complete Works of Geoffrey Chaucer*, vol. VII (Oxford, 1897), pp. 1–145.

Religious writing

BIBLIOGRAPHY

Edwards (ed.), Middle English Prose [see VI, 6]; [sections on the *Ancrene Wisse*; *The Cloud of Unknowing*; Walter Hilton; Julian of Norwich; Margery Kempe; and Wycliffite writings]

Lagorio, V.M. and Bradley, R. (eds.), *The Fourteenth Century English Mystics: a Comprehensive Annotated Bibliography* (London, 1981)

EDITIONS

Glasscoe, M. (ed.), *Julian of Norwich: a Revelation of Love* (Exeter, 1976)

Hudson, A. (ed.), *Selections from English Wycliffite Writings* (Cambridge, 1978)

Millett, B. and Unger-Browne, J., Bella Millett and Jocelyn Unger-Browne, *Medieval English Prose for Women* (Oxford, 1990) [ed. and parallel tr.]

Salu, M.B. (tr.), *The Ancrene Riwle* (1955)

Sherley-Price, L. (tr.), *The Ladder of Perfection* (Harmondsworth, 1985)

Windeatt, B.A. (tr.), *The Book of Margery Kempe* (Harmondsworth, 1985)

Wolters, C. (tr.), *The Cloud of Unknowing* (Harmondsworth, 1961)

Julian of Norwich, *Revelations of Divine Love* (Harmondsworth, 1966)

SECONDARY READING

Dobson, E.J., *The Origins of Ancrene Wisse* (Oxford, 1976) [important study]

Kenny, A. (ed.), *Wyclif in his Times* (Oxford, 1986)

Riehle, W., *The Middle English Mystics* (1981) [good bibliography]

Romance

[see also under the Gawain poet and Malory]

BIBLIOGRAPHY

Rice, J.A., *Middle English Romance: an Annotated Bibliography 1955–1983* (New York and London, 1985)

EDITIONS

Barron, W.R.J., and Weinberg, S.C., *Layamon's Arthur* (1989) [ed. and parallel tr. of the Arthurian section of Layamon's *Brut*]

Bliss, A.J. (ed.), *Sir Orfeo* (Oxford, 1954; repr. 1966)

Burgess, G.S. and Busby, K. (tr.), *The Lais of Marie de France* (Harmondsworth, 1986) [select bibliography]

Hamel, M. (ed.), *Morte Arthure: a Critical Edition* (New York and London, 1984)

Mills, M. (ed.), *Six Middle English Romances* (1973)

Schmidt, A.V.C. and Jacobs, N. (eds.), *Medieval Verse Romances*, 2 vols. (1980)

Thorpe, L. (tr.), *Geoffrey of Monmouth: the History of the Kings of Britain* (Harmondsworth, 1966)

SECONDARY READING

Barber, R., *King Arthur; Hero and Legend* (Woodbridge, 1986)

Barron, W.R.J., *English Medieval Romance* (1987)

Crane, S., *Insular Romance: Politics, Faith and Culture in Anglo-Norman and Middle English Literature* (Berkeley, 1986)

Loomis, R.S. (ed.), *Arthurian Literature in the Middle Ages* (Oxford, 1959) [standard reference work]

Mehl, D., *The Middle English Romances of the Thirteenth and Fourteenth Centuries* (1968)

Mills, M., Fellow, J. and Meale, C. (eds.), *Romance in Medieval England* (Cambridge, 1991)

Scottish and Welsh literature

BIBLIOGRAPHY

Scheps, W. and Looney, J.A. (eds.), *Middle Scots Poets: A Reference Guide* (Boston, Mass., 1986)

Stephens, M. (ed.), *The Oxford Companion to the Literature of Wales* (Oxford, 1986)

EDITIONS

Bewcutt, P. and Riddy, F., *Longer Scottish Poems*, vol. 1, *1375–1650* (Edinburgh, 1987)

Bromwich, R. (ed.), *Selected Poems of Dafydd ap Gwilym* (Harmondsworth, 1985) [text with parallel translation]

Caldwell, D.F.C. (ed.), *Gavin Douglas: Selections* (Oxford, 1964)

Fox, D. (ed.), *Robert Henryson: The Poems* (Oxford, 1987)

Kinsley, J. (ed.), *The Poems of William Dunbar* (Oxford, 1979) [selections]

Mackenzie, W. (ed.), *Dunbar: Works* (1932)

Norton-Smith, J. (ed.), *The Kingis Quair* (Oxford, 1971)

Thorpe, L. (tr.), *Gerald of Wales: the Journey through Wales and the Description of Wales* (Harmondsworth, 1978)

SECONDARY READING

Bawcutt, P., *Gavin Douglas: a Critical Study* (Edinburgh, 1976)

Bromwich, R., *Aspects of the Poetry of Dafydd ap Gwilym* (New York and London, 1985)

Gray, D., *Robert Henryson* (1980)

Jarman, A.O.H. and Hughes, G.R. (eds.), *A Guide to Welsh literature*, vols. I, II (Swansea, 1976, 1979)

Kratzmann, G., *Anglo-Scottish Literary Relations 1430–1550* (Cambridge, 1980)

Scott, T., *Dunbar: a Critical Exposition of the Poems* (Edinburgh, 1966)

Authors

Caxton, William (*c*.1420–91)

BIBLIOGRAPHY AND EDITION

Blake, N.F., *William Caxton: a Bibliographical Guide* (New York and London, 1985)

(ed.), *Caxton's Own Prose* (1973)

SECONDARY READING

Painter, G.D., *William Caxton: a Quincentenary Biography of England's First Printer* (1976)

Chaucer, Geoffrey (*c*.1340–1400)

BIOGRAPHY AND BIBLIOGRAPHY

Baird, L.Y., *A Bibliography of Chaucer 1964–73* (Boston and London, 1977)

Crow, M.M. and Olson, C.C. (eds.), *Chaucer Life-Records* (Oxford, 1966)

EDITIONS

Windeatt, B.A. (ed.), *Geoffrey Chaucer: Troilus and Criseyde. A new Edition of 'The Book of Troilus'* (1984) [indispensable: includes a parallel text of Boccaccio's *Il Filostrato*]

SECONDARY READING

Aers, D., *Chaucer, Langland and the Creative Imagination* (1980)

Geoffrey Chaucer (Brighton, 1986)

Barney, S.A. (ed.), *Chaucer's Troilus: Essays in Criticism* (1980)

Benson, C.D., *Chaucer's Troilus and Criseyde* (1990)

Blamires, A., *The Canterbury Tales* (1987) [guide to current critical trends]

Boitani, P. and Mann, J. (eds.), *The Cambridge Chaucer Companion* (Cambridge, 1986)

Brewer, D.S., (ed.) *Chaucer: the Critical Heritage*, 2 vols. (1978)

Cooper, H., *The Structure of the Canterbury Tales* (1983)

Dinshaw, C., *Chaucer's Sexual Poetics* (Wisconsin, 1989)

Mann, J., *Geoffrey Chaucer* (1991)

Mehl, D., *Geoffrey Chaucer: an Introduction to his Narrative Poetry* (Cambridge, 1986) [good introduction]

Muscatine, C., *Chaucer and the French Tradition* (Berkeley, 1957; repr. 1964)

Pearsall, D., *The Canterbury Tales* (1985)

Strohm, P., *Social Chaucer* (Harvard, 1989)

Wetherbee, W., *Chaucer: The Canterbury Tales* (Cambridge, 1989)

The Gawain poet (latter half of 14th century)

BIBLIOGRAPHY

Andrew, M., *The Gawain-Poet: an Annotated Bibliography* (New York and London, 1979)

EDITIONS

Andrew, M. and Waldron, R. (eds.), *The Poems of the Pearl Manuscript* (1978) [good introduction and notes]

Barron, W.R.J. (ed.), *Sir Gawain and the Green Knight* (Manchester, 1974) [includes a parallel translation]

SECONDARY READING

Burrow, J.A., *A Reading of Sir Gawain and the Green Knight* (1965) [influential study]

Davenport, W.A., *The Art of the Gawain-poet* (1978)

Kean, P.M., *The Pearl: an Interpretation* (1967)

Nicholls, J.W., *The Matter of Courtesy: a Study of Medieval Courtesy Books and the Gawain-poet* (Woodbridge, 1985)

Spearing, A.C., *The Gawain-poet: a Critical Study* (Cambridge, 1970)

Wilson, E., *The Gawain-poet* (Leiden, 1976)

Gower, John (*c.*1330–1408)

EDITION

Weinberg, C. (ed.), *John Gower: Selected Poetry* (Manchester, 1983)

SECONDARY READING

Fisher, J.H., *John Gower, Moral Philosopher and Friend of Chaucer* (New York, 1964)

Minnis, A.J. (ed.), *Gower's 'Confessio Amantis': Responses and Reassessments* (Woodbridge, 1983)

Nicholson, P. (ed.), *Gower's 'Confessio Amantis': A Critical Anthology* (Cambridge, 1991)

Hoccleve, Thomas (*c.*1368–*c.*1430)

EDITION

Seymour, M.C. (ed.), *Selections from Hoccleve* (Oxford, 1981)

SECONDARY READING

Mitchell, J., *Thomas Hoccleve: a Study in Early Fifteenth Century English Poetic* (Urbana, Chicago and London, 1968) [still the only book-length study]

Langland, William (b. *c.*1330)

BIBLIOGRAPHY

Pearsall, D., *An Annotated Critical Bibliography of Langland* (Brighton, 1990)

EDITIONS

Goodridge, J.F. (tr.), *Piers the Ploughman* (Harmondsworth, 1959) [translation of the B text]

Pearsall, D. (ed.), *Piers Plowman: an Edition of the C Text* (1978)

Schmidt, A.V.C. (ed.), *The Vision of Piers Plowman: a Complete Edition of the B Text* (1978) [good critical apparatus]

SECONDARY READING

Aers, D., *Piers Plowman and Christian Allegory* (1975)

Alford, J.A. (ed.), *A Companion to Piers Plowman* (Berkeley and Los Angeles, 1988)

Griffiths, L. *Personification in Piers Plowman* (Woodbridge, 1985)

Salter, E., *Piers Plowman: an Introduction* (Oxford, 1962)

Simpson, J., *Piers Plowman: An Introduction to the B-Text* (London and New York, 1990)

Lydgate, John (*c.*1370–*c.*1450)

EDITION

Norton-Smith, J. (ed.), *John Lydgate: Poems* (Oxford, 1966) [a selection including an extract from the *Life of Our Lady*]

SECONDARY READING

Pearsall, D., *John Lydgate* (1970)

Malory, Sir Thomas (d.1471)

BIBLIOGRAPHY

Life, P.W., *Sir Thomas Malory and the Morte D'Arthur: a Survey of Scholarship and Annotated Bibliography* (Charlottesville, Va, 1980)

EDITIONS

Cowen, J. (ed.), *The Morte D'Arthur*, 2 vols. (1969) [a modernised version based upon Caxton's edition of 1485]

Vinaver, E. (ed.), *The Works of Sir Thomas Malory* (2nd edn, 1971)

SECONDARY READING

Benson, L.D., *Malory's Morte D'Arthur* (Cambridge, Mass., 1976)

Kennedy, B., *Knighthood in the Morte d'Arthur* (Woodbridge, 1985)

Lambert, M., *Style and Vision in Malory's Morte D'Arthur* (New Haven, 1975)

Riddy, F., *Sir Thomas Malory* (Leiden, 1987)

Takamiya, T. and Brewer, D.S. (eds.), *Aspects of Malory* (Woodbridge, 1981).

Vinaver, E., *The Rise of Romance* (1971; repr. Woodbridge, 1984)

Whitaker, M, *Arthur's Kingdom of Adventure: the World of Malory's Morte D'Arthur* (Woodbridge, 1984)

Skelton, John (*c*.1460–1529)

BIBLIOGRAPHY

Kinsman, R.S., *John Skelton, Early Tudor Laureate: an Annotated Bibliography c.1488–1977* (1979)

EDITION

Scattergood, J. (ed.), *John Skelton: the Complete English Poems* (Harmondsworth, 1983)

SECONDARY READING

Edwards, A.S.G. (ed.), *Skelton: the Critical Heritage* (1981)

Edwards, H.L.R., *Skelton: the Life and Times of an Early Tudor Poet* (1949)

6 Music

Introduction

BIBLIOGRAPHY AND REFERENCE

Hughes, A., *Medieval Music: the Sixth Liberal Art*, Toronto Medieval Bibliographies, 4 (rev. edn, Toronto, 1980)

Roche, J. and Roche, E., *A Dictionary of Early Music* (1981)

Sadie, S. (ed.), *The New Grove Dictionary of Music and Musicians*, 20 vols. (1980) [indispensable: information on composers, manuscripts and instruments, bibliographical references]

INSTRUMENTS AND PERFORMANCE

Munrow, D., *Instruments of the Middle Ages and Renaissance* (1976) [illustrated; survey by the type of instrument]

Page, C., *Voices and Instruments of the Middle Ages* (1986)

Remnant, M., *English Bowed Instruments from Anglo-Saxon to Tudor Times* (Oxford, 1986)

Remnant, M. and Marks, R., 'A medieval "gittern"', *Music and Civilisation*, The British Museum Yearbook, 4 (1980), 83–134

Religious music

EDITIONS OF MUSIC

Marrocco, T.W. and Sandon, N. (eds.), *The Oxford Anthology of Music: Medieval Music* (1977) [includes English music from the thirteenth to the fifteenth centuries: pieces by Benet, Bedyngham, Dunstable]

SECONDARY READING

Cattin, G., *Music of the Middle Ages*, vol. I (Cambridge, 1984)

Gallo, F.A., *Music in the Middle Ages*, vol. II (Cambridge, 1985)

Hoppin, R.H., *Medieval Music* (New York, 1978)

Secular music

EDITIONS OF WORDS AND MUSIC

Bennett, J.A.W. and Smithers, G.V. (eds.), *Early Middle English Verse and Prose* (2nd edn, 1966) [romance, lyrics, saints' legends, etc.]

Brook (ed.), *The Harley Lyrics* [see 5]

Brown (ed.), *English Lyrics of the Thirteenth Century* [see 5]

Coussemaker, E. de (ed.), *Scriptorium de Musica medii Aevi Nova Series*, 4 vols. (Paris, 1864–76; repr. 1963)

Dobson, E.J. and Harrison, L.L. (eds.), *Medieval English Songs* (1979)

Greene (ed.), *Early English Carols* [see 5]
The Lyrics of the Red Book of Ossory, Medium Aevum Monographs NS 5 (1974)

SECONDARY READING

Boffey, J., *Manuscripts of English Courtly Love Lyrics in the Later Middle Ages* (Woodbridge, 1985) [transmission of lyrics and their audience; words and music]

Bullock-Davies, C., *Menestrellorum Multitudo* (Cardiff, 1978) [study of professional minstrels based on documentary sources]

Stevens, J., *Music and Poetry at the Early Tudor Court* (2nd edn, Cambridge, 1979)
Words and Music in the Middle Ages: Song, Narrative, Dance and Drama, 1050–1350 (Cambridge, 1986)

Wilkins, N. *Music in the Age of Chaucer* (Cambridge, 1979) [illustrated]

Wilson, *The Lost Literature of Medieval England* [see 1]

Composers

For additional information and bibliography see Sadie, *New Grove Dictionary of Music and Musicians* (20 vols., 1980)

Bedyngham, John (c.1420–1459/60) Composer. For some time verger at Collegiate Chapel of St Stephen, Westminster. Surviving works include 2 Masses, individual Mass movements, and around 8 songs, some of which share attributions to Dunstable, Dufay or Frye. Popular on Continent; music survives largely in foreign sources.

Cornysh, William (d.1523) Composer, poet, dramatist, and actor. Devised pageants and 'disguysings' for marriage festivities of Prince Arthur and Catherine of Aragon, 1501; imprisoned in the Fleet, 1504 (cause unknown) but thereafter a favourite of Henry VIII. September 1509 until death: Master of the Children of the Chapel Royal; in this capacity played a crucial role in court plays and entertainments. Accompanied Henry VIII on his French campaign of 1513, and to the Field of the Cloth of Gold in 1520.

Dunstable, John (c.1390–1453) Shared contemporary pre-eminence as a composer with Lionel Power. Nothing certain known about his life or career: may have been in service of John, Duke of Bedford, Regent of France (1422–35). Well-known on the Continent. Masses, motets and some few secular and vernacular pieces attributed to him.

Fayrfax, Robert (1464–1521) More music survives by him than by any other composer here listed. Particularly renowned for his cultivation of the cyclic Mass. Gentleman of the Chapel Royal by 1497; Mus.B. at Cambridge, 1501, Mus.D. Cambridge 1504; D.Mus. Oxford, 1511. Attended all major court functions from the funeral of Henry VII (1509) onwards. Favoured by Henry VIII. 29 compositions survive: 6 cyclic Masses; 2 Magnificat settings; 10 antiphons; 8 part-songs and 3 instrumental pieces. Noted for restraint and carefully wrought melodic lines.

Frye, Walter (fl.c.1450–75) Little known about his life: may have been in charge of the lay choir at Ely Cathedral,

1440s and 50s. Works survive almost exclusively in Continental sources, but the assumption made hitherto that he worked mainly abroad is unnecessary, since his musical language is ultimately free from Continental influences, closer to older English styles. Works thought to be by him include 4 Masses; 5 motets; and some English songs.

Power, Lionel (c.1370/85–1445) Composer and theorist. With Dunstable led English style 1410–40. Instructor of choristers and clerk of household chapel of Thomas, Duke of Clarence (d.1421). Thereafter Master of Lady Chapel at Canterbury Cathedral, where he was probably a teacher of the boys in the choir. This may account for the two surviving treatises attributed to him. 40 works are undoubtedly by him, another 17 at present attributed. No secular work survives. He made a substantial contribution to the Old Hall manuscript; later works known exclusively from Continental sources. Renowned for his love of sonorities, and for his refinement of harmony and texture.

7   Oxburgh Hall, Norfolk

Davis (ed.), *The Paston Letters* [see 5] [includes references to, and letters from, Sir Edmund Bedingfeld; gives a vivid picture of life at this time]

Oxburgh Hall, Norfolk, National Trust Guidebook (1980)

Zulueta, F. de, *Oxburgh Hall, Norfolk* (1953; rev. by A.L. Bedingfeld, 1968)

8   The Visual Arts and Crafts

General

Anderson, M.D., *The Imagery of British Churches* (1955)

English Romanesque Art 1066–1200, exhibition catalogue, Hayward Gallery (1984) [excellent critical bibliography]

Farmer, D.H., *The Oxford Dictionary of Saints* (2nd edn, Oxford, 1987)

Harvey, J.H., *Medieval Craftsmen* (1975)

Hudson, A., *Selections from English Wycliffite Writings* (Cambridge, 1978) [item 16, 'Images and pilgrimage']

Platt, C., *The Parish Churches of Medieval England* (1981) [a social study]

Ivories

Beckwith, J., *Ivory Carving in Early Medieval England* (1972)

Longhurst, M.H., *English Ivories* (1926) [this remains the general survey]
Williamson, P., *An Introduction to Medieval Ivory Carvings*, Victoria and Albert Museum (1982)

Manuscripts and painting

Binski, P., *The Painted Chamber at Westminster*, Society of Antiquaries (1986) [important new study on the artistic patronage of Henry III and Edward I]
Dodwell, C.R., *The Canterbury School of Illumination, 1066–1200* (1954)
Kauffmann, C.M., *Romanesque Manuscripts 1066–1200*, A Survey of Manuscripts Illuminated in the British Isles, **3** (1975)
McLachan, P., *The Scriptorium of Bury St Edmunds in the Twelfth Century* (New York and London, 1986)
Marks, R. and Morgan, N., *The Golden Age of English Manuscript Painting, 1200–1500* (1981)
Morgan, N.J., *Early Gothic Manuscripts*, vol. I, *1190–1250*, A Survey of Manuscripts Illuminated in the British Isles, **4** (1982), **5** (1978)
Pächt, O., Dodwell, C.R. and Wormald, F., *The Saint Albans Psalter (Albani Psalter)* (1960)
Sandler, L.F., *Gothic Manuscripts 1285–1385*, A Survey of Manuscripts Illuminated in the British Isles, **6, 7** (1986)
Scheller, R.W., *A Survey of Medieval Model Books* (Haarlem, 1963)
Talbot, C.H., *The Life of Christina of Markyate* (Oxford, 1959)
Tristram, E.W., *English Medieval Wall-Paintings:*
  The Twelfth Century (Oxford, 1944)
  The Thirteenth Century, 2 vols. (Oxford, 1950)
  The Fourteenth Century (Oxford, 1955)

Metalwork

Birch, W. de G., *Catalogue of Seals in the Department of Manuscripts in the British Museum*. 6 vols. (1887–1900)
Campbell, M., *An Introduction to Medieval Enamels*, Victoria and Albert Museum (1983)
Gardner, J.S., *Ironwork*, Victoria and Albert Museum (1927, repr. 1978)
Giuseppi, M.S. and Green, R.A., *An Appendix to a List of Monumental Brasses in the British Isles by Mill Stephenson* (1938)

Stephenson, M., *A List of Monumental Brasses in the British Isles* (1926; repr. 1964)

Opus Anglicanum

Christie, G., *English Medieval Embroidery* (1938)
Kendrick, A.F., *English Needlework* (2nd edn, 1967)
Opus Anglicanum, exhibition catalogue, Victoria and Albert Museum (1963)
Parker, R., *The Subversive Stitch* (1984) [feminist history; see esp. ch. 3 on medieval embroiderers]

Sculpture and carving

Cave, C.J.P., *Roof Bosses in Medieval Churches: an Aspect of Gothic Culture* (1948)
Cheetham, F., *English Medieval Alabasters, with a Catalogue of the Collection in the Victoria and Albert Museum* (1984)
Gardner, A., *English Medieval Sculpture* (1951)
Howard, F.E. and Crossley, F.H., *English Church Woodwork . . . 1250–1500*, (2nd edn, 1927)
Remnant, G.L., *A Catalogue of Misericords in Great Britain* (1969)
Vallence, A., *Greater English Church Screens* (1947)
Zarnecki, G., *English Romanesque Sculpture 1066–1140* (1951)
  Later English Romanesque Sculpture (1957)

Stained and painted glass

[see also under 3]
Caviness, M.H., *Stained Glass Before 1540: an Annotated Bibliography* (Boston, 1983)
  The Early Stained Glass of Canterbury Cathedral, c. 1175–1220 (1977)
Brown, S., and O'Connor, D., *Glass-Painters (Medieval Craftsmen)* (Toronto, 1991)
Woodforde, C., *English Stained and Painted Glass* (1954)

Textiles

Thomson, W.G., *A History of Tapestry* (1906; rev. edn, 1930) [still the standard work]

Tiles

Eames, E.S., *English Medieval Tiles*, British Museum (1985) [good, popular introduction]

Salle Church, Norfolk

Fawcett, R. and King, D., 'Salle church', *Archaeological Journal*, **137** (1980), 332–5

Greenwood, R. and Norris, M., *The Brasses of Norfolk Churches*, The Norfolk Churches Trust (Norwich, 1976)

Parsons, W.L.E., *Salle, the Story of a Norfolk Parish, its Church, Manors and People* (Norwich, 1937)

Westminster Abbey

Lethaby, W.R., *Westminster Abbey and the King's Craftsmen* (1906)
Westminster Abbey Re-Examined (1925)

Tanner, L.E. *Unknown Westminster Abbey* (1948)

Wilson, C. *et al.*, *Westminster Abbey*, New Bell's Cathedral Guides (1986)

9 The Working Landscape

Beresford, M.W., *The Lost Villages of Medieval England* (1954; repr. Gloucester, 1983)

Beresford, M.W. and St Joseph, K., *Medieval England: an Aerial Survey* (2nd edn, Cambridge, 1979)

Cantor, L. (ed.), *The English Medieval Landscape* (1982)

Hallam, P., *Rural England, 1066–1348* (1981) [good introduction; critical bibliography]

Hanawelt, B., *The Ties that Bound: Peasant Families in Medieval England* (New York, 1986)

Harvey, J., *Medieval Gardens* (1981) [chronological survey, lavishly illustrated; good bibliography]

Hilton, R.H., *The English Peasantry in the Later Middle Ages* (Oxford, 1975)

Hoskins, W.G., *The Making of the English Landscape* (1955)

Miller, E. and Hatcher, J., *Medieval England – Rural Society and Economic Change, 1086–1348* (1978)

Rackham, O., *Ancient Woodland: its History, Vegetation and Uses in England* (1980
The History of the Countryside (1986)

Williamson, T. and Bellamy, L., *Property and Landscape: A social history of land ownership and the English Countryside* (1987)

Young, C.R., *The Royal Forests of Medieval England* (Leicester, 1979)

Sources of Illustrations

Index